dEAd EyEs OpEn

BY MATTHEW SHEPHERD
AND ROY BONEY JR.

DEAD EYES OPEN

Dead Eyes Open collects the six-issue SLG miniseries *Dead Eyes Open* by Matthew Shepherd and Roy Boney, Jr.

First Printing: February 2008
ISBN 978-1-59362-100-1

Published by SLG Publishing
www.slgcomic.com

P.O. Box 26427
San Jose, CA 95159

Dan Vado - President and Publisher
Jennifer deGuzman - Editor-in-Chief
Scott Saavedra - Art Director

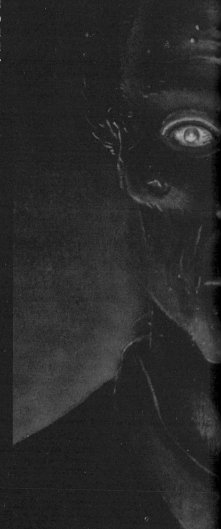

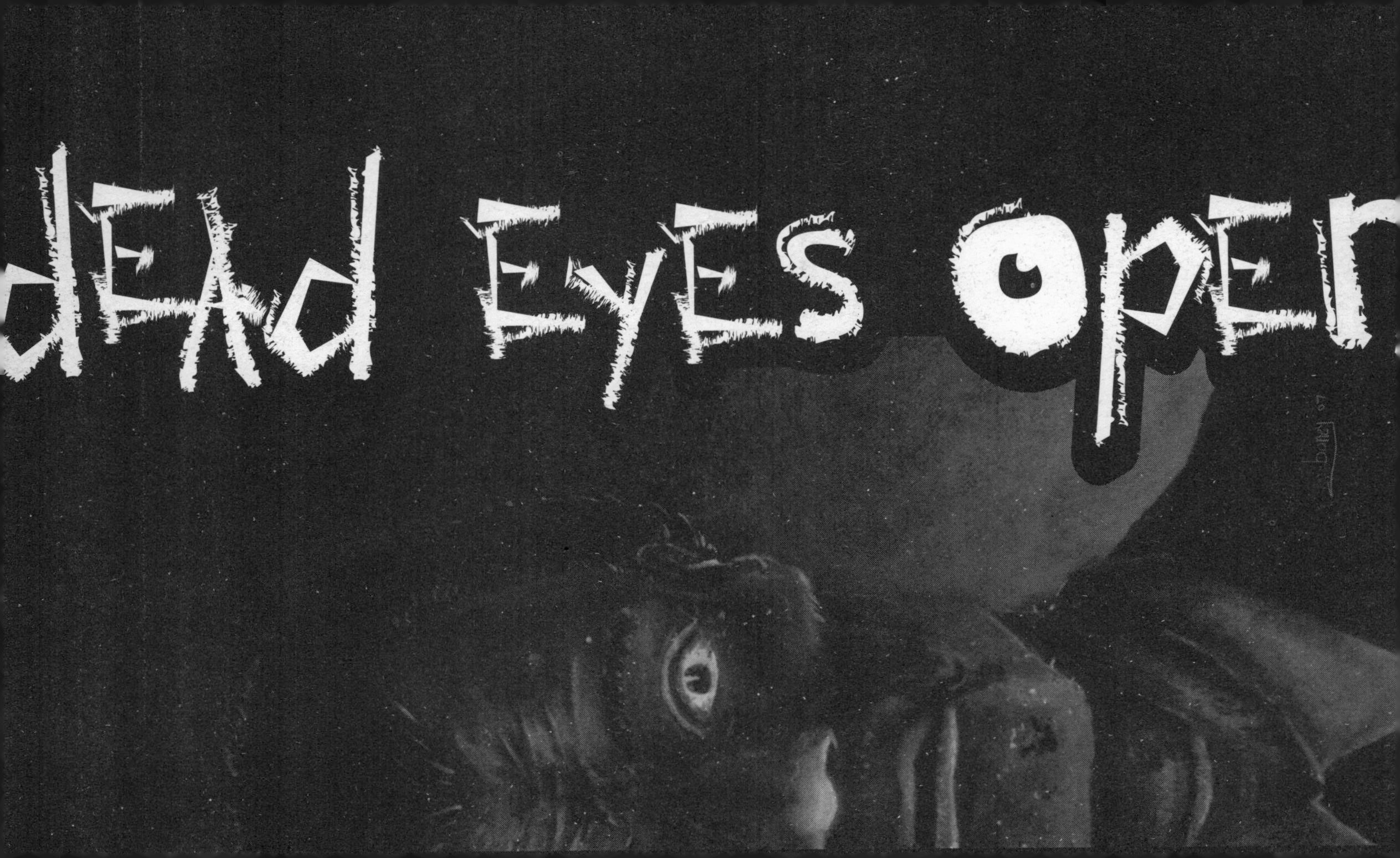
dead eyes open

CHAPTER ONE

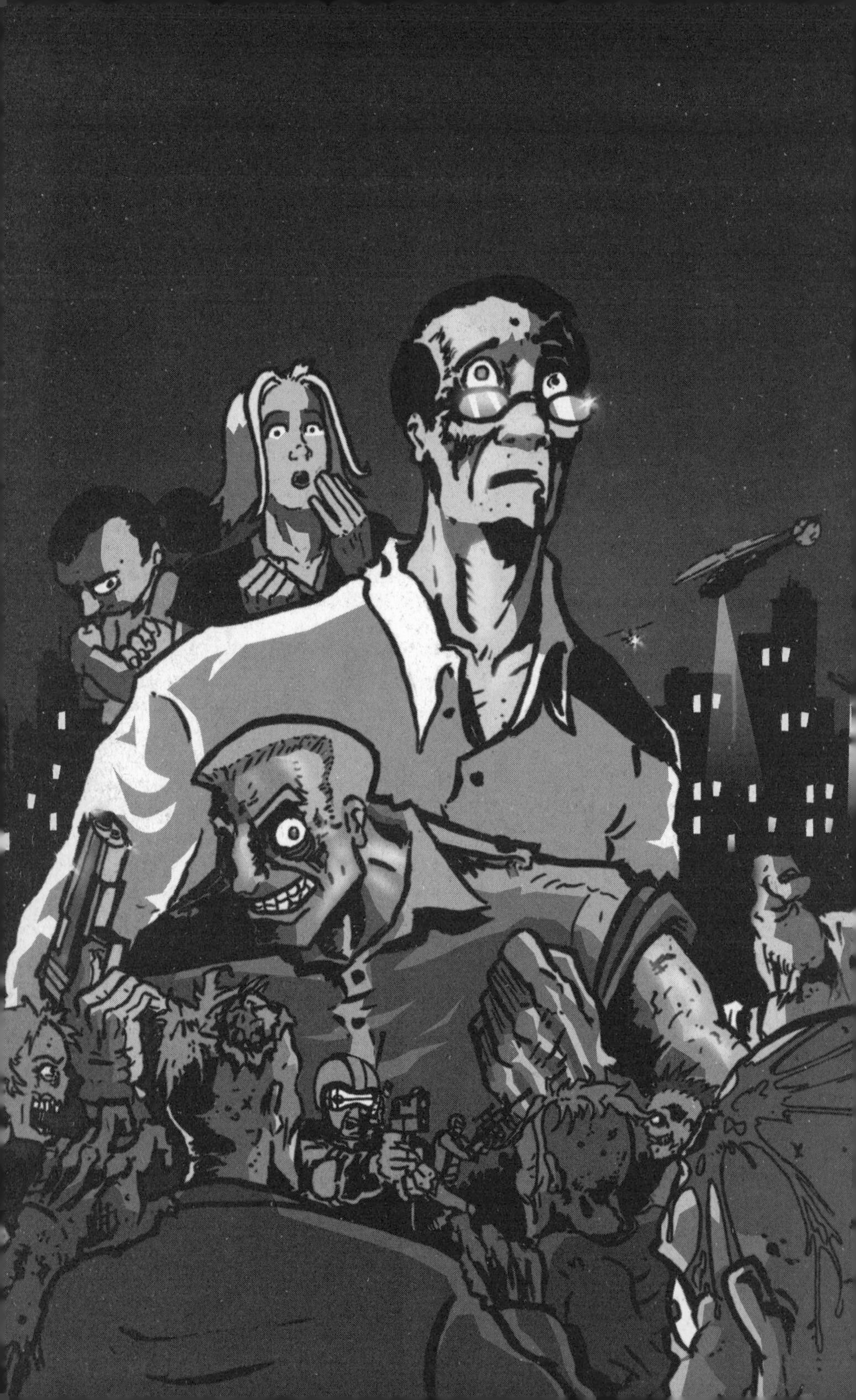

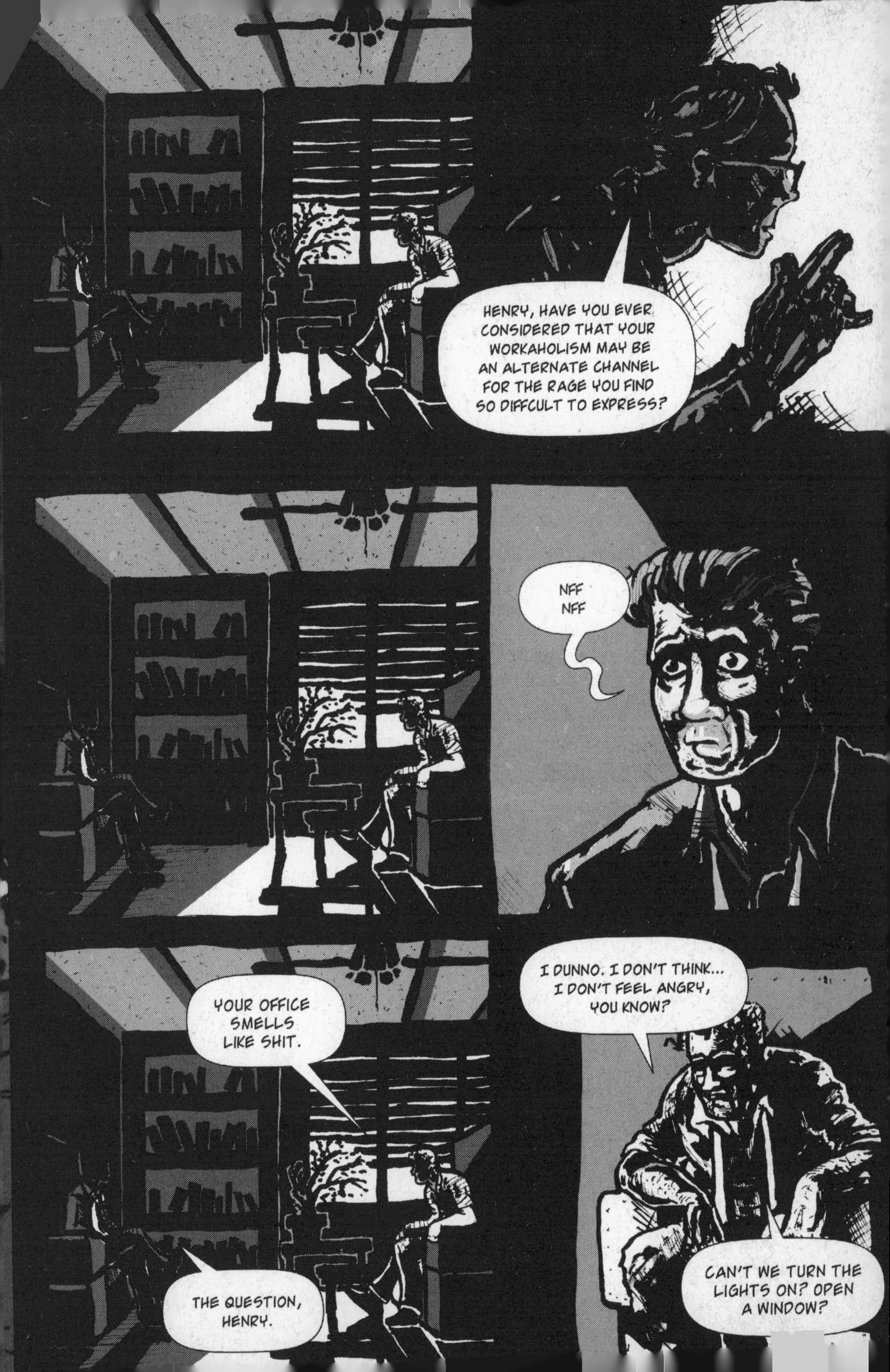
HENRY, HAVE YOU EVER CONSIDERED THAT YOUR WORKAHOLISM MAY BE AN ALTERNATE CHANNEL FOR THE RAGE YOU FIND SO DIFFCULT TO EXPRESS?
NFF NFF
YOUR OFFICE SMELLS LIKE SHIT.
THE QUESTION, HENRY.
I DUNNO. I DON'T THINK... I DON'T FEEL ANGRY, YOU KNOW?
CAN'T WE TURN THE LIGHTS ON? OPEN A WINDOW?

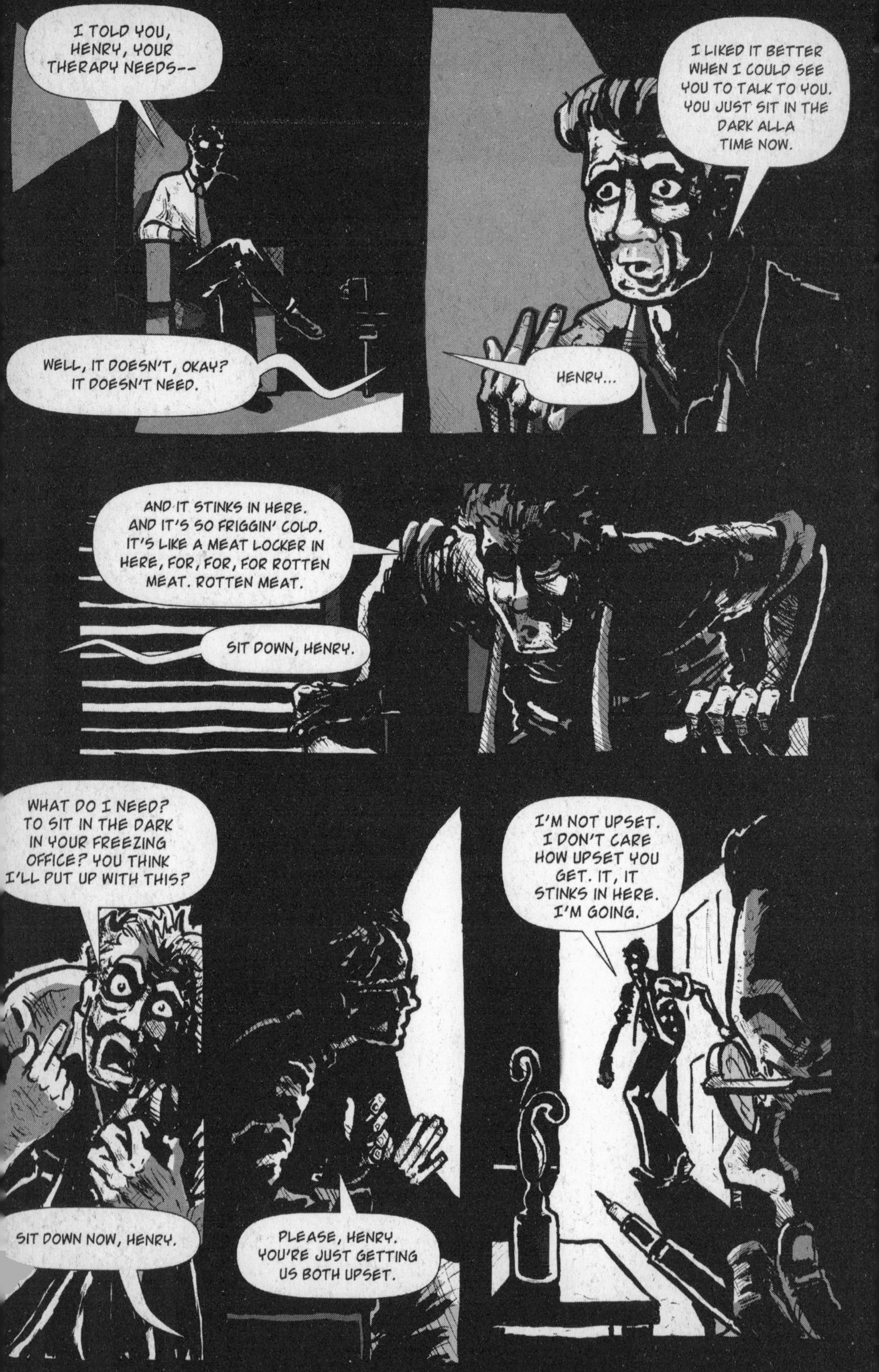
I TOLD YOU, HENRY, YOUR THERAPY NEEDS--
WELL, IT DOESN'T, OKAY? IT DOESN'T NEED.
I LIKED IT BETTER WHEN I COULD SEE YOU TO TALK TO YOU. YOU JUST SIT IN THE DARK ALLA TIME NOW.
HENRY...
AND IT STINKS IN HERE. AND IT'S SO FRIGGIN' COLD. IT'S LIKE A MEAT LOCKER IN HERE, FOR, FOR, FOR ROTTEN MEAT. ROTTEN MEAT.
SIT DOWN, HENRY.
WHAT DO I NEED? TO SIT IN THE DARK IN YOUR FREEZING OFFICE? YOU THINK I'LL PUT UP WITH THIS?
SIT DOWN NOW, HENRY.
PLEASE, HENRY. YOU'RE JUST GETTING US BOTH UPSET.
I'M NOT UPSET. I DON'T CARE HOW UPSET YOU GET. IT, IT STINKS IN HERE. I'M GOING.

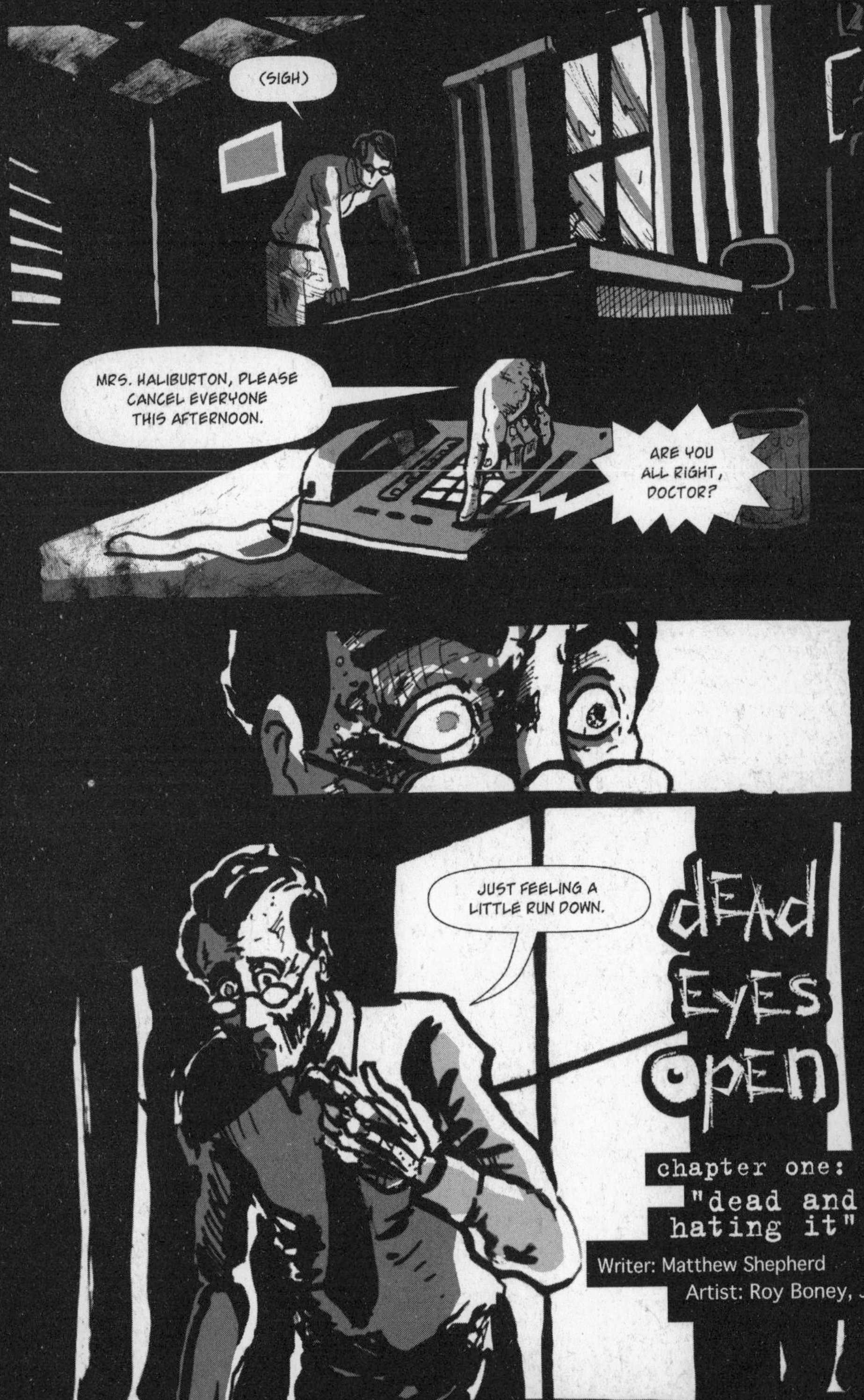
(SIGH)
MRS. HALIBURTON, PLEASE CANCEL EVERYONE THIS AFTERNOON.
ARE YOU ALL RIGHT, DOCTOR?
JUST FEELING A LITTLE RUN DOWN.
dEAd EYES OPEN
chapter one:
"dead and hating it"
Writer: Matthew Shepherd
Artist: Roy Boney, Jr.

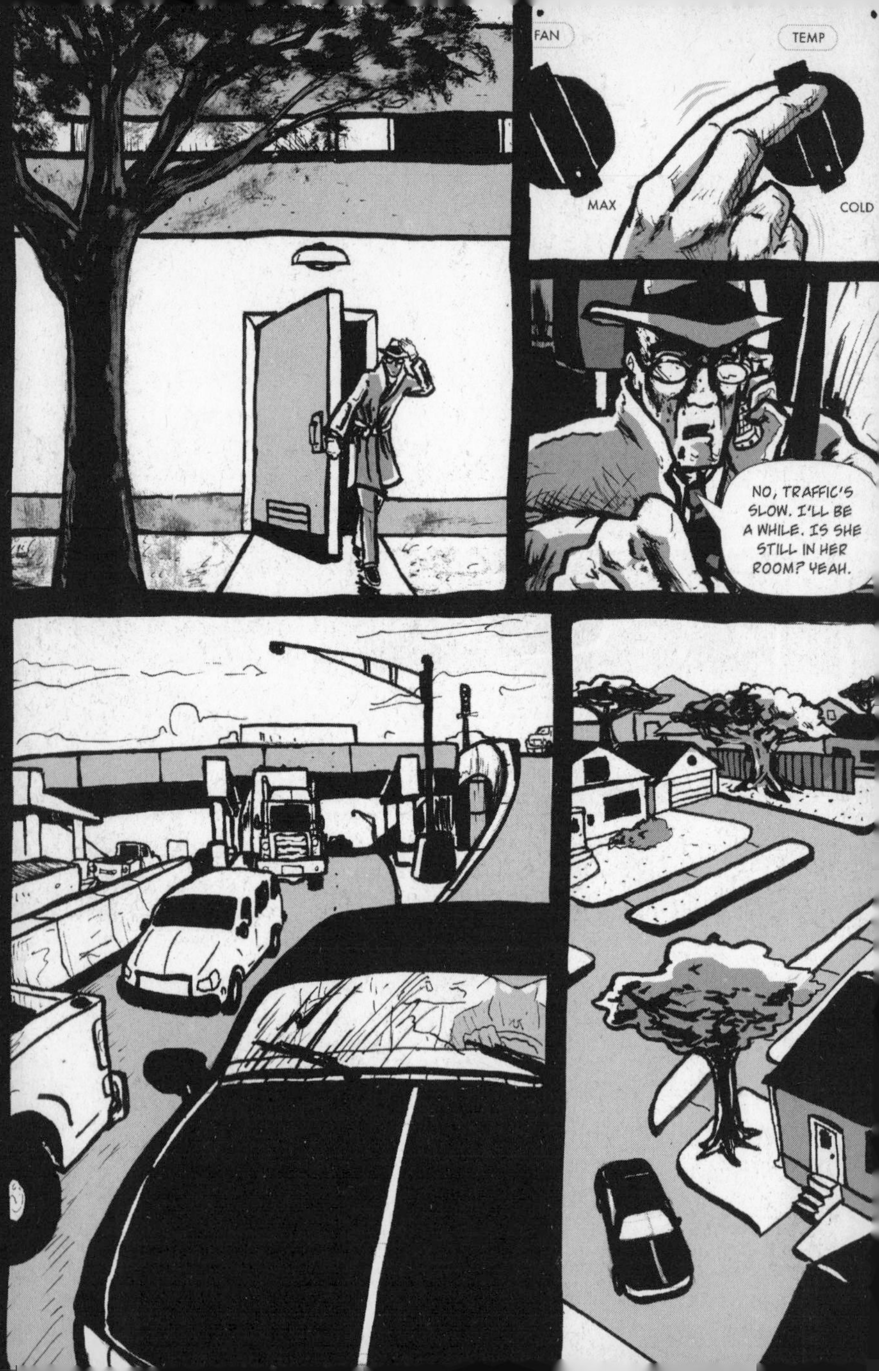
FAN
TEMP
MAX
COLD
NO, TRAFFIC'S SLOW. I'LL BE A WHILE. IS SHE STILL IN HER ROOM? YEAH.

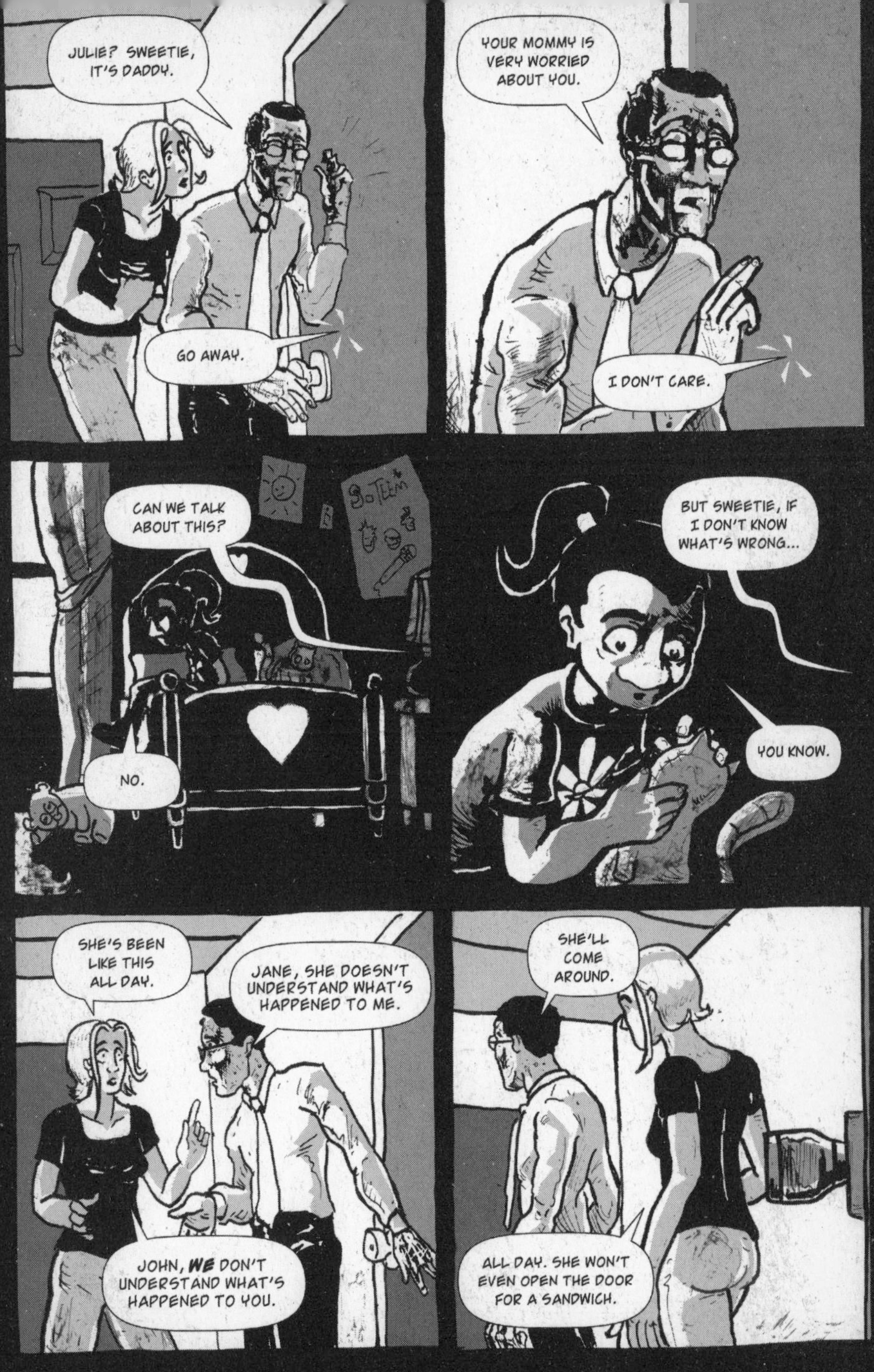
JULIE? SWEETIE, IT'S DADDY.
GO AWAY.
YOUR MOMMY IS VERY WORRIED ABOUT YOU.
I DON'T CARE.
CAN WE TALK ABOUT THIS?
NO.
BUT SWEETIE, IF I DON'T KNOW WHAT'S WRONG...
YOU KNOW.
SHE'S BEEN LIKE THIS ALL DAY.
JANE, SHE DOESN'T UNDERSTAND WHAT'S HAPPENED TO ME.
JOHN, WE DON'T UNDERSTAND WHAT'S HAPPENED TO YOU.
SHE'LL COME AROUND.
ALL DAY. SHE WON'T EVEN OPEN THE DOOR FOR A SANDWICH.

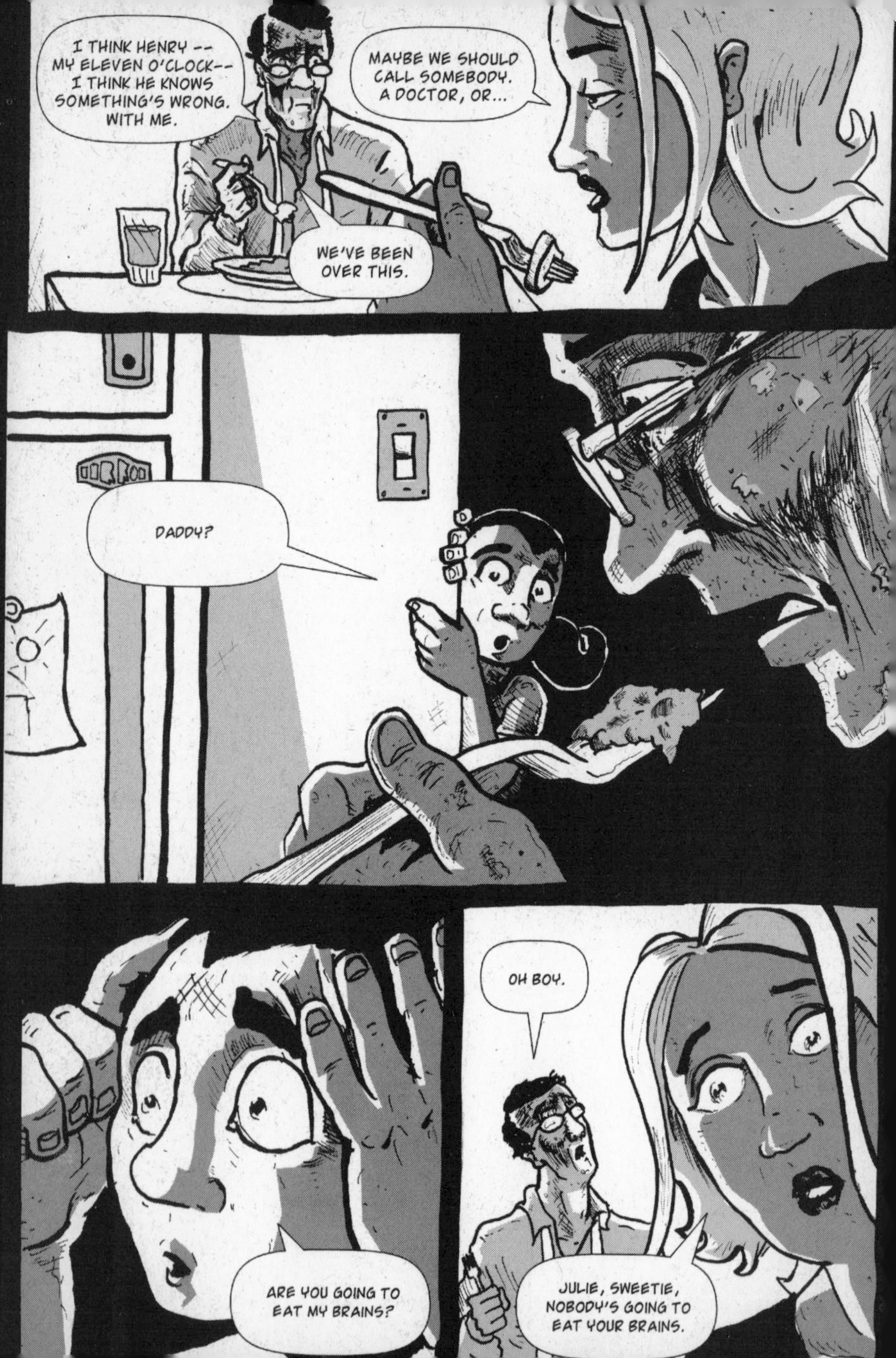
I THINK HENRY -- MY ELEVEN O'CLOCK-- I THINK HE KNOWS SOMETHING'S WRONG. WITH ME.
MAYBE WE SHOULD CALL SOMEBODY. A DOCTOR, OR...
WE'VE BEEN OVER THIS.
DADDY?
ARE YOU GOING TO EAT MY BRAINS?
OH BOY.
JULIE, SWEETIE, NOBODY'S GOING TO EAT YOUR BRAINS.

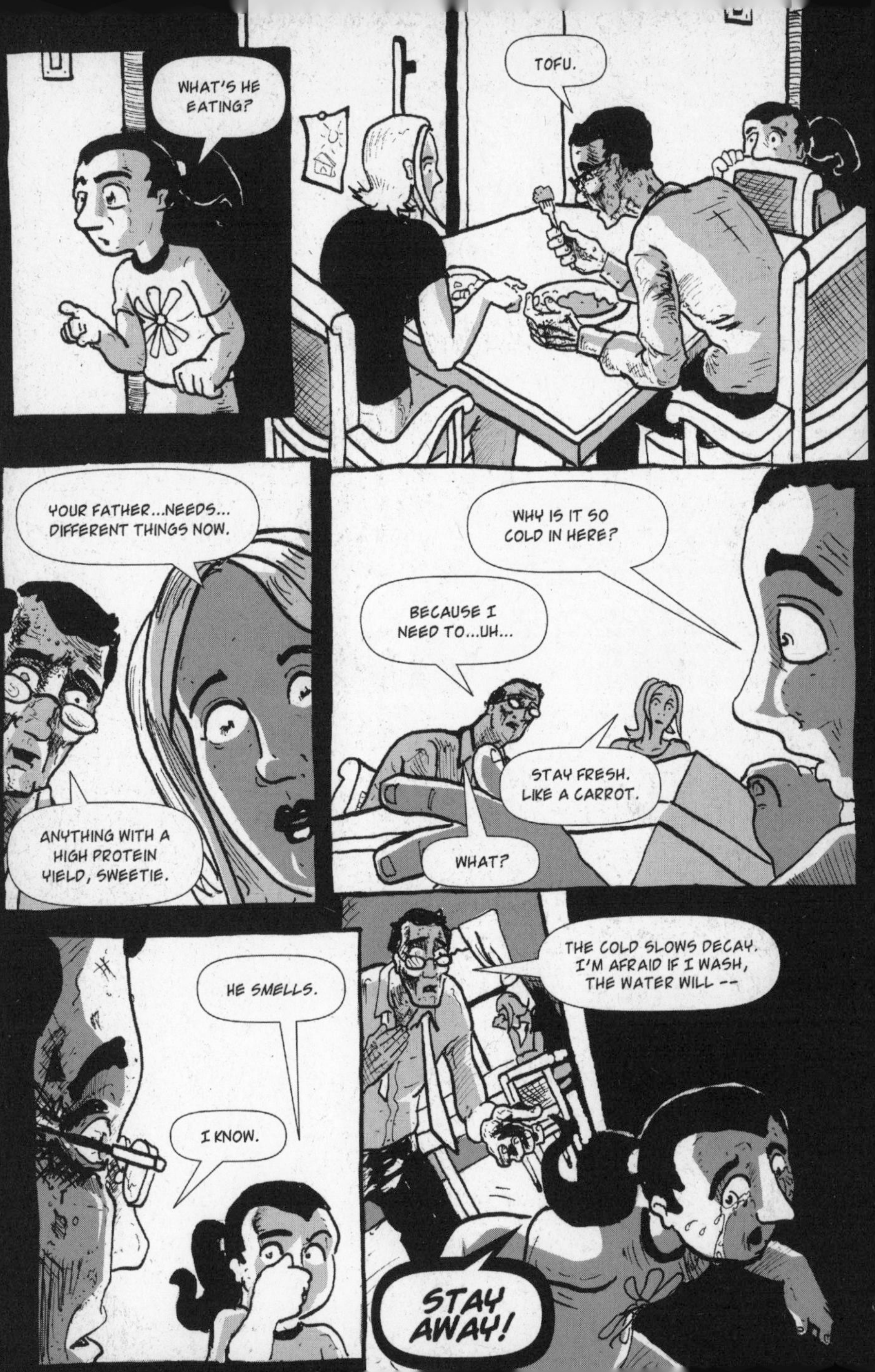
WHAT'S HE EATING?
TOFU.
YOUR FATHER...NEEDS... DIFFERENT THINGS NOW.
ANYTHING WITH A HIGH PROTEIN YIELD, SWEETIE.
WHY IS IT SO COLD IN HERE?
BECAUSE I NEED TO...UH...
STAY FRESH. LIKE A CARROT.
WHAT?
HE SMELLS.
I KNOW.
THE COLD SLOWS DECAY. I'M AFRAID IF I WASH, THE WATER WILL --
STAY AWAY!

KNOCK KNOCK. JULIE? SWEETIE?

I KNOW IT'S HARD TO UNDERSTAND WHY...THINGS HAVE CHANGED...

I'M GONNA TELL.

WHAT?

AT SCHOOL TOMORROW. I'M GONNA TELL *EVERYBODY*.

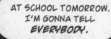

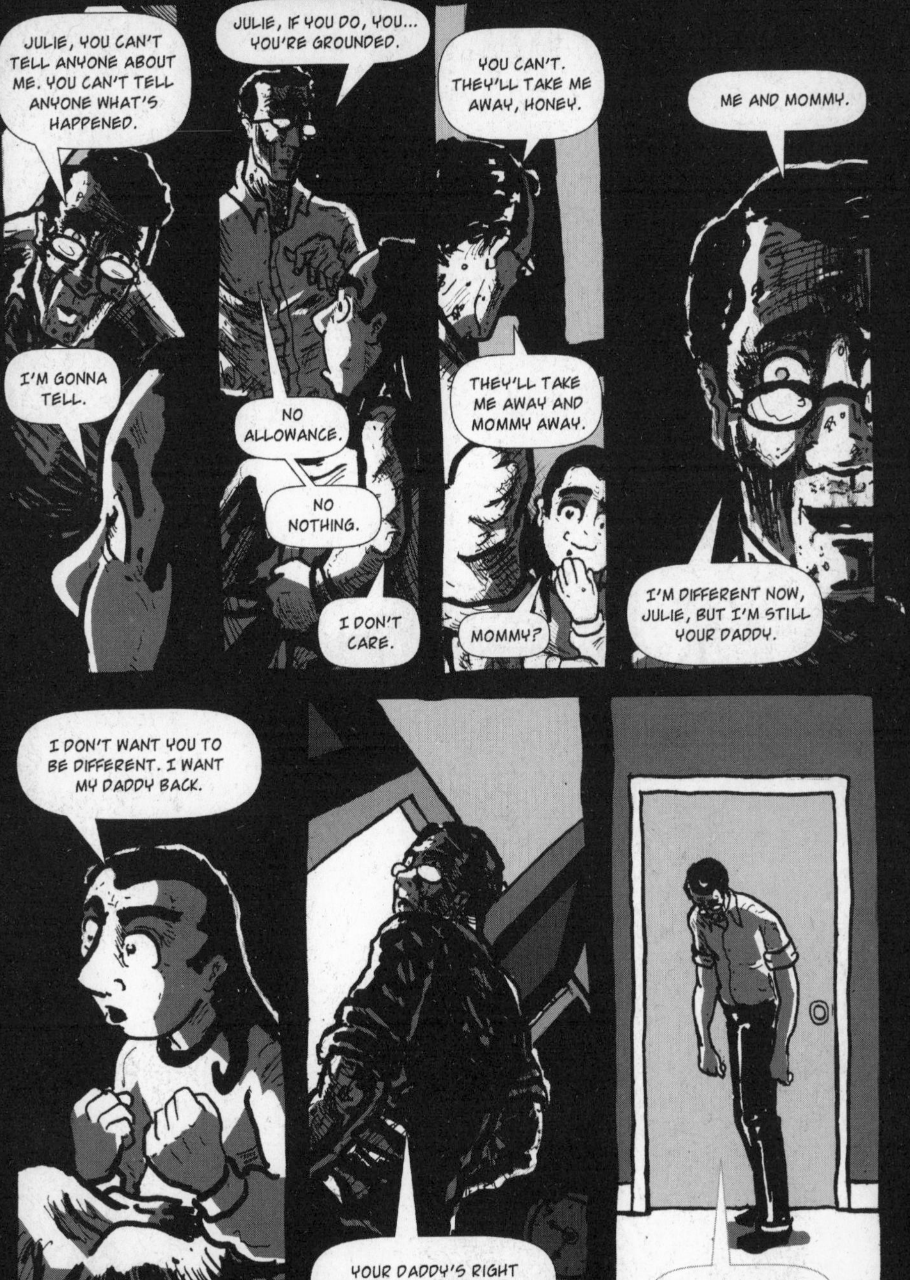
JULIE, YOU CAN'T TELL ANYONE ABOUT ME. YOU CAN'T TELL ANYONE WHAT'S HAPPENED.
I'M GONNA TELL.
JULIE, IF YOU DO, YOU... YOU'RE GROUNDED.
NO ALLOWANCE.
NO NOTHING.
I DON'T CARE.
YOU CAN'T. THEY'LL TAKE ME AWAY, HONEY.
THEY'LL TAKE ME AWAY AND MOMMY AWAY.
MOMMY?
ME AND MOMMY.
I'M DIFFERENT NOW, JULIE, BUT I'M STILL YOUR DADDY.
I DON'T WANT YOU TO BE DIFFERENT. I WANT MY DADDY BACK.
YOUR DADDY'S RIGHT HERE. I NEVER LEFT.
I NEVER LEFT. GOD HELP ME.

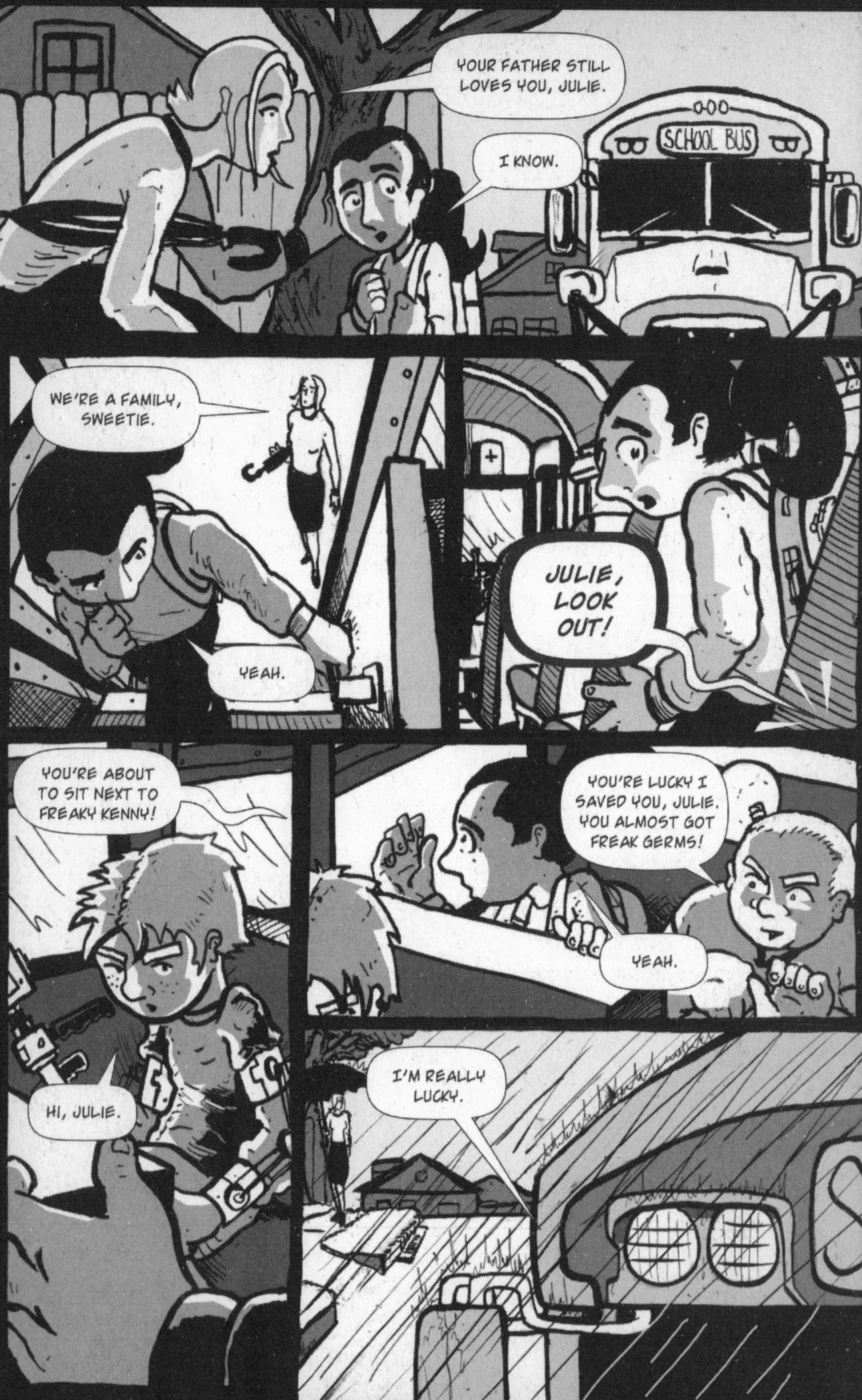
YOUR FATHER STILL LOVES YOU, JULIE.
I KNOW.
WE'RE A FAMILY, SWEETIE.
YEAH.
JULIE, LOOK OUT!
YOU'RE ABOUT TO SIT NEXT TO FREAKY KENNY!
HI, JULIE.
YOU'RE LUCKY I SAVED YOU, JULIE. YOU ALMOST GOT FREAK GERMS!
YEAH.
I'M REALLY LUCKY.
SCHOOL BUS

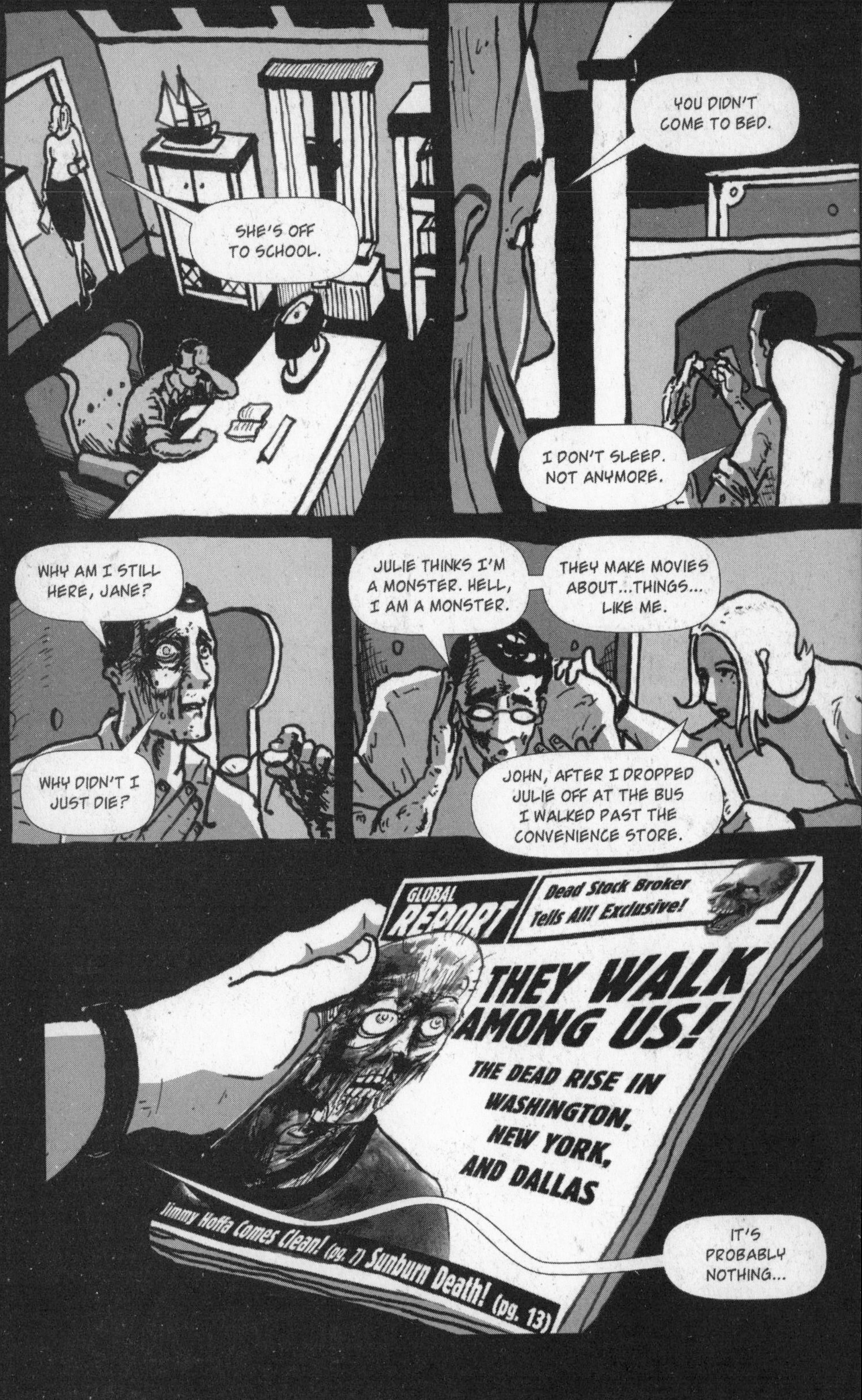
SHE'S OFF TO SCHOOL.
YOU DIDN'T COME TO BED.
I DON'T SLEEP. NOT ANYMORE.
WHY AM I STILL HERE, JANE?
WHY DIDN'T I JUST DIE?
JULIE THINKS I'M A MONSTER. HELL, I AM A MONSTER.
THEY MAKE MOVIES ABOUT...THINGS... LIKE ME.
JOHN, AFTER I DROPPED JULIE OFF AT THE BUS I WALKED PAST THE CONVENIENCE STORE.
GLOBAL REPORT
Dead Stock Broker Tells All! Exclusive!
THEY WALK AMONG US!
THE DEAD RISE IN WASHINGTON, NEW YORK, AND DALLAS
Jimmy Hoffa Comes Clean! (pg. 7) Sunburn Death! (pg. 13)
IT'S PROBABLY NOTHING...

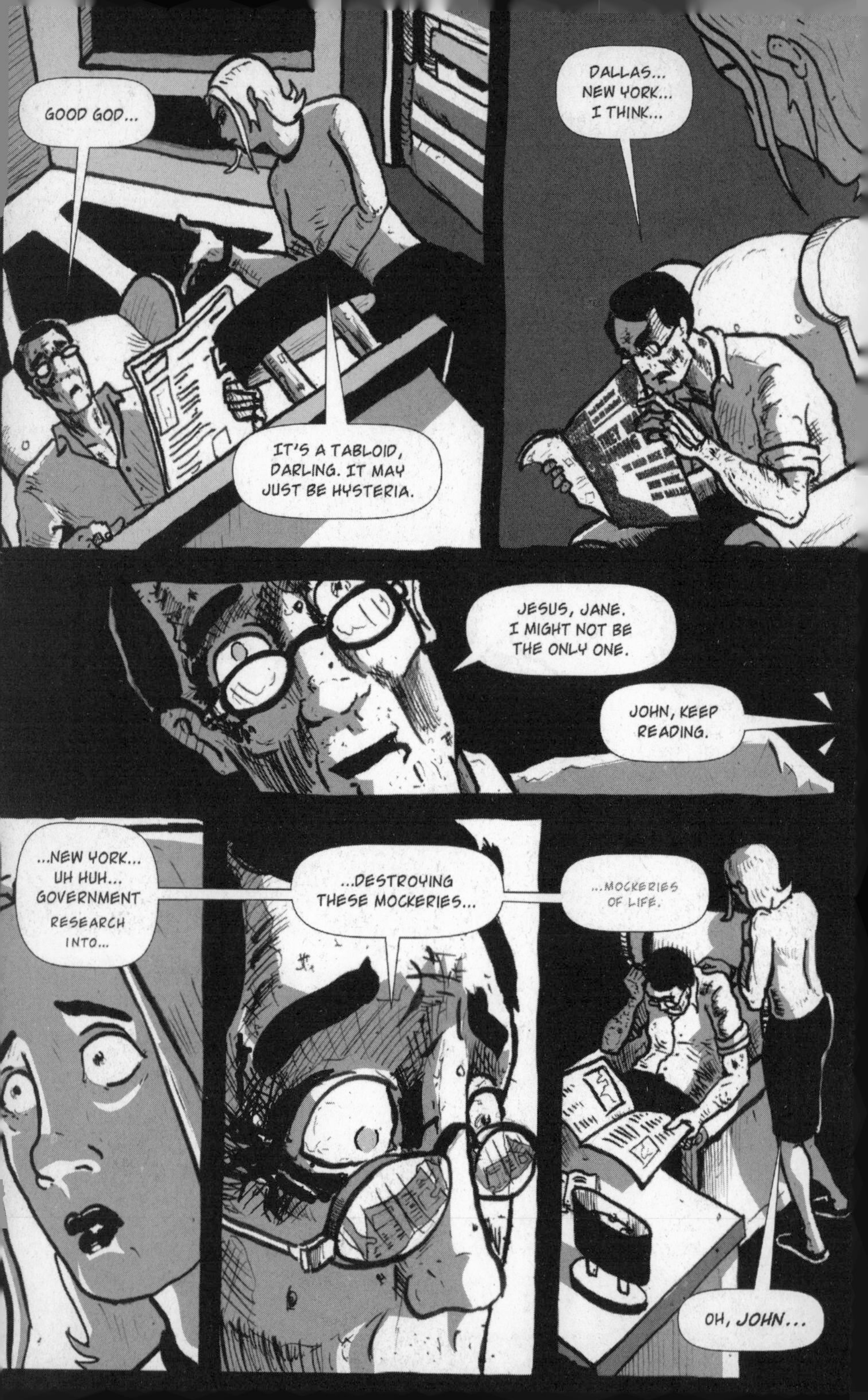
GOOD GOD...
IT'S A TABLOID, DARLING. IT MAY JUST BE HYSTERIA.
DALLAS... NEW YORK... I THINK...
JESUS, JANE. I MIGHT NOT BE THE ONLY ONE.
JOHN, KEEP READING.
...NEW YORK... UH HUH... GOVERNMENT RESEARCH INTO...
...DESTROYING THESE MOCKERIES...
...MOCKERIES OF LIFE.
OH, JOHN...

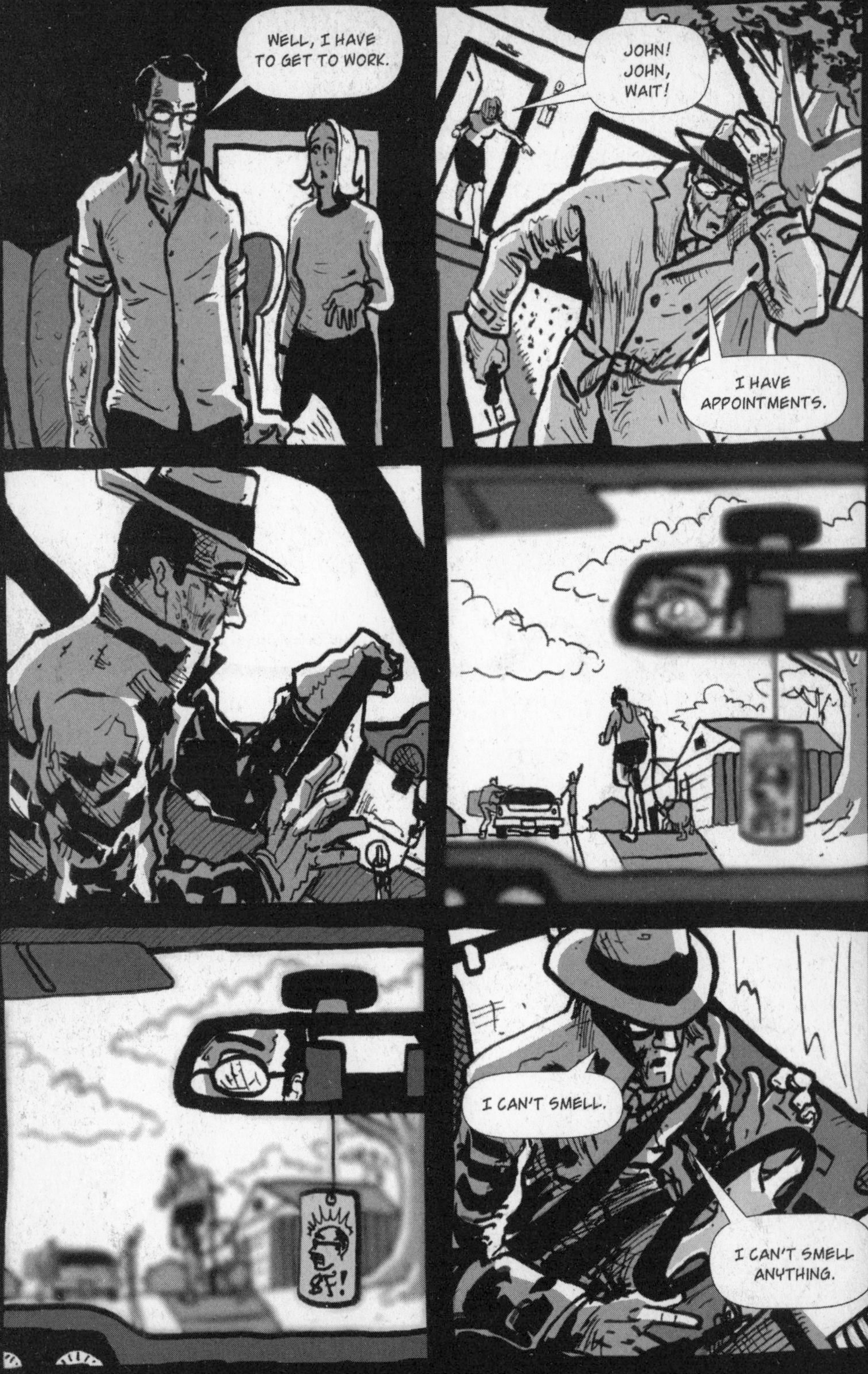
WELL, I HAVE TO GET TO WORK.
JOHN! JOHN, WAIT!
I HAVE APPOINTMENTS.
SF!
I CAN'T SMELL.
I CAN'T SMELL ANYTHING.

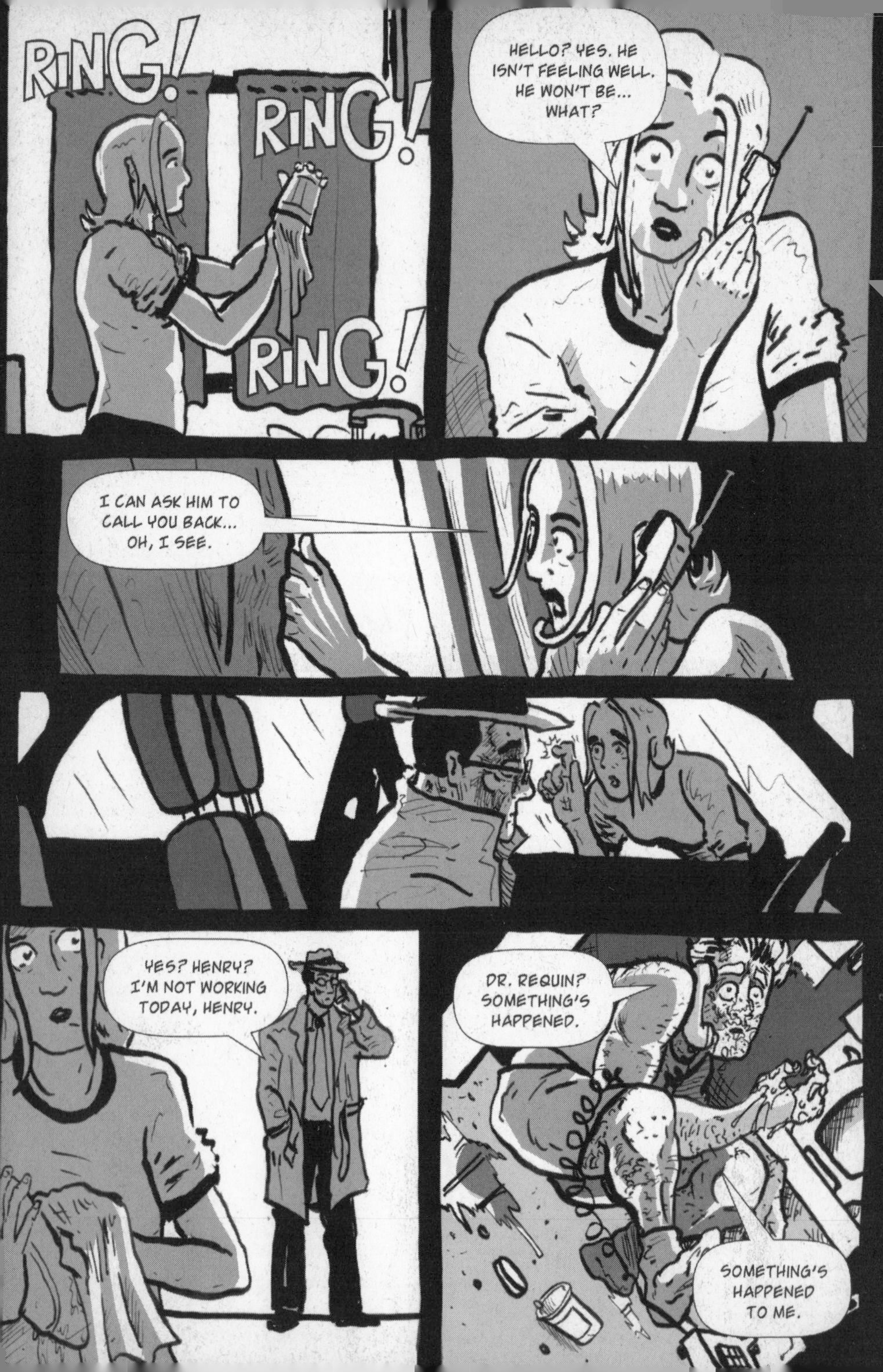
RING!
RING!
RING!
HELLO? YES. HE ISN'T FEELING WELL. HE WON'T BE... WHAT?
I CAN ASK HIM TO CALL YOU BACK... OH, I SEE.
YES? HENRY? I'M NOT WORKING TODAY, HENRY.
DR. REQUIN? SOMETHING'S HAPPENED.
SOMETHING'S HAPPENED TO ME.

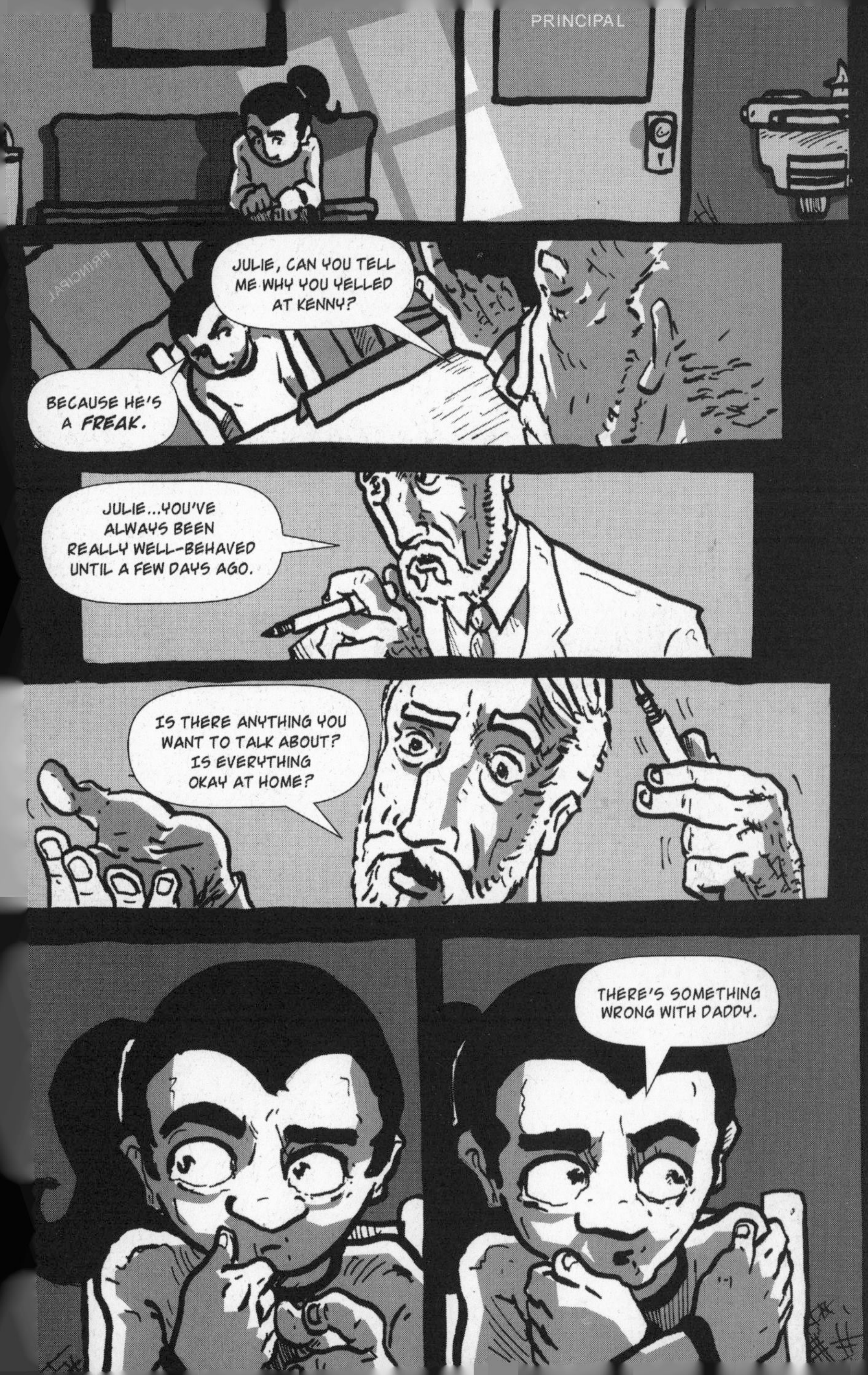
PRINCIPAL
JULIE, CAN YOU TELL ME WHY YOU YELLED AT KENNY?
BECAUSE HE'S A FREAK.
JULIE...YOU'VE ALWAYS BEEN REALLY WELL-BEHAVED UNTIL A FEW DAYS AGO.
IS THERE ANYTHING YOU WANT TO TALK ABOUT? IS EVERYTHING OKAY AT HOME?
THERE'S SOMETHING WRONG WITH DADDY.

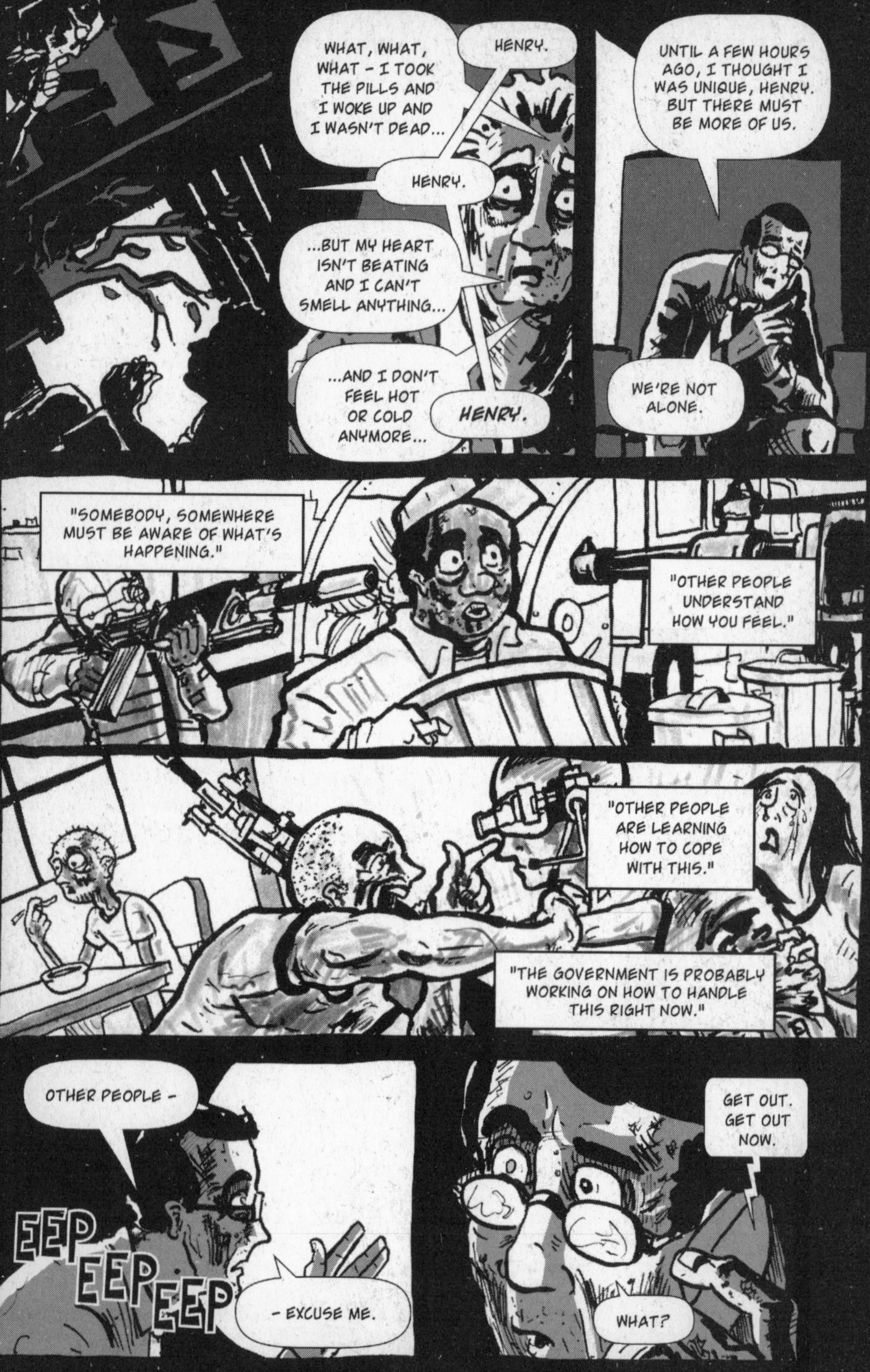
WHAT, WHAT, WHAT - I TOOK THE PILLS AND I WOKE UP AND I WASN'T DEAD...
HENRY.
HENRY.
...BUT MY HEART ISN'T BEATING AND I CAN'T SMELL ANYTHING...
...AND I DON'T FEEL HOT OR COLD ANYMORE...
HENRY.
UNTIL A FEW HOURS AGO, I THOUGHT I WAS UNIQUE, HENRY. BUT THERE MUST BE MORE OF US.
WE'RE NOT ALONE.
"SOMEBODY, SOMEWHERE MUST BE AWARE OF WHAT'S HAPPENING."
"OTHER PEOPLE UNDERSTAND HOW YOU FEEL."
"OTHER PEOPLE ARE LEARNING HOW TO COPE WITH THIS."
"THE GOVERNMENT IS PROBABLY WORKING ON HOW TO HANDLE THIS RIGHT NOW."
OTHER PEOPLE -
EEP EEP EEP
- EXCUSE ME.
GET OUT. GET OUT NOW.
WHAT?

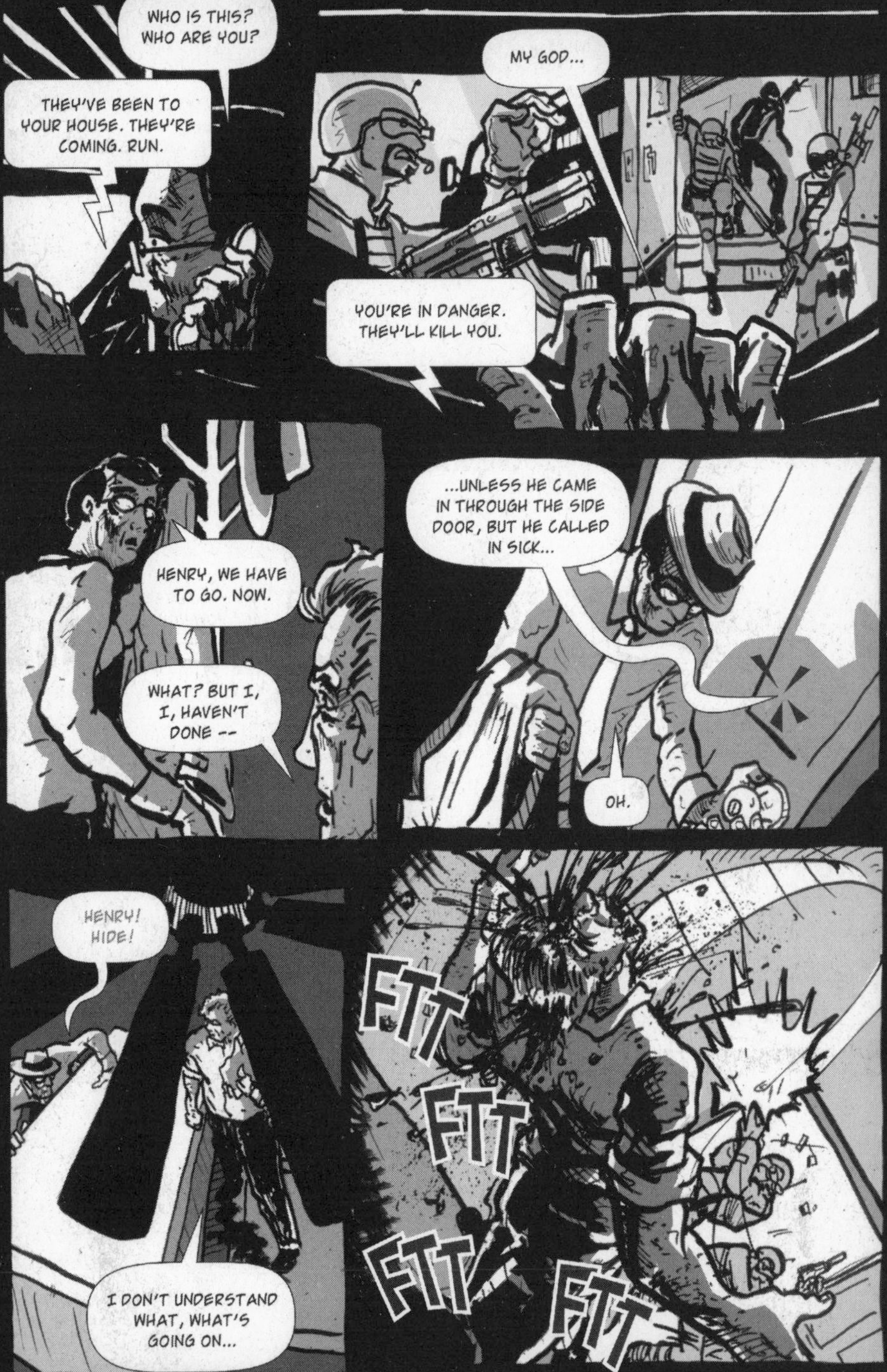
WHO IS THIS? WHO ARE YOU?
THEY'VE BEEN TO YOUR HOUSE. THEY'RE COMING. RUN.
MY GOD...
YOU'RE IN DANGER. THEY'LL KILL YOU.
HENRY, WE HAVE TO GO. NOW.
WHAT? BUT I, I, HAVEN'T DONE --
...UNLESS HE CAME IN THROUGH THE SIDE DOOR, BUT HE CALLED IN SICK...
OH.
HENRY! HIDE!
I DON'T UNDERSTAND WHAT, WHAT'S GOING ON...
FTT
FTT
FTT
FTT

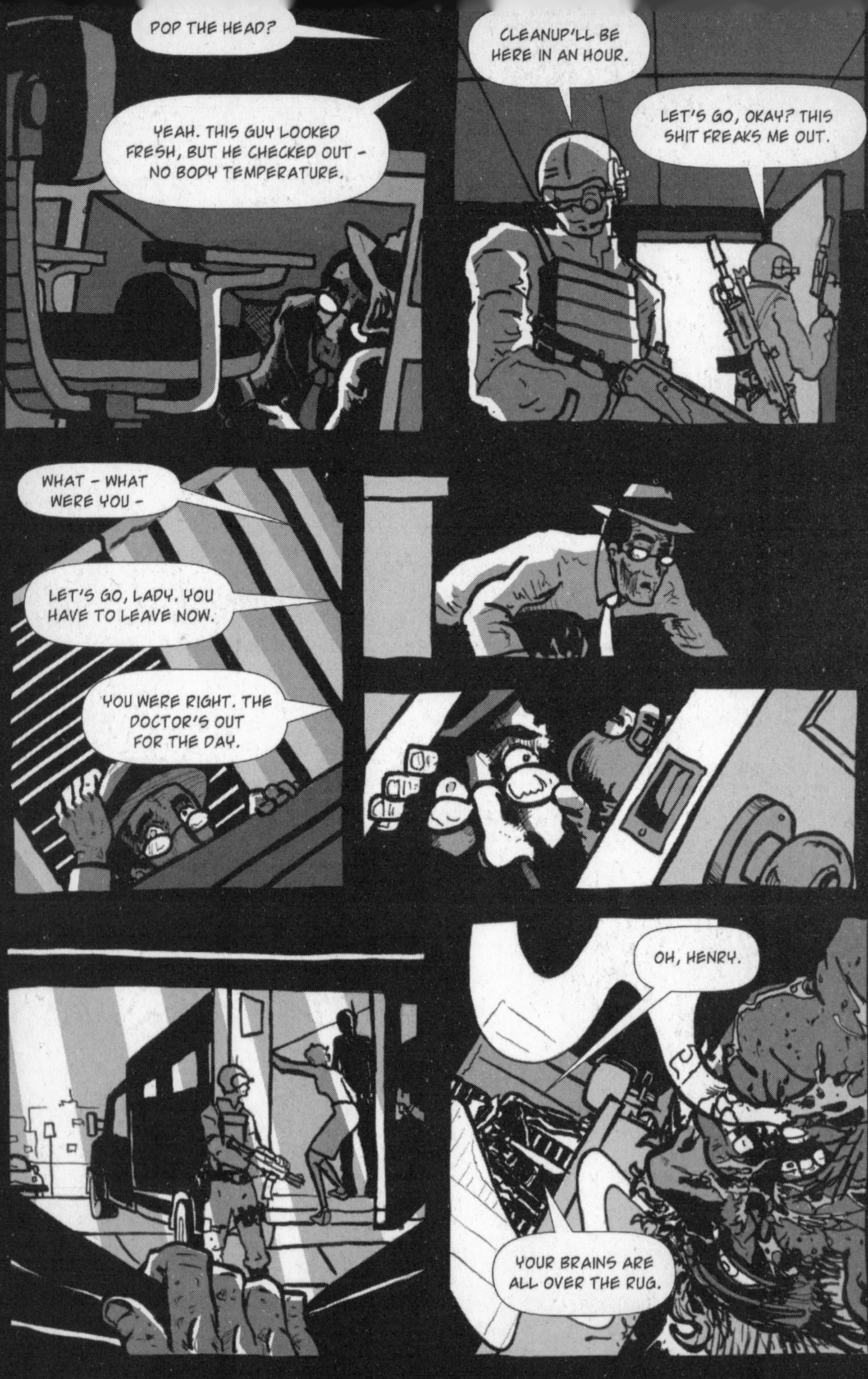
POP THE HEAD?
YEAH. THIS GUY LOOKED FRESH, BUT HE CHECKED OUT - NO BODY TEMPERATURE.
CLEANUP'LL BE HERE IN AN HOUR.
LET'S GO, OKAY? THIS SHIT FREAKS ME OUT.
WHAT - WHAT WERE YOU -
LET'S GO, LADY. YOU HAVE TO LEAVE NOW.
YOU WERE RIGHT. THE DOCTOR'S OUT FOR THE DAY.
OH, HENRY.
YOUR BRAINS ARE ALL OVER THE RUG.

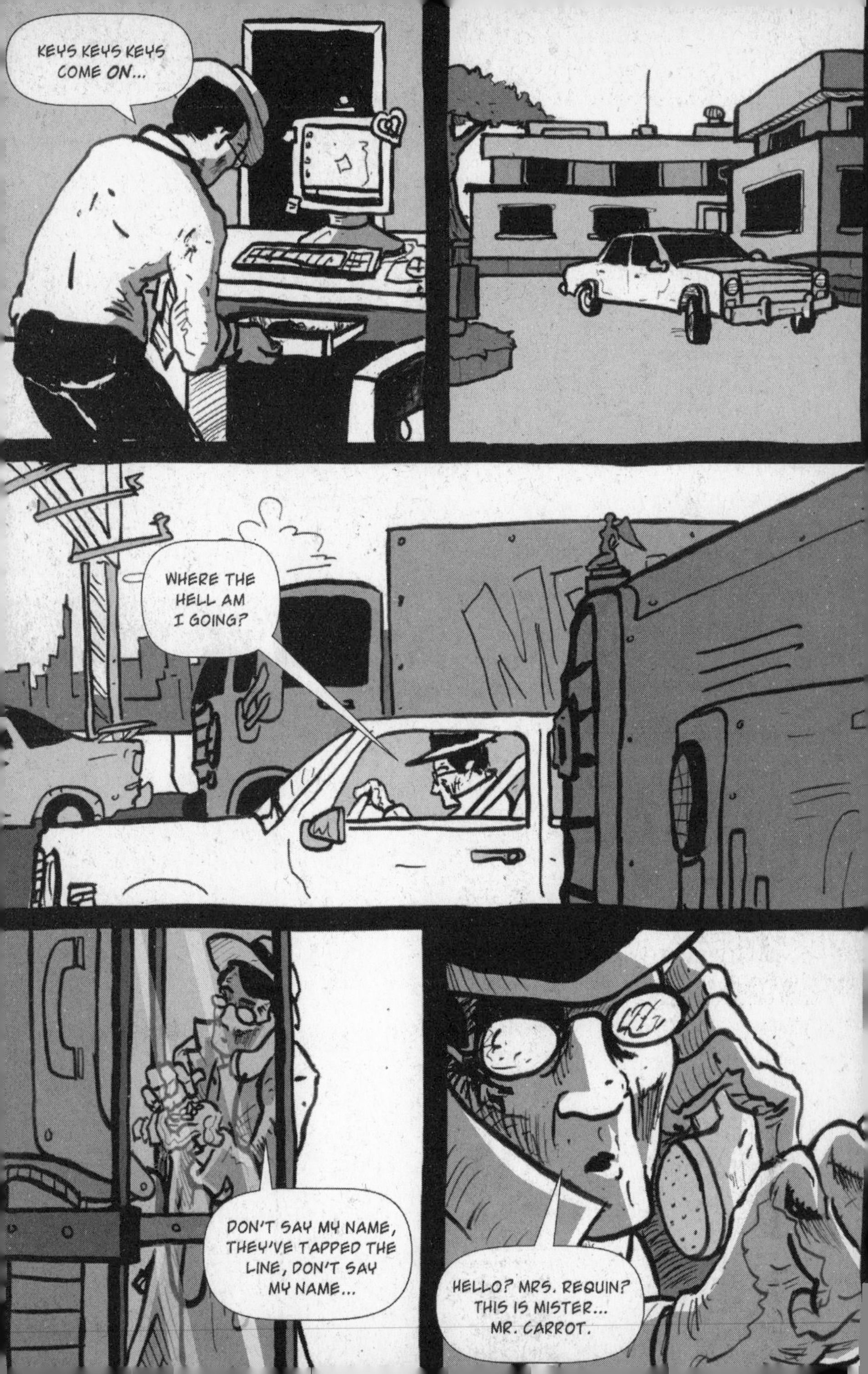
KEYS KEYS KEYS COME ON...
WHERE THE HELL AM I GOING?
DON'T SAY MY NAME, THEY'VE TAPPED THE LINE, DON'T SAY MY NAME...
HELLO? MRS. REQUIN? THIS IS MISTER... MR. CARROT.

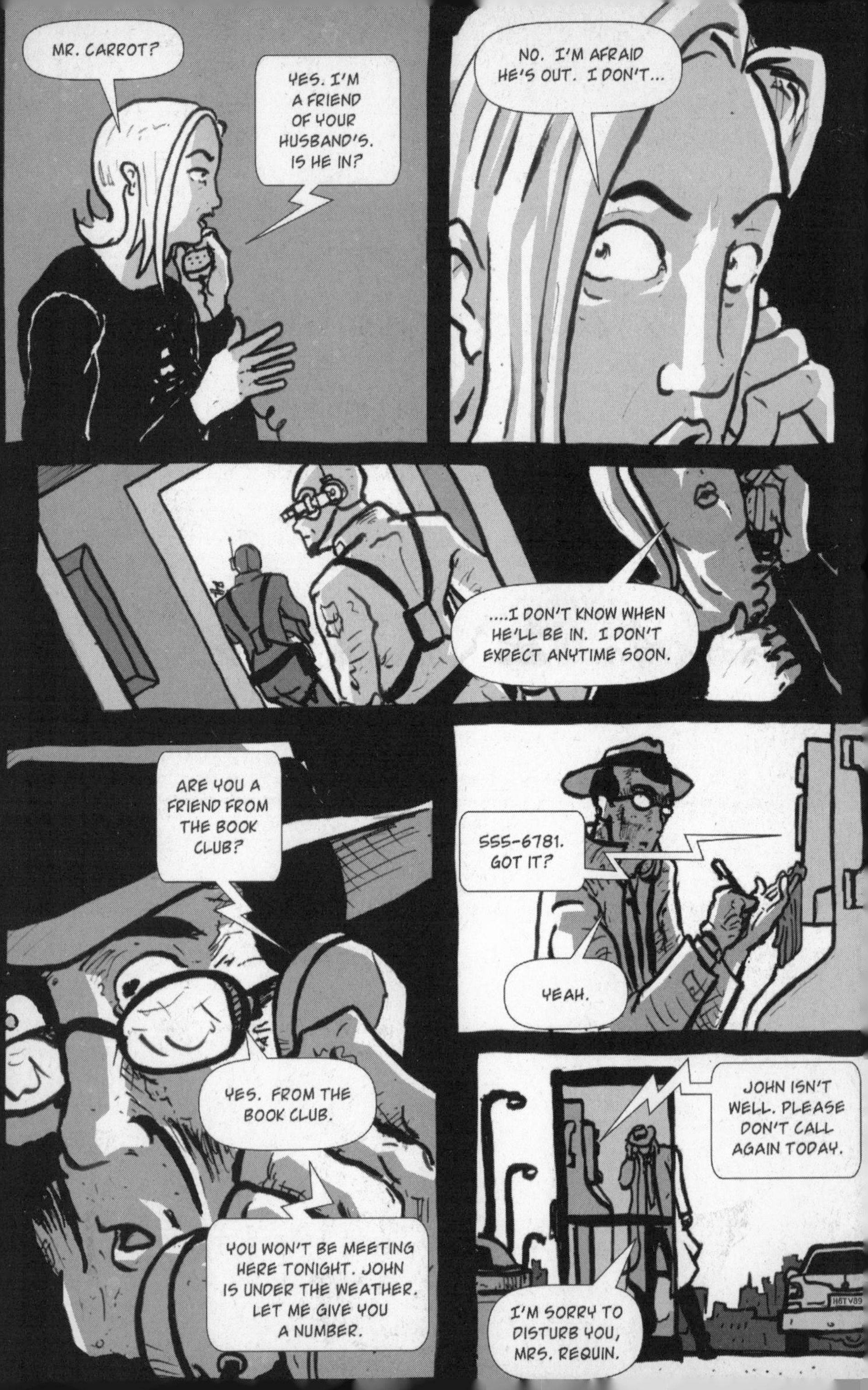
MR. CARROT?
YES. I'M A FRIEND OF YOUR HUSBAND'S. IS HE IN?
NO. I'M AFRAID HE'S OUT. I DON'T...
....I DON'T KNOW WHEN HE'LL BE IN. I DON'T EXPECT ANYTIME SOON.
ARE YOU A FRIEND FROM THE BOOK CLUB?
YES. FROM THE BOOK CLUB.
YOU WON'T BE MEETING HERE TONIGHT. JOHN IS UNDER THE WEATHER. LET ME GIVE YOU A NUMBER.
555-6781. GOT IT?
YEAH.
JOHN ISN'T WELL. PLEASE DON'T CALL AGAIN TODAY.
I'M SORRY TO DISTURB YOU, MRS. REQUIN.
H6TV89

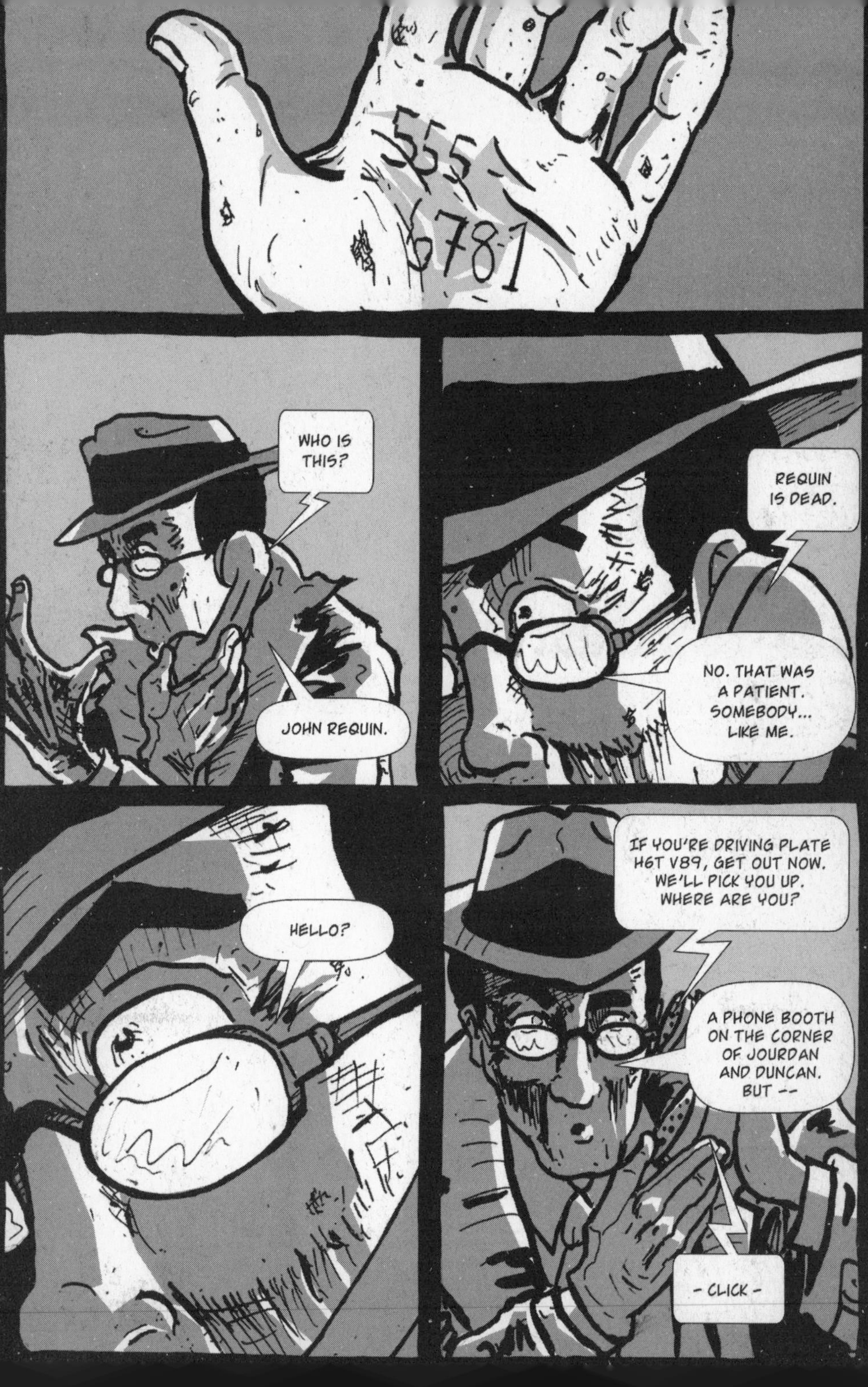
555
6781
WHO IS THIS?
JOHN REQUIN.
REQUIN IS DEAD.
NO. THAT WAS A PATIENT. SOMEBODY... LIKE ME.
HELLO?
IF YOU'RE DRIVING PLATE H6T V89, GET OUT NOW. WE'LL PICK YOU UP. WHERE ARE YOU?
A PHONE BOOTH ON THE CORNER OF JOURDAN AND DUNCAN. BUT --
- CLICK -

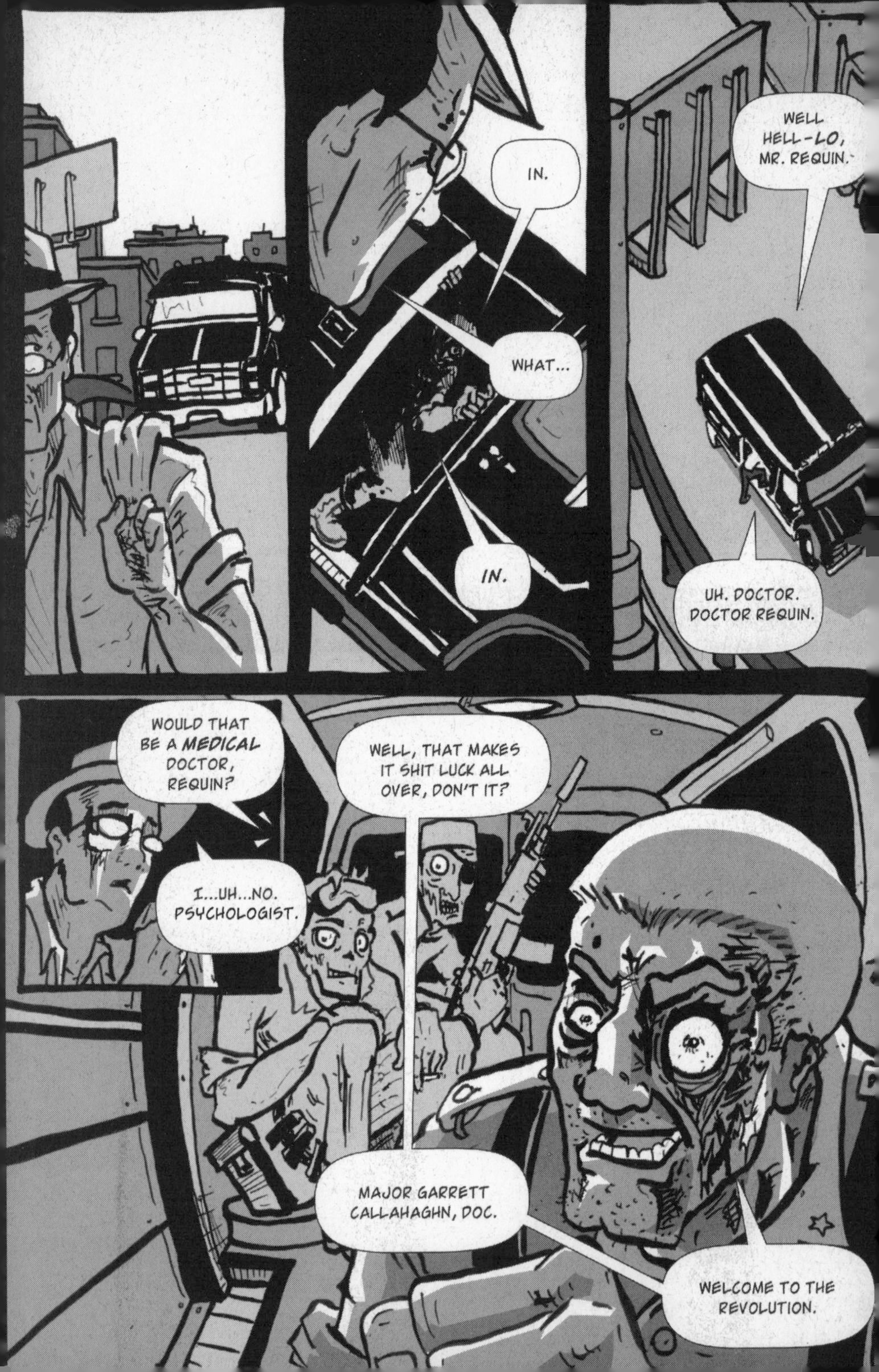
IN.
WHAT...
IN.
WELL HELL-*LO*, MR. REQUIN.
UH. DOCTOR. DOCTOR REQUIN.
WOULD THAT BE A *MEDICAL* DOCTOR, REQUIN?
I...UH...NO. PSYCHOLOGIST.
WELL, THAT MAKES IT SHIT LUCK ALL OVER, DON'T IT?
MAJOR GARRETT CALLAHAGHN, DOC.
WELCOME TO THE REVOLUTION.

CHAPTER TWO

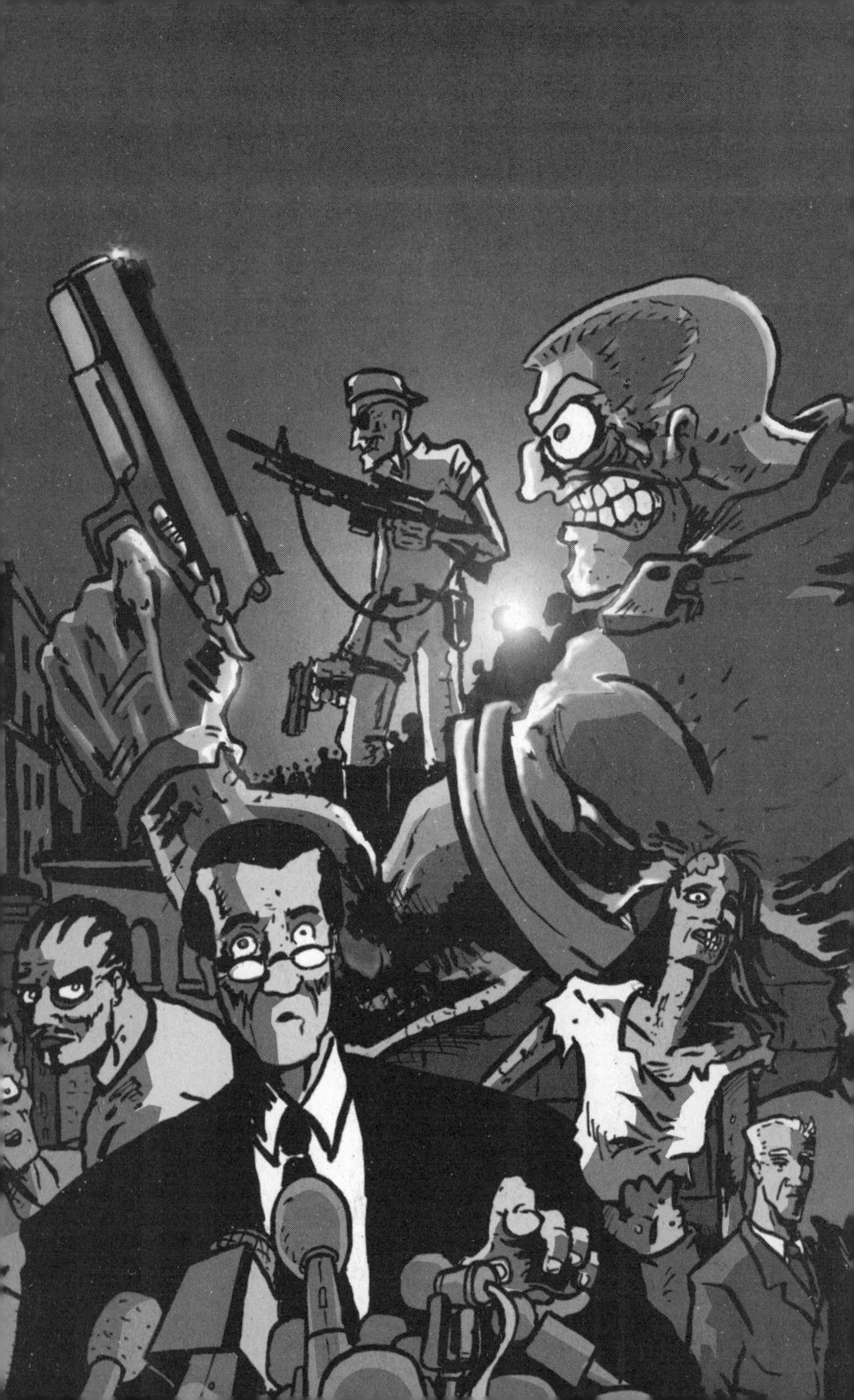

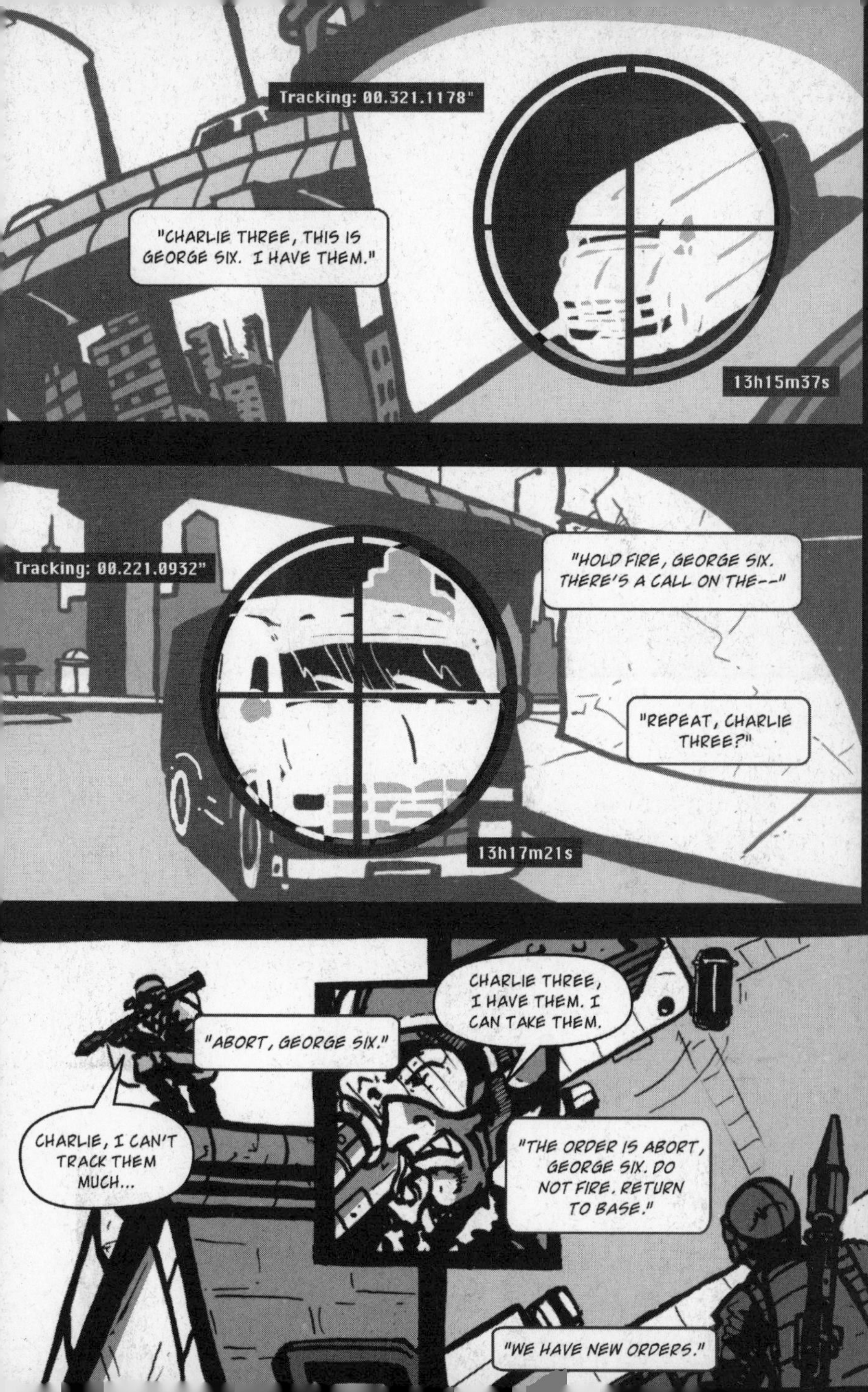
Tracking: 00.321.1178"
"CHARLIE THREE, THIS IS GEORGE SIX. I HAVE THEM."
13h15m37s
Tracking: 00.221.0932"
"HOLD FIRE, GEORGE SIX. THERE'S A CALL ON THE--"
"REPEAT, CHARLIE THREE?"
13h17m21s
CHARLIE THREE, I HAVE THEM. I CAN TAKE THEM.
"ABORT, GEORGE SIX."
CHARLIE, I CAN'T TRACK THEM MUCH...
"THE ORDER IS ABORT, GEORGE SIX. DO NOT FIRE. RETURN TO BASE."
"WE HAVE NEW ORDERS."

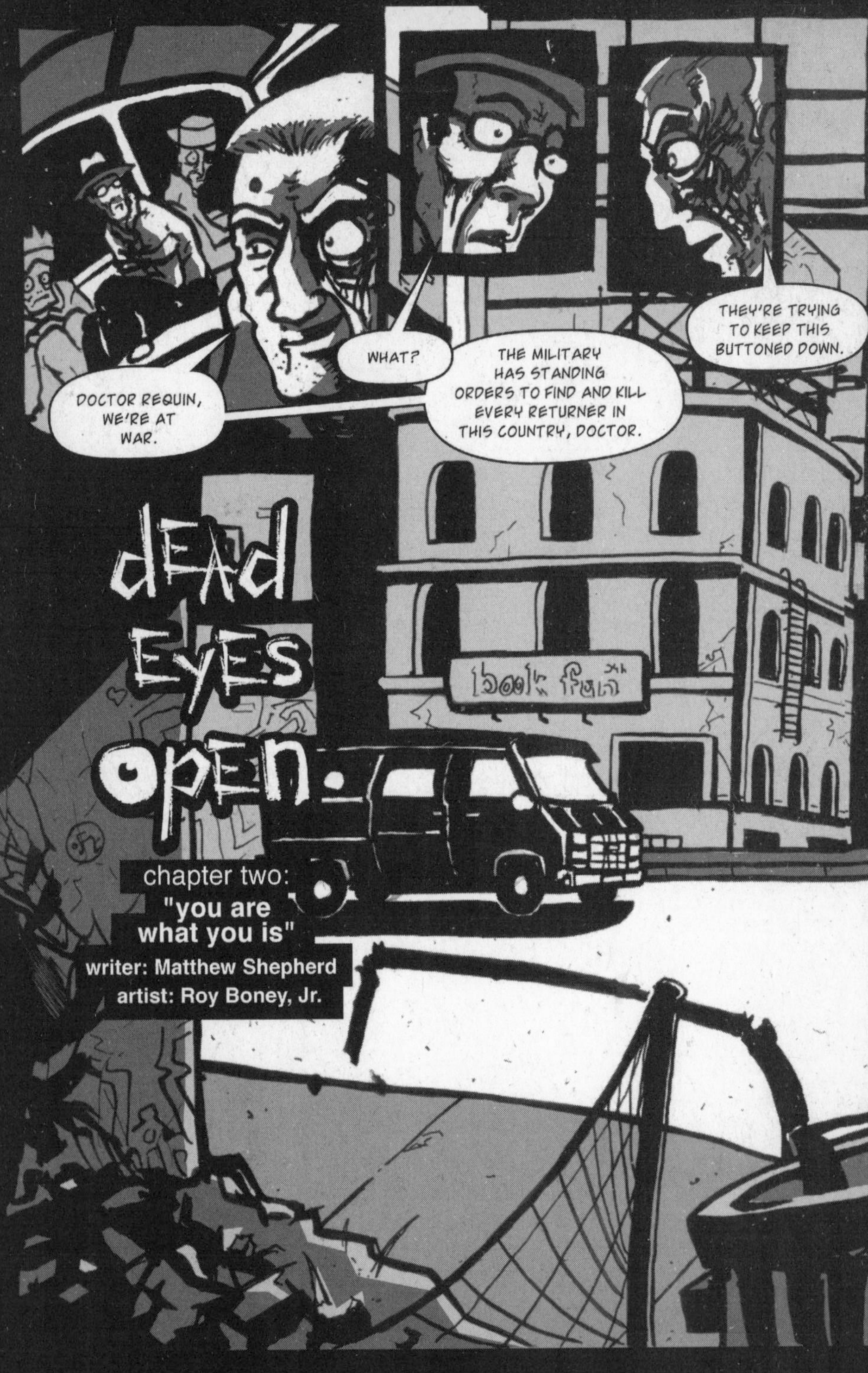
DOCTOR REQUIN, WE'RE AT WAR.
WHAT?
THE MILITARY HAS STANDING ORDERS TO FIND AND KILL EVERY RETURNER IN THIS COUNTRY, DOCTOR.
THEY'RE TRYING TO KEEP THIS BUTTONED DOWN.
dead EYES OPEN
chapter two:
"you are what you is"
writer: Matthew Shepherd
artist: Roy Boney, Jr.

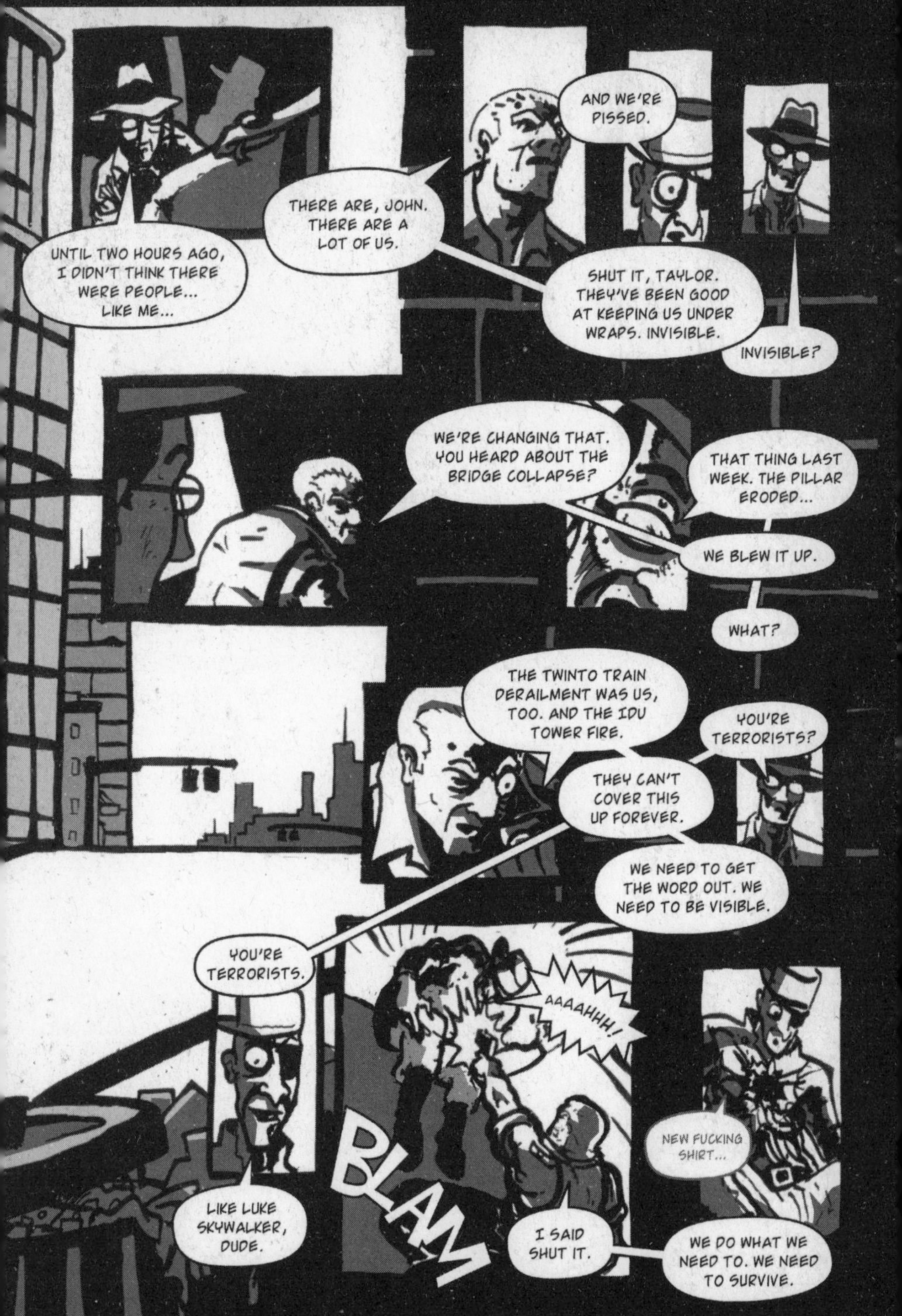
UNTIL TWO HOURS AGO, I DIDN'T THINK THERE WERE PEOPLE... LIKE ME...
THERE ARE, JOHN. THERE ARE A LOT OF US.
AND WE'RE PISSED.
SHUT IT, TAYLOR. THEY'VE BEEN GOOD AT KEEPING US UNDER WRAPS. INVISIBLE.
INVISIBLE?
WE'RE CHANGING THAT. YOU HEARD ABOUT THE BRIDGE COLLAPSE?
THAT THING LAST WEEK. THE PILLAR ERODED...
WE BLEW IT UP.
WHAT?
THE TWINTO TRAIN DERAILMENT WAS US, TOO. AND THE IDU TOWER FIRE.
YOU'RE TERRORISTS?
THEY CAN'T COVER THIS UP FOREVER.
WE NEED TO GET THE WORD OUT. WE NEED TO BE VISIBLE.
YOU'RE TERRORISTS.
LIKE LUKE SKYWALKER, DUDE.
AAAAHHH!
BLAM
I SAID SHUT IT.
NEW FUCKING SHIRT...
WE DO WHAT WE NEED TO. WE NEED TO SURVIVE.

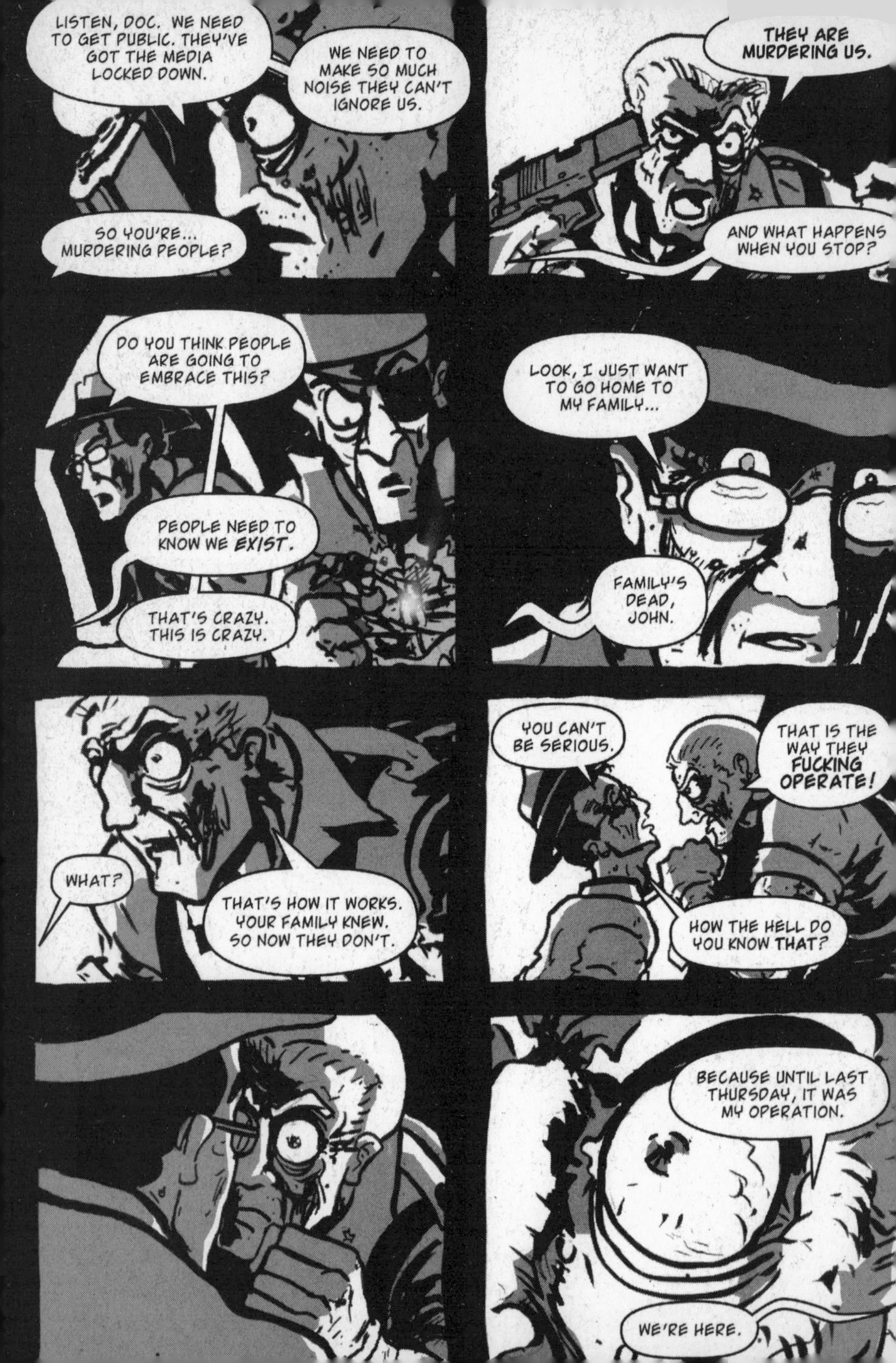
LISTEN, DOC. WE NEED TO GET PUBLIC. THEY'VE GOT THE MEDIA LOCKED DOWN.
WE NEED TO MAKE SO MUCH NOISE THEY CAN'T IGNORE US.
SO YOU'RE... MURDERING PEOPLE?
THEY ARE MURDERING US.
AND WHAT HAPPENS WHEN YOU STOP?
DO YOU THINK PEOPLE ARE GOING TO EMBRACE THIS?
PEOPLE NEED TO KNOW WE EXIST.
THAT'S CRAZY. THIS IS CRAZY.
LOOK, I JUST WANT TO GO HOME TO MY FAMILY...
FAMILY'S DEAD, JOHN.
WHAT?
THAT'S HOW IT WORKS. YOUR FAMILY KNEW. SO NOW THEY DON'T.
YOU CAN'T BE SERIOUS.
THAT IS THE WAY THEY FUCKING OPERATE!
HOW THE HELL DO YOU KNOW THAT?
BECAUSE UNTIL LAST THURSDAY, IT WAS MY OPERATION.
WE'RE HERE.

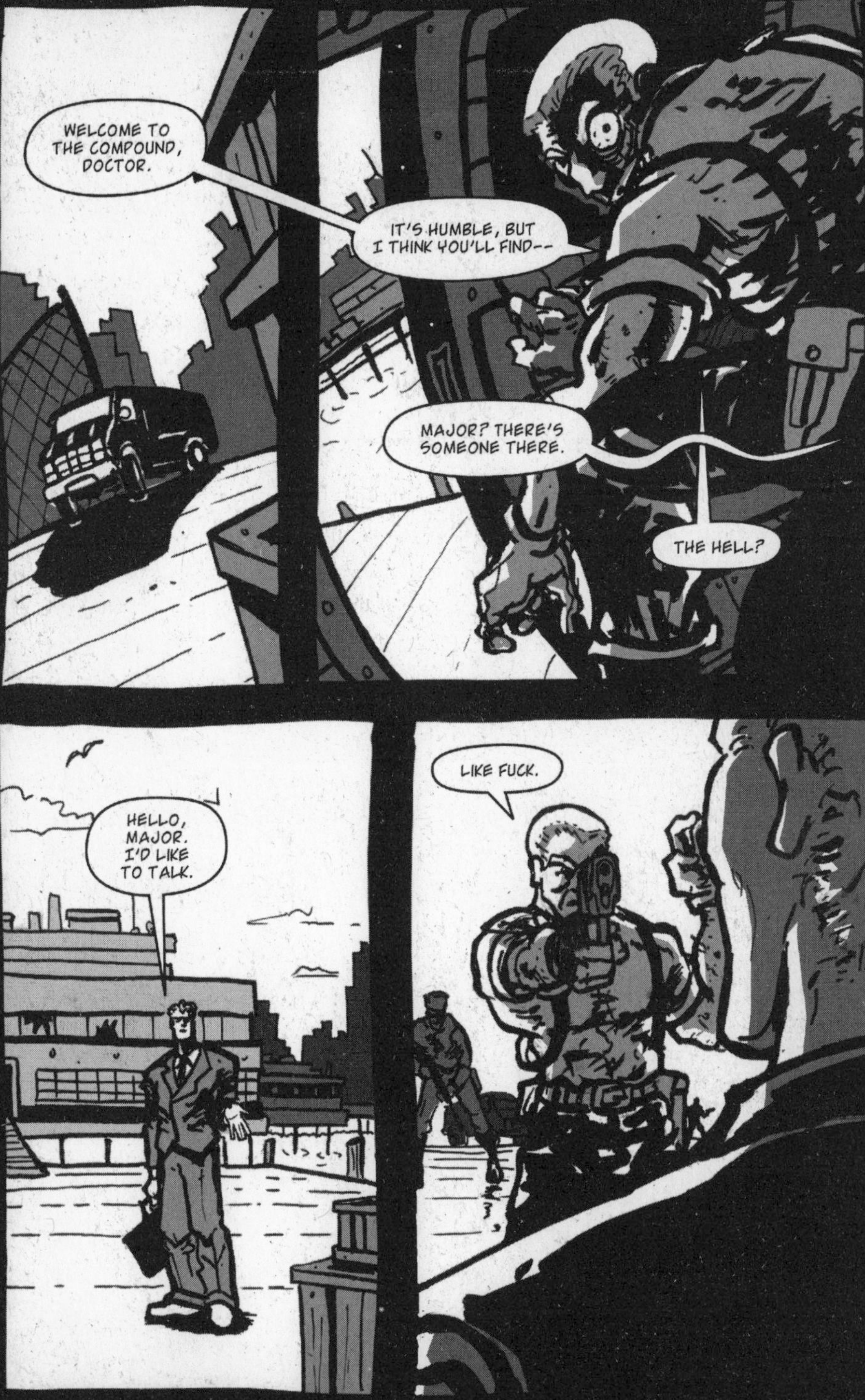
WELCOME TO THE COMPOUND, DOCTOR.
IT'S HUMBLE, BUT I THINK YOU'LL FIND--
MAJOR? THERE'S SOMEONE THERE.
THE HELL?
HELLO, MAJOR. I'D LIKE TO TALK.
LIKE FUCK.

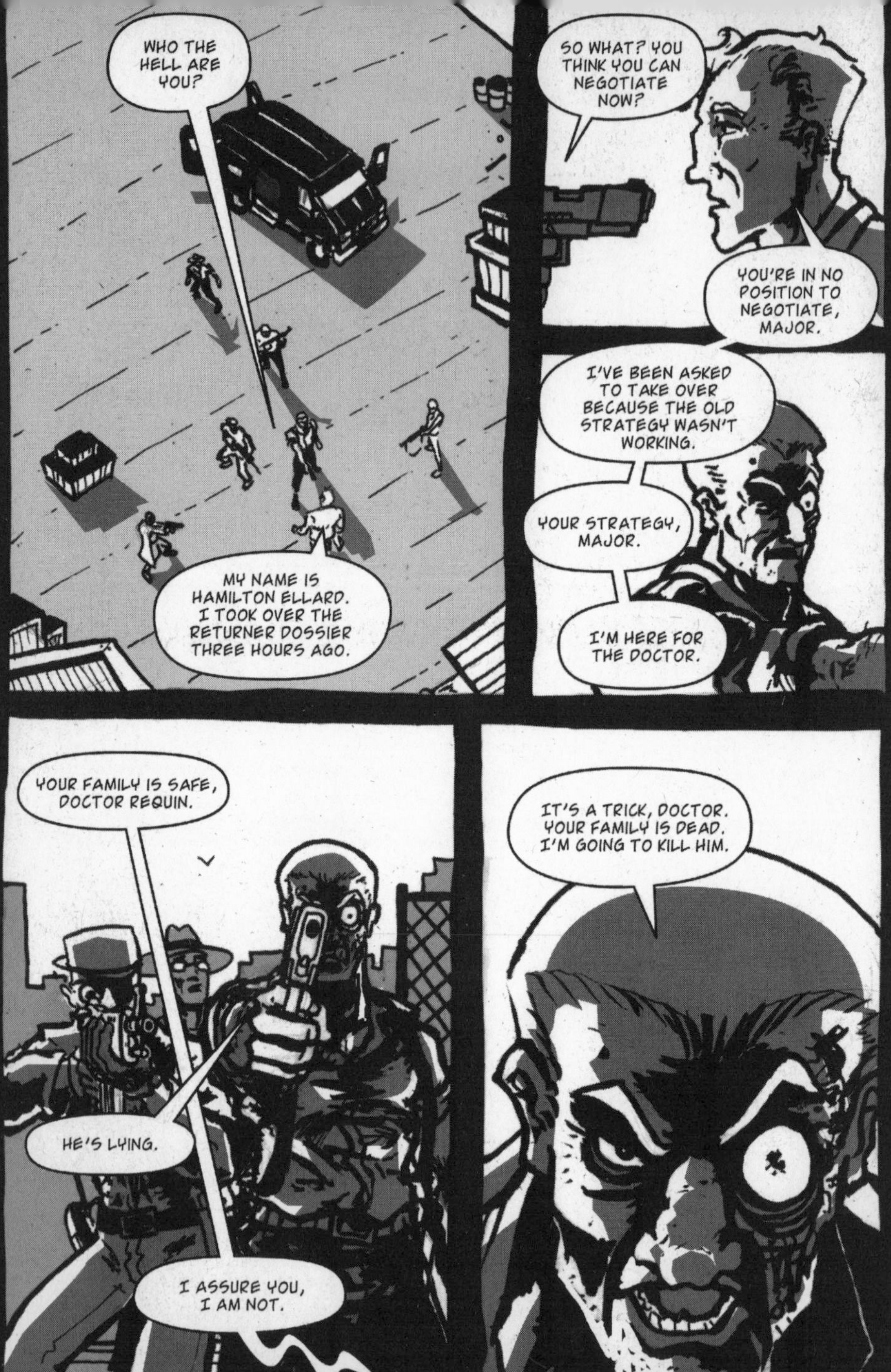
WHO THE HELL ARE YOU?
MY NAME IS HAMILTON ELLARD. I TOOK OVER THE RETURNER DOSSIER THREE HOURS AGO.
SO WHAT? YOU THINK YOU CAN NEGOTIATE NOW?
YOU'RE IN NO POSITION TO NEGOTIATE, MAJOR.
I'VE BEEN ASKED TO TAKE OVER BECAUSE THE OLD STRATEGY WASN'T WORKING.
YOUR STRATEGY, MAJOR.
I'M HERE FOR THE DOCTOR.
YOUR FAMILY IS SAFE, DOCTOR REQUIN.
HE'S LYING.
I ASSURE YOU, I AM NOT.
IT'S A TRICK, DOCTOR. YOUR FAMILY IS DEAD. I'M GOING TO KILL HIM.

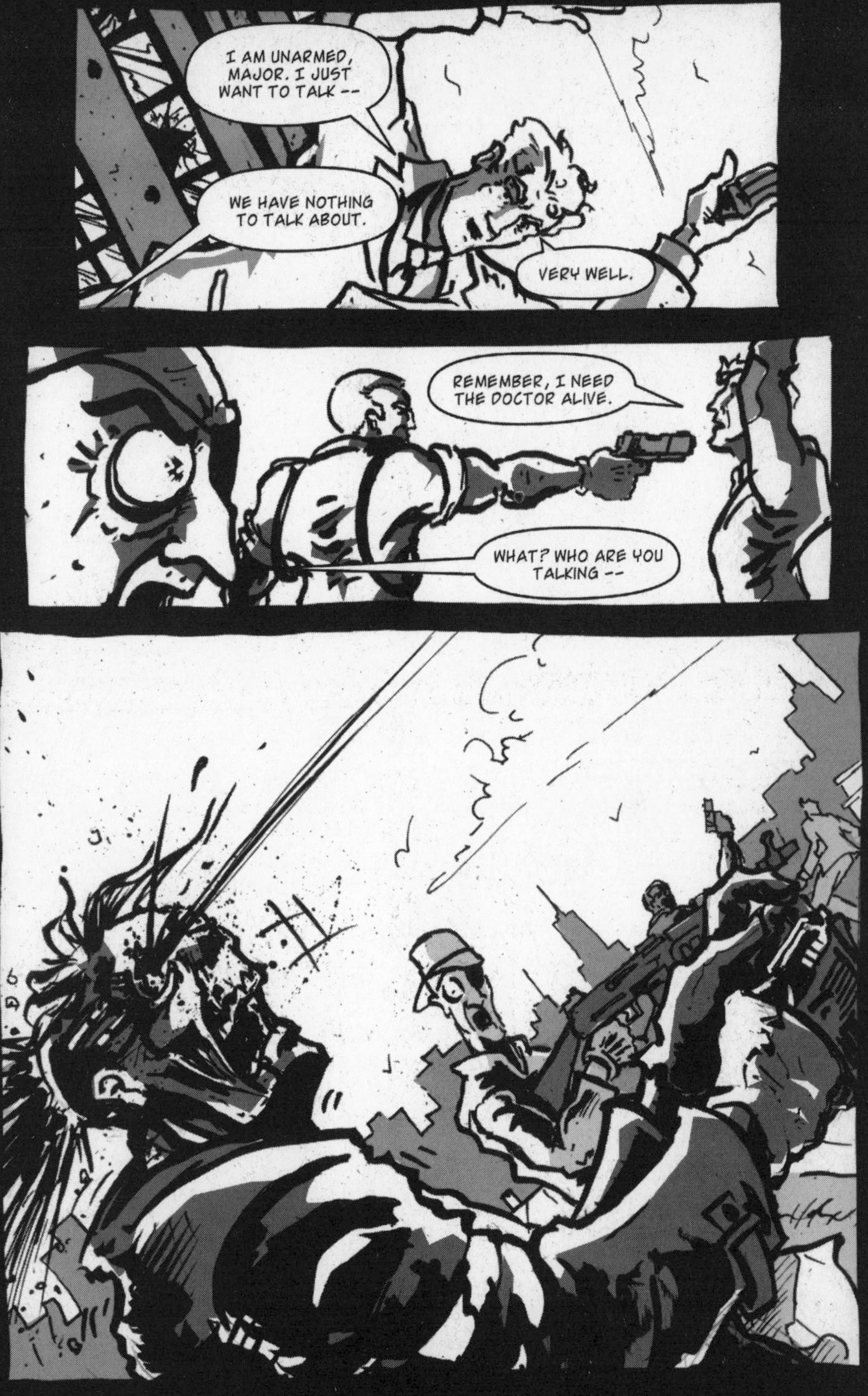
I AM UNARMED, MAJOR. I JUST WANT TO TALK --
WE HAVE NOTHING TO TALK ABOUT.
VERY WELL.
REMEMBER, I NEED THE DOCTOR ALIVE.
WHAT? WHO ARE YOU TALKING --

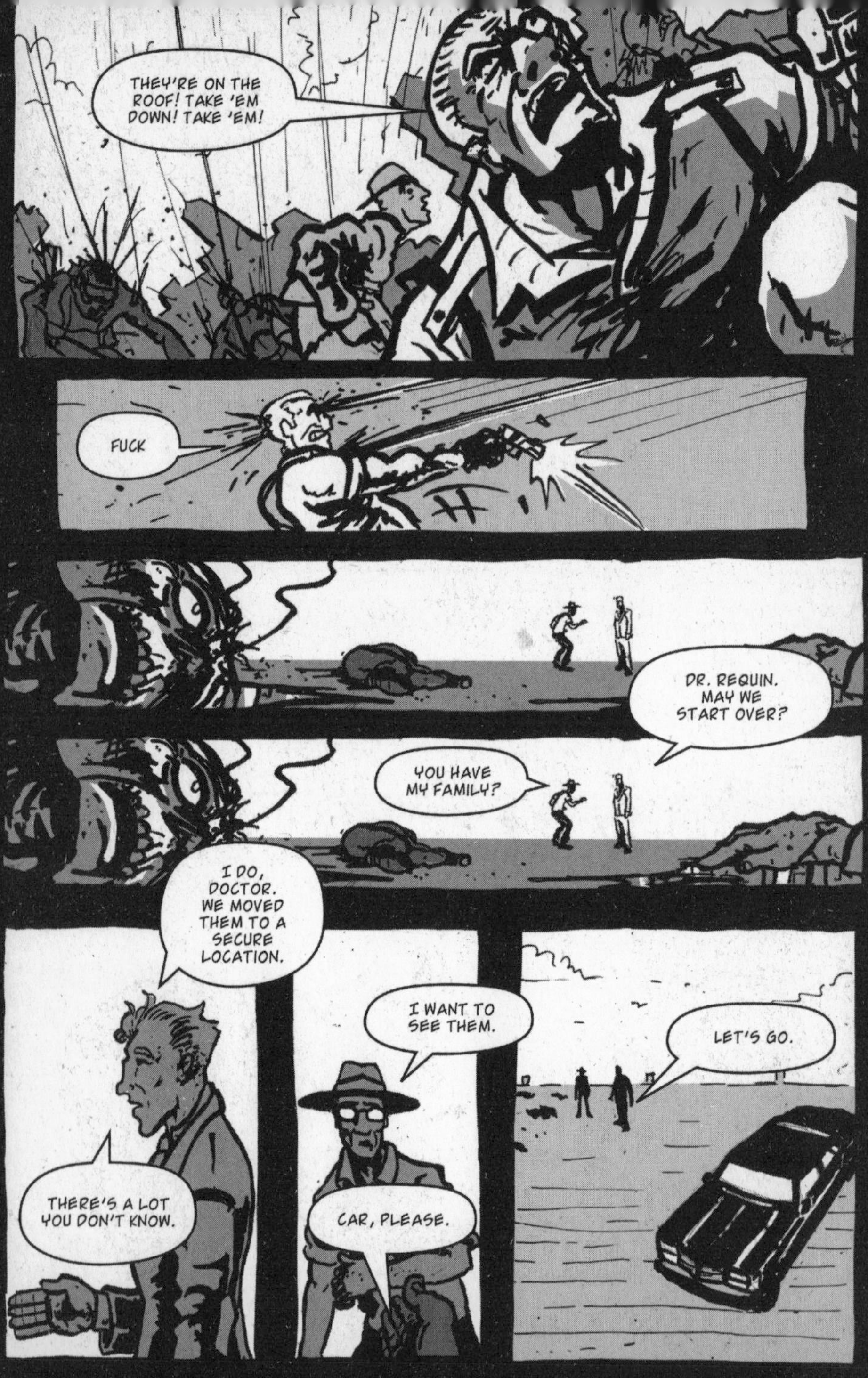
THEY'RE ON THE ROOF! TAKE 'EM DOWN! TAKE 'EM!
FUCK
DR. REQUIN. MAY WE START OVER?
YOU HAVE MY FAMILY?
I DO, DOCTOR. WE MOVED THEM TO A SECURE LOCATION.
THERE'S A LOT YOU DON'T KNOW.
I WANT TO SEE THEM.
CAR, PLEASE.
LET'S GO.

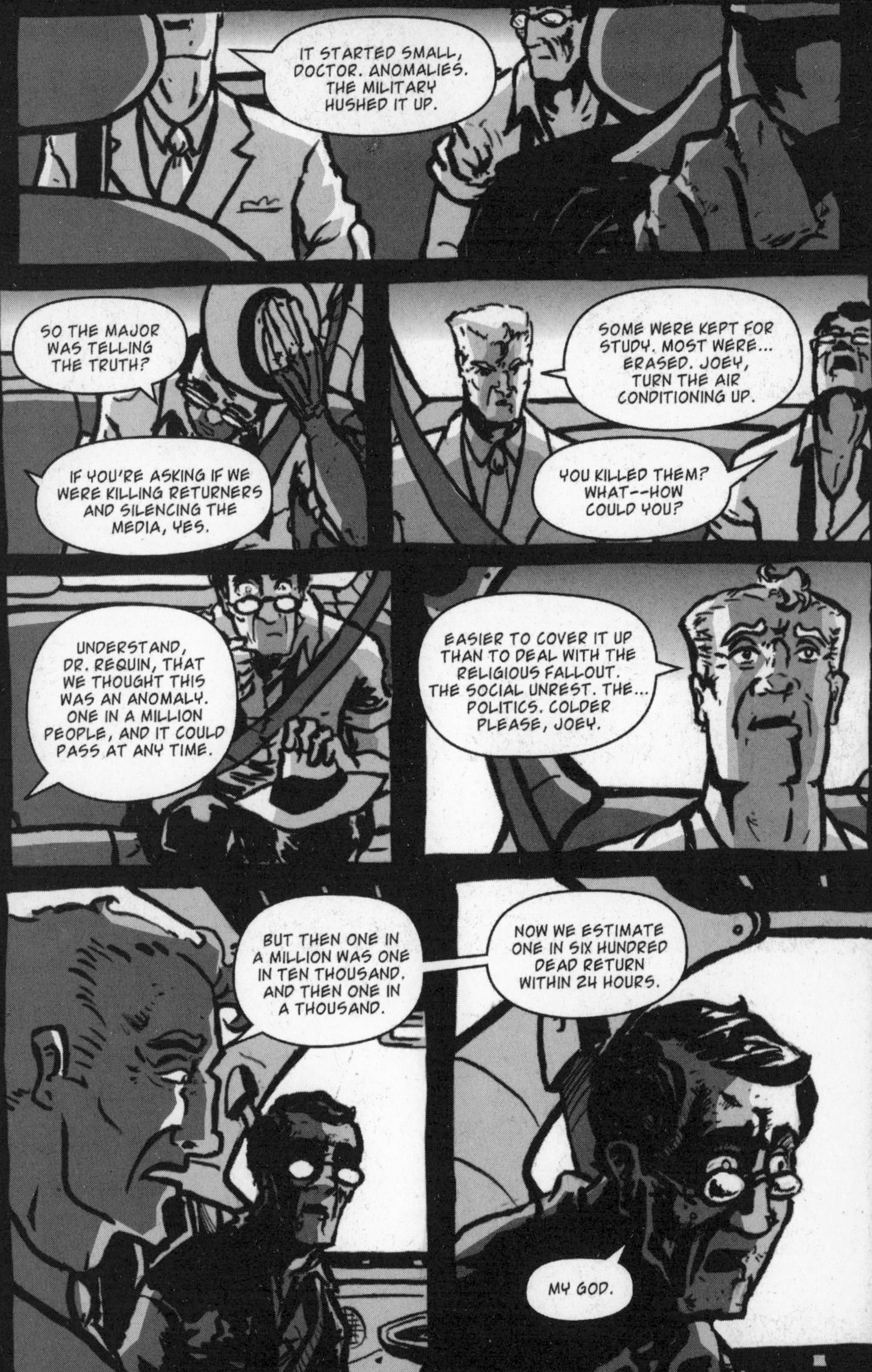
IT STARTED SMALL, DOCTOR. ANOMALIES. THE MILITARY HUSHED IT UP.
SO THE MAJOR WAS TELLING THE TRUTH?
IF YOU'RE ASKING IF WE WERE KILLING RETURNERS AND SILENCING THE MEDIA, YES.
SOME WERE KEPT FOR STUDY. MOST WERE... ERASED. JOEY, TURN THE AIR CONDITIONING UP.
YOU KILLED THEM? WHAT--HOW COULD YOU?
UNDERSTAND, DR. REQUIN, THAT WE THOUGHT THIS WAS AN ANOMALY. ONE IN A MILLION PEOPLE, AND IT COULD PASS AT ANY TIME.
EASIER TO COVER IT UP THAN TO DEAL WITH THE RELIGIOUS FALLOUT. THE SOCIAL UNREST. THE... POLITICS. COLDER PLEASE, JOEY.
BUT THEN ONE IN A MILLION WAS ONE IN TEN THOUSAND. AND THEN ONE IN A THOUSAND.
NOW WE ESTIMATE ONE IN SIX HUNDRED DEAD RETURN WITHIN 24 HOURS.
MY GOD.

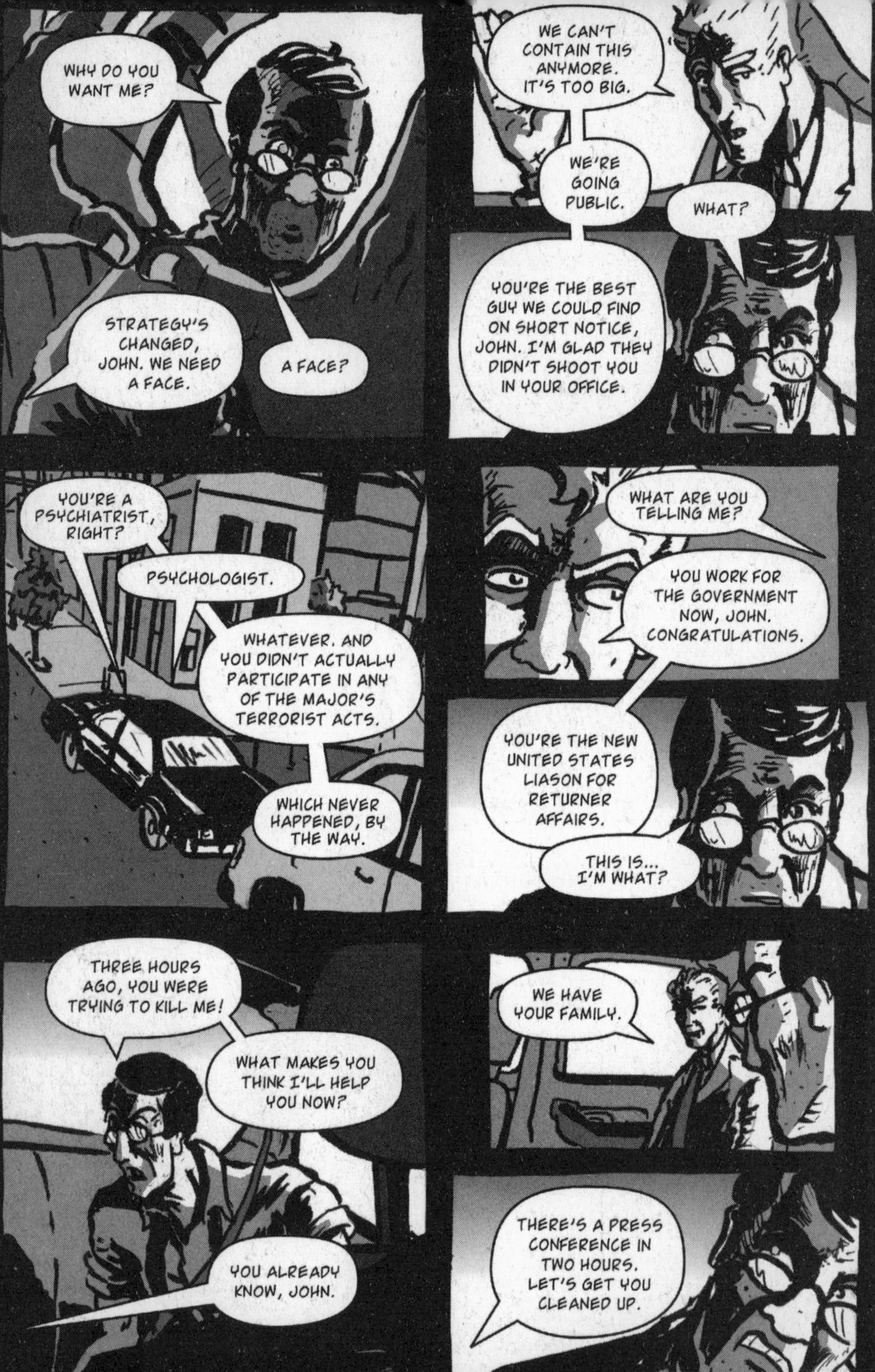
WHY DO YOU WANT ME?
STRATEGY'S CHANGED, JOHN. WE NEED A FACE.
A FACE?
WE CAN'T CONTAIN THIS ANYMORE. IT'S TOO BIG.
WE'RE GOING PUBLIC.
WHAT?
YOU'RE THE BEST GUY WE COULD FIND ON SHORT NOTICE, JOHN. I'M GLAD THEY DIDN'T SHOOT YOU IN YOUR OFFICE.
YOU'RE A PSYCHIATRIST, RIGHT?
PSYCHOLOGIST.
WHATEVER. AND YOU DIDN'T ACTUALLY PARTICIPATE IN ANY OF THE MAJOR'S TERRORIST ACTS.
WHICH NEVER HAPPENED, BY THE WAY.
WHAT ARE YOU TELLING ME?
YOU WORK FOR THE GOVERNMENT NOW, JOHN. CONGRATULATIONS.
YOU'RE THE NEW UNITED STATES LIASON FOR RETURNER AFFAIRS.
THIS IS... I'M WHAT?
THREE HOURS AGO, YOU WERE TRYING TO KILL ME!
WHAT MAKES YOU THINK I'LL HELP YOU NOW?
YOU ALREADY KNOW, JOHN.
WE HAVE YOUR FAMILY.
THERE'S A PRESS CONFERENCE IN TWO HOURS. LET'S GET YOU CLEANED UP.

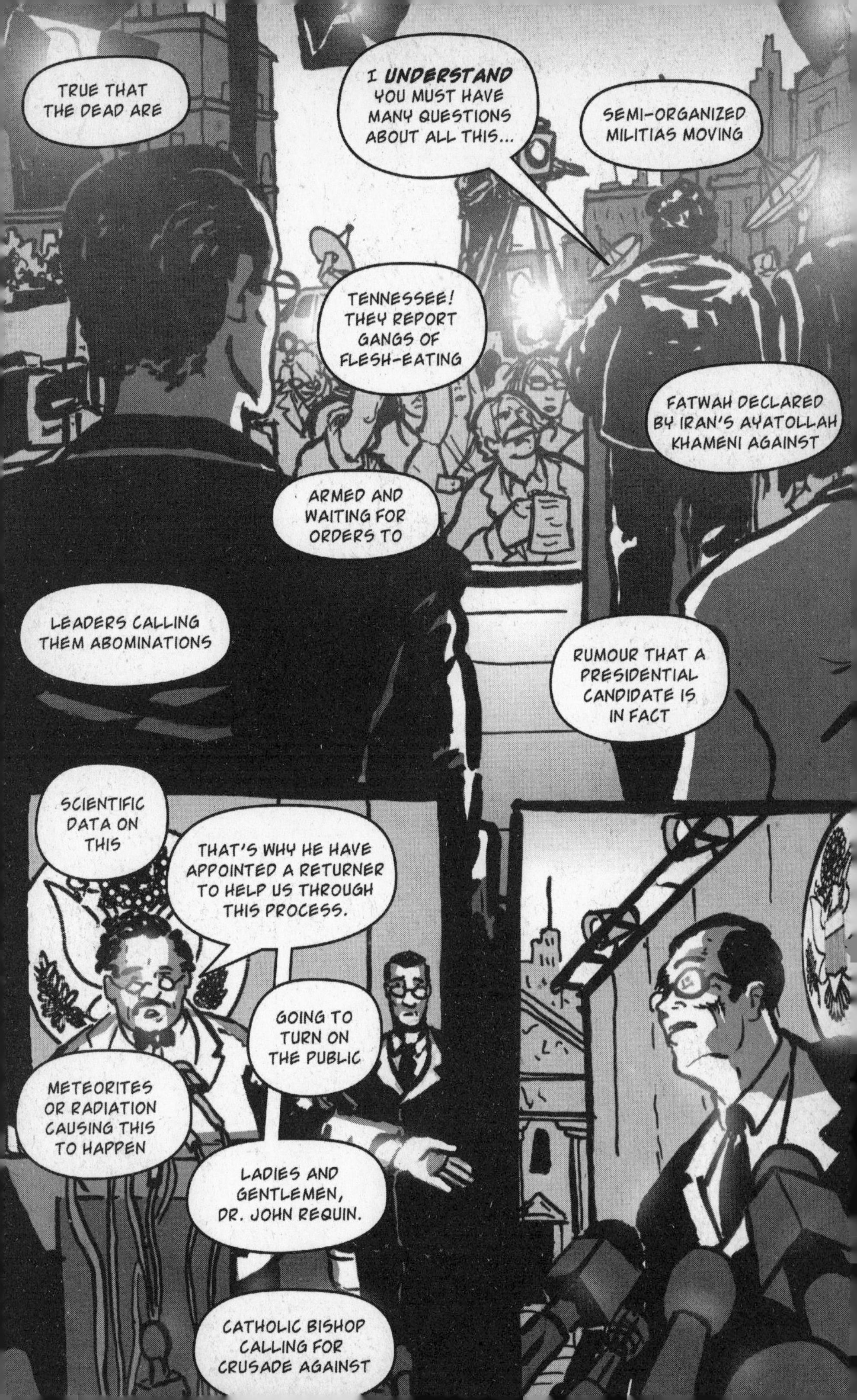
TRUE THAT THE DEAD ARE
I UNDERSTAND YOU MUST HAVE MANY QUESTIONS ABOUT ALL THIS...
SEMI-ORGANIZED MILITIAS MOVING
TENNESSEE! THEY REPORT GANGS OF FLESH-EATING
FATWAH DECLARED BY IRAN'S AYATOLLAH KHAMENI AGAINST
ARMED AND WAITING FOR ORDERS TO
LEADERS CALLING THEM ABOMINATIONS
RUMOUR THAT A PRESIDENTIAL CANDIDATE IS IN FACT
SCIENTIFIC DATA ON THIS
THAT'S WHY HE HAVE APPOINTED A RETURNER TO HELP US THROUGH THIS PROCESS.
GOING TO TURN ON THE PUBLIC
METEORITES OR RADIATION CAUSING THIS TO HAPPEN
LADIES AND GENTLEMEN, DR. JOHN REQUIN.
CATHOLIC BISHOP CALLING FOR CRUSADE AGAINST

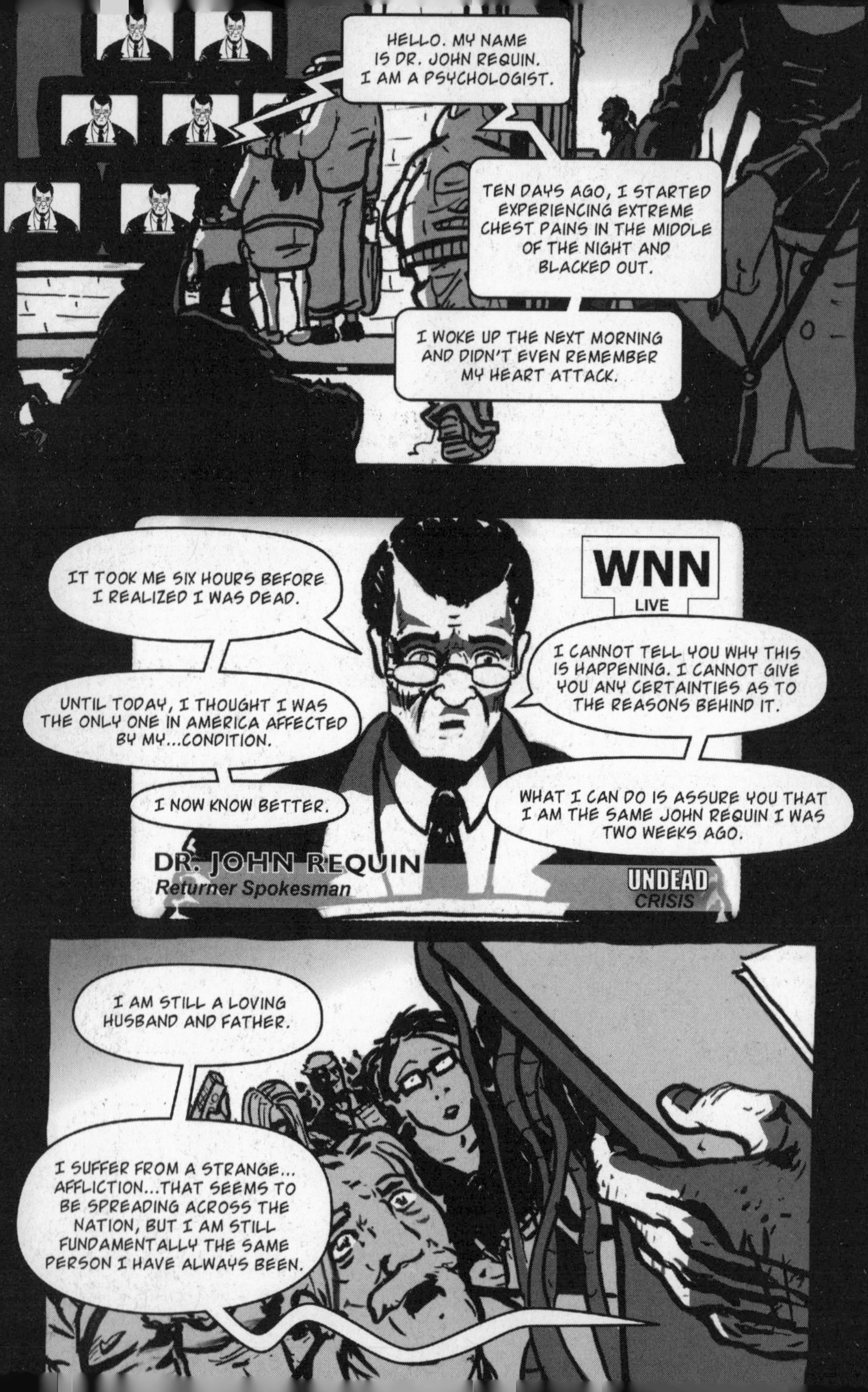
HELLO. MY NAME IS DR. JOHN REQUIN. I AM A PSYCHOLOGIST.
TEN DAYS AGO, I STARTED EXPERIENCING EXTREME CHEST PAINS IN THE MIDDLE OF THE NIGHT AND BLACKED OUT.
I WOKE UP THE NEXT MORNING AND DIDN'T EVEN REMEMBER MY HEART ATTACK.
WNN
LIVE
IT TOOK ME SIX HOURS BEFORE I REALIZED I WAS DEAD.
UNTIL TODAY, I THOUGHT I WAS THE ONLY ONE IN AMERICA AFFECTED BY MY...CONDITION.
I NOW KNOW BETTER.
I CANNOT TELL YOU WHY THIS IS HAPPENING. I CANNOT GIVE YOU ANY CERTAINTIES AS TO THE REASONS BEHIND IT.
WHAT I CAN DO IS ASSURE YOU THAT I AM THE SAME JOHN REQUIN I WAS TWO WEEKS AGO.
DR. JOHN REQUIN
Returner Spokesman
UNDEAD
CRISIS
I AM STILL A LOVING HUSBAND AND FATHER.
I SUFFER FROM A STRANGE... AFFLICTION...THAT SEEMS TO BE SPREADING ACROSS THE NATION, BUT I AM STILL FUNDAMENTALLY THE SAME PERSON I HAVE ALWAYS BEEN.

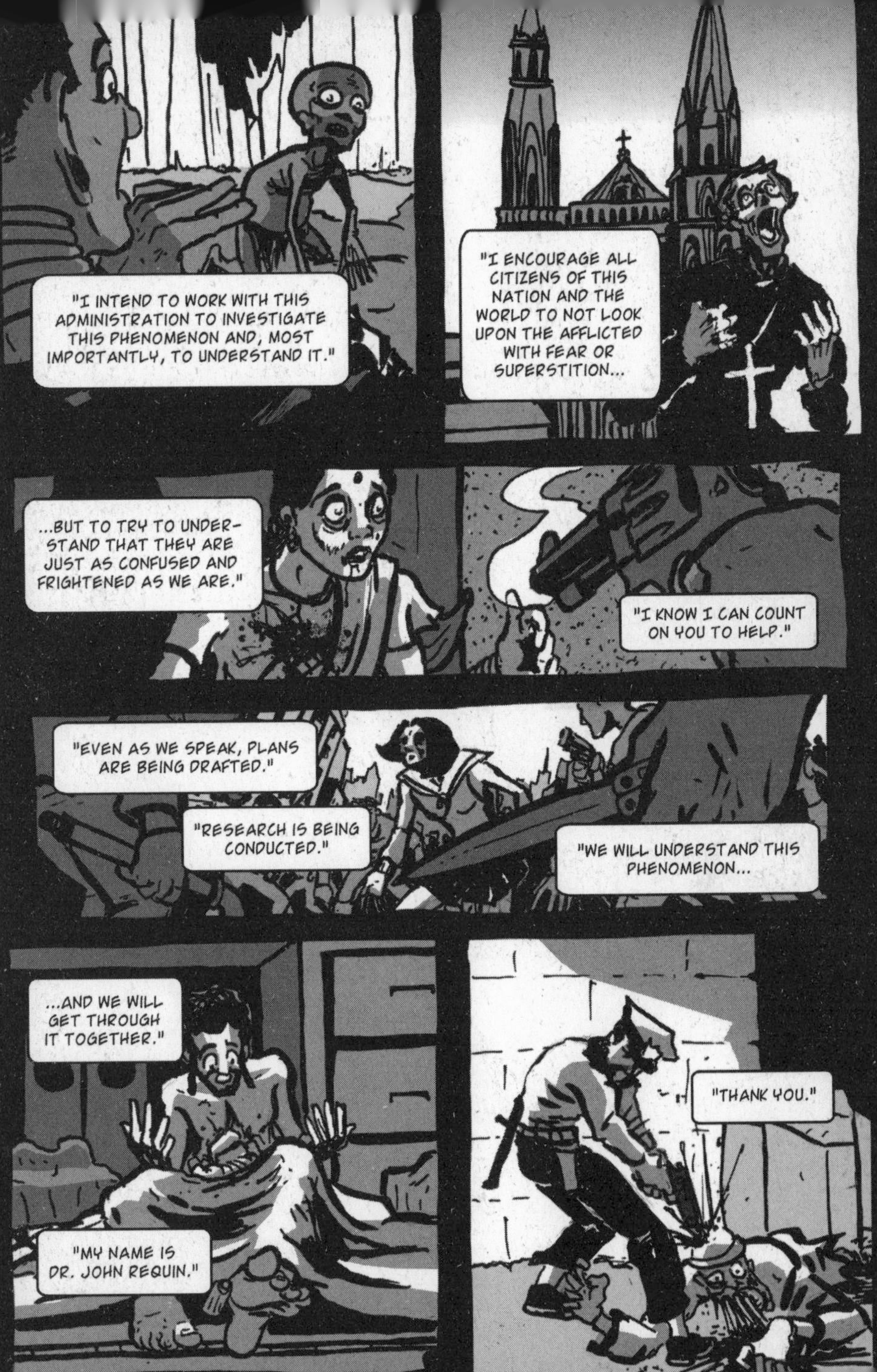
"I INTEND TO WORK WITH THIS ADMINISTRATION TO INVESTIGATE THIS PHENOMENON AND, MOST IMPORTANTLY, TO UNDERSTAND IT."
"I ENCOURAGE ALL CITIZENS OF THIS NATION AND THE WORLD TO NOT LOOK UPON THE AFFLICTED WITH FEAR OR SUPERSTITION...
...BUT TO TRY TO UNDERSTAND THAT THEY ARE JUST AS CONFUSED AND FRIGHTENED AS WE ARE."
"I KNOW I CAN COUNT ON YOU TO HELP."
"EVEN AS WE SPEAK, PLANS ARE BEING DRAFTED."
"RESEARCH IS BEING CONDUCTED."
"WE WILL UNDERSTAND THIS PHENOMENON...
...AND WE WILL GET THROUGH IT TOGETHER."
"MY NAME IS DR. JOHN REQUIN."
"THANK YOU."

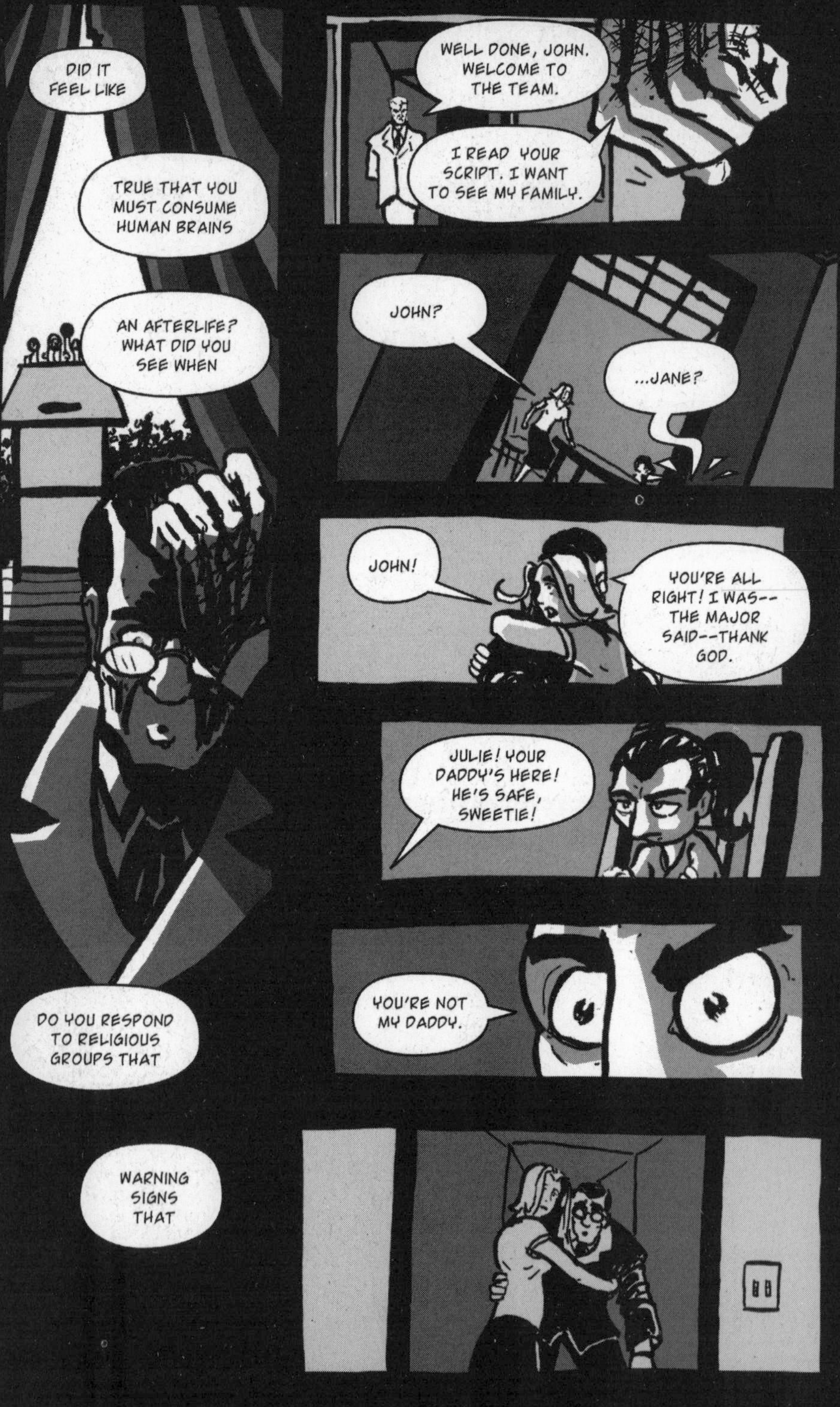
DID IT FEEL LIKE
TRUE THAT YOU MUST CONSUME HUMAN BRAINS
AN AFTERLIFE? WHAT DID YOU SEE WHEN
WELL DONE, JOHN. WELCOME TO THE TEAM.
I READ YOUR SCRIPT. I WANT TO SEE MY FAMILY.
JOHN?
...JANE?
JOHN!
YOU'RE ALL RIGHT! I WAS-- THE MAJOR SAID--THANK GOD.
JULIE! YOUR DADDY'S HERE! HE'S SAFE, SWEETIE!
YOU'RE NOT MY DADDY.
DO YOU RESPOND TO RELIGIOUS GROUPS THAT
WARNING SIGNS THAT

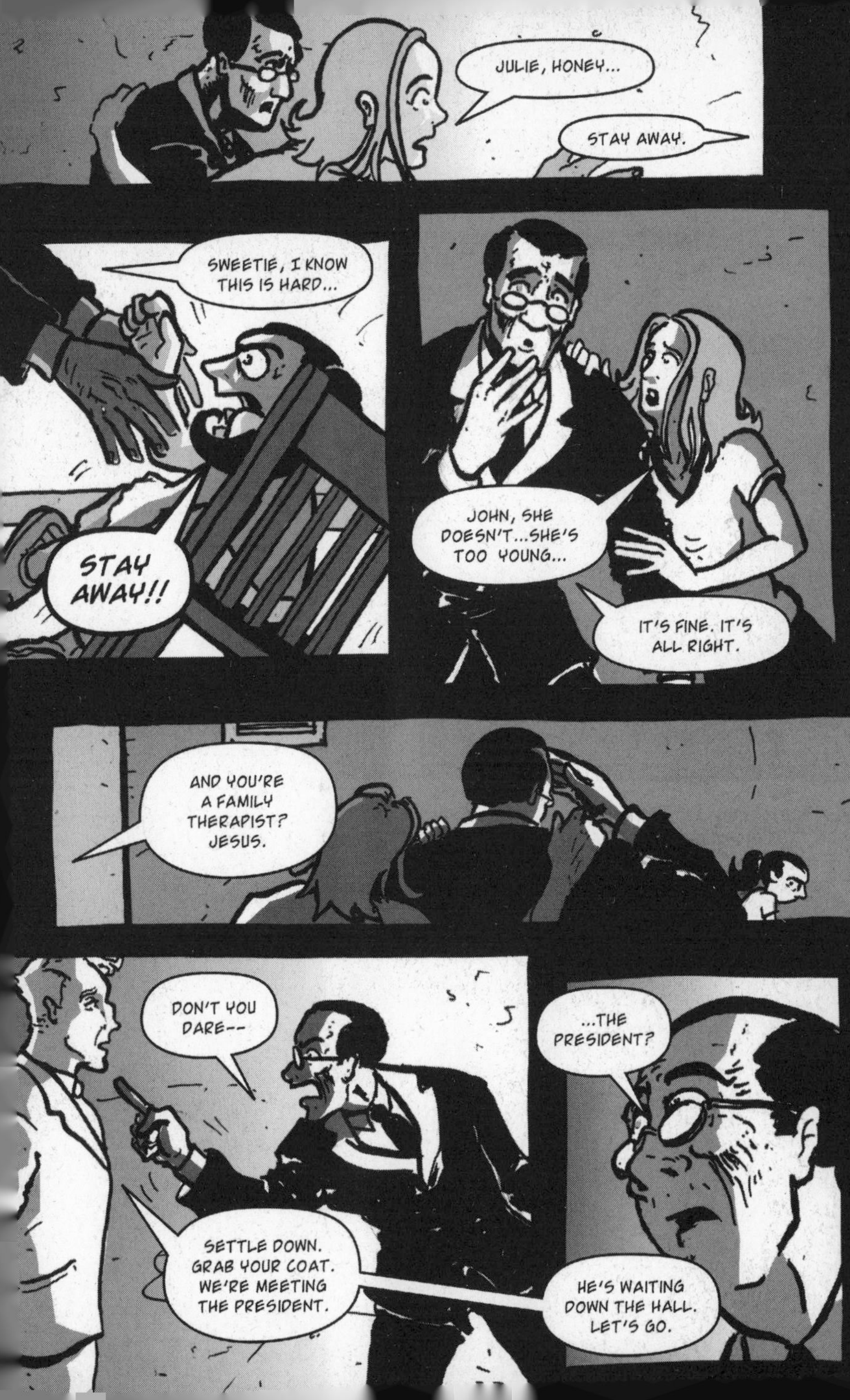
JULIE, HONEY...
STAY AWAY.
SWEETIE, I KNOW THIS IS HARD...
STAY AWAY!!
JOHN, SHE DOESN'T...SHE'S TOO YOUNG...
IT'S FINE. IT'S ALL RIGHT.
AND YOU'RE A FAMILY THERAPIST? JESUS.
DON'T YOU DARE--
SETTLE DOWN. GRAB YOUR COAT. WE'RE MEETING THE PRESIDENT.
...THE PRESIDENT?
HE'S WAITING DOWN THE HALL. LET'S GO.

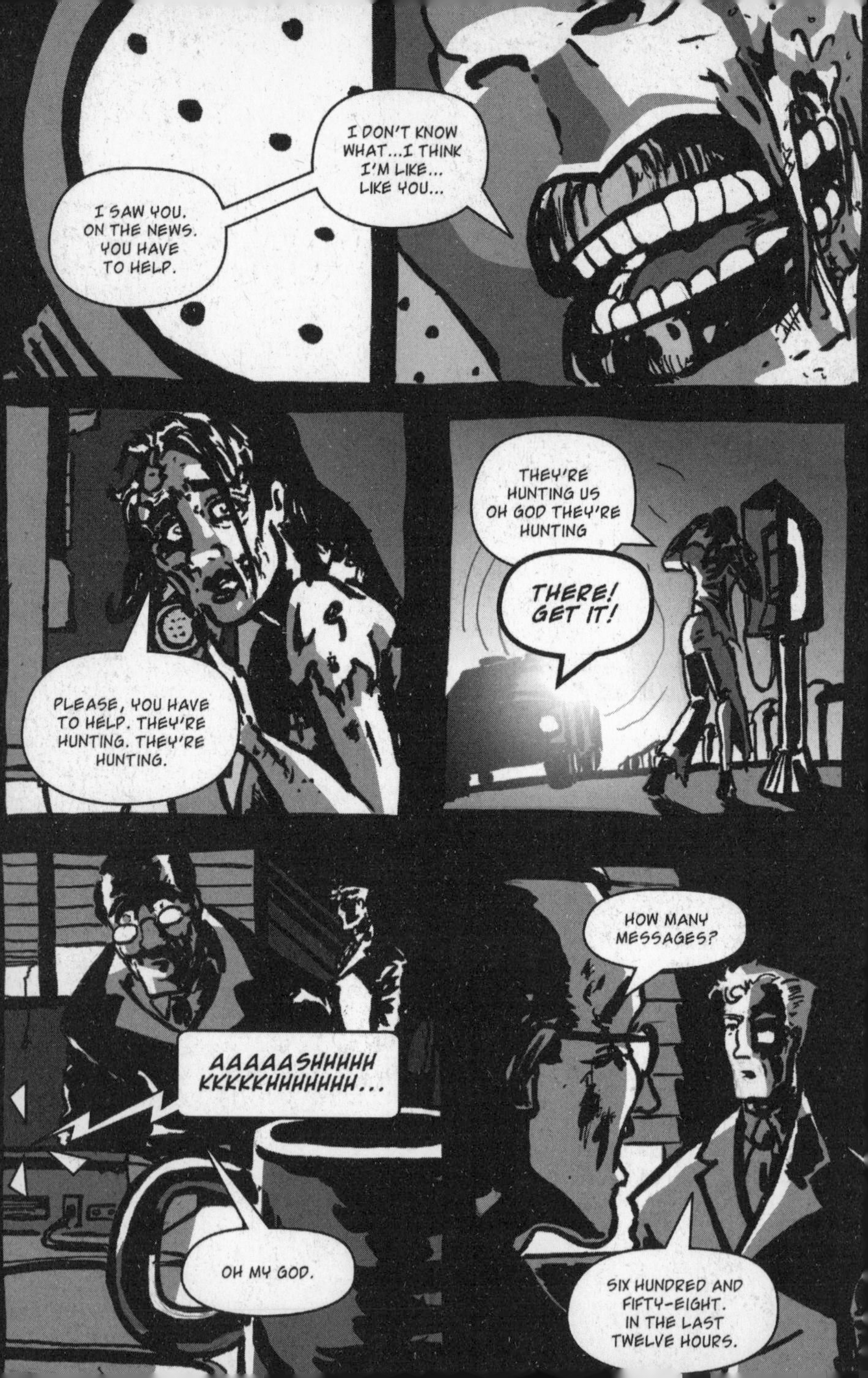
I SAW YOU. ON THE NEWS. YOU HAVE TO HELP.
I DON'T KNOW WHAT...I THINK I'M LIKE... LIKE YOU...
PLEASE, YOU HAVE TO HELP. THEY'RE HUNTING. THEY'RE HUNTING.
THEY'RE HUNTING US OH GOD THEY'RE HUNTING
THERE! GET IT!
AAAAASHHHHH KKKKKHHHHHHH...
OH MY GOD.
HOW MANY MESSAGES?
SIX HUNDRED AND FIFTY-EIGHT. IN THE LAST TWELVE HOURS.

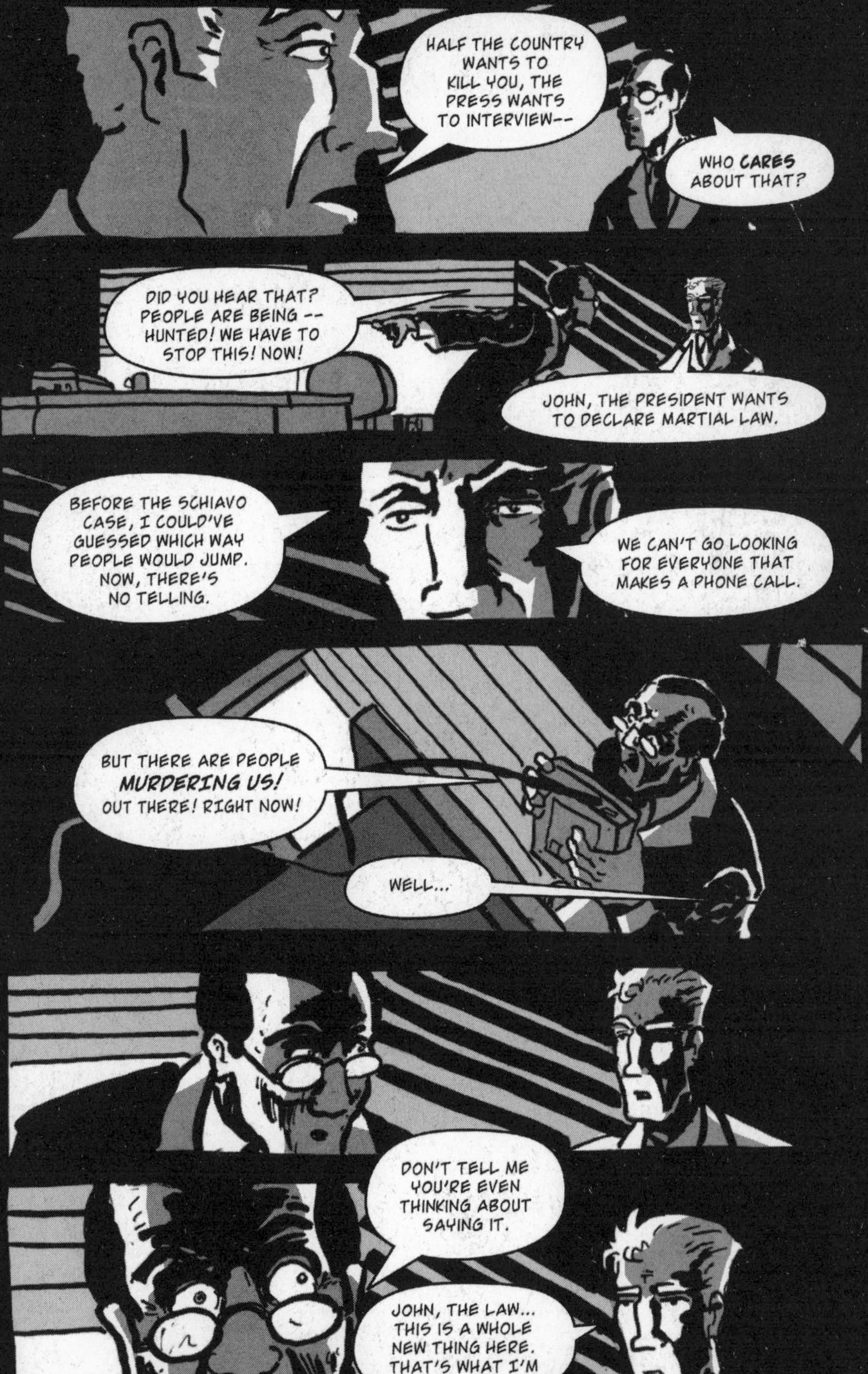
HALF THE COUNTRY WANTS TO KILL YOU, THE PRESS WANTS TO INTERVIEW--
WHO **CARES** ABOUT THAT?
DID YOU HEAR THAT? PEOPLE ARE BEING -- HUNTED! WE HAVE TO STOP THIS! NOW!
JOHN, THE PRESIDENT WANTS TO DECLARE MARTIAL LAW.
BEFORE THE SCHIAVO CASE, I COULD'VE GUESSED WHICH WAY PEOPLE WOULD JUMP. NOW, THERE'S NO TELLING.
WE CAN'T GO LOOKING FOR EVERYONE THAT MAKES A PHONE CALL.
BUT THERE ARE PEOPLE ***MURDERING US!*** OUT THERE! RIGHT NOW!
WELL...
DON'T TELL ME YOU'RE EVEN THINKING ABOUT SAYING IT.
JOHN, THE LAW... THIS IS A WHOLE NEW THING HERE. THAT'S WHAT I'M SAYING.

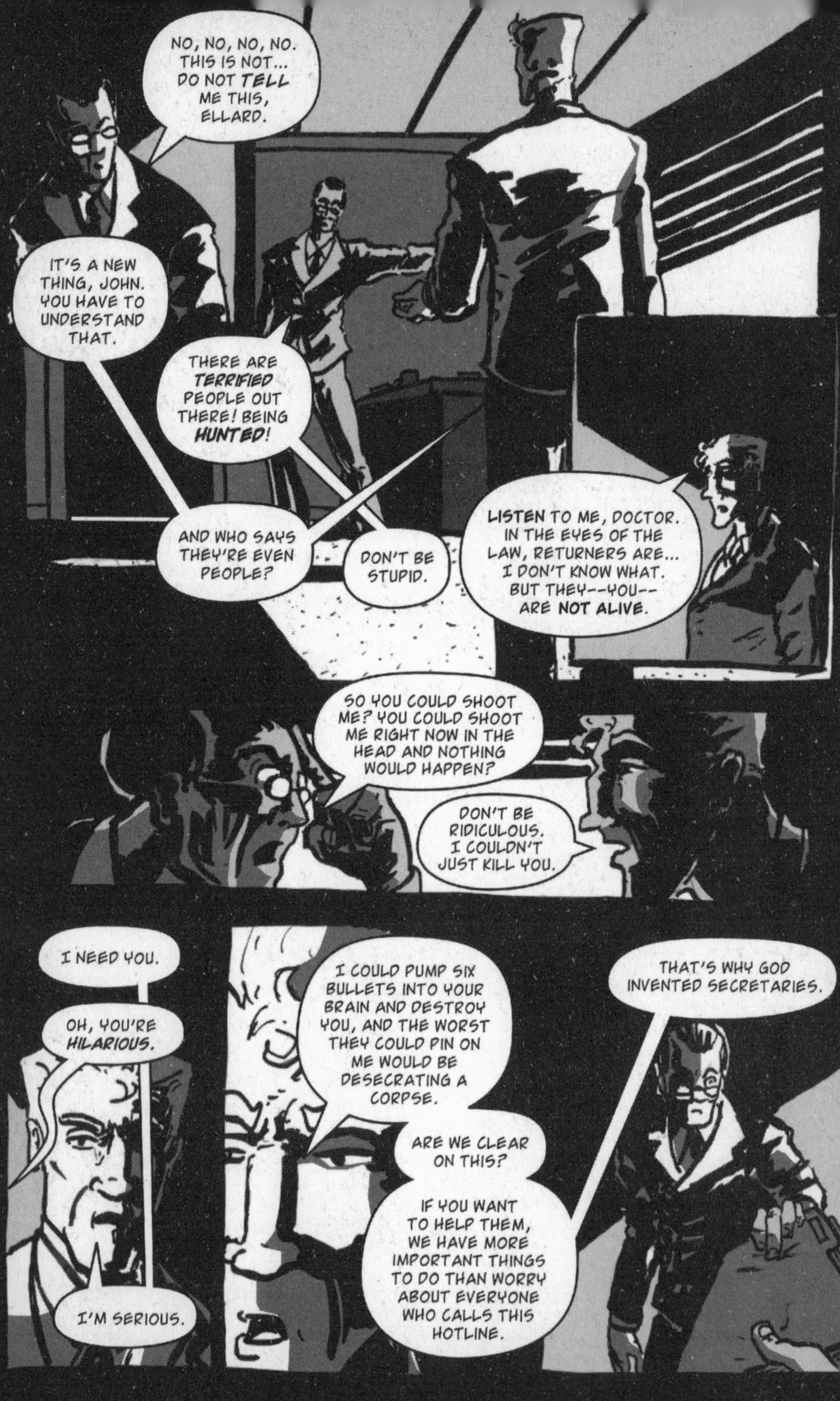
NO, NO, NO, NO. THIS IS NOT... DO NOT TELL ME THIS, ELLARD.
IT'S A NEW THING, JOHN. YOU HAVE TO UNDERSTAND THAT.
THERE ARE TERRIFIED PEOPLE OUT THERE! BEING HUNTED!
AND WHO SAYS THEY'RE EVEN PEOPLE?
DON'T BE STUPID.
LISTEN TO ME, DOCTOR. IN THE EYES OF THE LAW, RETURNERS ARE... I DON'T KNOW WHAT. BUT THEY--YOU--ARE NOT ALIVE.
SO YOU COULD SHOOT ME? YOU COULD SHOOT ME RIGHT NOW IN THE HEAD AND NOTHING WOULD HAPPEN?
DON'T BE RIDICULOUS. I COULDN'T JUST KILL YOU.
I NEED YOU.
OH, YOU'RE HILARIOUS.
I'M SERIOUS.
I COULD PUMP SIX BULLETS INTO YOUR BRAIN AND DESTROY YOU, AND THE WORST THEY COULD PIN ON ME WOULD BE DESECRATING A CORPSE.
ARE WE CLEAR ON THIS?
IF YOU WANT TO HELP THEM, WE HAVE MORE IMPORTANT THINGS TO DO THAN WORRY ABOUT EVERYONE WHO CALLS THIS HOTLINE.
THAT'S WHY GOD INVENTED SECRETARIES.

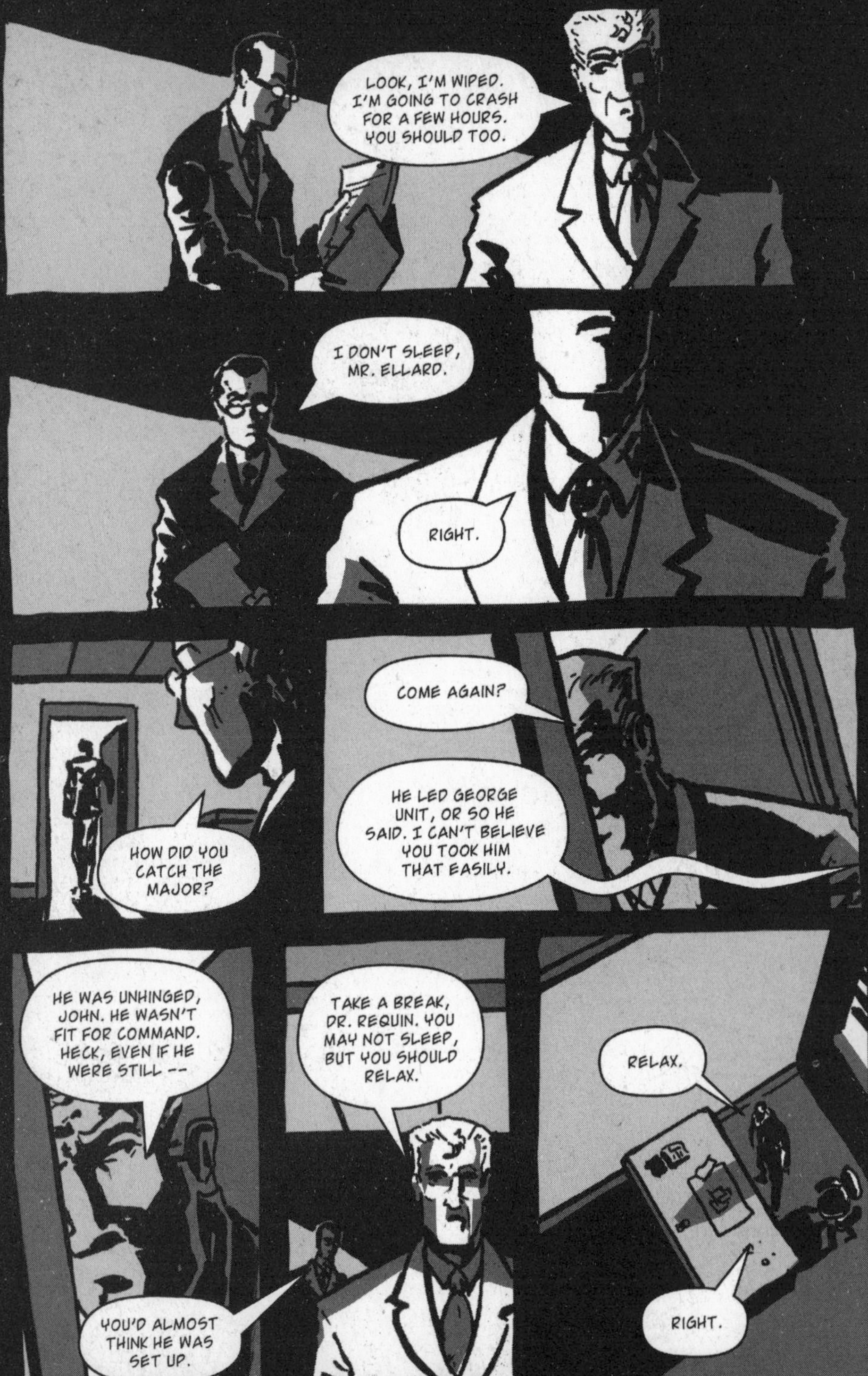
LOOK, I'M WIPED. I'M GOING TO CRASH FOR A FEW HOURS. YOU SHOULD TOO.
I DON'T SLEEP, MR. ELLARD.
RIGHT.
HOW DID YOU CATCH THE MAJOR?
COME AGAIN?
HE LED GEORGE UNIT, OR SO HE SAID. I CAN'T BELIEVE YOU TOOK HIM THAT EASILY.
HE WAS UNHINGED, JOHN. HE WASN'T FIT FOR COMMAND. HECK, EVEN IF HE WERE STILL --
YOU'D ALMOST THINK HE WAS SET UP.
TAKE A BREAK, DR. REQUIN. YOU MAY NOT SLEEP, BUT YOU SHOULD RELAX.
RELAX.
RIGHT.

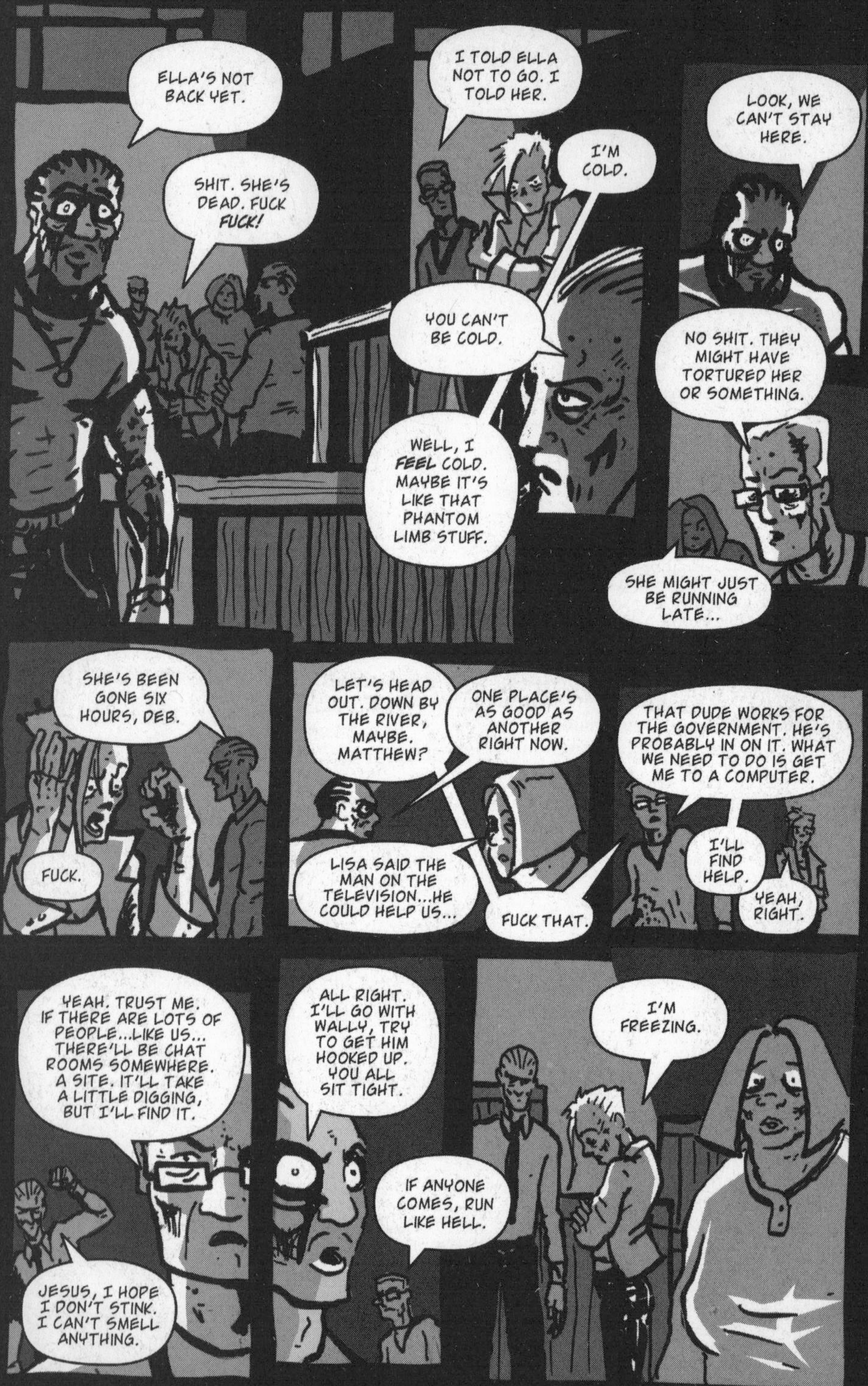
ELLA'S NOT BACK YET.
SHIT. SHE'S DEAD. FUCK FUCK!
I TOLD ELLA NOT TO GO. I TOLD HER.
I'M COLD.
YOU CAN'T BE COLD.
WELL, I FEEL COLD. MAYBE IT'S LIKE THAT PHANTOM LIMB STUFF.
LOOK, WE CAN'T STAY HERE.
NO SHIT. THEY MIGHT HAVE TORTURED HER OR SOMETHING.
SHE MIGHT JUST BE RUNNING LATE...
SHE'S BEEN GONE SIX HOURS, DEB.
FUCK.
LET'S HEAD OUT. DOWN BY THE RIVER, MAYBE. MATTHEW?
ONE PLACE'S AS GOOD AS ANOTHER RIGHT NOW.
LISA SAID THE MAN ON THE TELEVISION...HE COULD HELP US...
FUCK THAT.
THAT DUDE WORKS FOR THE GOVERNMENT. HE'S PROBABLY IN ON IT. WHAT WE NEED TO DO IS GET ME TO A COMPUTER.
I'LL FIND HELP.
YEAH, RIGHT.
YEAH. TRUST ME. IF THERE ARE LOTS OF PEOPLE...LIKE US... THERE'LL BE CHAT ROOMS SOMEWHERE. A SITE. IT'LL TAKE A LITTLE DIGGING, BUT I'LL FIND IT.
JESUS, I HOPE I DON'T STINK. I CAN'T SMELL ANYTHING.
ALL RIGHT. I'LL GO WITH WALLY, TRY TO GET HIM HOOKED UP. YOU ALL SIT TIGHT.
IF ANYONE COMES, RUN LIKE HELL.
I'M FREEZING.

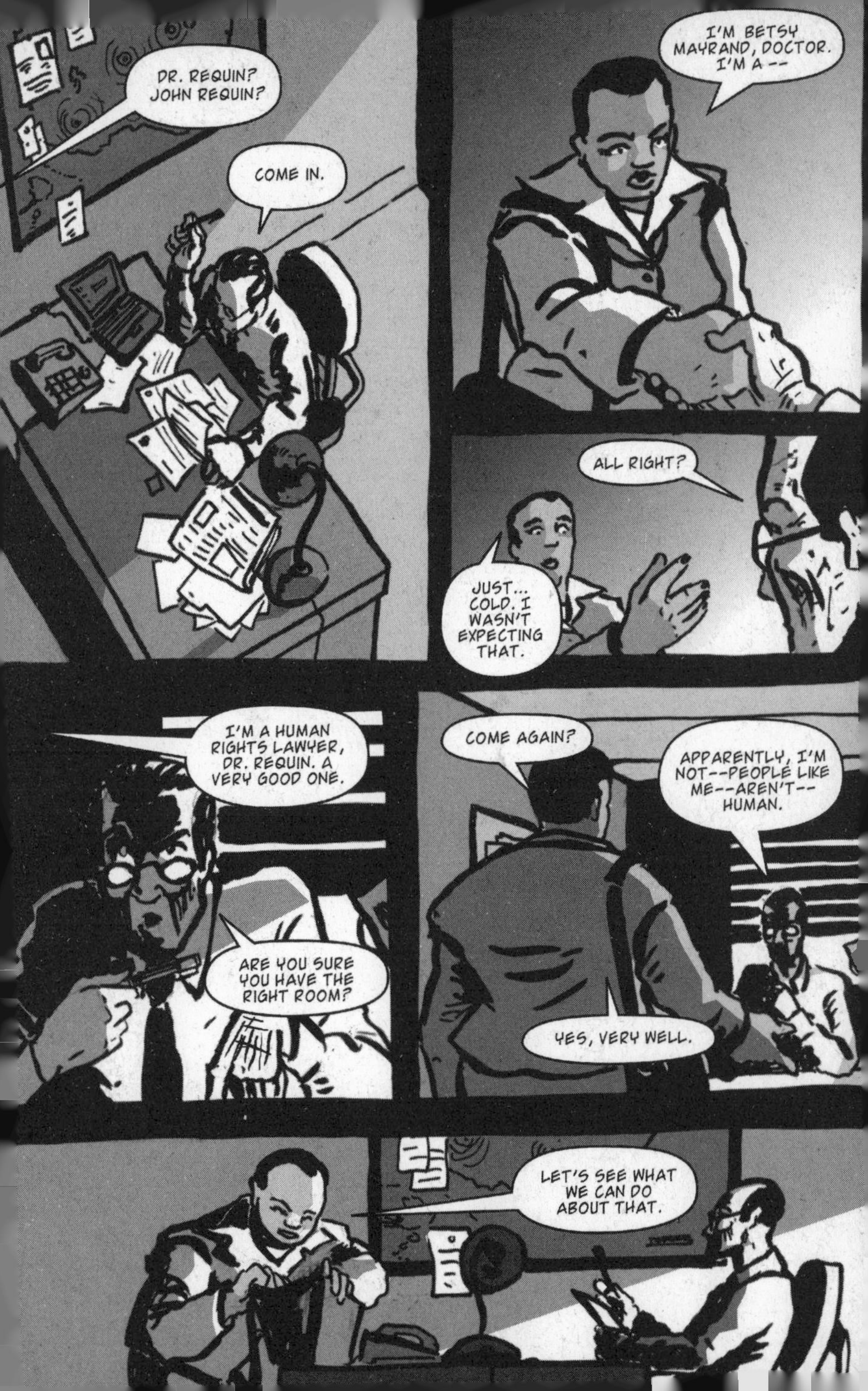
DR. REQUIN? JOHN REQUIN?
COME IN.
I'M BETSY MAYRAND, DOCTOR. I'M A --
ALL RIGHT?
JUST... COLD. I WASN'T EXPECTING THAT.
I'M A HUMAN RIGHTS LAWYER, DR. REQUIN. A VERY GOOD ONE.
ARE YOU SURE YOU HAVE THE RIGHT ROOM?
COME AGAIN?
APPARENTLY, I'M NOT--PEOPLE LIKE ME--AREN'T--HUMAN.
YES, VERY WELL.
LET'S SEE WHAT WE CAN DO ABOUT THAT.

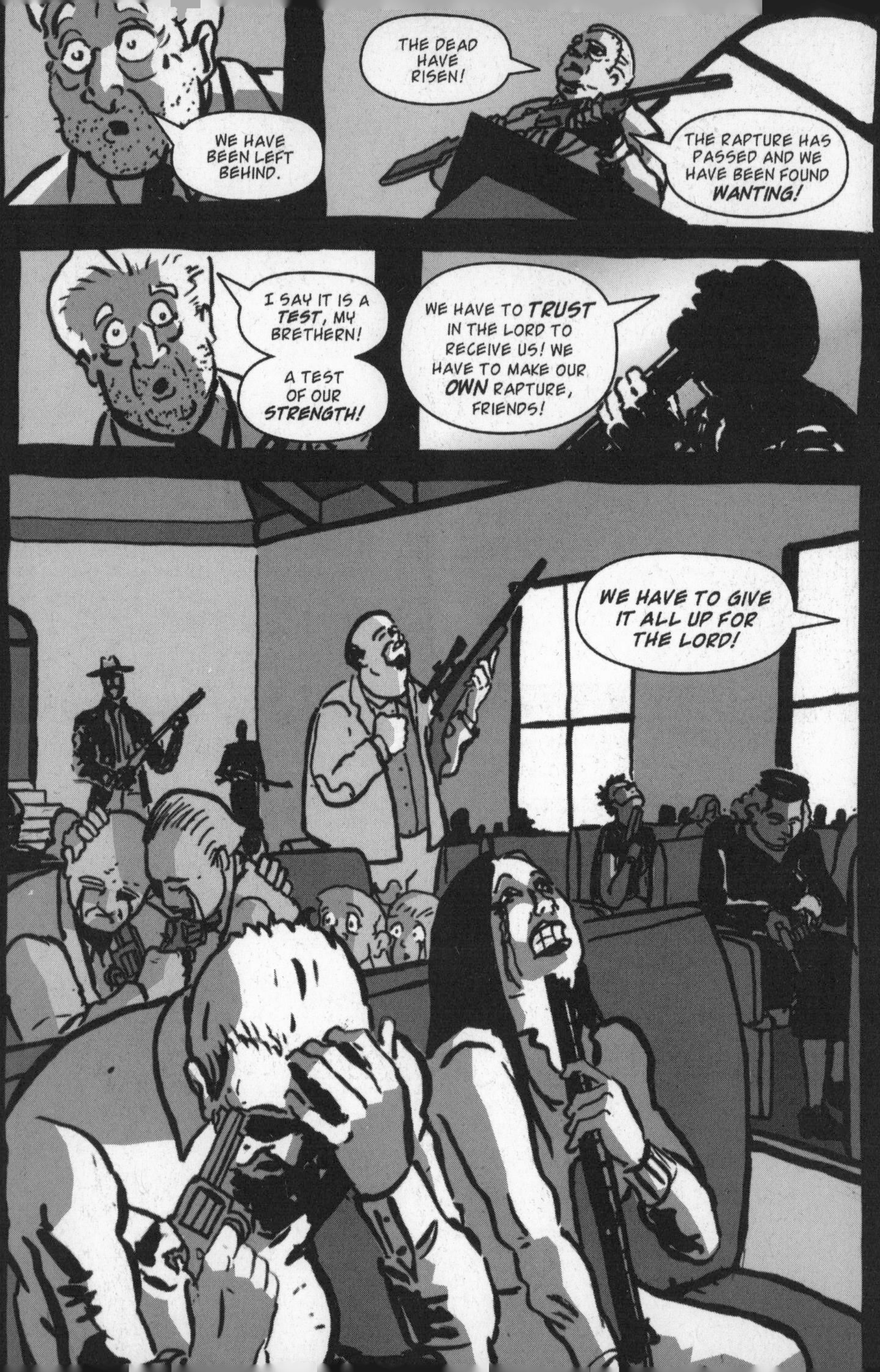
WE HAVE BEEN LEFT BEHIND.
THE DEAD HAVE RISEN!
THE RAPTURE HAS PASSED AND WE HAVE BEEN FOUND WANTING!
I SAY IT IS A TEST, MY BRETHERN!
A TEST OF OUR STRENGTH!
WE HAVE TO TRUST IN THE LORD TO RECEIVE US! WE HAVE TO MAKE OUR OWN RAPTURE, FRIENDS!
WE HAVE TO GIVE IT ALL UP FOR THE LORD!

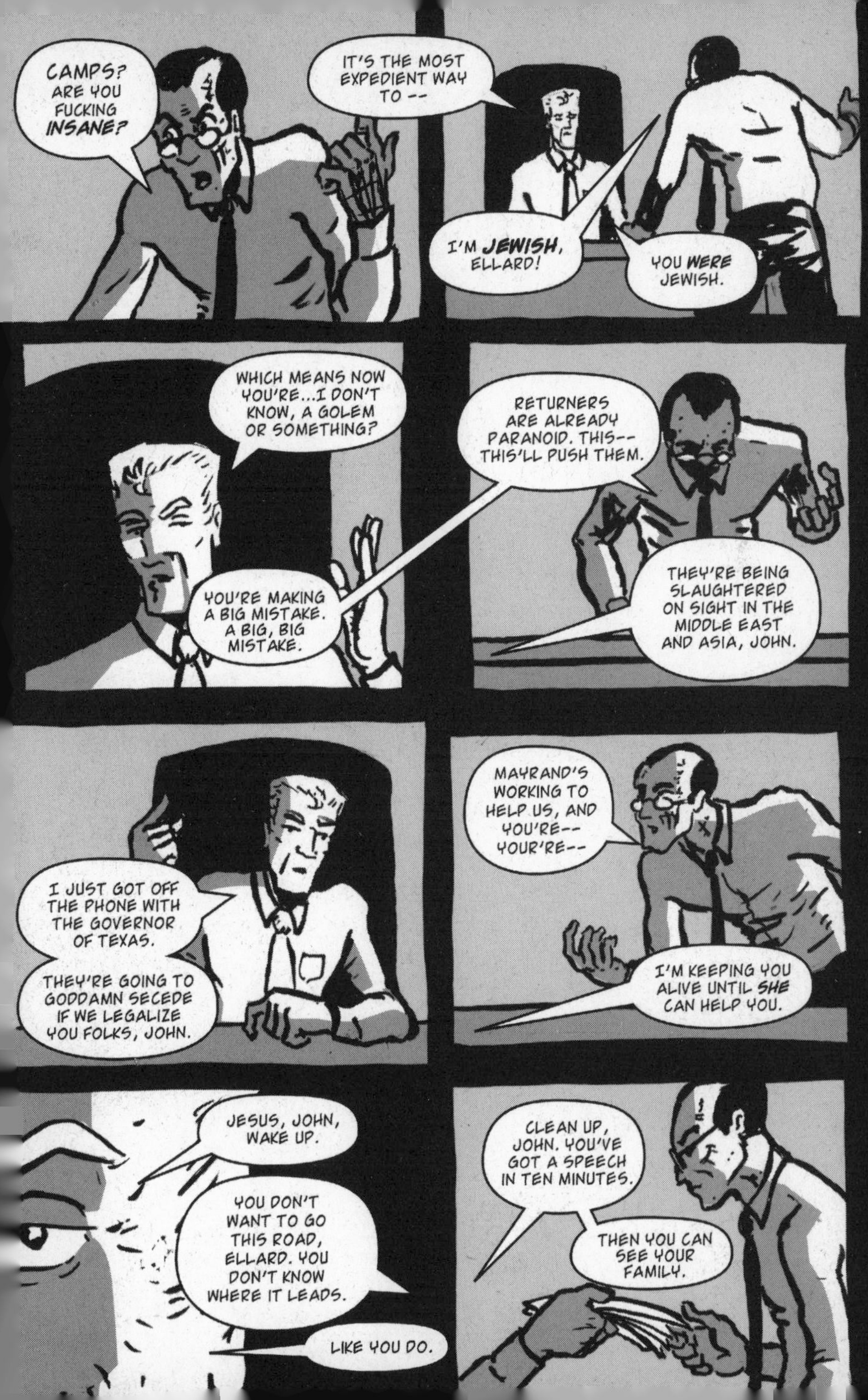
CAMPS? ARE YOU FUCKING INSANE?
IT'S THE MOST EXPEDIENT WAY TO --
I'M JEWISH, ELLARD!
YOU WERE JEWISH.
WHICH MEANS NOW YOU'RE...I DON'T KNOW, A GOLEM OR SOMETHING?
YOU'RE MAKING A BIG MISTAKE. A BIG, BIG MISTAKE.
RETURNERS ARE ALREADY PARANOID. THIS-- THIS'LL PUSH THEM.
THEY'RE BEING SLAUGHTERED ON SIGHT IN THE MIDDLE EAST AND ASIA, JOHN.
I JUST GOT OFF THE PHONE WITH THE GOVERNOR OF TEXAS.
THEY'RE GOING TO GODDAMN SECEDE IF WE LEGALIZE YOU FOLKS, JOHN.
MAYRAND'S WORKING TO HELP US, AND YOU'RE-- YOUR'RE--
I'M KEEPING YOU ALIVE UNTIL SHE CAN HELP YOU.
JESUS, JOHN, WAKE UP.
YOU DON'T WANT TO GO THIS ROAD, ELLARD. YOU DON'T KNOW WHERE IT LEADS.
LIKE YOU DO.
CLEAN UP, JOHN. YOU'VE GOT A SPEECH IN TEN MINUTES.
THEN YOU CAN SEE YOUR FAMILY.

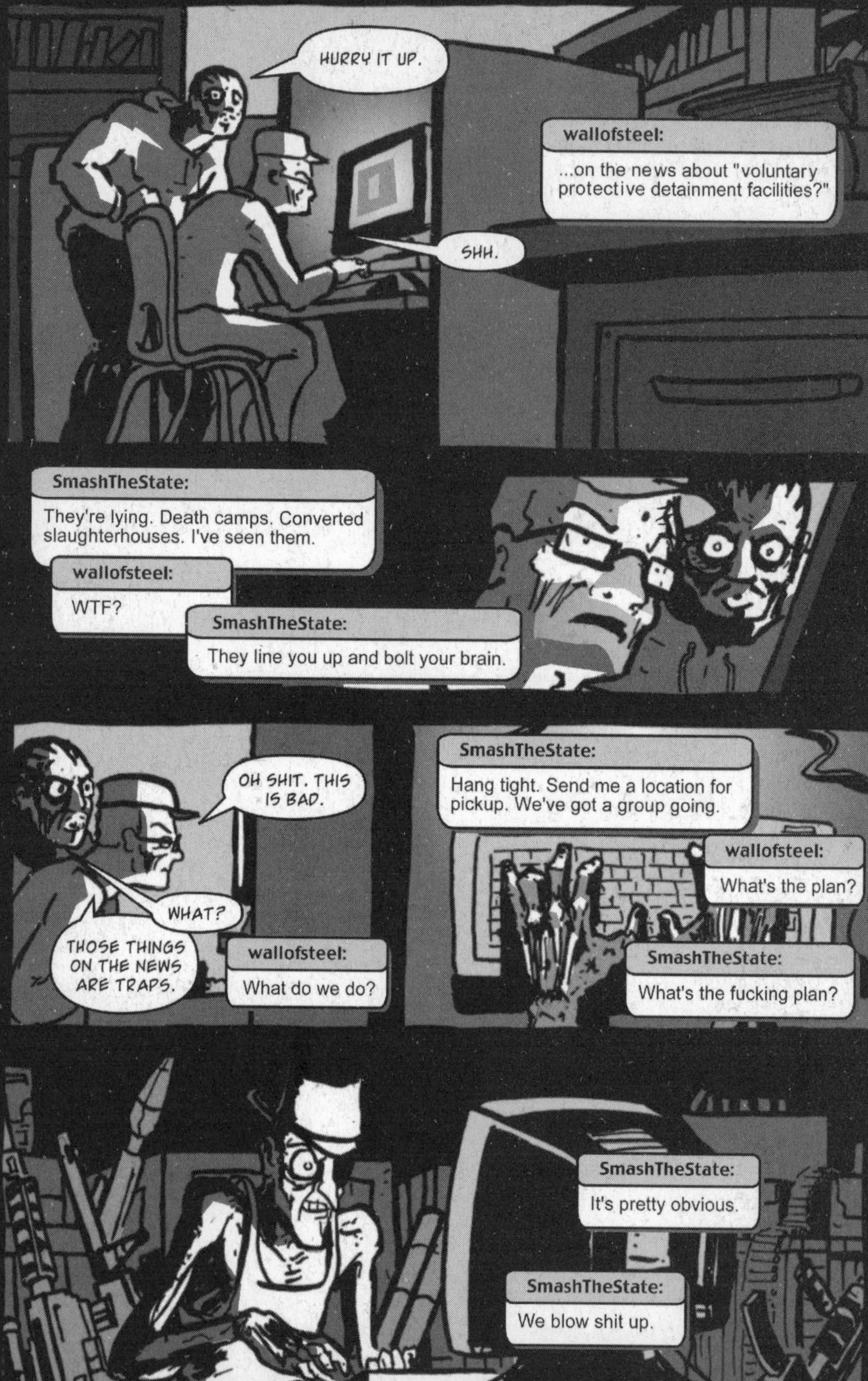
HURRY IT UP.
wallofsteel:
...on the news about "voluntary protective detainment facilities?"
SHH.
SmashTheState:
They're lying. Death camps. Converted slaughterhouses. I've seen them.
wallofsteel:
WTF?
SmashTheState:
They line you up and bolt your brain.
OH SHIT. THIS IS BAD.
WHAT?
THOSE THINGS ON THE NEWS ARE TRAPS.
wallofsteel:
What do we do?
SmashTheState:
Hang tight. Send me a location for pickup. We've got a group going.
wallofsteel:
What's the plan?
SmashTheState:
What's the fucking plan?
SmashTheState:
It's pretty obvious.
SmashTheState:
We blow shit up.

CHAPTER THREE

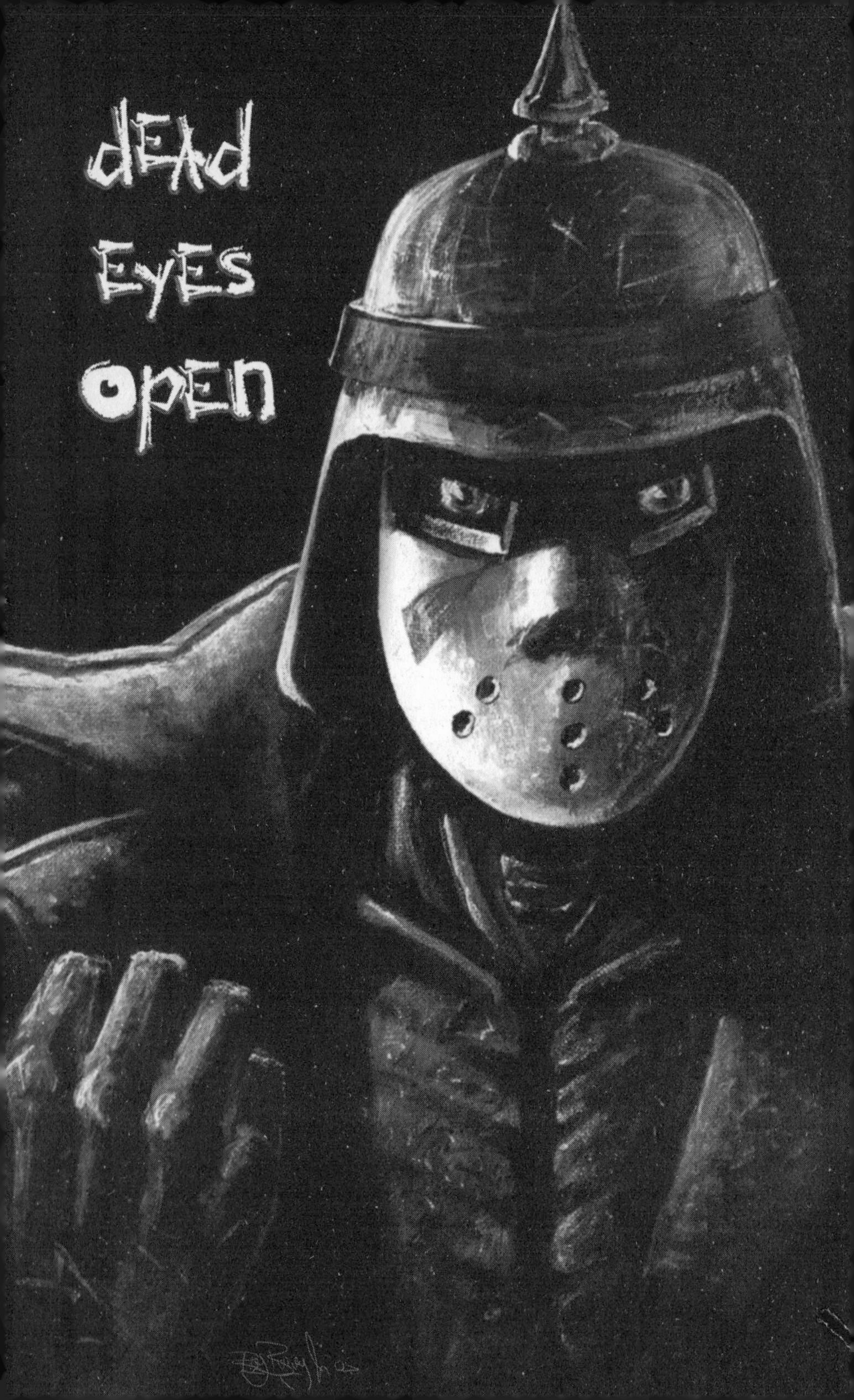
dEAd
EYES
OPEN

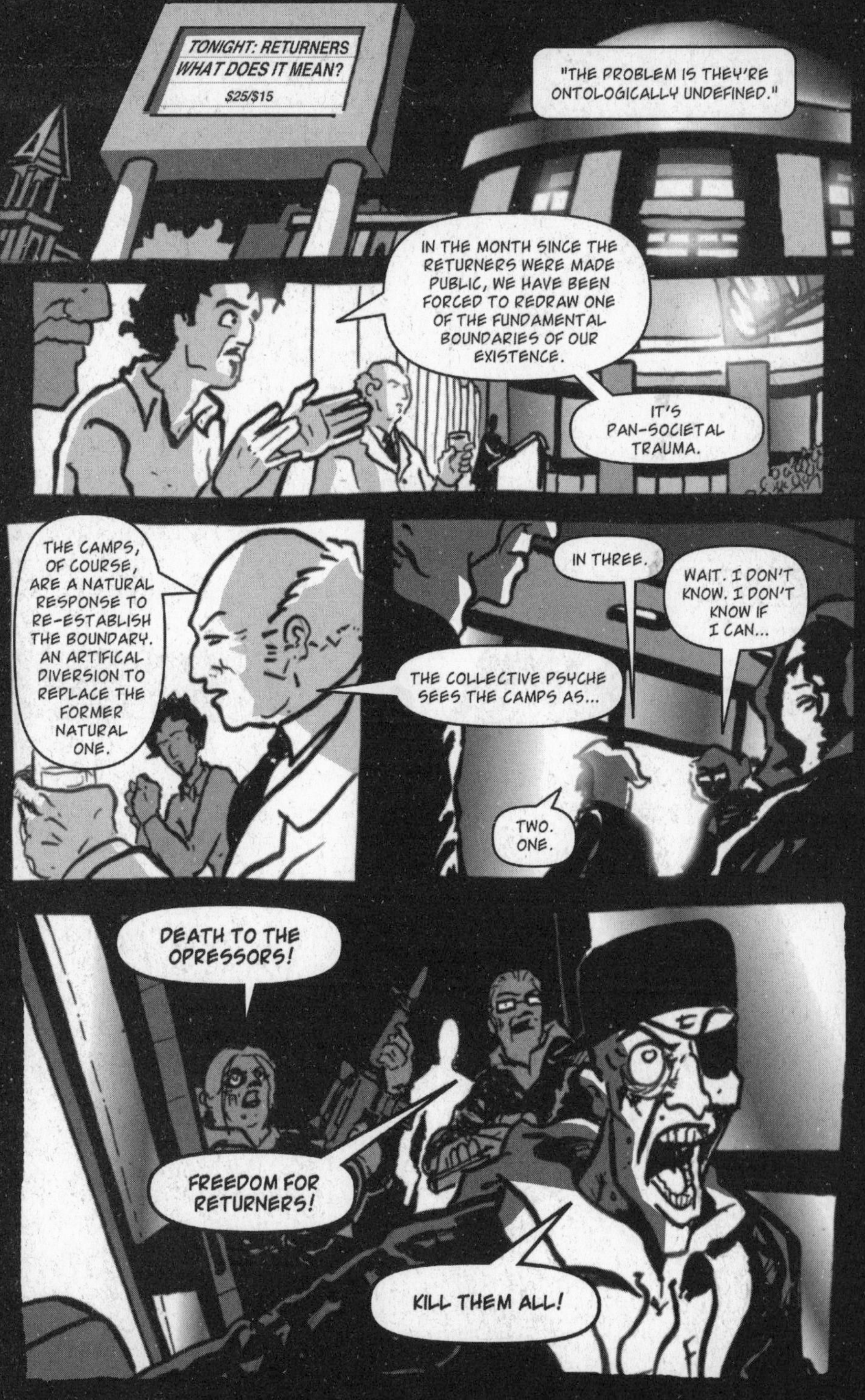
TONIGHT: RETURNERS
WHAT DOES IT MEAN?
$25/$15
"THE PROBLEM IS THEY'RE ONTOLOGICALLY UNDEFINED."
IN THE MONTH SINCE THE RETURNERS WERE MADE PUBLIC, WE HAVE BEEN FORCED TO REDRAW ONE OF THE FUNDAMENTAL BOUNDARIES OF OUR EXISTENCE.
IT'S PAN-SOCIETAL TRAUMA.
THE CAMPS, OF COURSE, ARE A NATURAL RESPONSE TO RE-ESTABLISH THE BOUNDARY. AN ARTIFICAL DIVERSION TO REPLACE THE FORMER NATURAL ONE.
THE COLLECTIVE PSYCHE SEES THE CAMPS AS...
IN THREE.
WAIT. I DON'T KNOW. I DON'T KNOW IF I CAN...
TWO. ONE.
DEATH TO THE OPRESSORS!
FREEDOM FOR RETURNERS!
KILL THEM ALL!

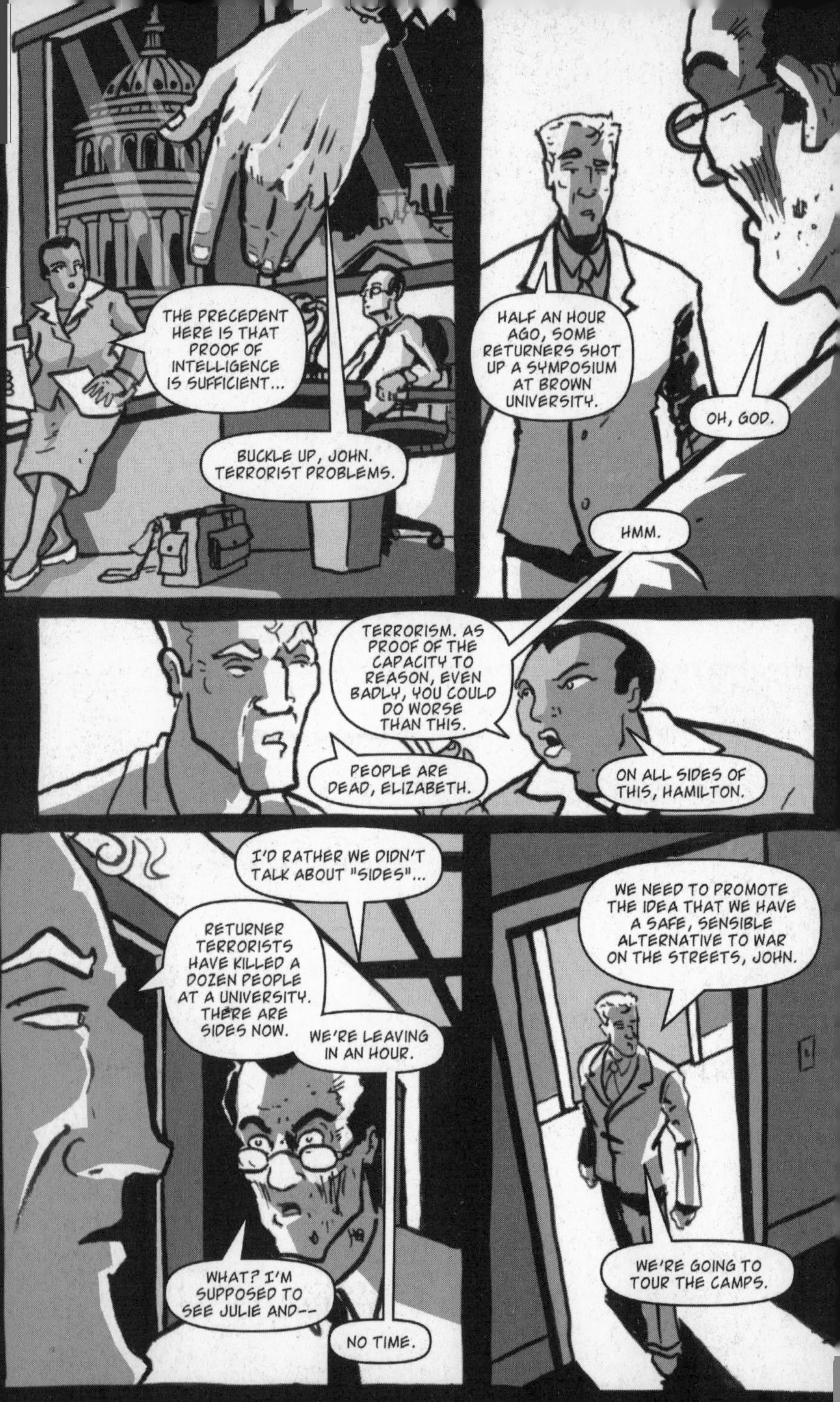
THE PRECEDENT HERE IS THAT PROOF OF INTELLIGENCE IS SUFFICIENT...
BUCKLE UP, JOHN. TERRORIST PROBLEMS.
HALF AN HOUR AGO, SOME RETURNERS SHOT UP A SYMPOSIUM AT BROWN UNIVERSITY.
OH, GOD.
HMM.
TERRORISM. AS PROOF OF THE CAPACITY TO REASON, EVEN BADLY, YOU COULD DO WORSE THAN THIS.
PEOPLE ARE DEAD, ELIZABETH.
ON ALL SIDES OF THIS, HAMILTON.
I'D RATHER WE DIDN'T TALK ABOUT "SIDES"...
RETURNER TERRORISTS HAVE KILLED A DOZEN PEOPLE AT A UNIVERSITY. THERE ARE SIDES NOW.
WE'RE LEAVING IN AN HOUR.
WHAT? I'M SUPPOSED TO SEE JULIE AND--
NO TIME.
WE NEED TO PROMOTE THE IDEA THAT WE HAVE A SAFE, SENSIBLE ALTERNATIVE TO WAR ON THE STREETS, JOHN.
WE'RE GOING TO TOUR THE CAMPS.

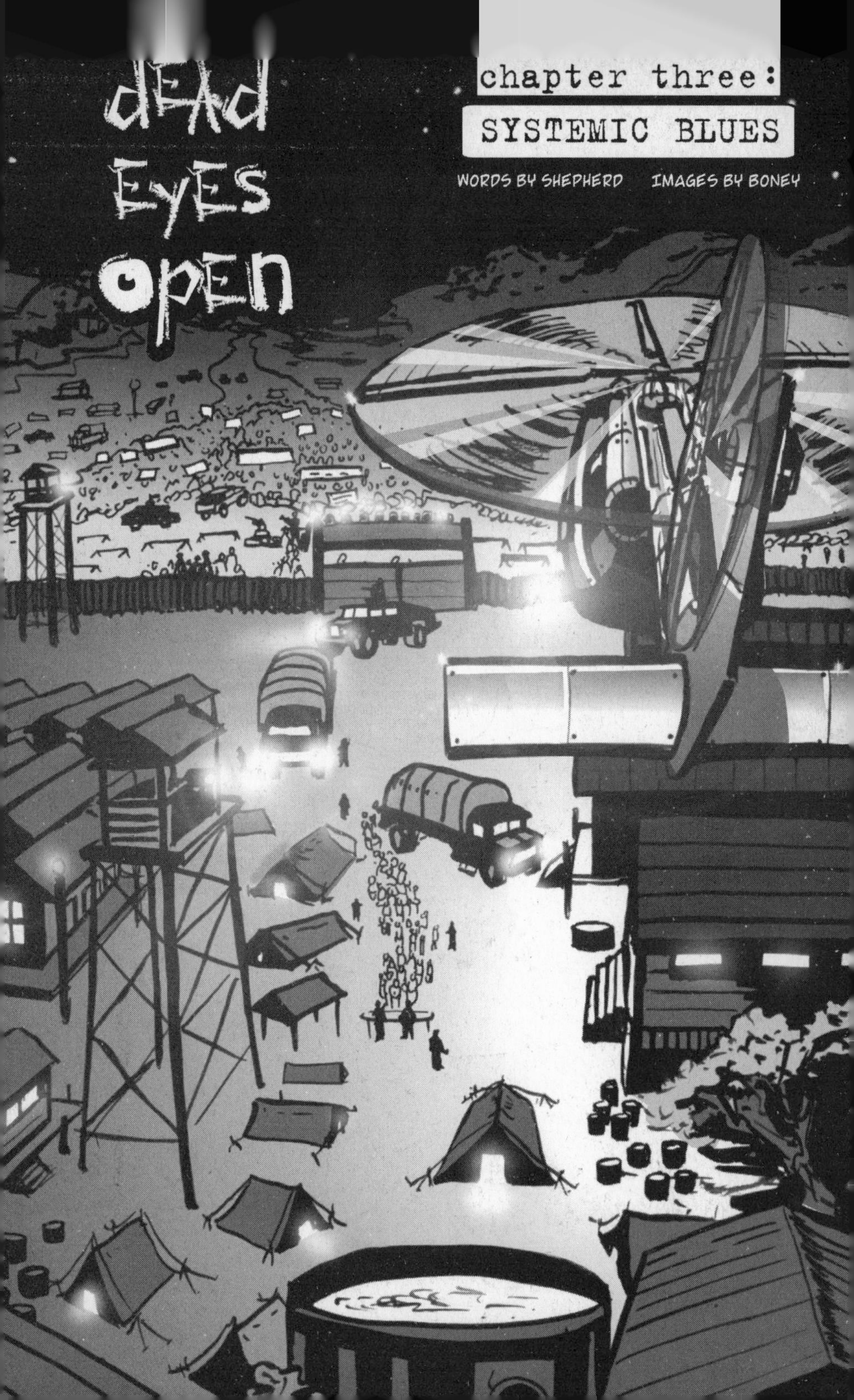
dead eyes open
chapter three:
SYSTEMIC BLUES
WORDS BY SHEPHERD
IMAGES BY BONEY

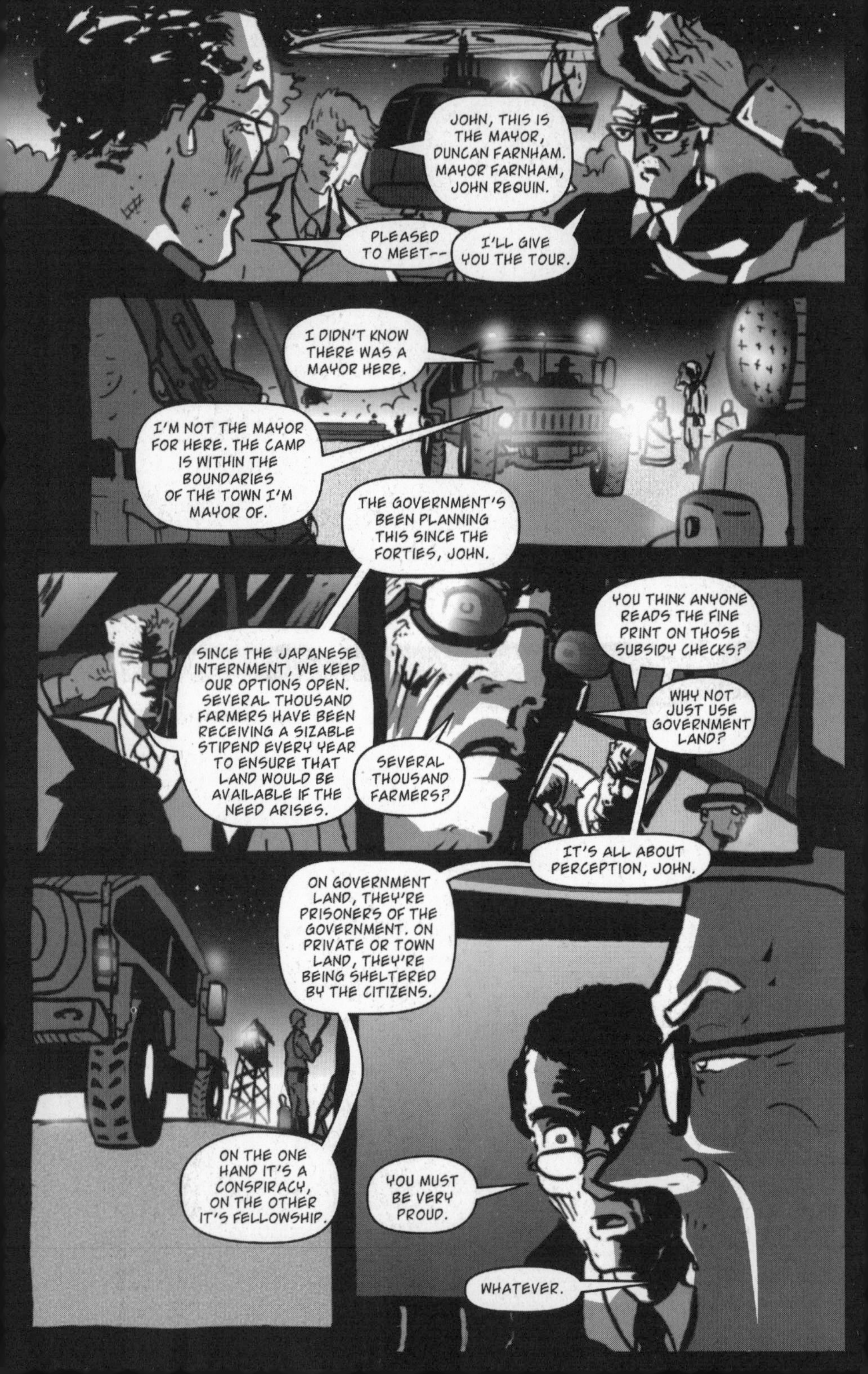
JOHN, THIS IS THE MAYOR, DUNCAN FARNHAM. MAYOR FARNHAM, JOHN REQUIN.
PLEASED TO MEET--
I'LL GIVE YOU THE TOUR.
I DIDN'T KNOW THERE WAS A MAYOR HERE.
I'M NOT THE MAYOR FOR HERE. THE CAMP IS WITHIN THE BOUNDARIES OF THE TOWN I'M MAYOR OF.
THE GOVERNMENT'S BEEN PLANNING THIS SINCE THE FORTIES, JOHN.
SINCE THE JAPANESE INTERNMENT, WE KEEP OUR OPTIONS OPEN. SEVERAL THOUSAND FARMERS HAVE BEEN RECEIVING A SIZABLE STIPEND EVERY YEAR TO ENSURE THAT LAND WOULD BE AVAILABLE IF THE NEED ARISES.
SEVERAL THOUSAND FARMERS?
YOU THINK ANYONE READS THE FINE PRINT ON THOSE SUBSIDY CHECKS?
WHY NOT JUST USE GOVERNMENT LAND?
IT'S ALL ABOUT PERCEPTION, JOHN.
ON GOVERNMENT LAND, THEY'RE PRISONERS OF THE GOVERNMENT. ON PRIVATE OR TOWN LAND, THEY'RE BEING SHELTERED BY THE CITIZENS.
ON THE ONE HAND IT'S A CONSPIRACY, ON THE OTHER IT'S FELLOWSHIP.
YOU MUST BE VERY PROUD.
WHATEVER.

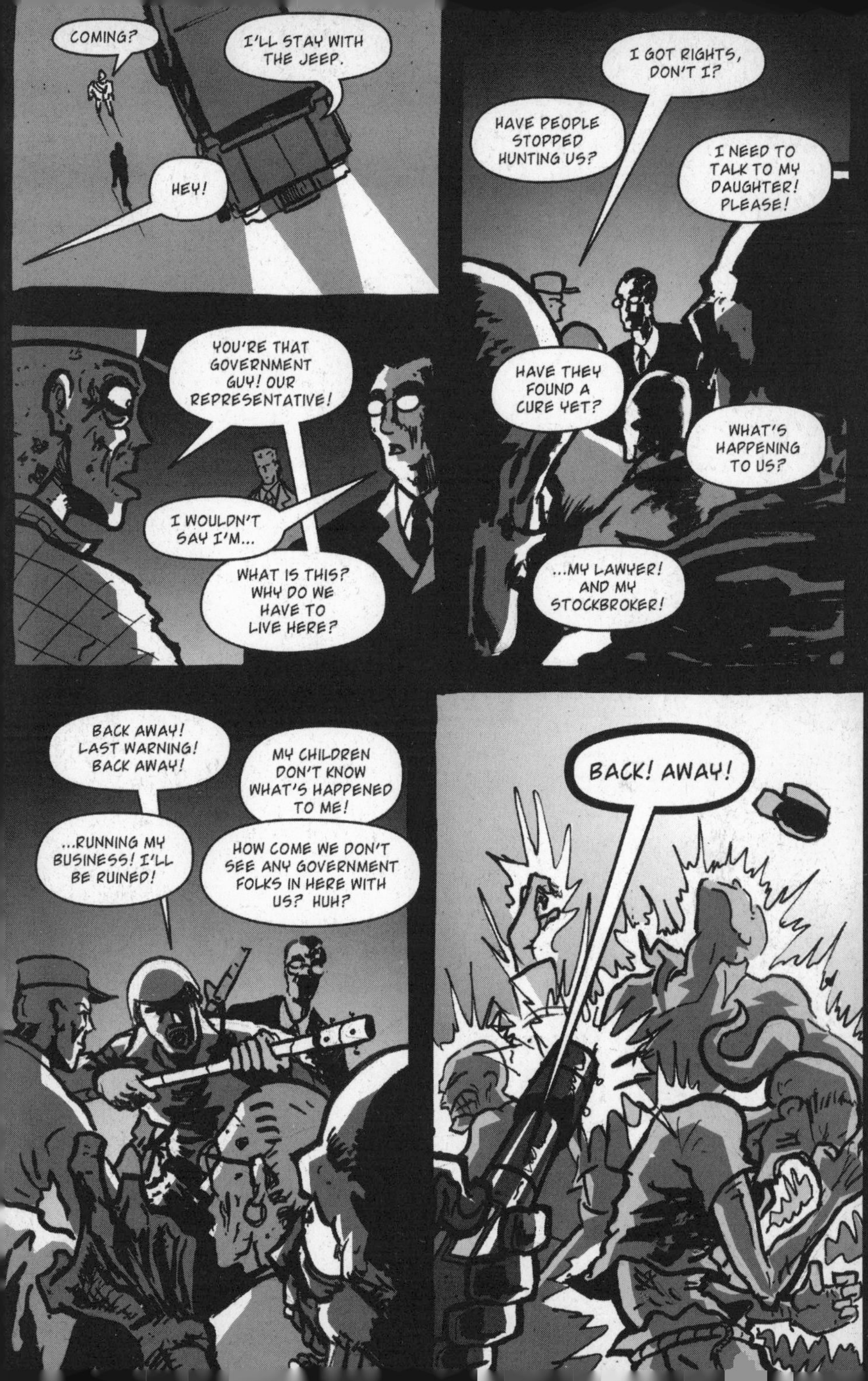
COMING?
I'LL STAY WITH THE JEEP.
HEY!
I GOT RIGHTS, DON'T I?
HAVE PEOPLE STOPPED HUNTING US?
I NEED TO TALK TO MY DAUGHTER! PLEASE!
YOU'RE THAT GOVERNMENT GUY! OUR REPRESENTATIVE!
I WOULDN'T SAY I'M...
WHAT IS THIS? WHY DO WE HAVE TO LIVE HERE?
HAVE THEY FOUND A CURE YET?
WHAT'S HAPPENING TO US?
...MY LAWYER! AND MY STOCKBROKER!
BACK AWAY! LAST WARNING! BACK AWAY!
MY CHILDREN DON'T KNOW WHAT'S HAPPENED TO ME!
...RUNNING MY BUSINESS! I'LL BE RUINED!
HOW COME WE DON'T SEE ANY GOVERNMENT FOLKS IN HERE WITH US? HUH?
BACK! AWAY!

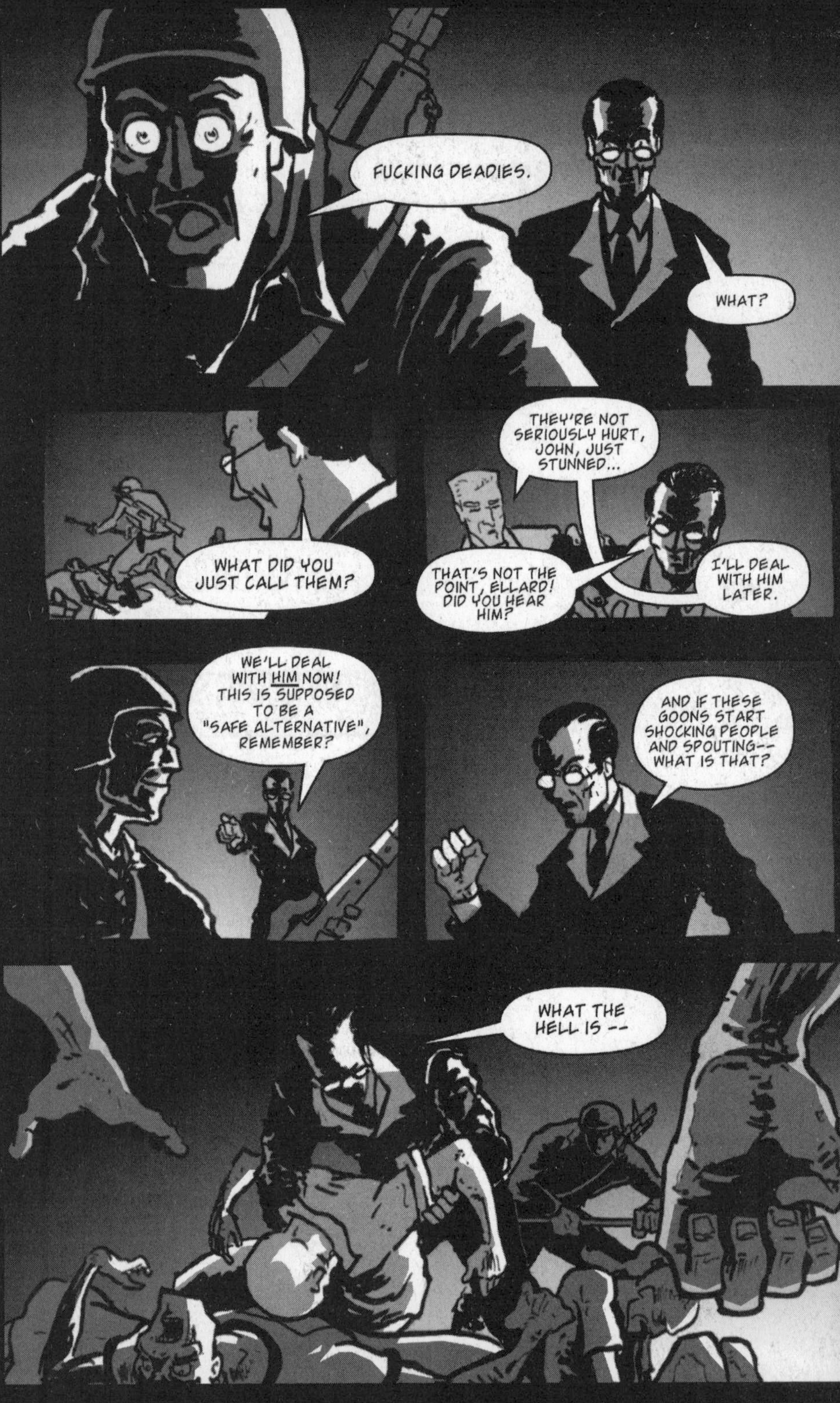
FUCKING DEADIES.
WHAT?
WHAT DID YOU JUST CALL THEM?
THEY'RE NOT SERIOUSLY HURT, JOHN, JUST STUNNED...
THAT'S NOT THE POINT, ELLARD! DID YOU HEAR HIM?
I'LL DEAL WITH HIM LATER.
WE'LL DEAL WITH HIM NOW! THIS IS SUPPOSED TO BE A "SAFE ALTERNATIVE", REMEMBER?
AND IF THESE GOONS START SHOCKING PEOPLE AND SPOUTING--WHAT IS THAT?
WHAT THE HELL IS --

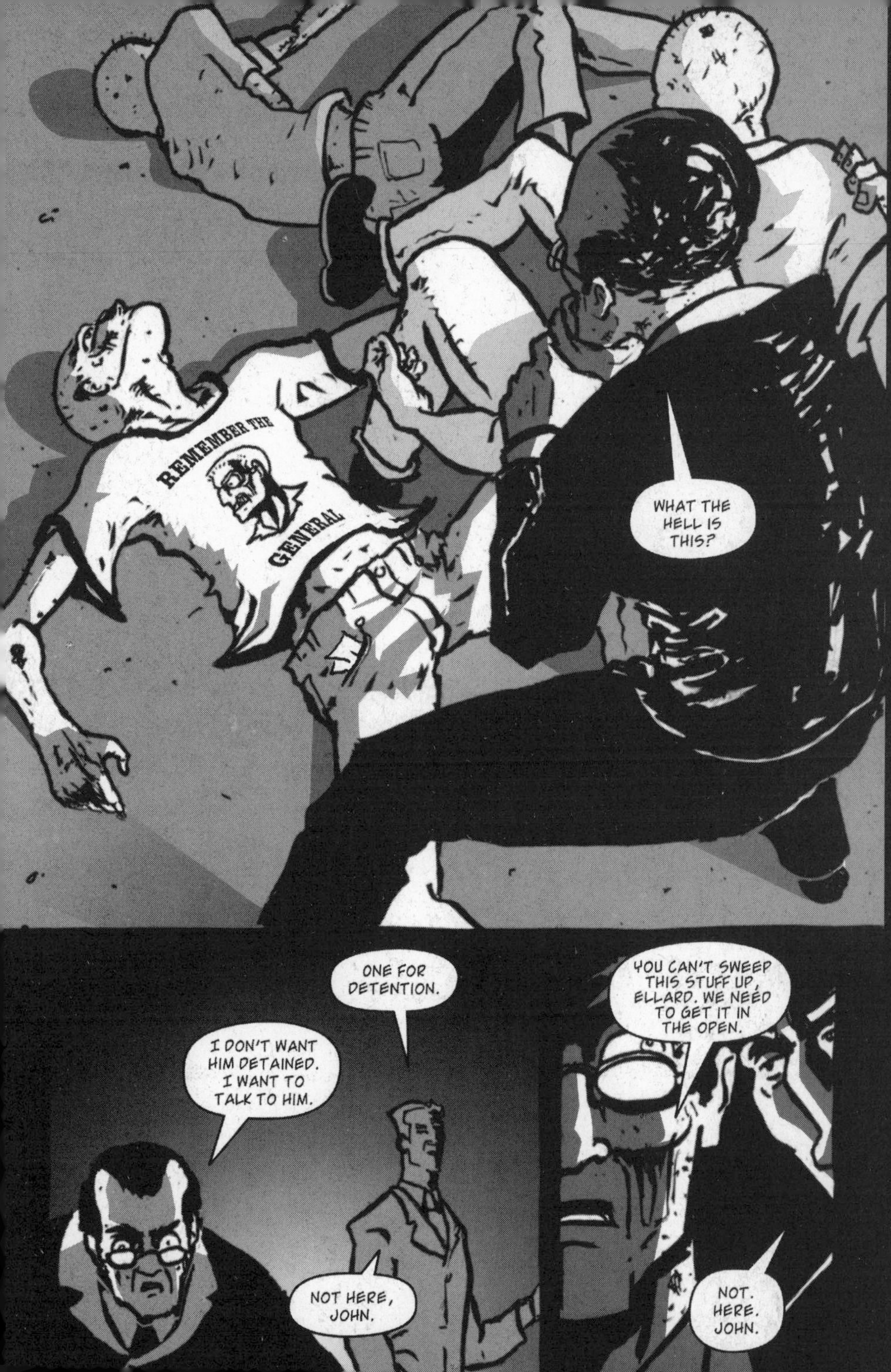
REMEMBER THE GENERAL
WHAT THE HELL IS THIS?
ONE FOR DETENTION.
I DON'T WANT HIM DETAINED. I WANT TO TALK TO HIM.
NOT HERE, JOHN.
YOU CAN'T SWEEP THIS STUFF UP, ELLARD. WE NEED TO GET IT IN THE OPEN.
NOT. HERE. JOHN.

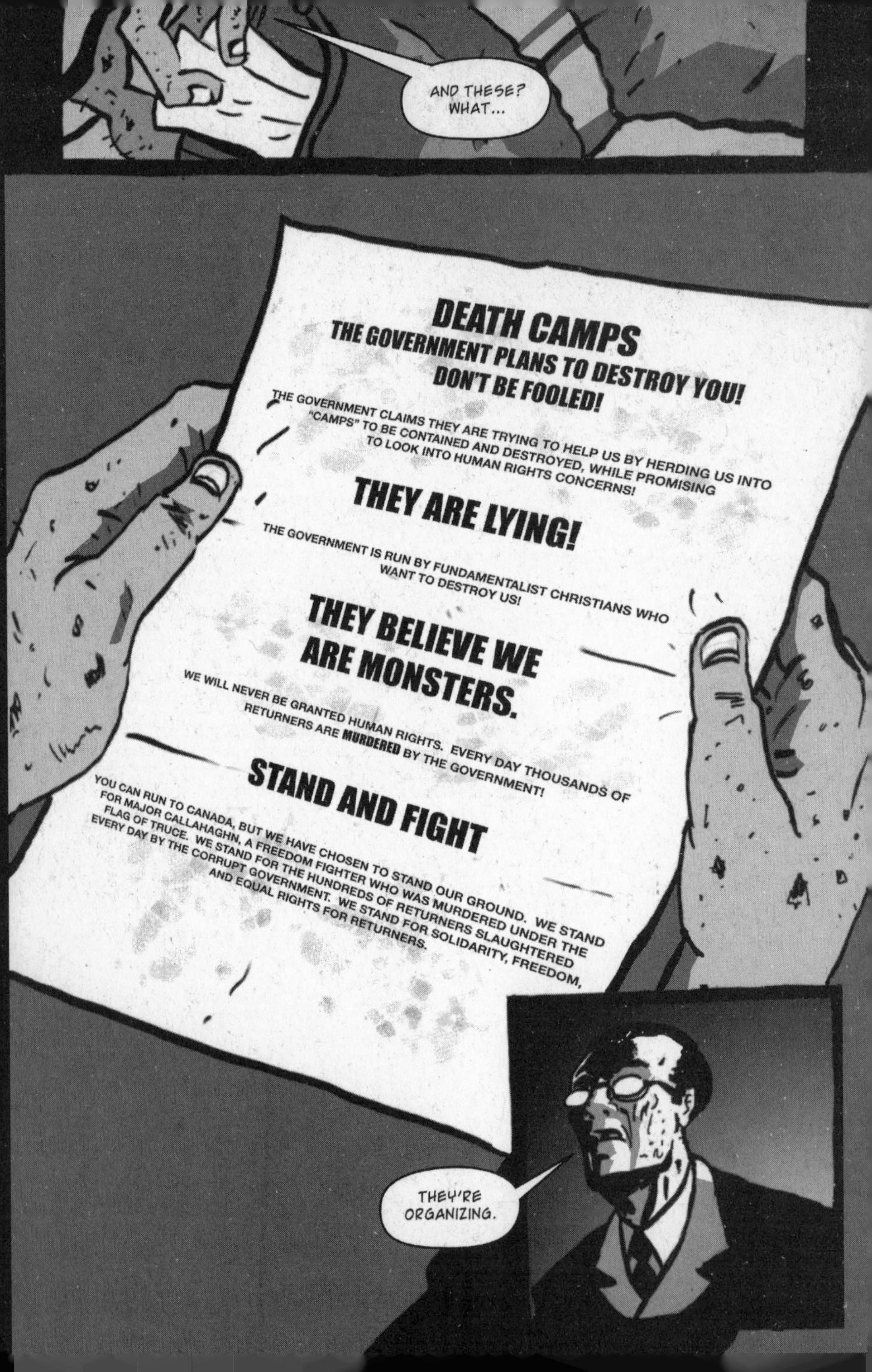
AND THESE? WHAT...
DEATH CAMPS
THE GOVERNMENT PLANS TO DESTROY YOU!
DON'T BE FOOLED!
THE GOVERNMENT CLAIMS THEY ARE TRYING TO HELP US BY HERDING US INTO "CAMPS" TO BE CONTAINED AND DESTROYED, WHILE PROMISING TO LOOK INTO HUMAN RIGHTS CONCERNS!
THEY ARE LYING!
THE GOVERNMENT IS RUN BY FUNDAMENTALIST CHRISTIANS WHO WANT TO DESTROY US!
THEY BELIEVE WE ARE MONSTERS.
WE WILL NEVER BE GRANTED HUMAN RIGHTS. EVERY DAY THOUSANDS OF RETURNERS ARE MURDERED BY THE GOVERNMENT!
STAND AND FIGHT
YOU CAN RUN TO CANADA, BUT WE HAVE CHOSEN TO STAND OUR GROUND. WE STAND FOR MAJOR CALLAHAGHN, A FREEDOM FIGHTER WHO WAS MURDERED UNDER THE FLAG OF TRUCE. WE STAND FOR THE HUNDREDS OF RETURNERS SLAUGHTERED EVERY DAY BY THE CORRUPT GOVERNMENT. WE STAND FOR SOLIDARITY, FREEDOM, AND EQUAL RIGHTS FOR RETURNERS.
THEY'RE ORGANIZING.

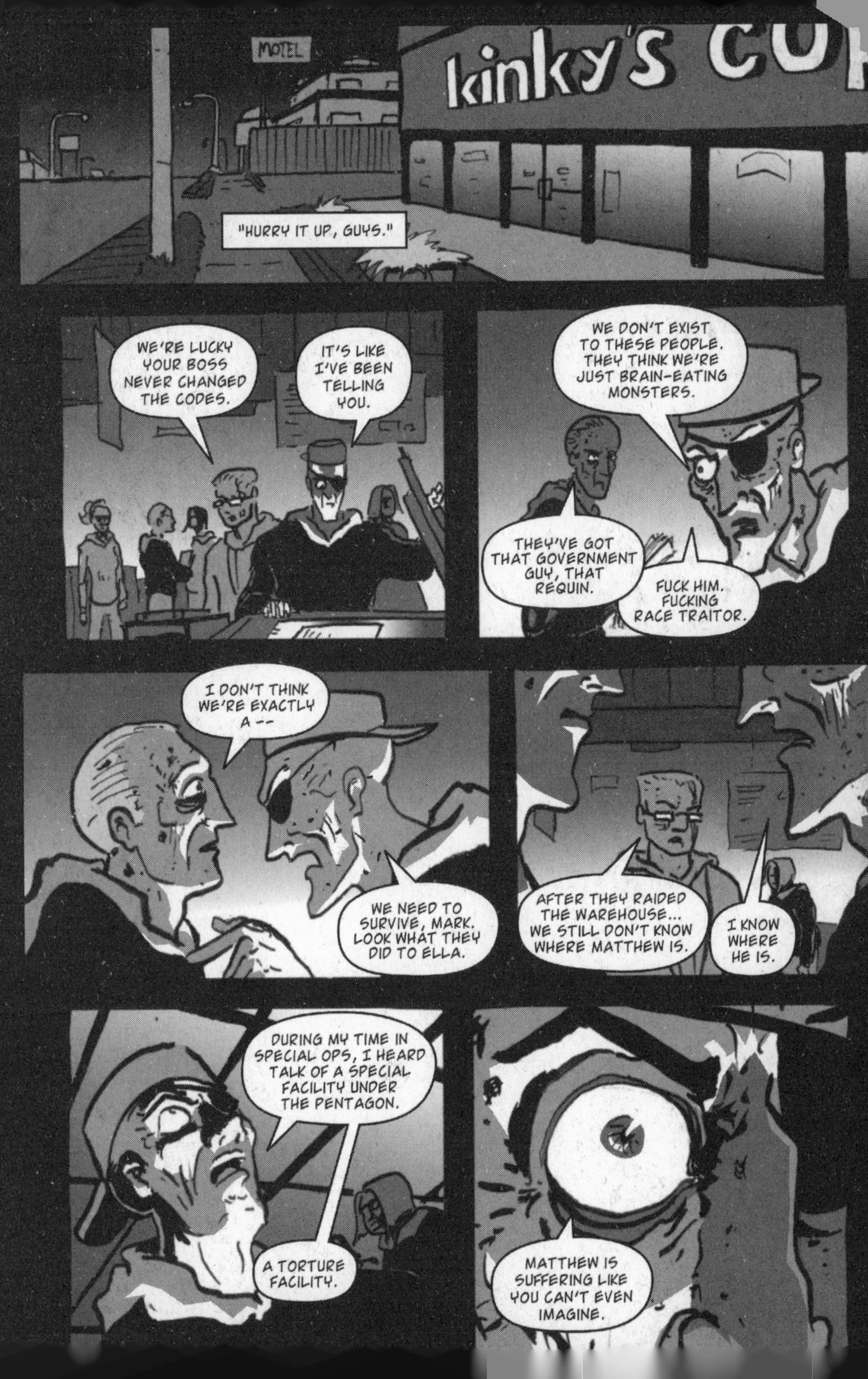
MOTEL
kinky's CO
"HURRY IT UP, GUYS."
WE'RE LUCKY YOUR BOSS NEVER CHANGED THE CODES.
IT'S LIKE I'VE BEEN TELLING YOU.
WE DON'T EXIST TO THESE PEOPLE. THEY THINK WE'RE JUST BRAIN-EATING MONSTERS.
THEY'VE GOT THAT GOVERNMENT GUY, THAT REQUIN.
FUCK HIM. FUCKING RACE TRAITOR.
I DON'T THINK WE'RE EXACTLY A --
WE NEED TO SURVIVE, MARK. LOOK WHAT THEY DID TO ELLA.
AFTER THEY RAIDED THE WAREHOUSE... WE STILL DON'T KNOW WHERE MATTHEW IS.
I KNOW WHERE HE IS.
DURING MY TIME IN SPECIAL OPS, I HEARD TALK OF A SPECIAL FACILITY UNDER THE PENTAGON.
A TORTURE FACILITY.
MATTHEW IS SUFFERING LIKE YOU CAN'T EVEN IMAGINE.

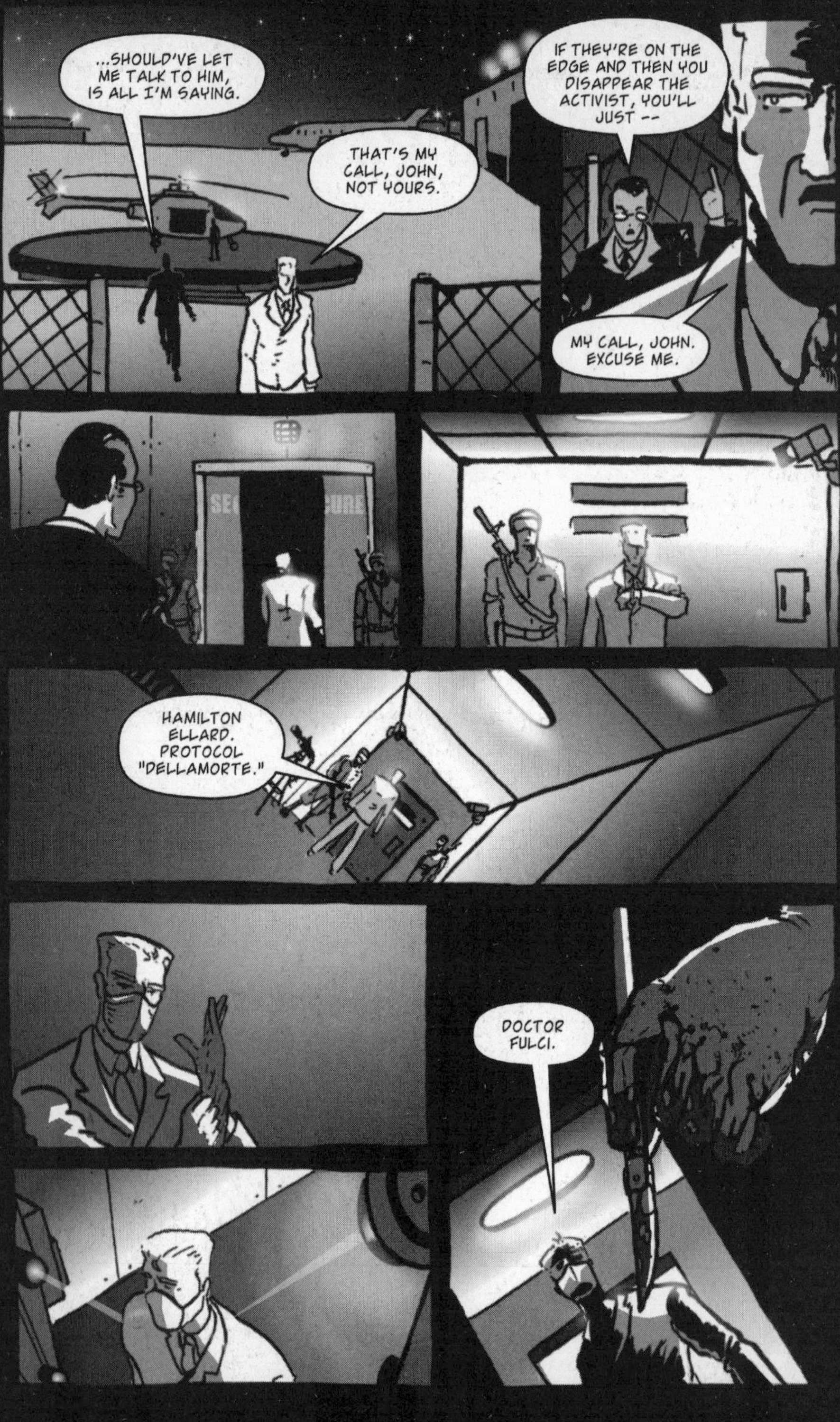
...SHOULD'VE LET ME TALK TO HIM, IS ALL I'M SAYING.
THAT'S MY CALL, JOHN, NOT YOURS.
IF THEY'RE ON THE EDGE AND THEN YOU DISAPPEAR THE ACTIVIST, YOU'LL JUST --
MY CALL, JOHN. EXCUSE ME.
HAMILTON ELLARD. PROTOCOL "DELLAMORTE."
DOCTOR FULCI.

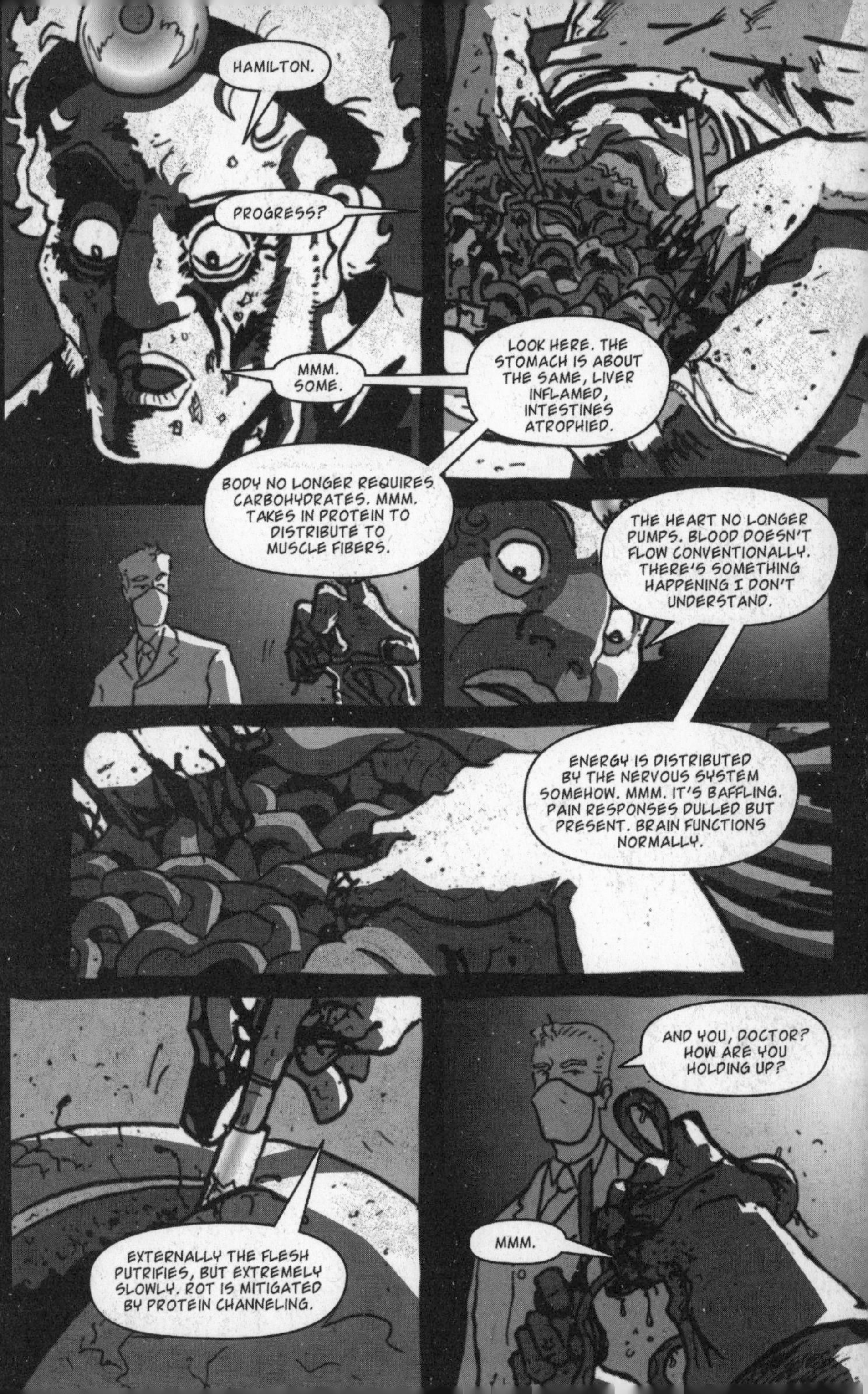
HAMILTON.
PROGRESS?
MMM. SOME.
LOOK HERE. THE STOMACH IS ABOUT THE SAME, LIVER INFLAMED, INTESTINES ATROPHIED.
BODY NO LONGER REQUIRES CARBOHYDRATES. MMM. TAKES IN PROTEIN TO DISTRIBUTE TO MUSCLE FIBERS.
THE HEART NO LONGER PUMPS. BLOOD DOESN'T FLOW CONVENTIONALLY. THERE'S SOMETHING HAPPENING I DON'T UNDERSTAND.
ENERGY IS DISTRIBUTED BY THE NERVOUS SYSTEM SOMEHOW. MMM. IT'S BAFFLING. PAIN RESPONSES DULLED BUT PRESENT. BRAIN FUNCTIONS NORMALLY.
EXTERNALLY THE FLESH PUTRIFIES, BUT EXTREMELY SLOWLY. ROT IS MITIGATED BY PROTEIN CHANNELING.
AND YOU, DOCTOR? HOW ARE YOU HOLDING UP?
MMM.

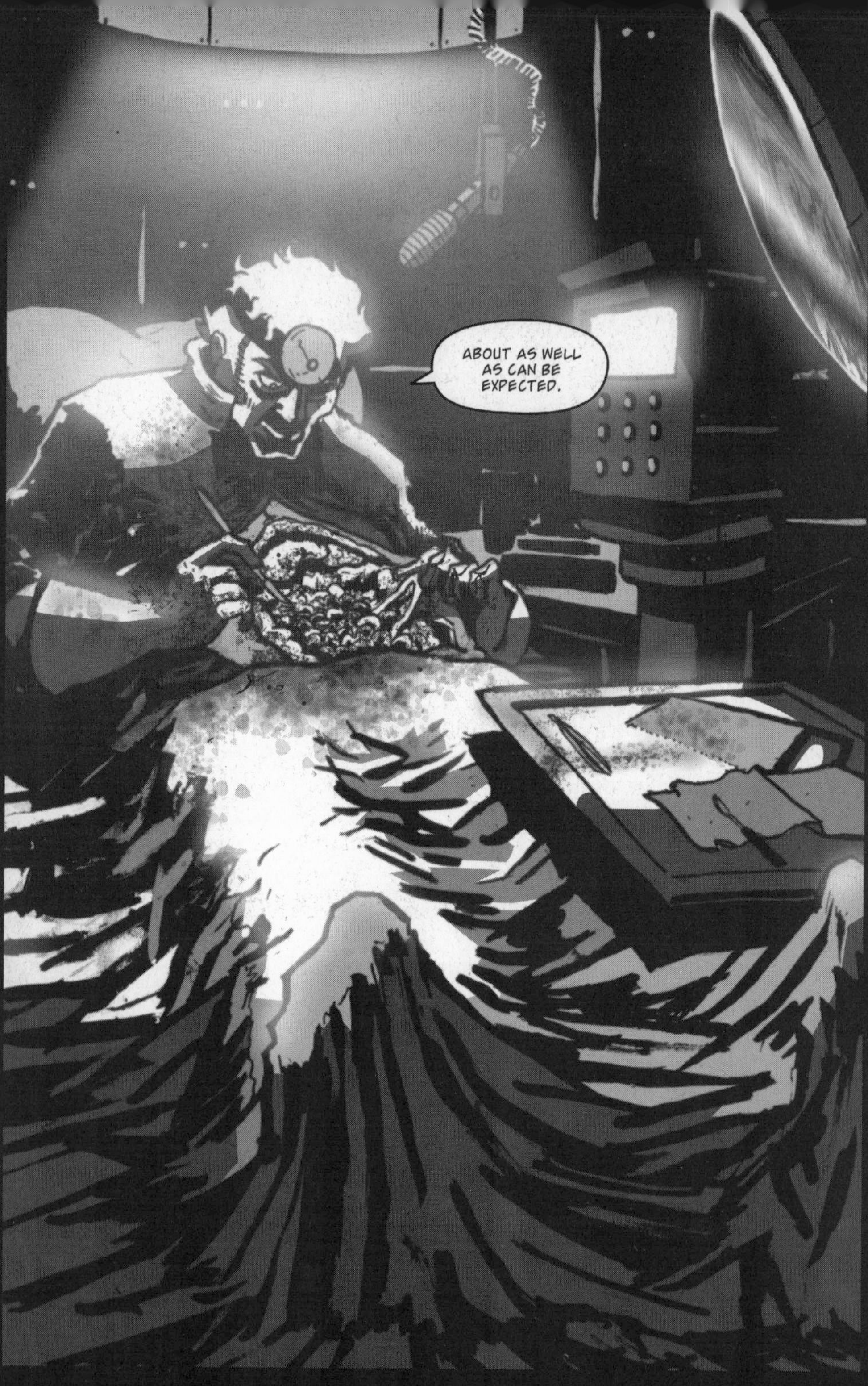
ABOUT AS WELL AS CAN BE EXPECTED.

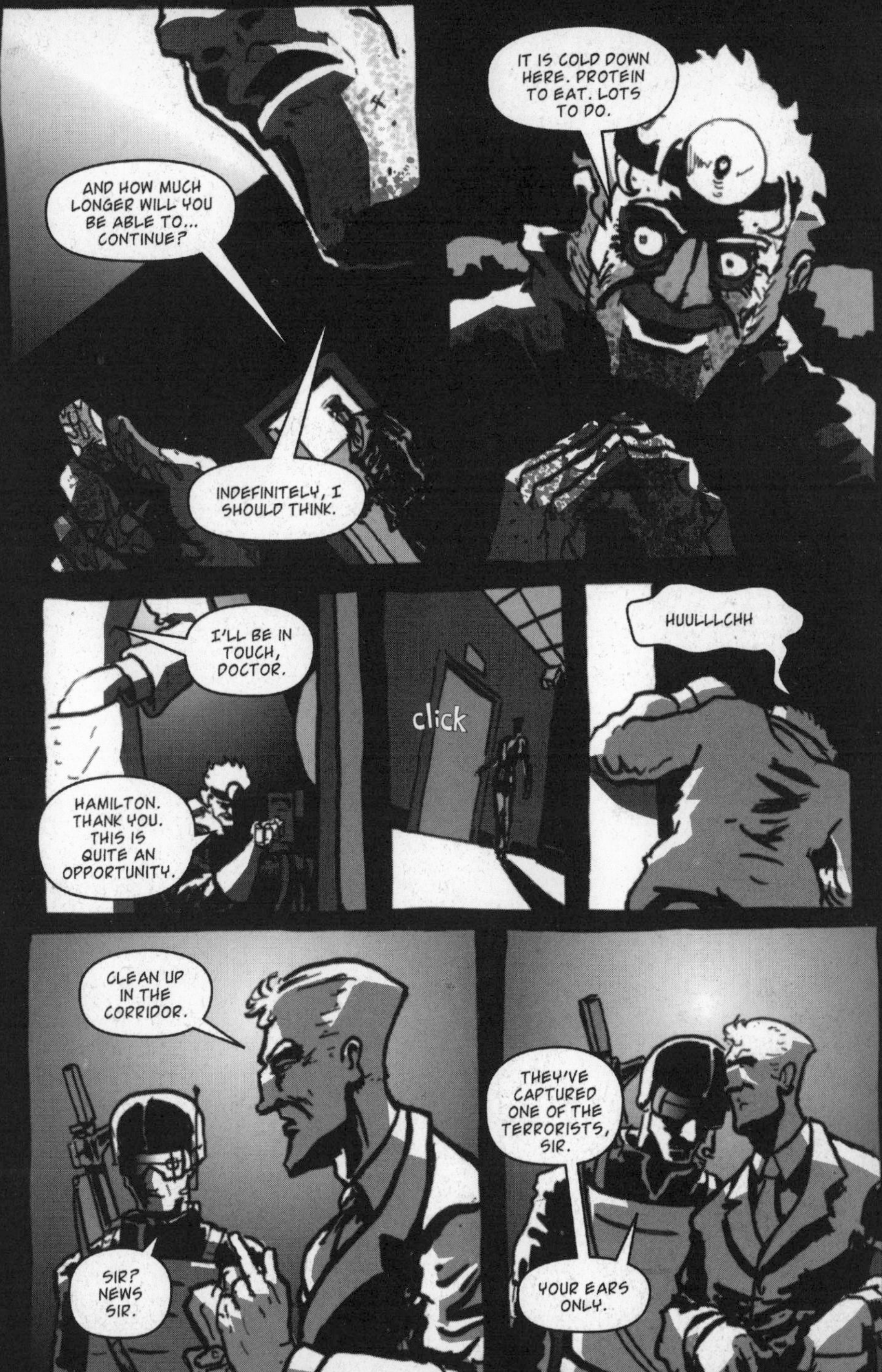
AND HOW MUCH LONGER WILL YOU BE ABLE TO... CONTINUE?
IT IS COLD DOWN HERE. PROTEIN TO EAT. LOTS TO DO.
INDEFINITELY, I SHOULD THINK.
I'LL BE IN TOUCH, DOCTOR.
HAMILTON. THANK YOU. THIS IS QUITE AN OPPORTUNITY.
click
HUULLLCHH
CLEAN UP IN THE CORRIDOR.
SIR? NEWS SIR.
THEY'VE CAPTURED ONE OF THE TERRORISTS, SIR.
YOUR EARS ONLY.

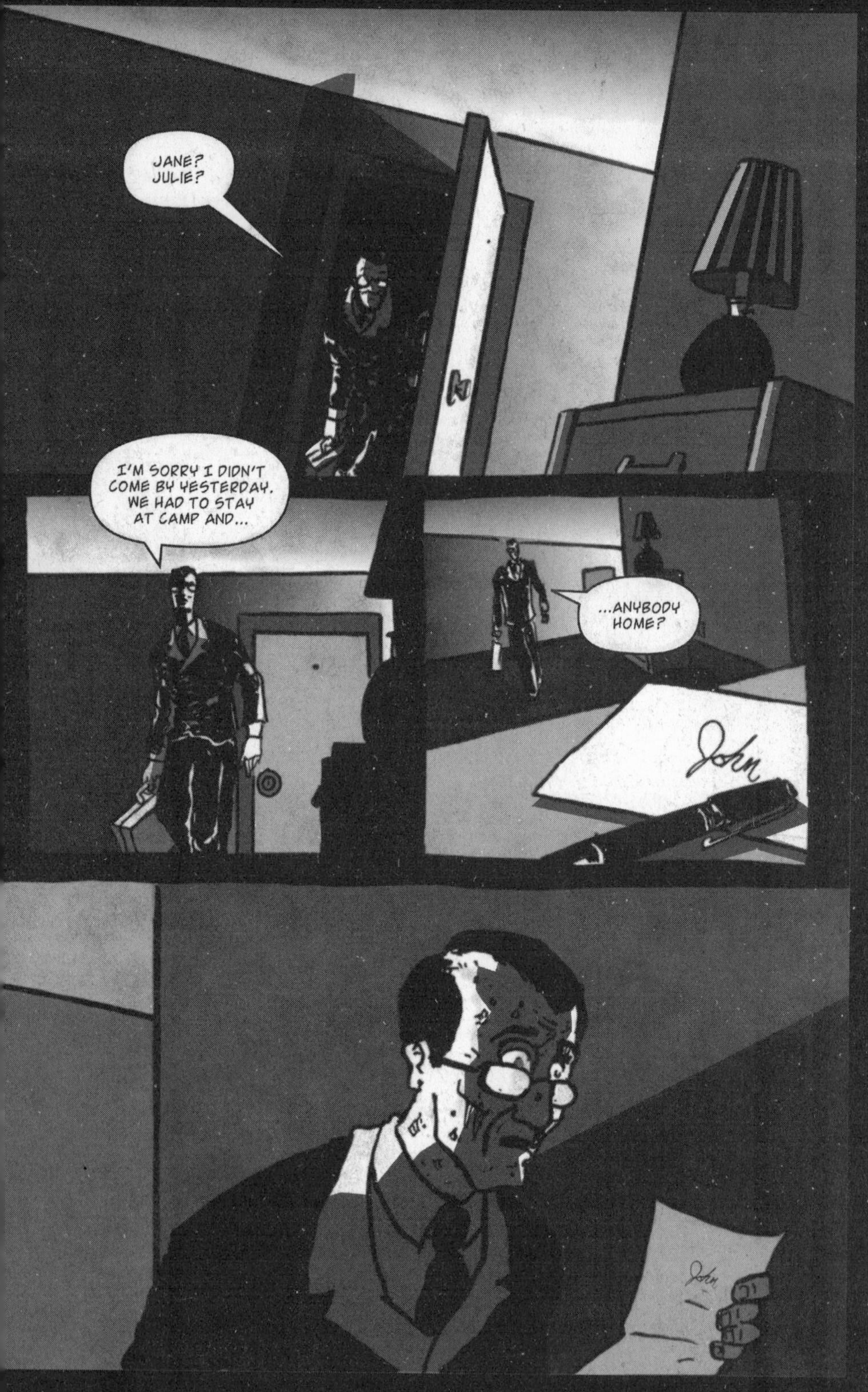
JANE? JULIE?
I'M SORRY I DIDN'T COME BY YESTERDAY. WE HAD TO STAY AT CAMP AND...
...ANYBODY HOME?
John
John

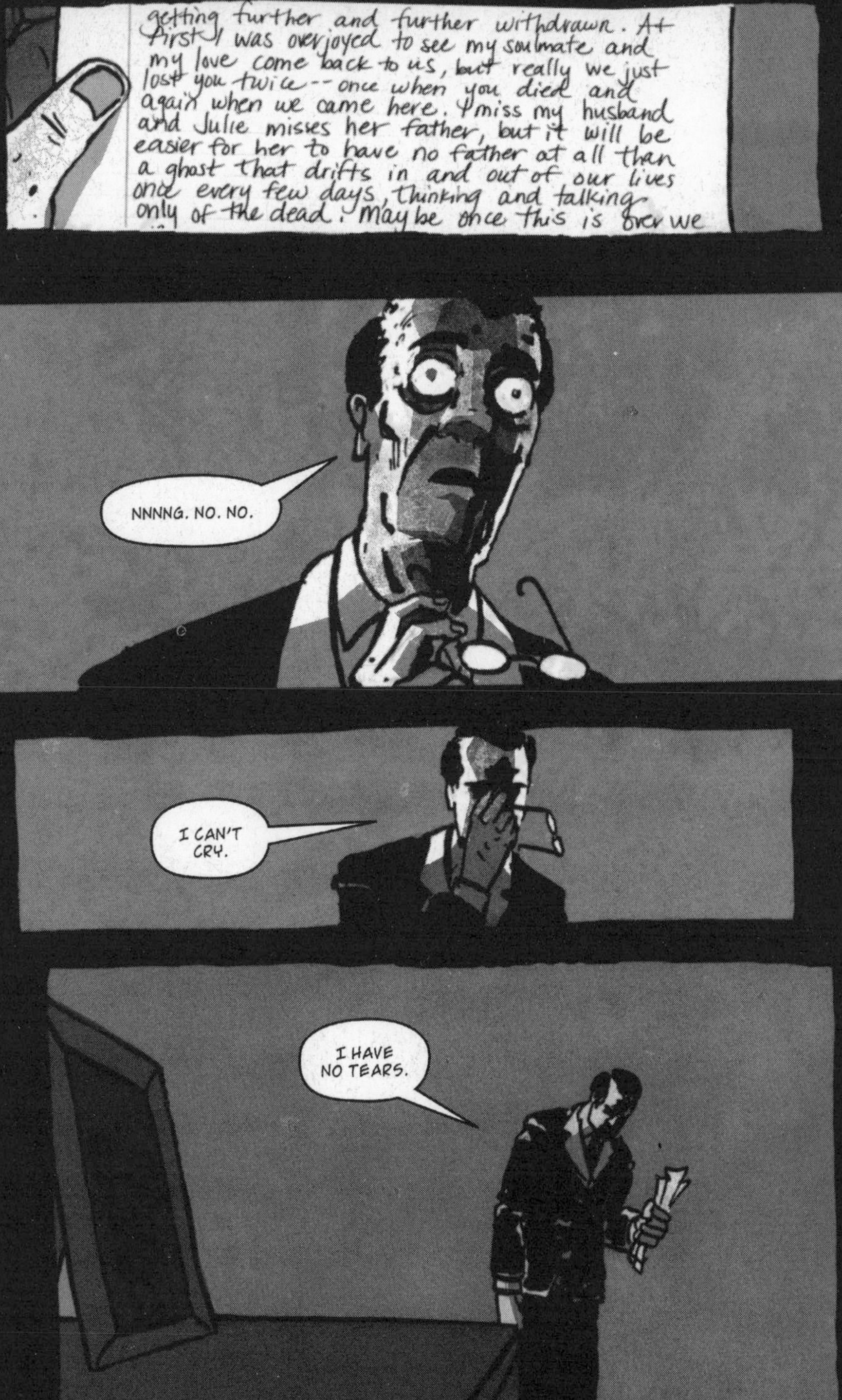
getting further and further withdrawn. At first I was overjoyed to see my soulmate and my love come back to us, but really we just lost you twice -- once when you died and again when we came here. I miss my husband and Julie misses her father, but it will be easier for her to have no father at all than a ghost that drifts in and out of our lives once every few days, thinking and talking only of the dead. Maybe once this is over we
NNNNG. NO. NO.
I CAN'T CRY.
I HAVE NO TEARS.

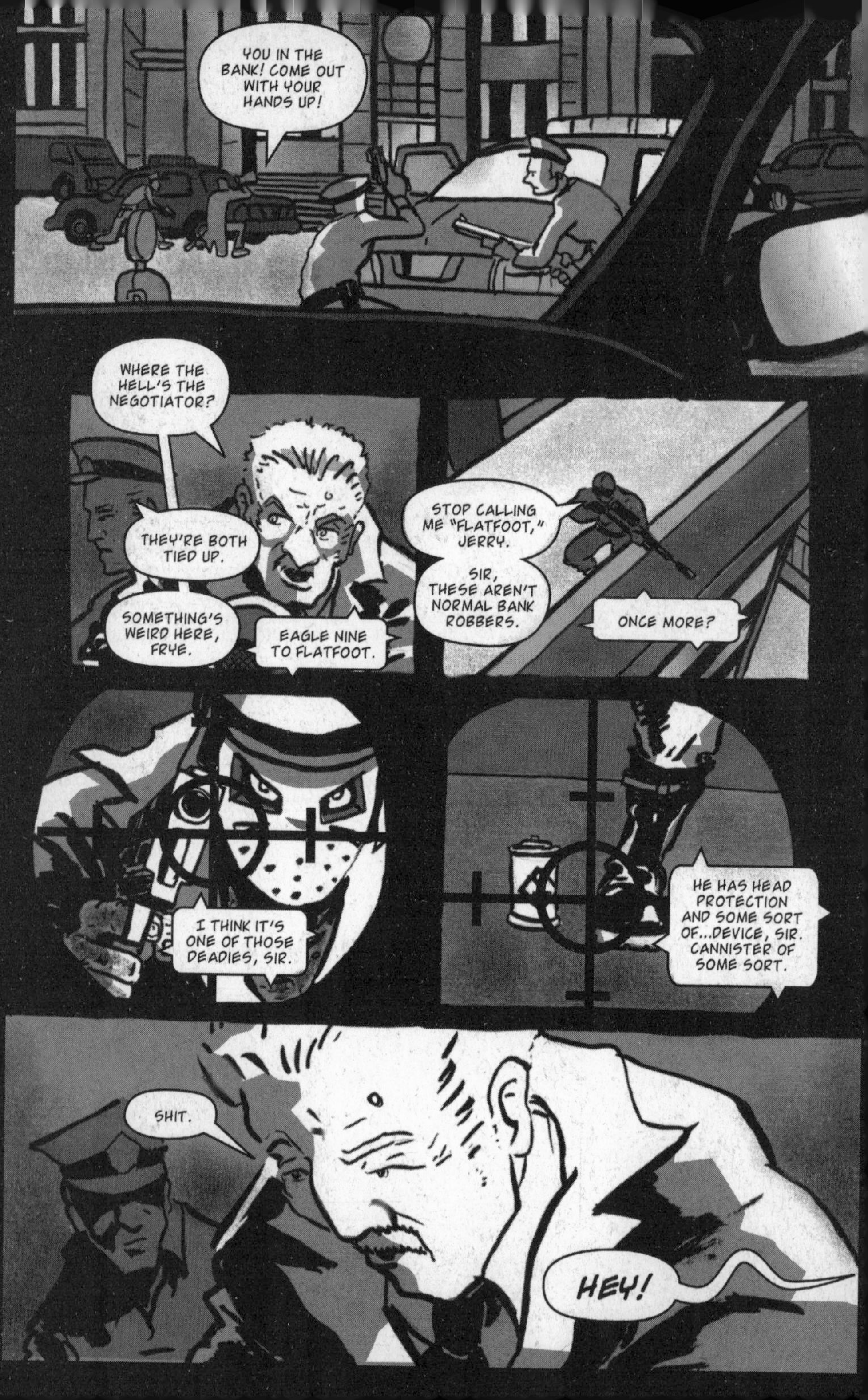
YOU IN THE BANK! COME OUT WITH YOUR HANDS UP!
WHERE THE HELL'S THE NEGOTIATOR?
THEY'RE BOTH TIED UP.
SOMETHING'S WEIRD HERE, FRYE.
EAGLE NINE TO FLATFOOT.
STOP CALLING ME "FLATFOOT," JERRY.
SIR, THESE AREN'T NORMAL BANK ROBBERS.
ONCE MORE?
I THINK IT'S ONE OF THOSE DEADIES, SIR.
HE HAS HEAD PROTECTION AND SOME SORT OF...DEVICE, SIR. CANNISTER OF SOME SORT.
SHIT.
HEY!

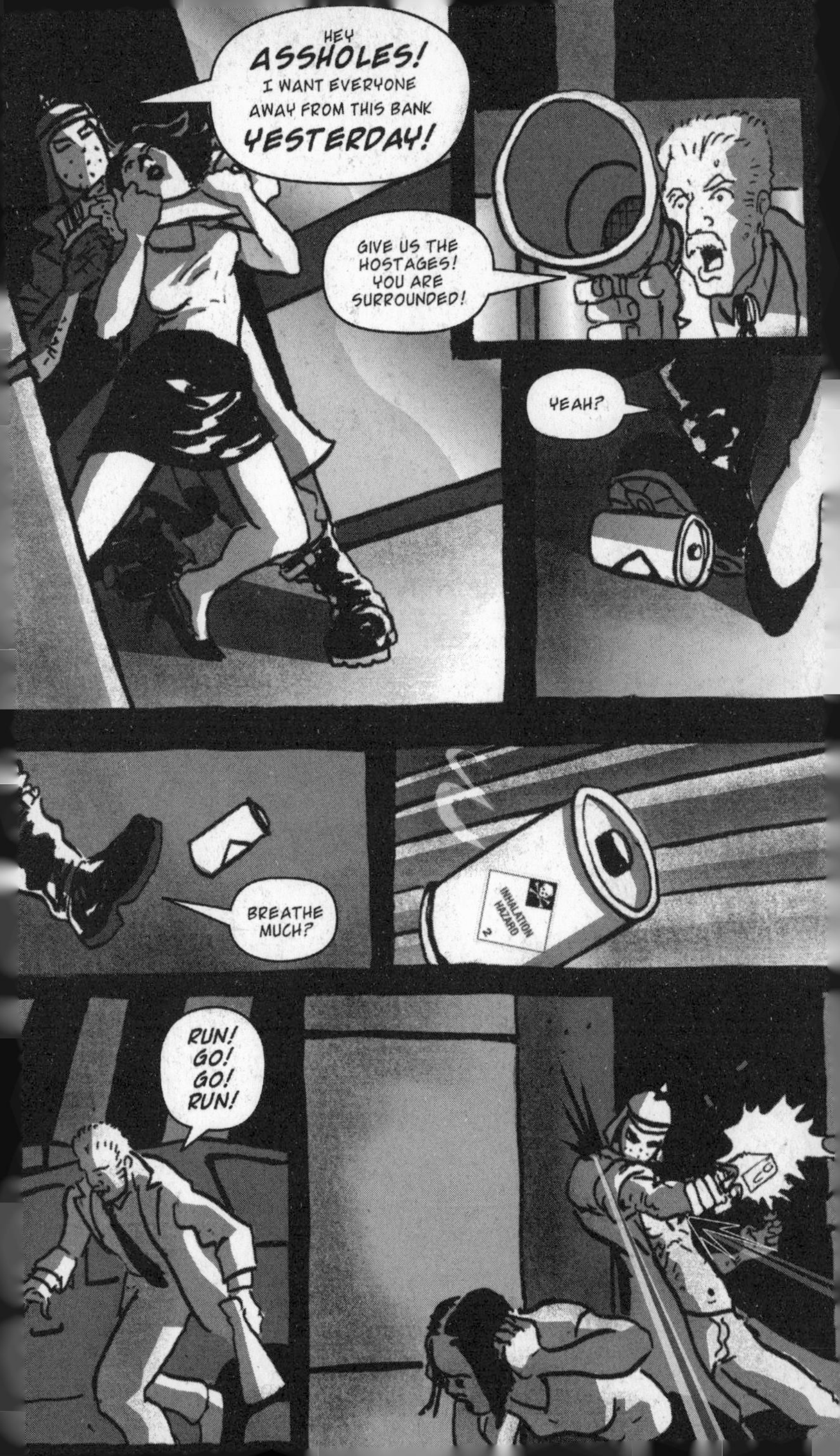
HEY ASSHOLES! I WANT EVERYONE AWAY FROM THIS BANK YESTERDAY!
GIVE US THE HOSTAGES! YOU ARE SURROUNDED!
YEAH?
BREATHE MUCH?
INHALATION HAZARD 2
RUN! GO! GO! RUN!

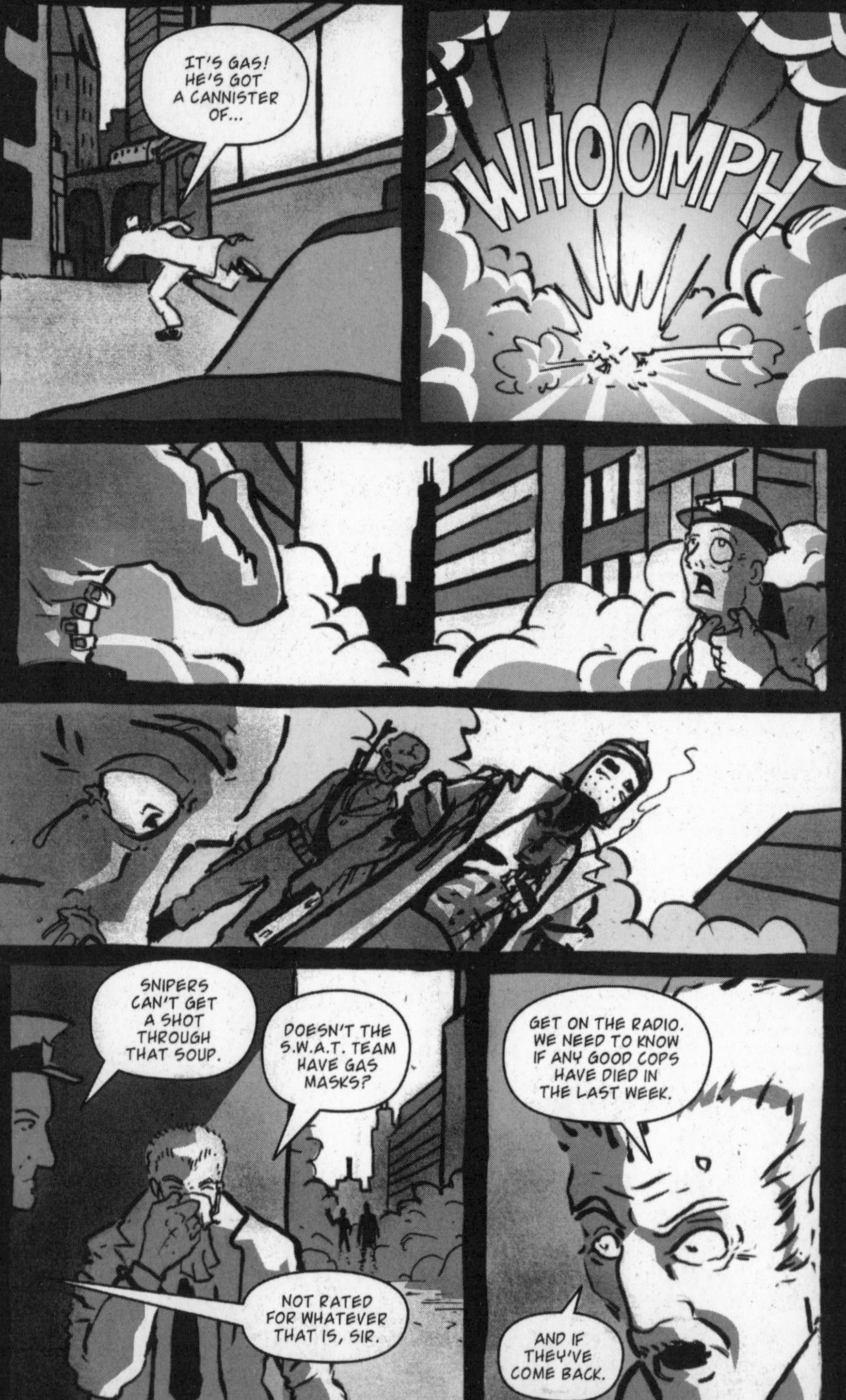
IT'S GAS! HE'S GOT A CANNISTER OF...
WHOOMPH
SNIPERS CAN'T GET A SHOT THROUGH THAT SOUP.
DOESN'T THE S.W.A.T. TEAM HAVE GAS MASKS?
NOT RATED FOR WHATEVER THAT IS, SIR.
GET ON THE RADIO. WE NEED TO KNOW IF ANY GOOD COPS HAVE DIED IN THE LAST WEEK.
AND IF THEY'VE COME BACK.

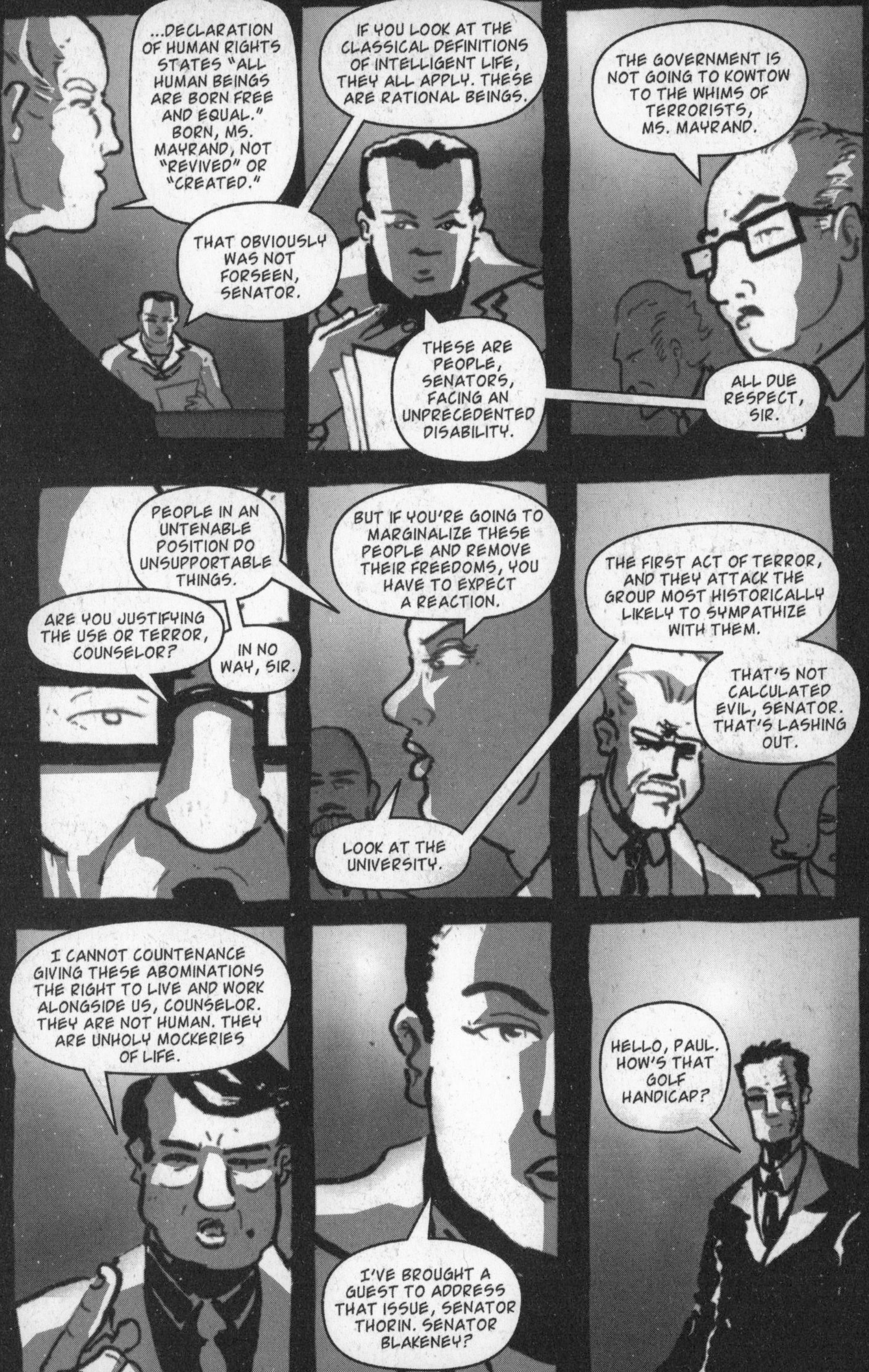
...DECLARATION OF HUMAN RIGHTS STATES "ALL HUMAN BEINGS ARE BORN FREE AND EQUAL." BORN, MS. MAYRAND, NOT "REVIVED" OR "CREATED."
THAT OBVIOUSLY WAS NOT FORSEEN, SENATOR.
IF YOU LOOK AT THE CLASSICAL DEFINITIONS OF INTELLIGENT LIFE, THEY ALL APPLY. THESE ARE RATIONAL BEINGS.
THESE ARE PEOPLE, SENATORS, FACING AN UNPRECEDENTED DISABILITY.
THE GOVERNMENT IS NOT GOING TO KOWTOW TO THE WHIMS OF TERRORISTS, MS. MAYRAND.
ALL DUE RESPECT, SIR.
PEOPLE IN AN UNTENABLE POSITION DO UNSUPPORTABLE THINGS.
ARE YOU JUSTIFYING THE USE OR TERROR, COUNSELOR?
IN NO WAY, SIR.
BUT IF YOU'RE GOING TO MARGINALIZE THESE PEOPLE AND REMOVE THEIR FREEDOMS, YOU HAVE TO EXPECT A REACTION.
LOOK AT THE UNIVERSITY.
THE FIRST ACT OF TERROR, AND THEY ATTACK THE GROUP MOST HISTORICALLY LIKELY TO SYMPATHIZE WITH THEM.
THAT'S NOT CALCULATED EVIL, SENATOR. THAT'S LASHING OUT.
I CANNOT COUNTENANCE GIVING THESE ABOMINATIONS THE RIGHT TO LIVE AND WORK ALONGSIDE US, COUNSELOR. THEY ARE NOT HUMAN. THEY ARE UNHOLY MOCKERIES OF LIFE.
I'VE BROUGHT A GUEST TO ADDRESS THAT ISSUE, SENATOR THORIN. SENATOR BLAKENEY?
HELLO, PAUL. HOW'S THAT GOLF HANDICAP?

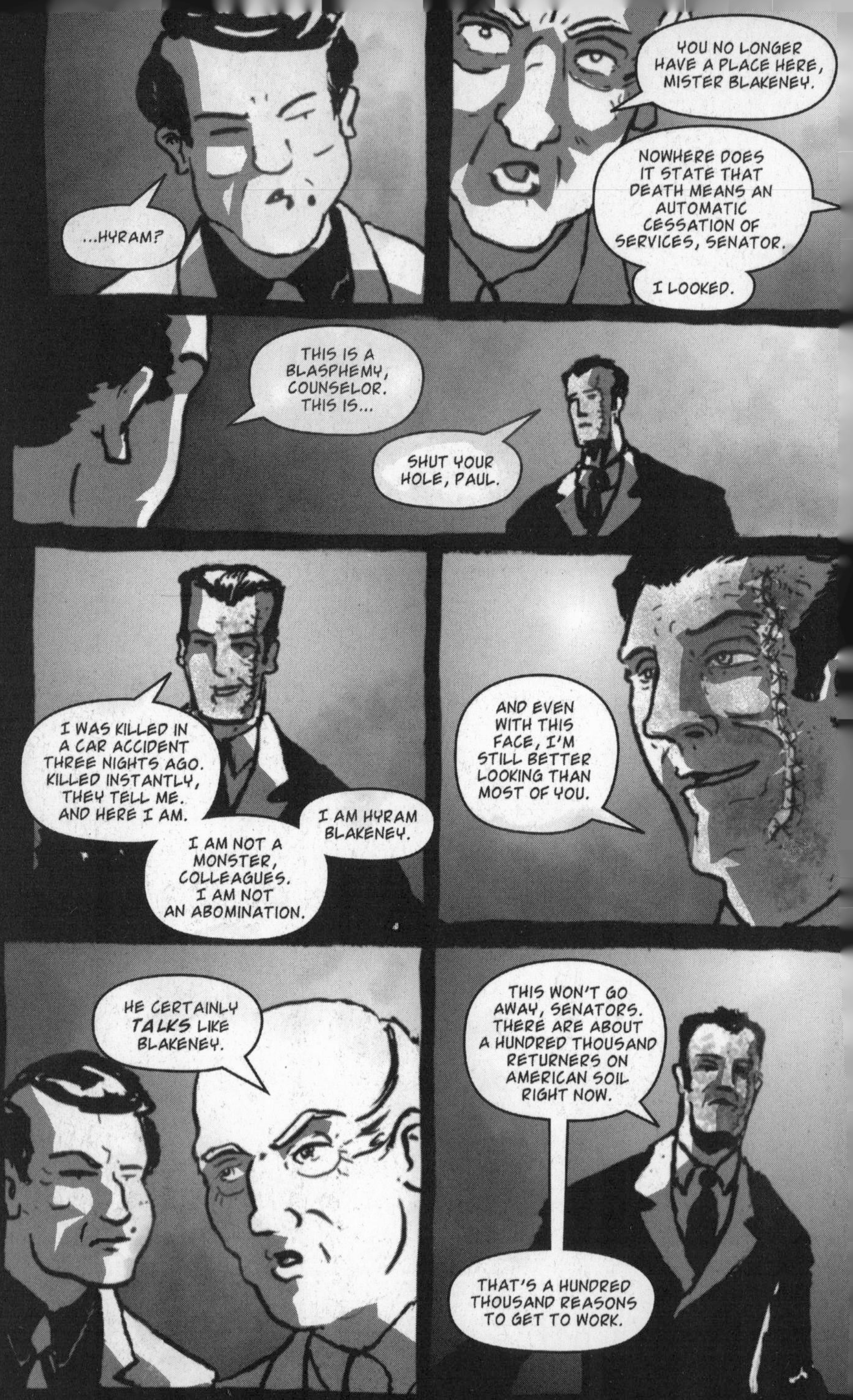
...HYRAM?
YOU NO LONGER HAVE A PLACE HERE, MISTER BLAKENEY.
NOWHERE DOES IT STATE THAT DEATH MEANS AN AUTOMATIC CESSATION OF SERVICES, SENATOR.
I LOOKED.
THIS IS A BLASPHEMY, COUNSELOR. THIS IS...
SHUT YOUR HOLE, PAUL.
I WAS KILLED IN A CAR ACCIDENT THREE NIGHTS AGO. KILLED INSTANTLY, THEY TELL ME. AND HERE I AM.
I AM NOT A MONSTER, COLLEAGUES. I AM NOT AN ABOMINATION.
I AM HYRAM BLAKENEY.
AND EVEN WITH THIS FACE, I'M STILL BETTER LOOKING THAN MOST OF YOU.
HE CERTAINLY *TALKS* LIKE BLAKENEY.
THIS WON'T GO AWAY, SENATORS. THERE ARE ABOUT A HUNDRED THOUSAND RETURNERS ON AMERICAN SOIL RIGHT NOW.
THAT'S A HUNDRED THOUSAND REASONS TO GET TO WORK.

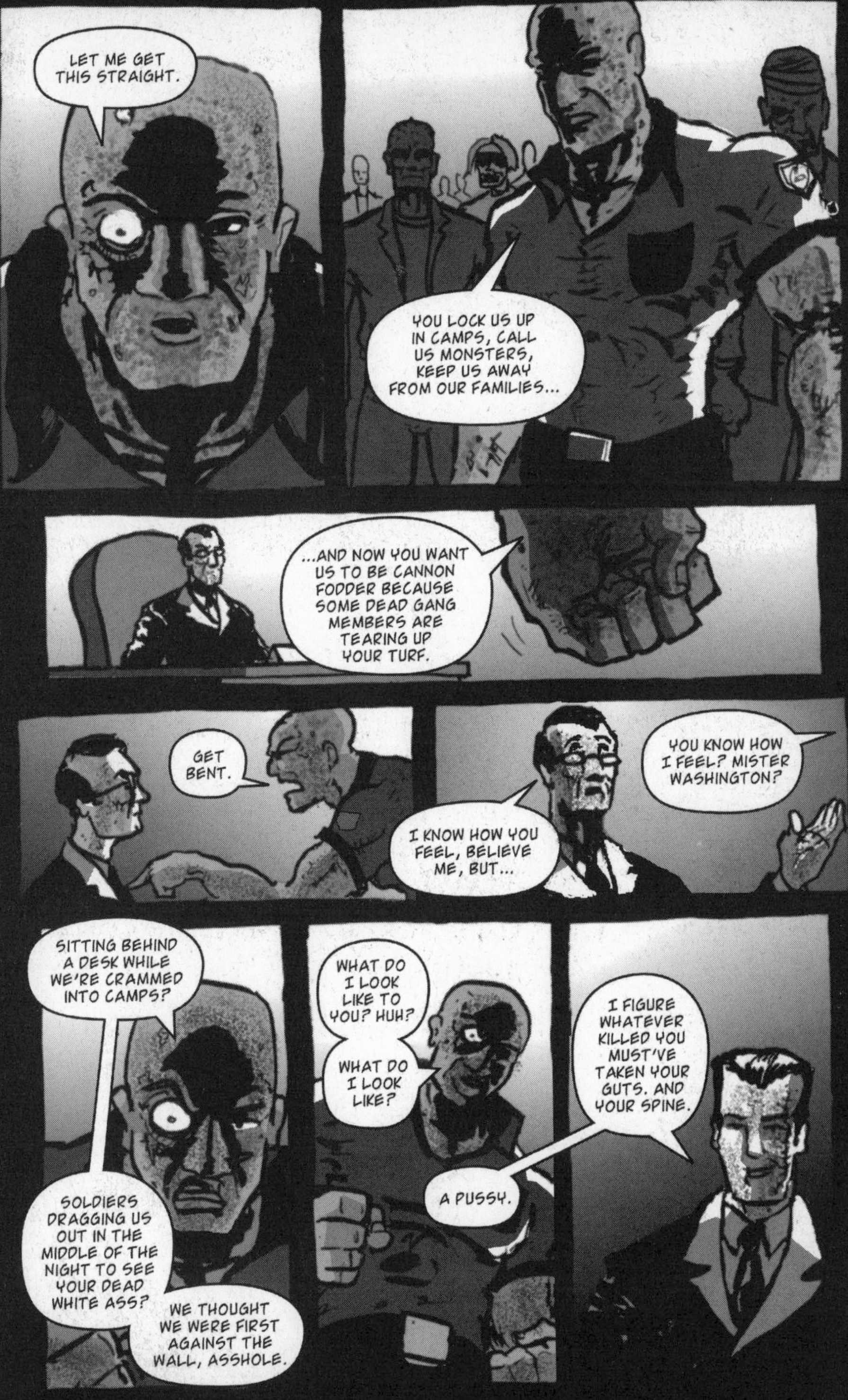
LET ME GET THIS STRAIGHT.
YOU LOCK US UP IN CAMPS, CALL US MONSTERS, KEEP US AWAY FROM OUR FAMILIES...
...AND NOW YOU WANT US TO BE CANNON FODDER BECAUSE SOME DEAD GANG MEMBERS ARE TEARING UP YOUR TURF.
GET BENT.
I KNOW HOW YOU FEEL, BELIEVE ME, BUT...
YOU KNOW HOW I FEEL? MISTER WASHINGTON?
SITTING BEHIND A DESK WHILE WE'RE CRAMMED INTO CAMPS?
SOLDIERS DRAGGING US OUT IN THE MIDDLE OF THE NIGHT TO SEE YOUR DEAD WHITE ASS?
WE THOUGHT WE WERE FIRST AGAINST THE WALL, ASSHOLE.
WHAT DO I LOOK LIKE TO YOU? HUH?
WHAT DO I LOOK LIKE?
I FIGURE WHATEVER KILLED YOU MUST'VE TAKEN YOUR GUTS. AND YOUR SPINE.
A PUSSY.

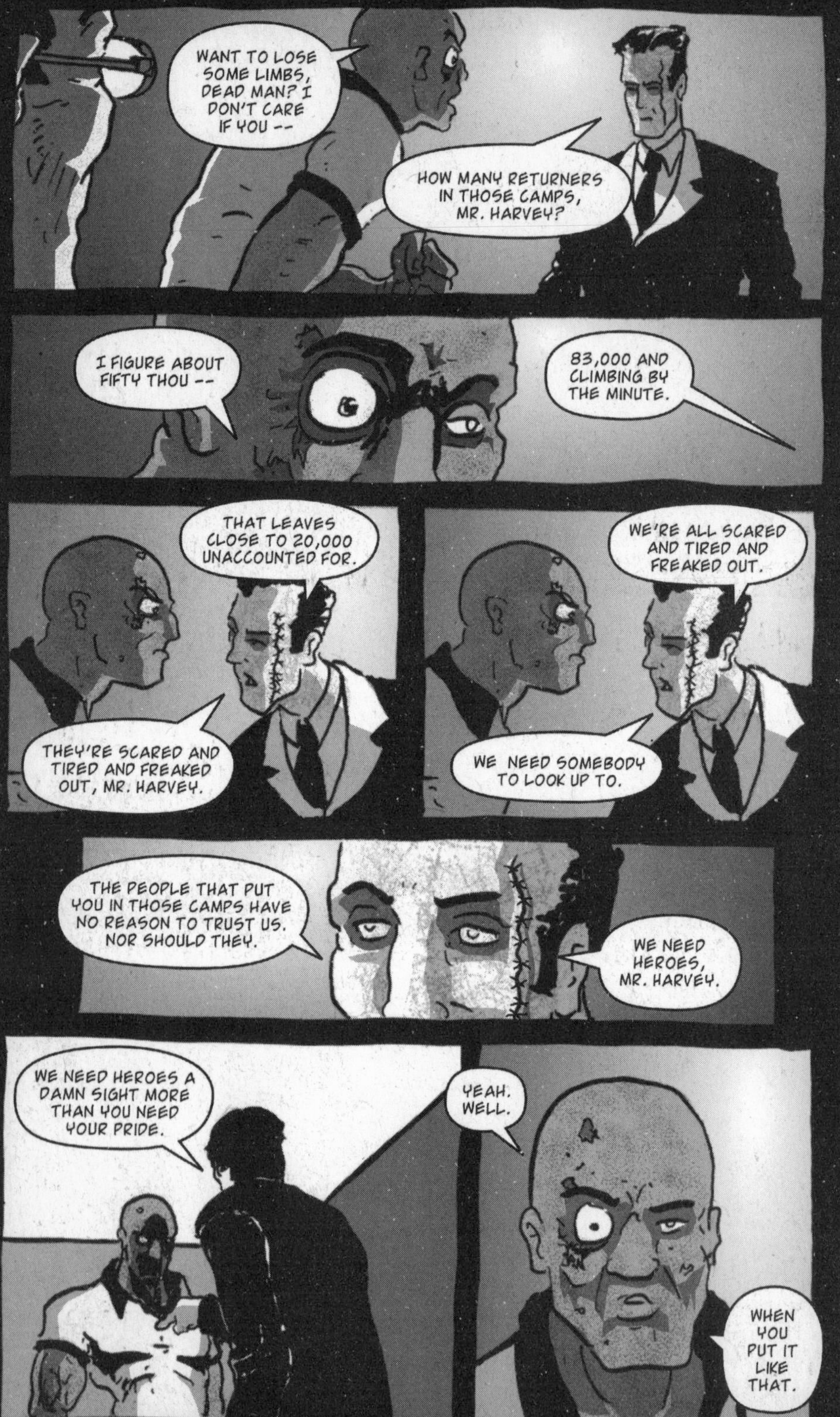
WANT TO LOSE SOME LIMBS, DEAD MAN? I DON'T CARE IF YOU --
HOW MANY RETURNERS IN THOSE CAMPS, MR. HARVEY?
I FIGURE ABOUT FIFTY THOU --
83,000 AND CLIMBING BY THE MINUTE.
THAT LEAVES CLOSE TO 20,000 UNACCOUNTED FOR.
THEY'RE SCARED AND TIRED AND FREAKED OUT, MR. HARVEY.
WE'RE ALL SCARED AND TIRED AND FREAKED OUT.
WE NEED SOMEBODY TO LOOK UP TO.
THE PEOPLE THAT PUT YOU IN THOSE CAMPS HAVE NO REASON TO TRUST US. NOR SHOULD THEY.
WE NEED HEROES, MR. HARVEY.
WE NEED HEROES A DAMN SIGHT MORE THAN YOU NEED YOUR PRIDE.
YEAH. WELL.
WHEN YOU PUT IT LIKE THAT.

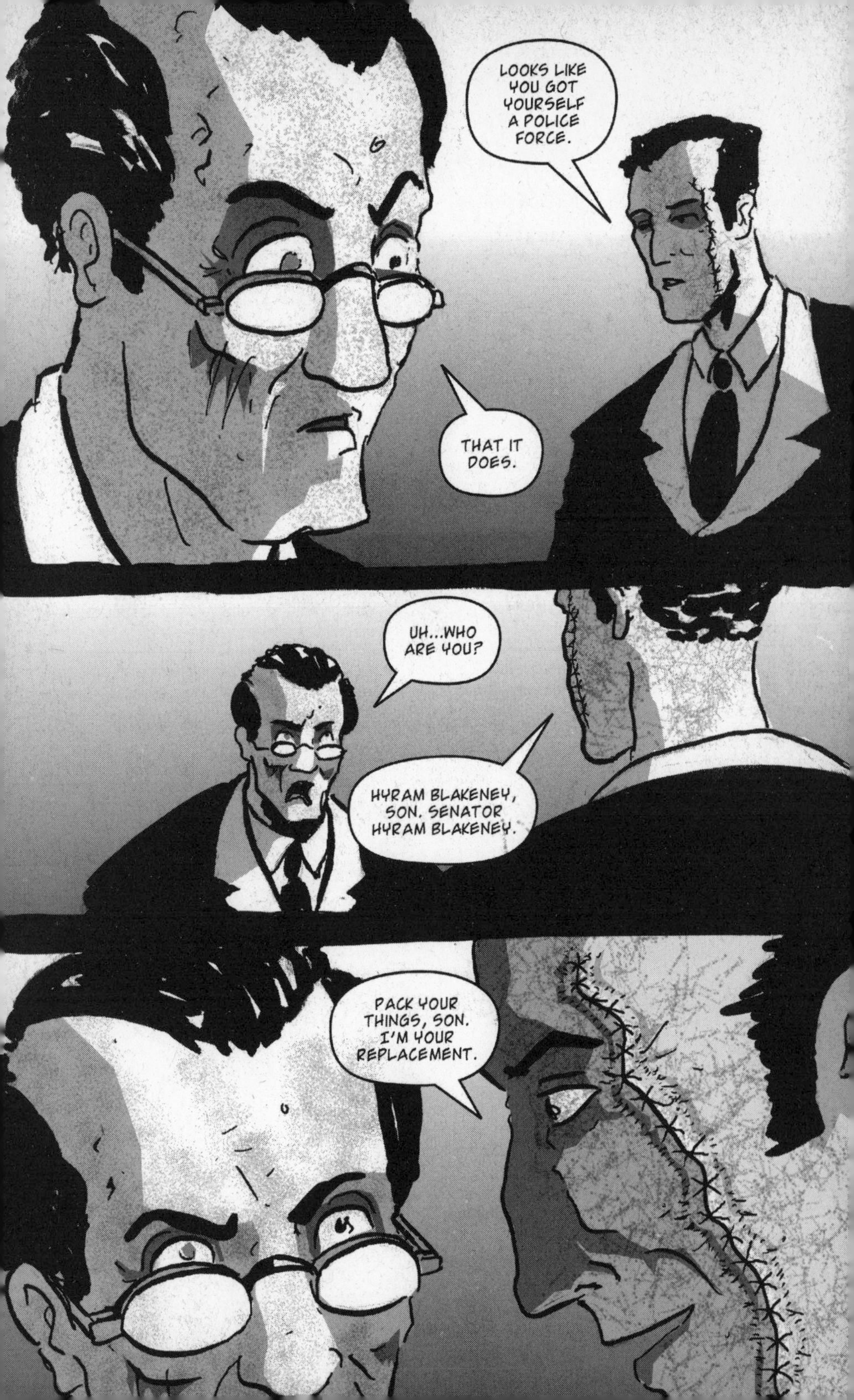
LOOKS LIKE YOU GOT YOURSELF A POLICE FORCE.
THAT IT DOES.
UH...WHO ARE YOU?
HYRAM BLAKENEY, SON. SENATOR HYRAM BLAKENEY.
PACK YOUR THINGS, SON. I'M YOUR REPLACEMENT.

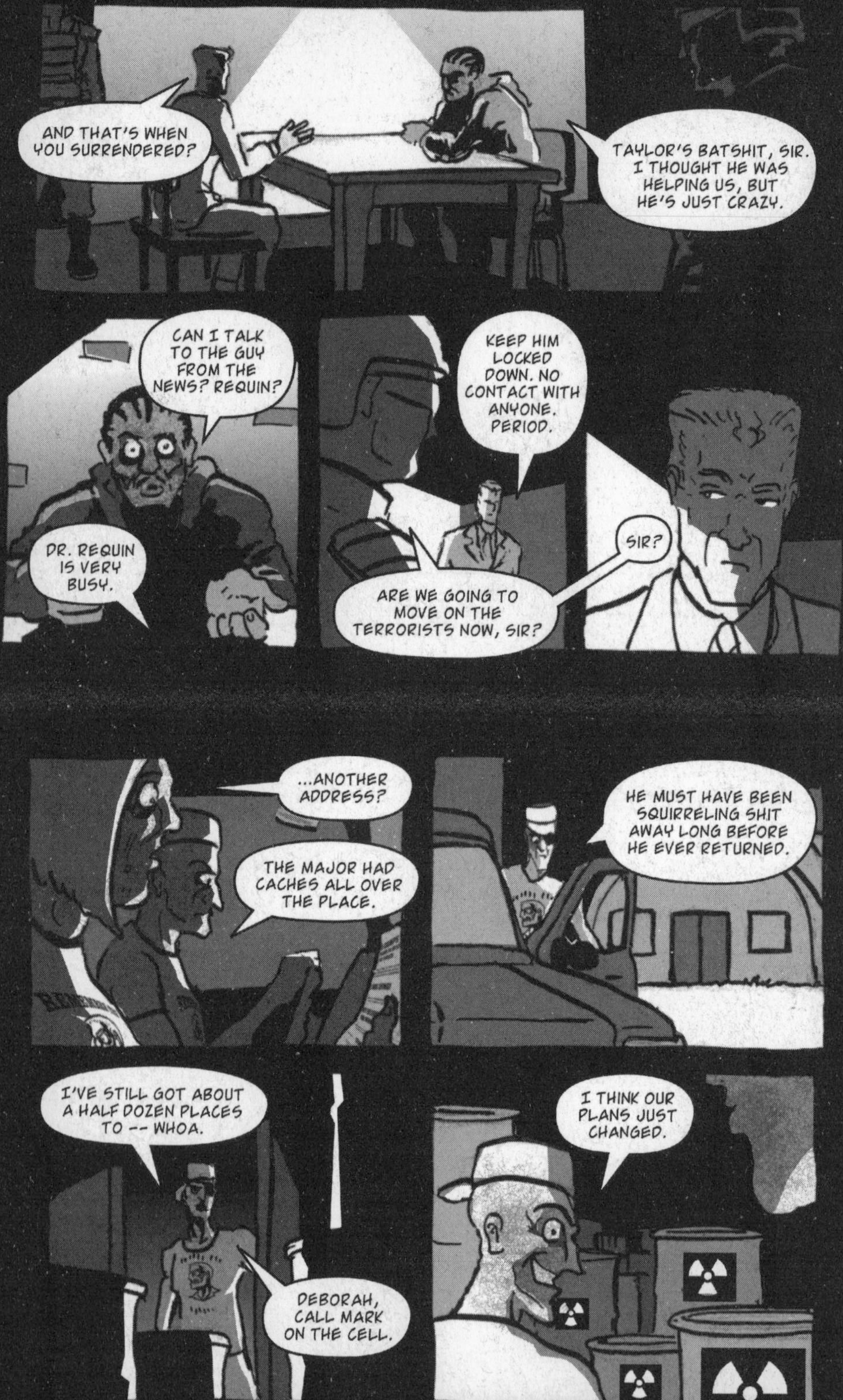
AND THAT'S WHEN YOU SURRENDERED?
TAYLOR'S BATSHIT, SIR. I THOUGHT HE WAS HELPING US, BUT HE'S JUST CRAZY.
CAN I TALK TO THE GUY FROM THE NEWS? REQUIN?
DR. REQUIN IS VERY BUSY.
KEEP HIM LOCKED DOWN. NO CONTACT WITH ANYONE. PERIOD.
ARE WE GOING TO MOVE ON THE TERRORISTS NOW, SIR?
SIR?
...ANOTHER ADDRESS?
THE MAJOR HAD CACHES ALL OVER THE PLACE.
HE MUST HAVE BEEN SQUIRRELING SHIT AWAY LONG BEFORE HE EVER RETURNED.
I'VE STILL GOT ABOUT A HALF DOZEN PLACES TO -- WHOA.
DEBORAH, CALL MARK ON THE CELL.
I THINK OUR PLANS JUST CHANGED.

CHAPTER FOUR

dEAd EYES OpEN

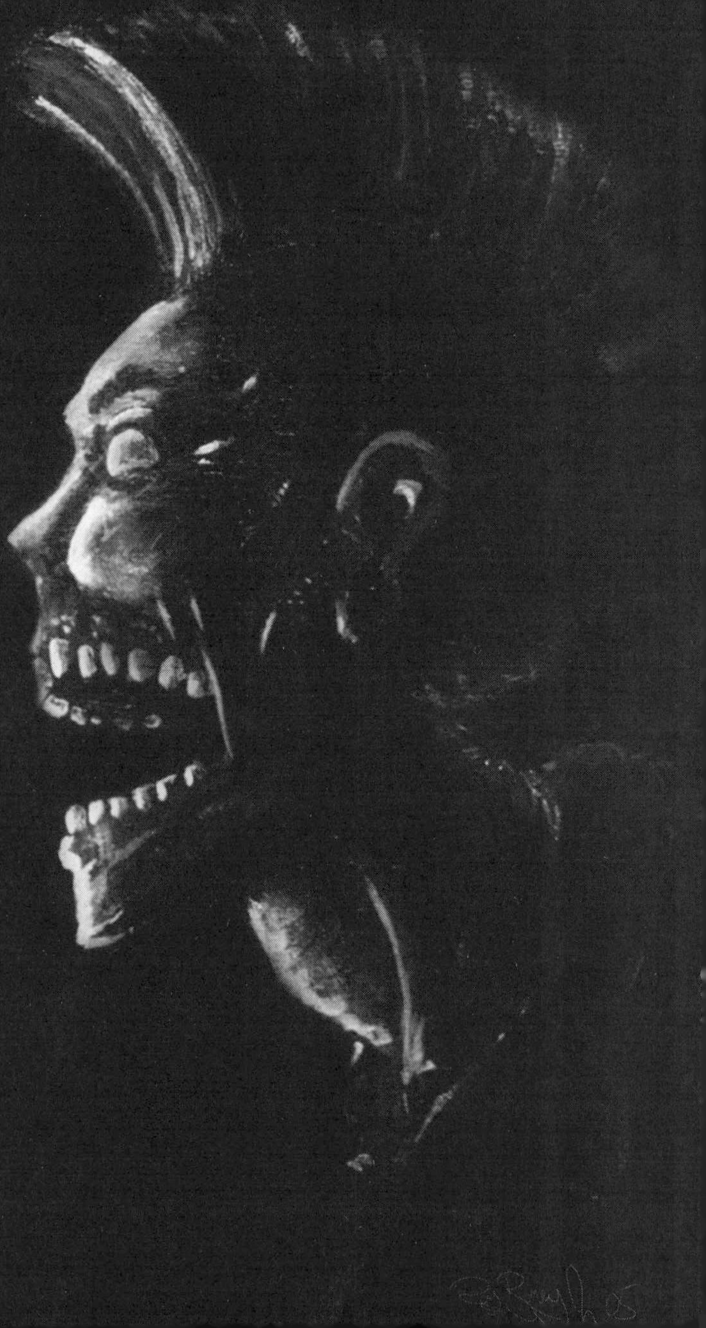

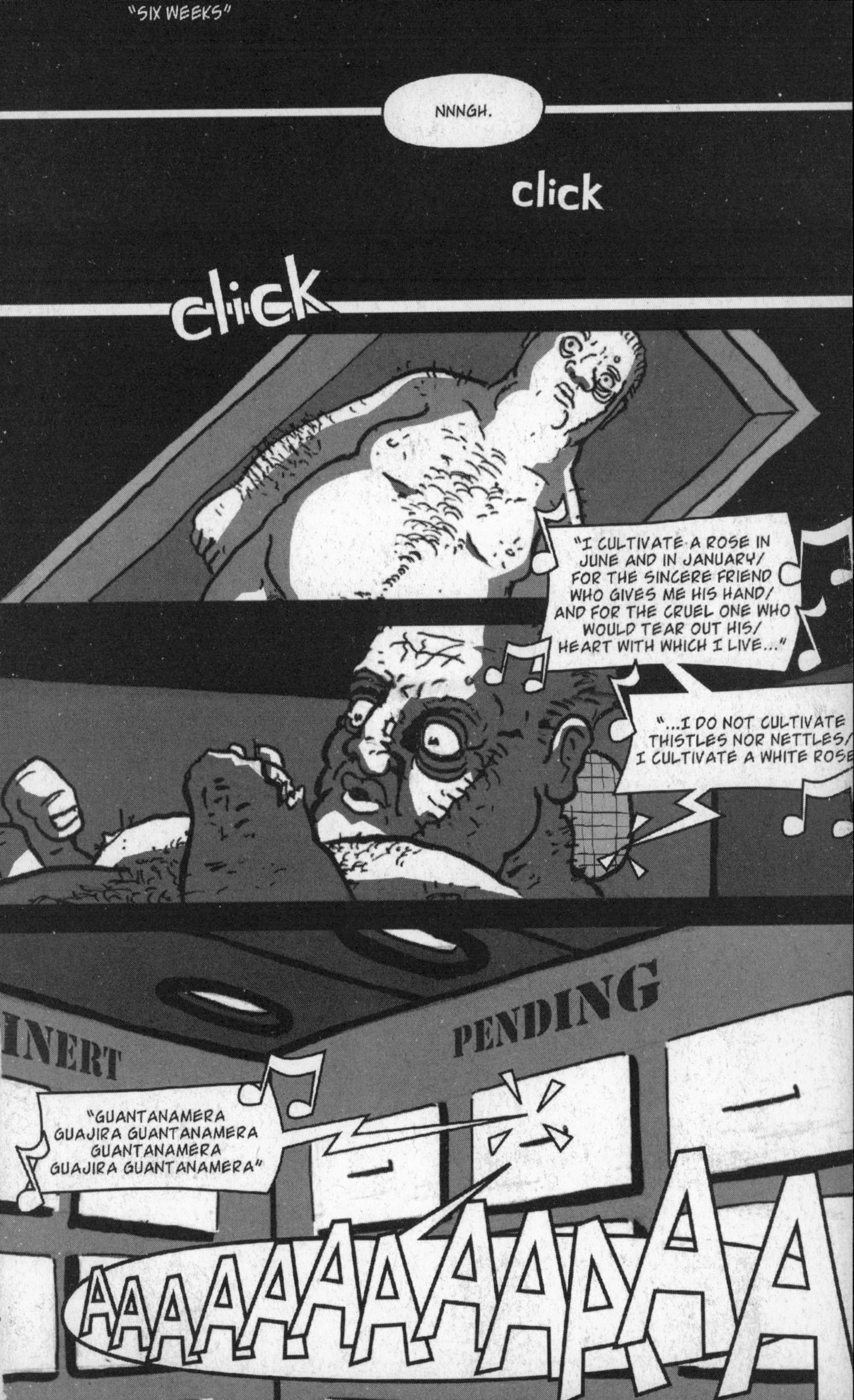
"SIX WEEKS"
NNNGH.
click
click
"I CULTIVATE A ROSE IN JUNE AND IN JANUARY/ FOR THE SINCERE FRIEND WHO GIVES ME HIS HAND/ AND FOR THE CRUEL ONE WHO WOULD TEAR OUT HIS/ HEART WITH WHICH I LIVE..."
"...I DO NOT CULTIVATE THISTLES NOR NETTLES/ I CULTIVATE A WHITE ROSE
INERT
PENDING
"GUANTANAMERA GUAJIRA GUANTANAMERA GUANTANAMERA GUAJIRA GUANTANAMERA"
AAAAAAAAAAAA

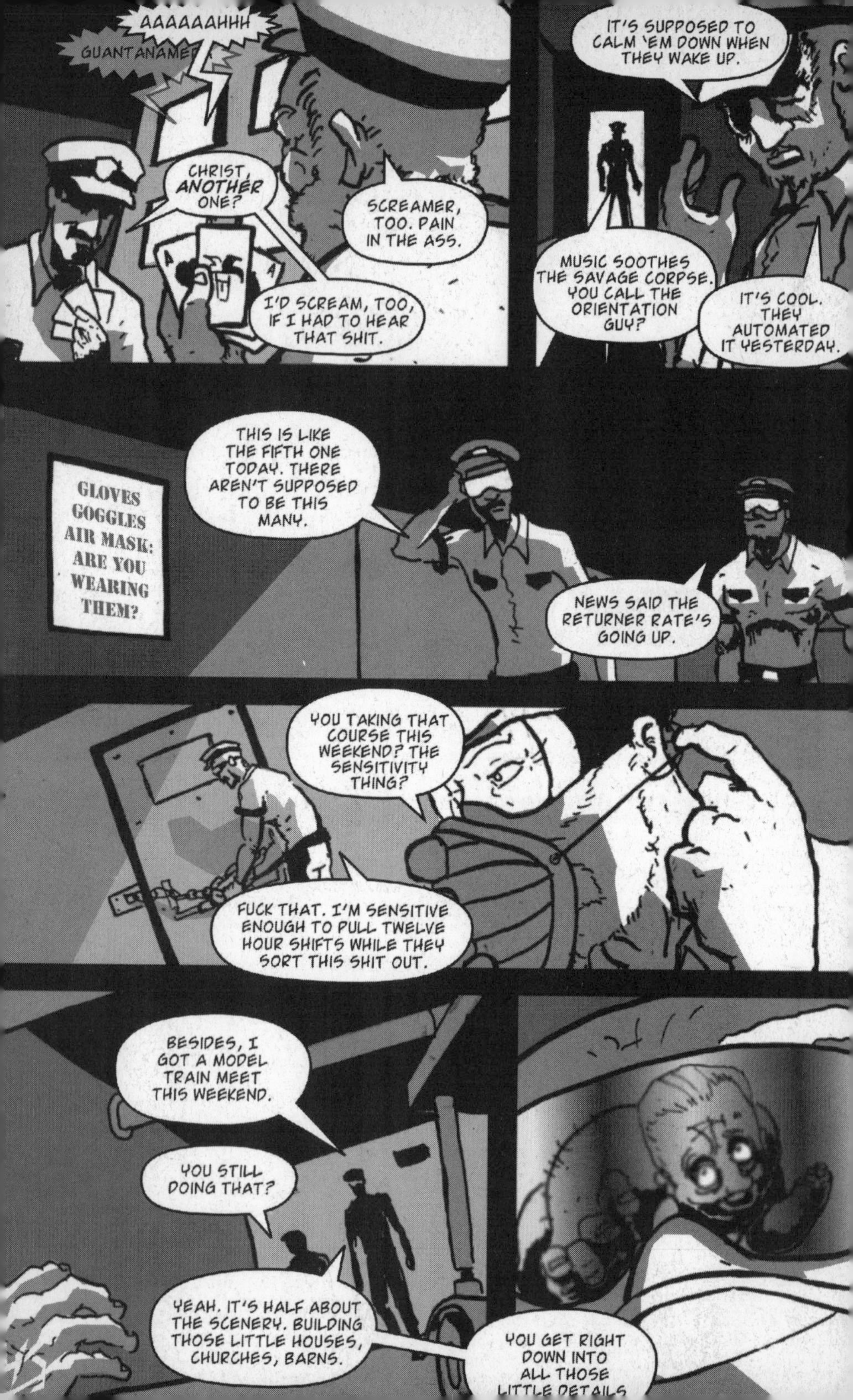
AAAAAAHHH
GUANTANAMER
CHRIST, ANOTHER ONE?
SCREAMER, TOO. PAIN IN THE ASS.
I'D SCREAM, TOO, IF I HAD TO HEAR THAT SHIT.
IT'S SUPPOSED TO CALM 'EM DOWN WHEN THEY WAKE UP.
MUSIC SOOTHES THE SAVAGE CORPSE. YOU CALL THE ORIENTATION GUY?
IT'S COOL. THEY AUTOMATED IT YESTERDAY.
GLOVES GOGGLES AIR MASK: ARE YOU WEARING THEM?
THIS IS LIKE THE FIFTH ONE TODAY. THERE AREN'T SUPPOSED TO BE THIS MANY.
NEWS SAID THE RETURNER RATE'S GOING UP.
YOU TAKING THAT COURSE THIS WEEKEND? THE SENSITIVITY THING?
FUCK THAT. I'M SENSITIVE ENOUGH TO PULL TWELVE HOUR SHIFTS WHILE THEY SORT THIS SHIT OUT.
BESIDES, I GOT A MODEL TRAIN MEET THIS WEEKEND.
YOU STILL DOING THAT?
YEAH. IT'S HALF ABOUT THE SCENERY. BUILDING THOSE LITTLE HOUSES, CHURCHES, BARNS.
YOU GET RIGHT DOWN INTO ALL THOSE LITTLE DETAILS

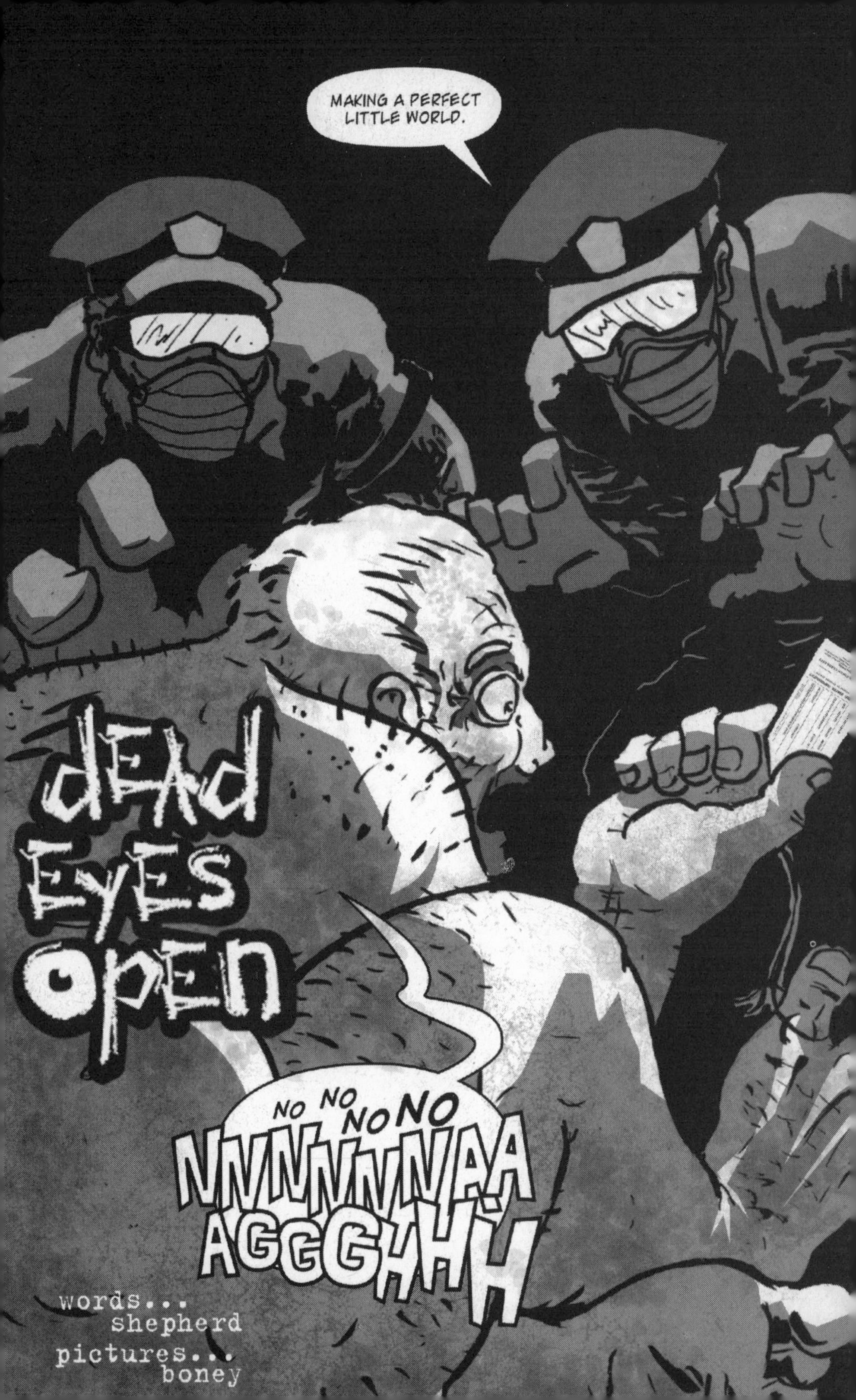
MAKING A PERFECT LITTLE WORLD.
dEAd EyEs OPEn
NO NO NO NO
NNNNNNNAA AGGGHHH
words... shepherd
pictures... boney

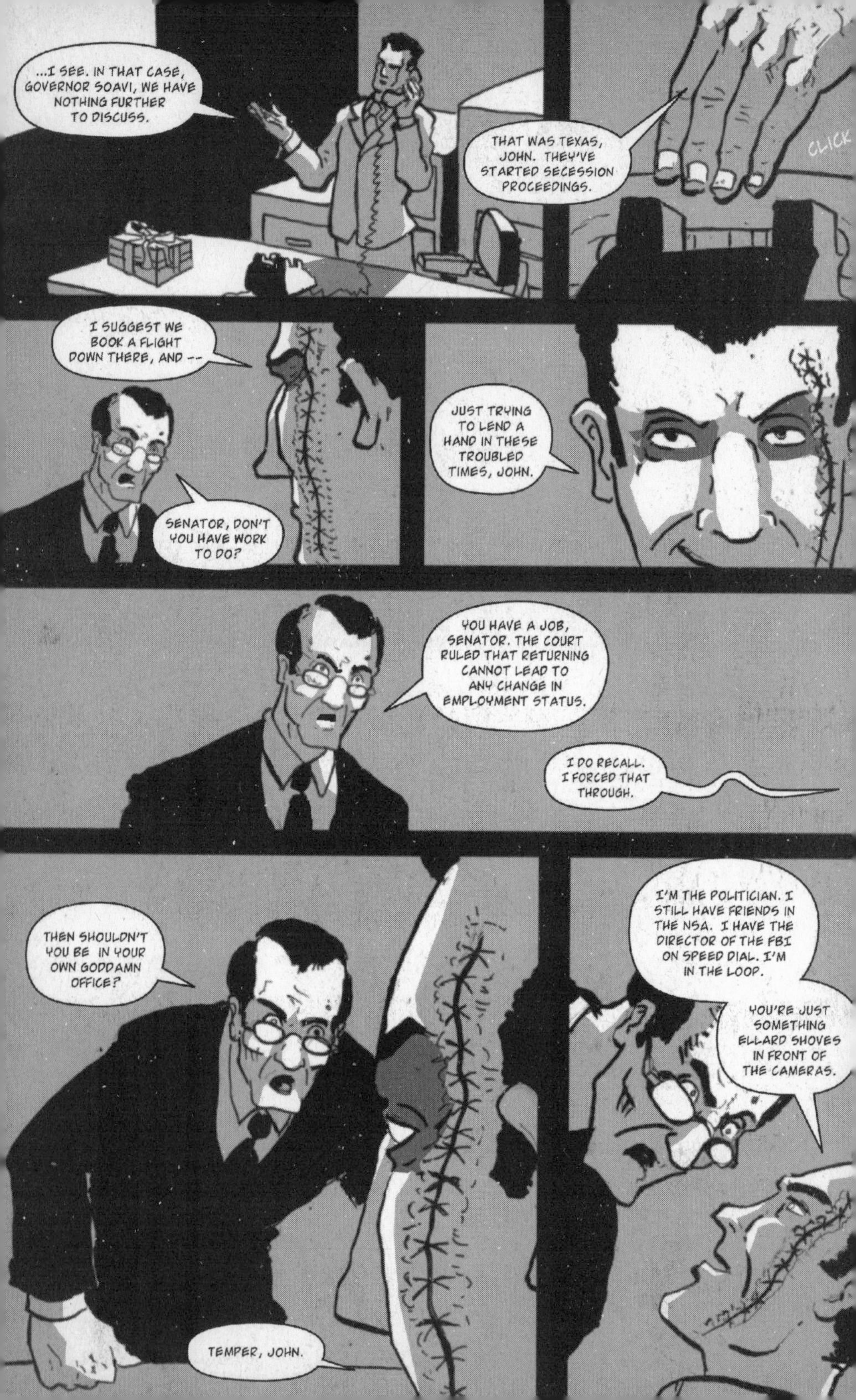
...I SEE. IN THAT CASE, GOVERNOR SOAVI, WE HAVE NOTHING FURTHER TO DISCUSS.
THAT WAS TEXAS, JOHN. THEY'VE STARTED SECESSION PROCEEDINGS.
CLICK
I SUGGEST WE BOOK A FLIGHT DOWN THERE, AND --
SENATOR, DON'T YOU HAVE WORK TO DO?
JUST TRYING TO LEND A HAND IN THESE TROUBLED TIMES, JOHN.
YOU HAVE A JOB, SENATOR. THE COURT RULED THAT RETURNING CANNOT LEAD TO ANY CHANGE IN EMPLOYMENT STATUS.
I DO RECALL. I FORCED THAT THROUGH.
THEN SHOULDN'T YOU BE IN YOUR OWN GODDAMN OFFICE?
TEMPER, JOHN.
I'M THE POLITICIAN. I STILL HAVE FRIENDS IN THE NSA. I HAVE THE DIRECTOR OF THE FBI ON SPEED DIAL. I'M IN THE LOOP.
YOU'RE JUST SOMETHING ELLARD SHOVES IN FRONT OF THE CAMERAS.

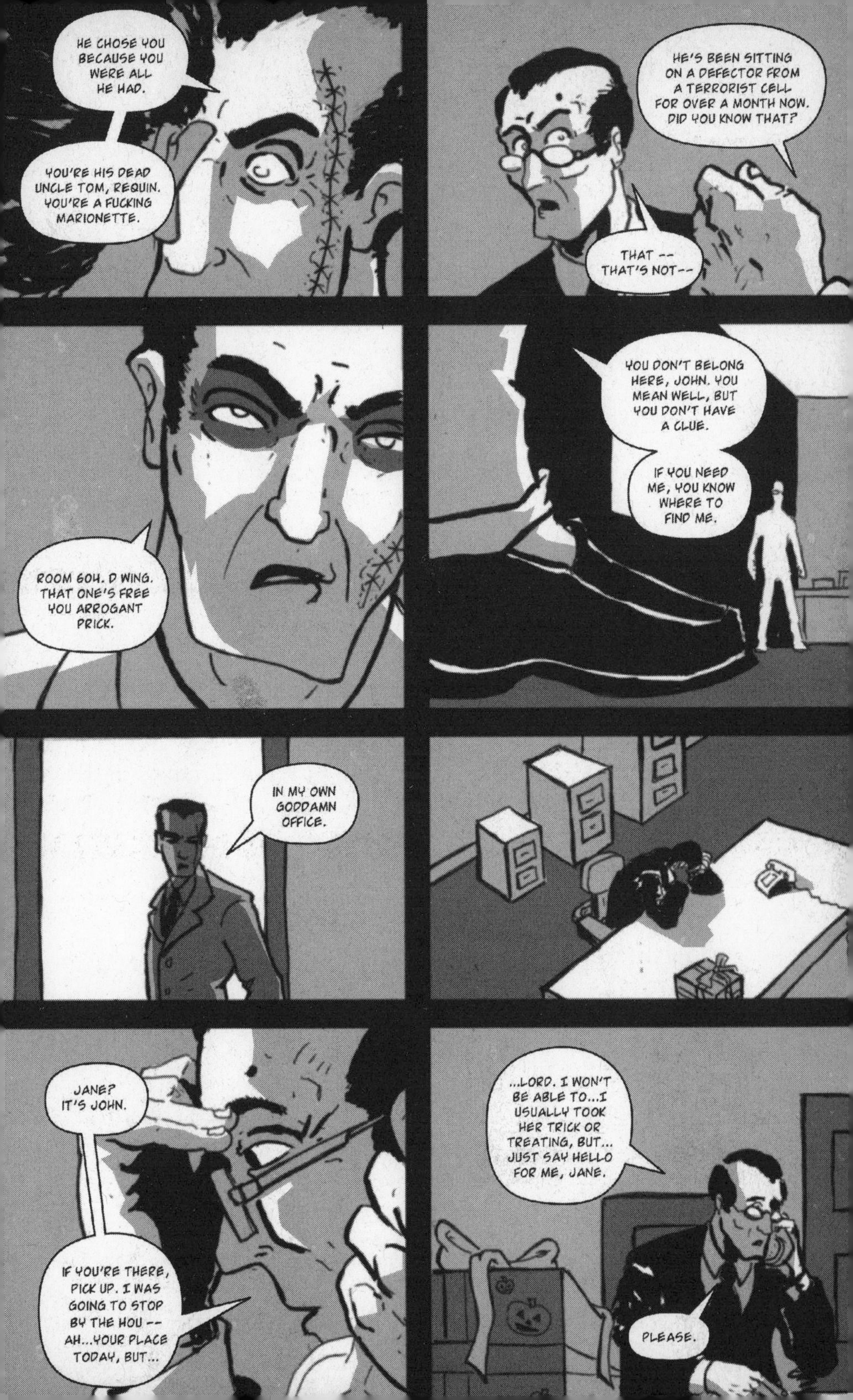
HE CHOSE YOU BECAUSE YOU WERE ALL HE HAD.
YOU'RE HIS DEAD UNCLE TOM, REQUIN. YOU'RE A FUCKING MARIONETTE.
HE'S BEEN SITTING ON A DEFECTOR FROM A TERRORIST CELL FOR OVER A MONTH NOW. DID YOU KNOW THAT?
THAT -- THAT'S NOT--
ROOM 604. D WING. THAT ONE'S FREE YOU ARROGANT PRICK.
YOU DON'T BELONG HERE, JOHN. YOU MEAN WELL, BUT YOU DON'T HAVE A CLUE.
IF YOU NEED ME, YOU KNOW WHERE TO FIND ME.
IN MY OWN GODDAMN OFFICE.
JANE? IT'S JOHN.
IF YOU'RE THERE, PICK UP. I WAS GOING TO STOP BY THE HOU -- AH...YOUR PLACE TODAY, BUT...
...LORD. I WON'T BE ABLE TO...I USUALLY TOOK HER TRICK OR TREATING, BUT... JUST SAY HELLO FOR ME, JANE.
PLEASE.

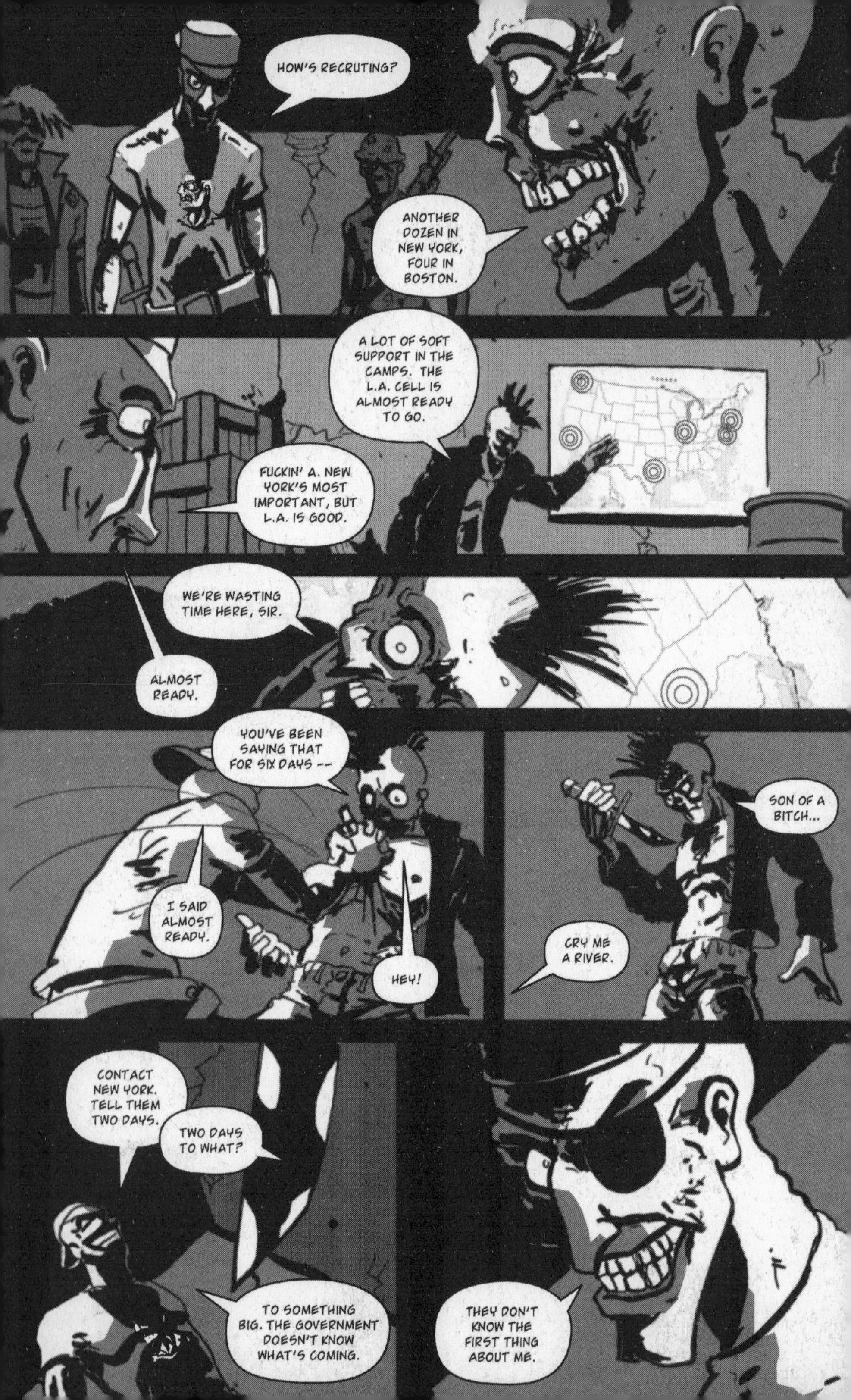
HOW'S RECRUTING?
ANOTHER DOZEN IN NEW YORK, FOUR IN BOSTON.
A LOT OF SOFT SUPPORT IN THE CAMPS. THE L.A. CELL IS ALMOST READY TO GO.
FUCKIN' A. NEW YORK'S MOST IMPORTANT, BUT L.A. IS GOOD.
WE'RE WASTING TIME HERE, SIR.
ALMOST READY.
YOU'VE BEEN SAYING THAT FOR SIX DAYS --
I SAID ALMOST READY.
HEY!
SON OF A BITCH...
CRY ME A RIVER.
CONTACT NEW YORK. TELL THEM TWO DAYS.
TWO DAYS TO WHAT?
TO SOMETHING BIG. THE GOVERNMENT DOESN'T KNOW WHAT'S COMING.
THEY DON'T KNOW THE FIRST THING ABOUT ME.

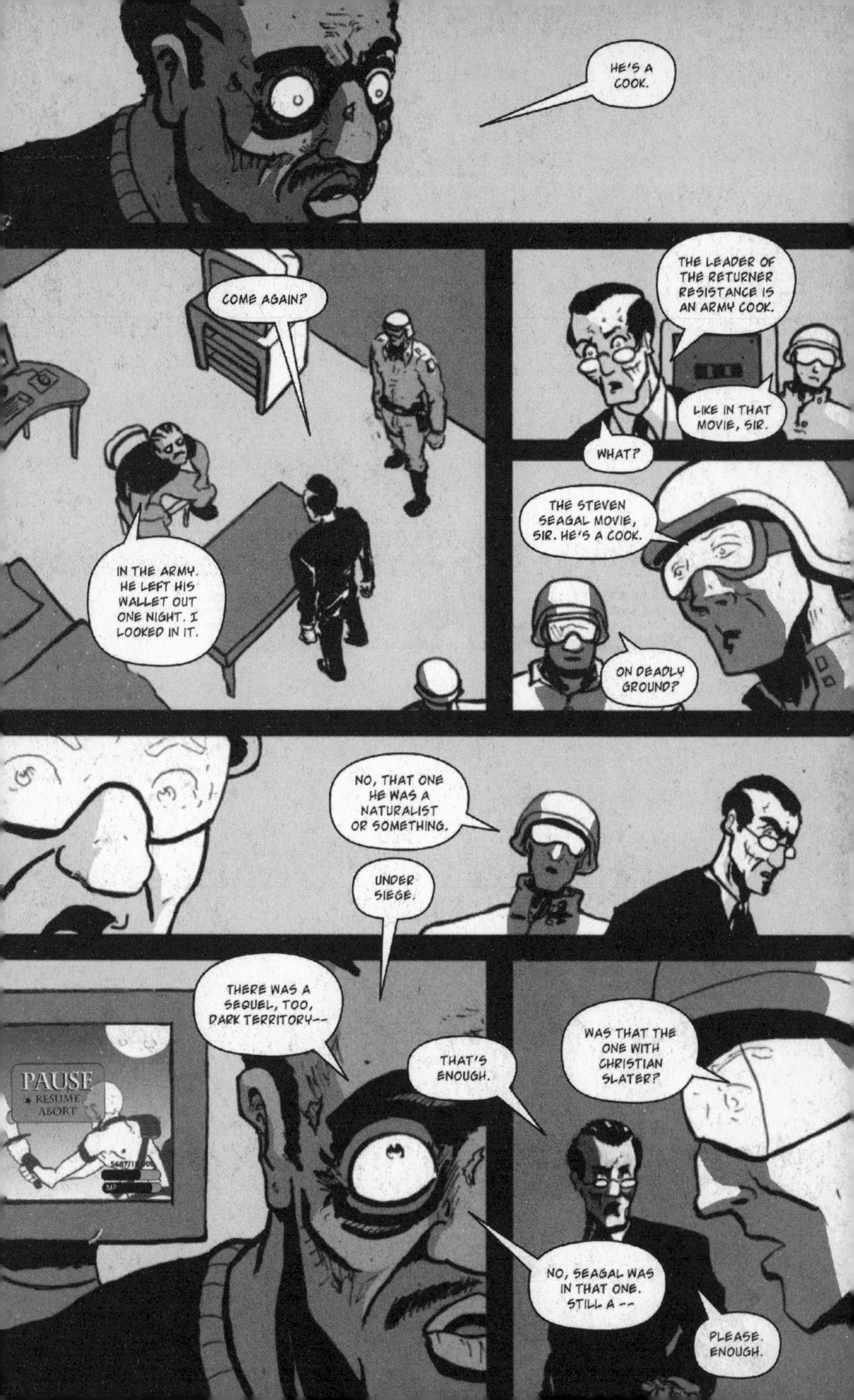
HE'S A COOK.
COME AGAIN?
IN THE ARMY. HE LEFT HIS WALLET OUT ONE NIGHT. I LOOKED IN IT.
THE LEADER OF THE RETURNER RESISTANCE IS AN ARMY COOK.
LIKE IN THAT MOVIE, SIR.
WHAT?
THE STEVEN SEAGAL MOVIE, SIR. HE'S A COOK.
ON DEADLY GROUND?
NO, THAT ONE HE WAS A NATURALIST OR SOMETHING.
UNDER SIEGE.
PAUSE
RESUME
ABORT
THERE WAS A SEQUEL, TOO, DARK TERRITORY--
THAT'S ENOUGH.
WAS THAT THE ONE WITH CHRISTIAN SLATER?
NO, SEAGAL WAS IN THAT ONE. STILL A --
PLEASE. ENOUGH.

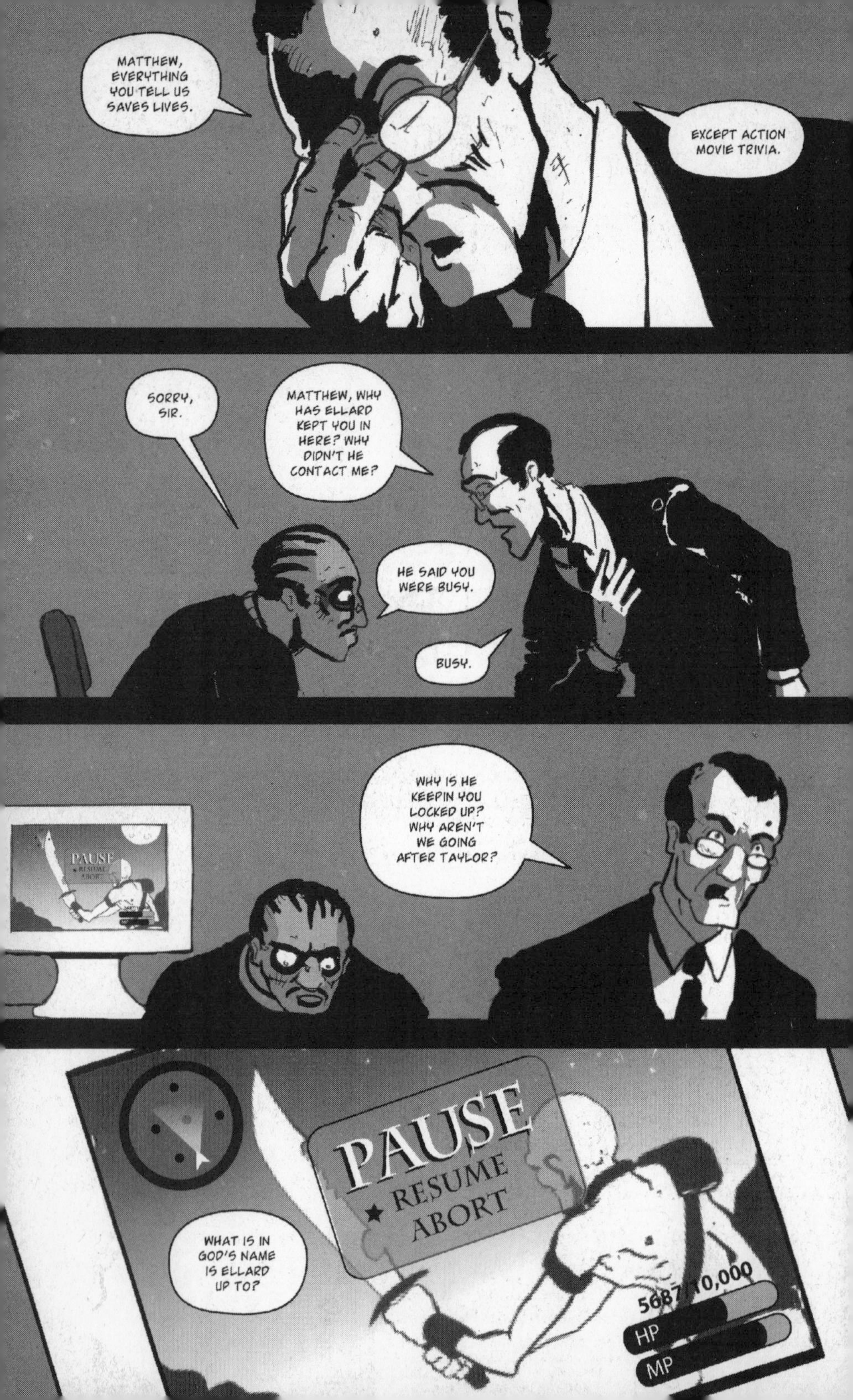
MATTHEW, EVERYTHING YOU TELL US SAVES LIVES.
EXCEPT ACTION MOVIE TRIVIA.
SORRY, SIR.
MATTHEW, WHY HAS ELLARD KEPT YOU IN HERE? WHY DIDN'T HE CONTACT ME?
HE SAID YOU WERE BUSY.
BUSY.
WHY IS HE KEEPIN YOU LOCKED UP? WHY AREN'T WE GOING AFTER TAYLOR?
PAUSE
RESUME
ABORT
WHAT IS IN GOD'S NAME IS ELLARD UP TO?
5687 10,000
HP
MP

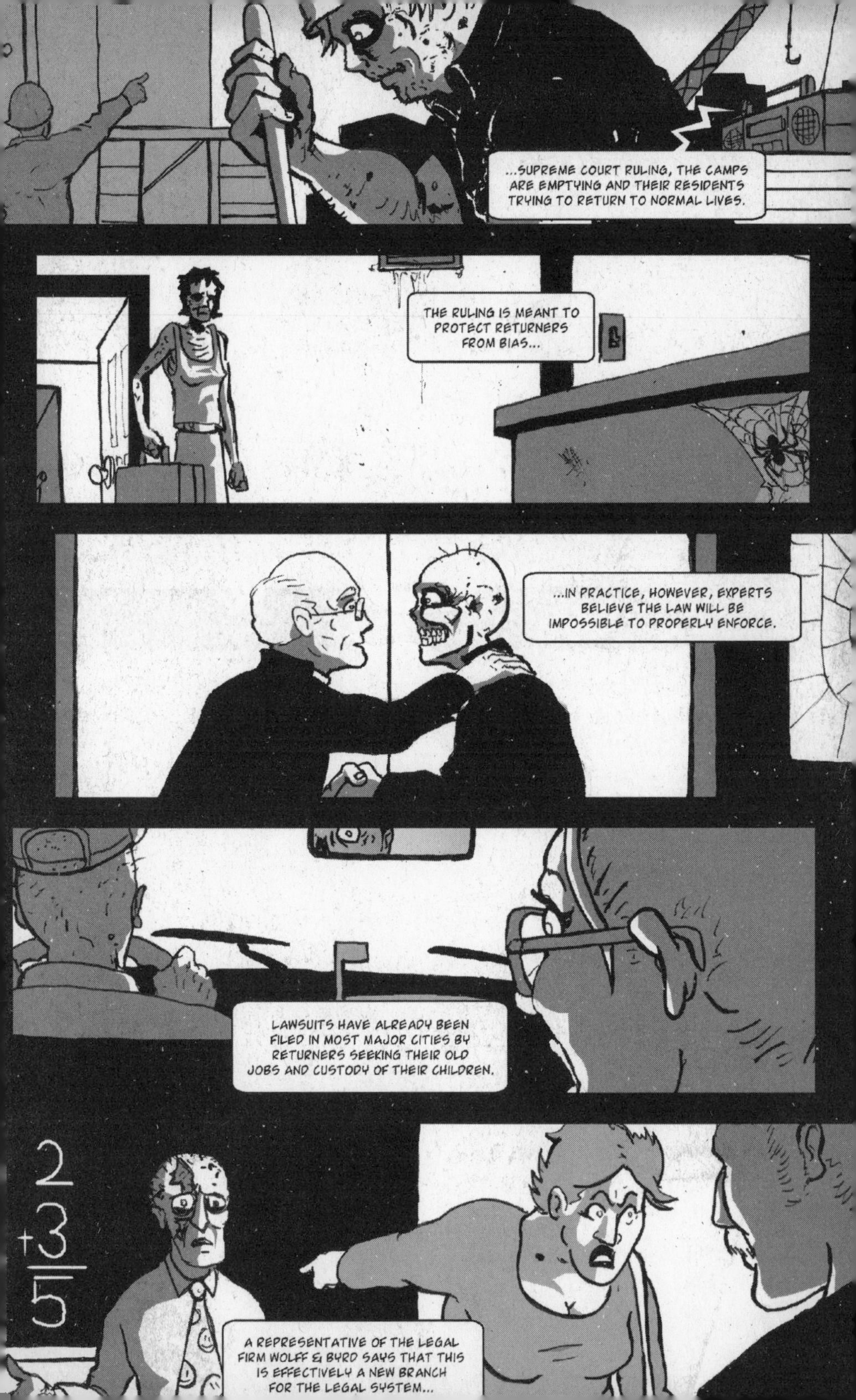
...SUPREME COURT RULING, THE CAMPS ARE EMPTYING AND THEIR RESIDENTS TRYING TO RETURN TO NORMAL LIVES.
THE RULING IS MEANT TO PROTECT RETURNERS FROM BIAS...
...IN PRACTICE, HOWEVER, EXPERTS BELIEVE THE LAW WILL BE IMPOSSIBLE TO PROPERLY ENFORCE.
LAWSUITS HAVE ALREADY BEEN FILED IN MOST MAJOR CITIES BY RETURNERS SEEKING THEIR OLD JOBS AND CUSTODY OF THEIR CHILDREN.
A REPRESENTATIVE OF THE LEGAL FIRM WOLFF & BYRD SAYS THAT THIS IS EFFECTIVELY A NEW BRANCH FOR THE LEGAL SYSTEM...

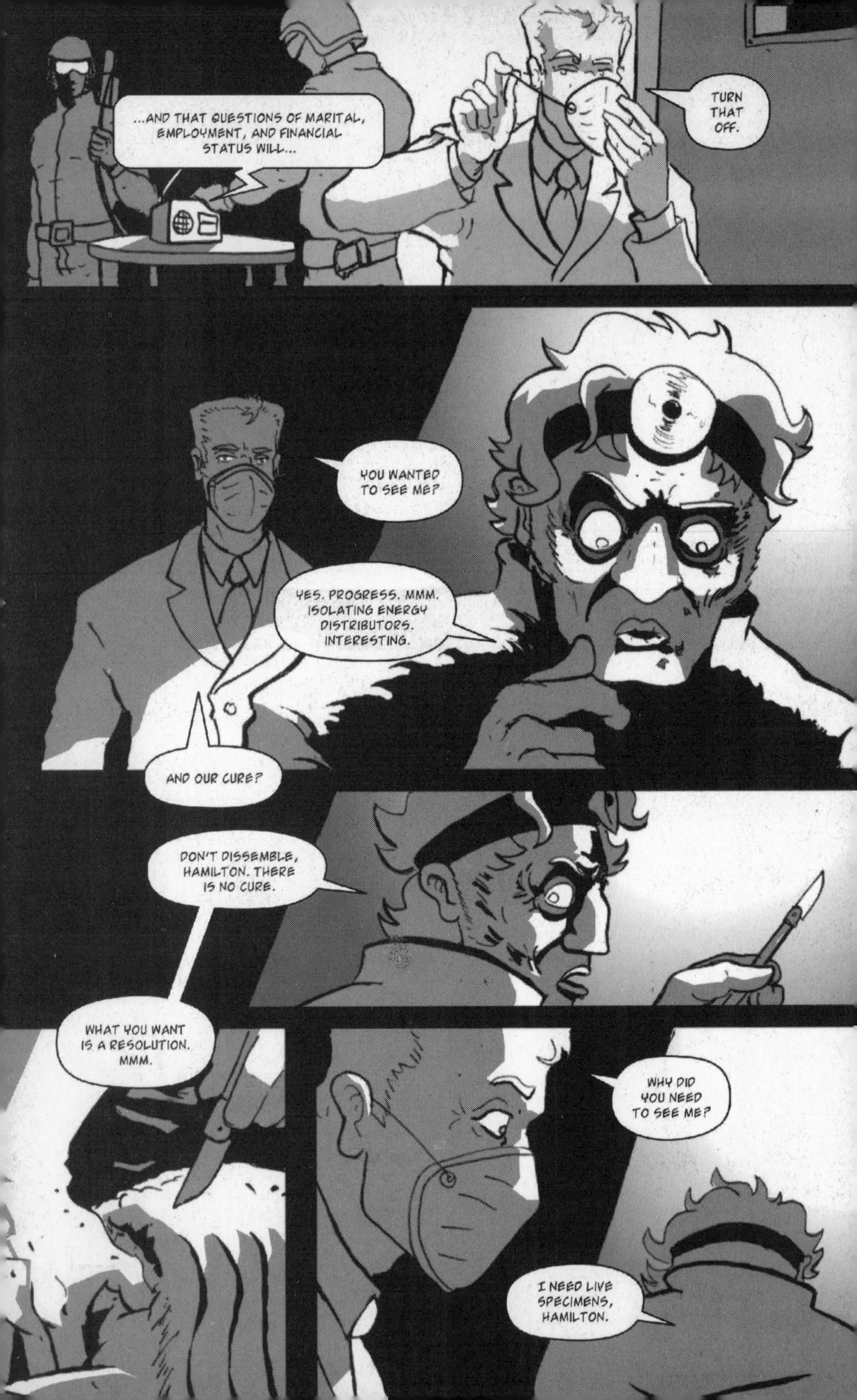
...AND THAT QUESTIONS OF MARITAL, EMPLOYMENT, AND FINANCIAL STATUS WILL...
TURN THAT OFF.
YOU WANTED TO SEE ME?
YES. PROGRESS. MMM. ISOLATING ENERGY DISTRIBUTORS. INTERESTING.
AND OUR CURE?
DON'T DISSEMBLE, HAMILTON. THERE IS NO CURE.
WHAT YOU WANT IS A RESOLUTION. MMM.
WHY DID YOU NEED TO SEE ME?
I NEED LIVE SPECIMENS, HAMILTON.

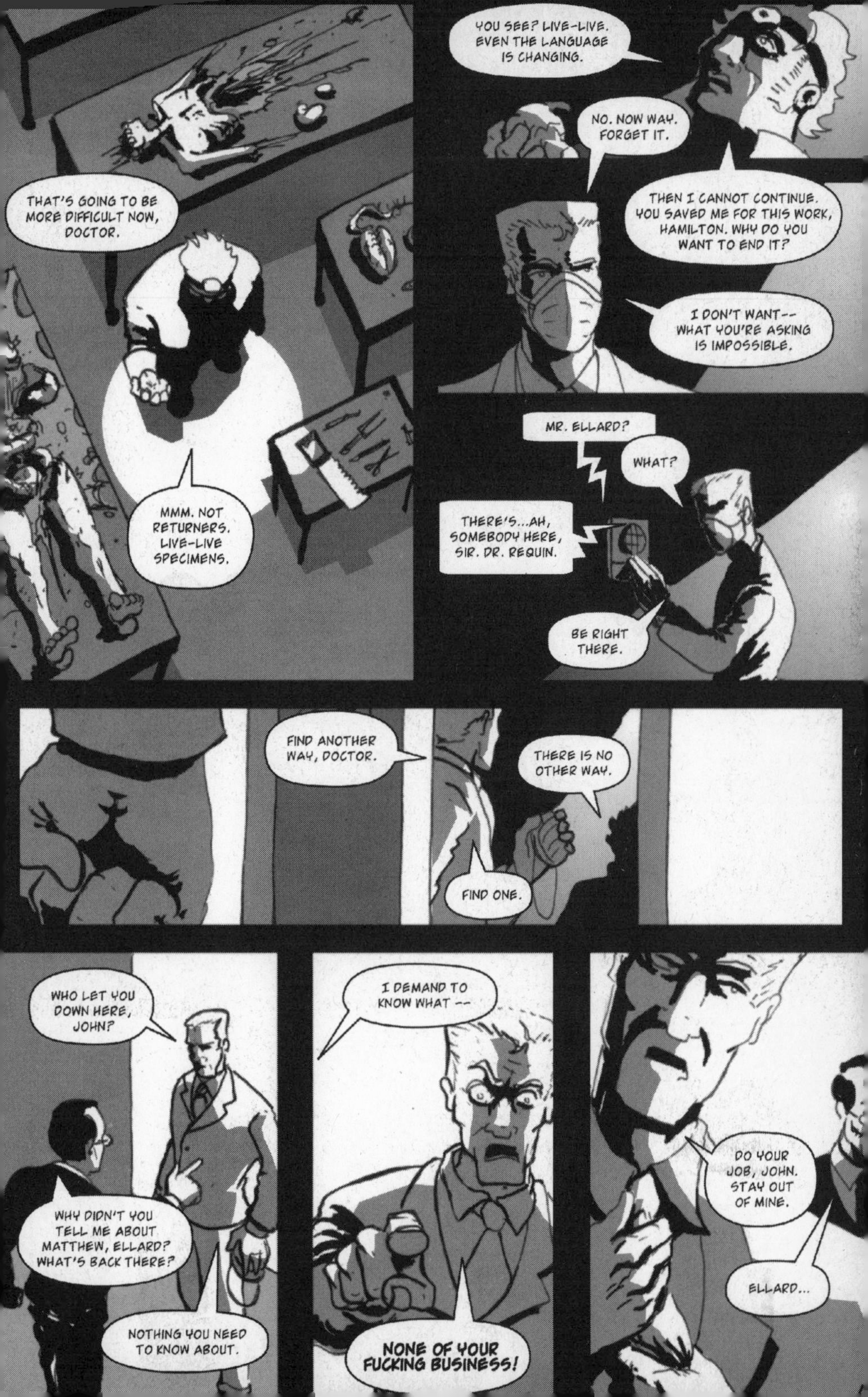
THAT'S GOING TO BE MORE DIFFICULT NOW, DOCTOR.
MMM. NOT RETURNERS. LIVE-LIVE SPECIMENS.
YOU SEE? LIVE-LIVE. EVEN THE LANGUAGE IS CHANGING.
NO. NOW WAY. FORGET IT.
THEN I CANNOT CONTINUE. YOU SAVED ME FOR THIS WORK, HAMILTON. WHY DO YOU WANT TO END IT?
I DON'T WANT-- WHAT YOU'RE ASKING IS IMPOSSIBLE.
MR. ELLARD?
WHAT?
THERE'S...AH, SOMEBODY HERE, SIR. DR. REQUIN.
BE RIGHT THERE.
FIND ANOTHER WAY, DOCTOR.
THERE IS NO OTHER WAY.
FIND ONE.
WHO LET YOU DOWN HERE, JOHN?
WHY DIDN'T YOU TELL ME ABOUT MATTHEW, ELLARD? WHAT'S BACK THERE?
NOTHING YOU NEED TO KNOW ABOUT.
I DEMAND TO KNOW WHAT --
NONE OF YOUR FUCKING BUSINESS!
DO YOUR JOB, JOHN. STAY OUT OF MINE.
ELLARD...

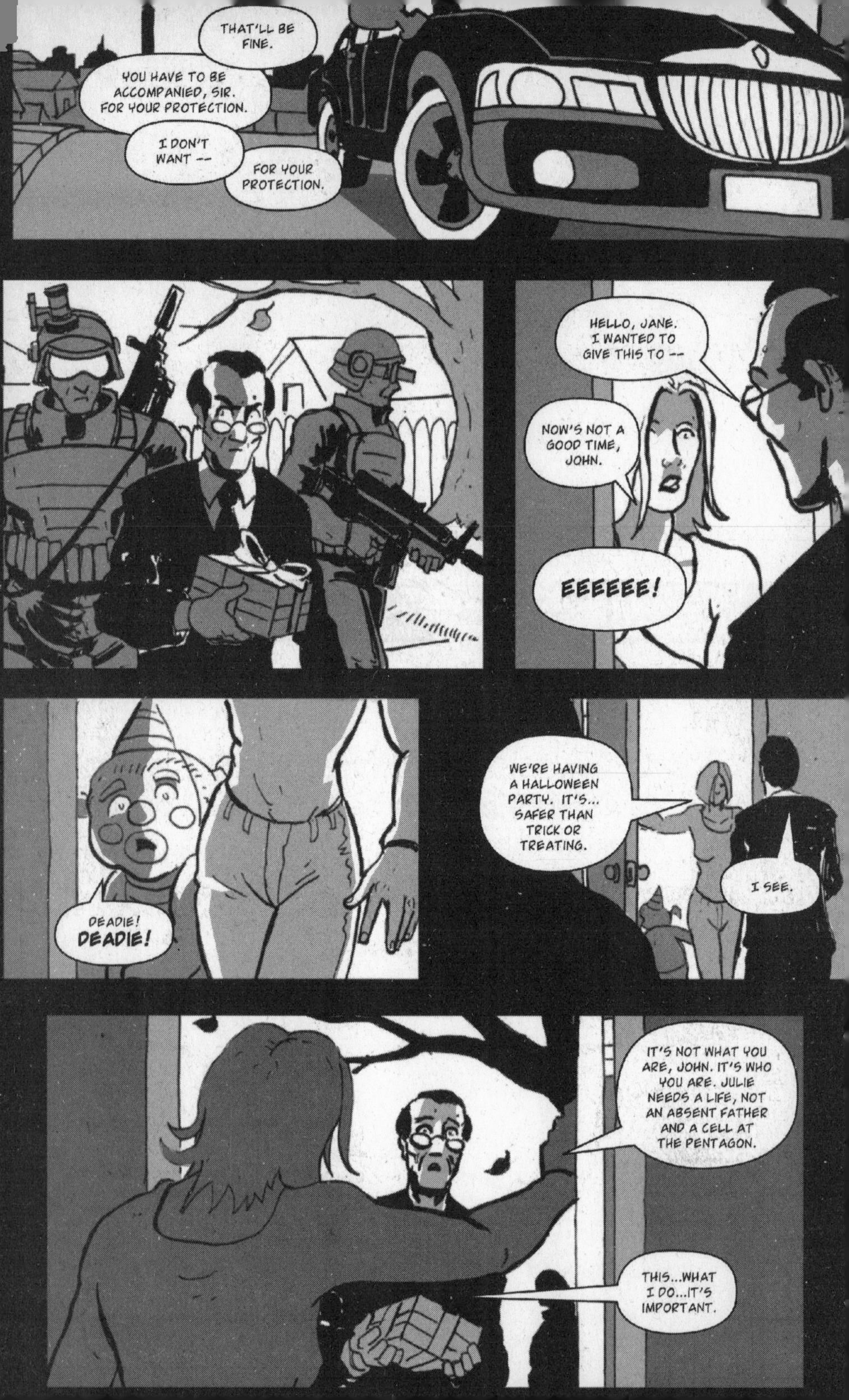
THAT'LL BE FINE.
YOU HAVE TO BE ACCOMPANIED, SIR. FOR YOUR PROTECTION.
I DON'T WANT --
FOR YOUR PROTECTION.
HELLO, JANE. I WANTED TO GIVE THIS TO --
NOW'S NOT A GOOD TIME, JOHN.
EEEEEE!
DEADIE! DEADIE!
WE'RE HAVING A HALLOWEEN PARTY. IT'S... SAFER THAN TRICK OR TREATING.
I SEE.
IT'S NOT WHAT YOU ARE, JOHN. IT'S WHO YOU ARE. JULIE NEEDS A LIFE, NOT AN ABSENT FATHER AND A CELL AT THE PENTAGON.
THIS...WHAT I DO...IT'S IMPORTANT.

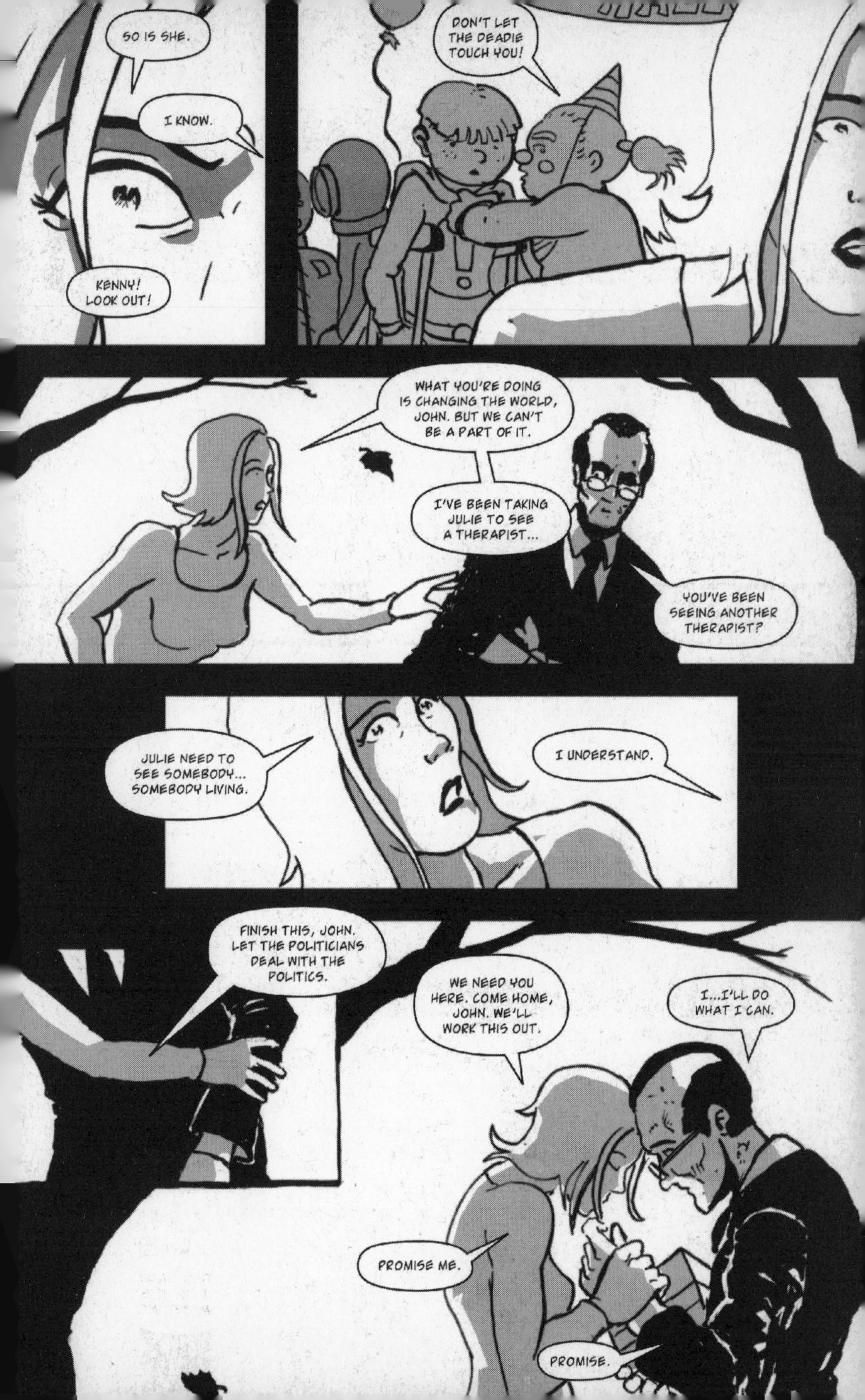
SO IS SHE.
I KNOW.
KENNY! LOOK OUT!
DON'T LET THE DEADIE TOUCH YOU!
WHAT YOU'RE DOING IS CHANGING THE WORLD, JOHN. BUT WE CAN'T BE A PART OF IT.
I'VE BEEN TAKING JULIE TO SEE A THERAPIST...
YOU'VE BEEN SEEING ANOTHER THERAPIST?
JULIE NEED TO SEE SOMEBODY... SOMEBODY LIVING.
I UNDERSTAND.
FINISH THIS, JOHN. LET THE POLITICIANS DEAL WITH THE POLITICS.
WE NEED YOU HERE. COME HOME, JOHN. WE'LL WORK THIS OUT.
I...I'LL DO WHAT I CAN.
PROMISE ME.
PROMISE.

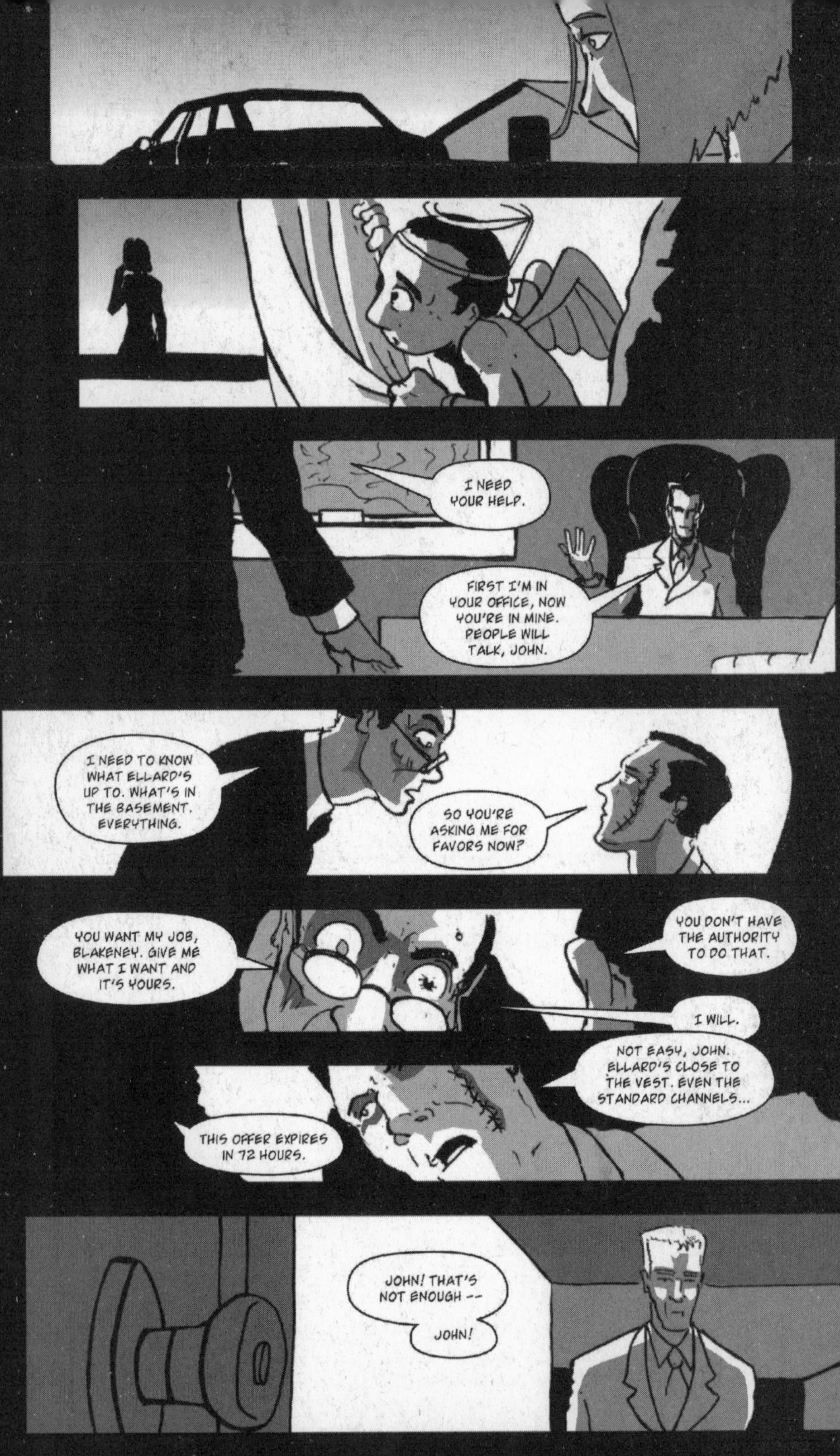

I NEED YOUR HELP.
FIRST I'M IN YOUR OFFICE, NOW YOU'RE IN MINE. PEOPLE WILL TALK, JOHN.
I NEED TO KNOW WHAT ELLARD'S UP TO. WHAT'S IN THE BASEMENT. EVERYTHING.
SO YOU'RE ASKING ME FOR FAVORS NOW?
YOU WANT MY JOB, BLAKENEY. GIVE ME WHAT I WANT AND IT'S YOURS.
YOU DON'T HAVE THE AUTHORITY TO DO THAT.
I WILL.
NOT EASY, JOHN. ELLARD'S CLOSE TO THE VEST. EVEN THE STANDARD CHANNELS...
THIS OFFER EXPIRES IN 72 HOURS.
JOHN! THAT'S NOT ENOUGH --
JOHN!

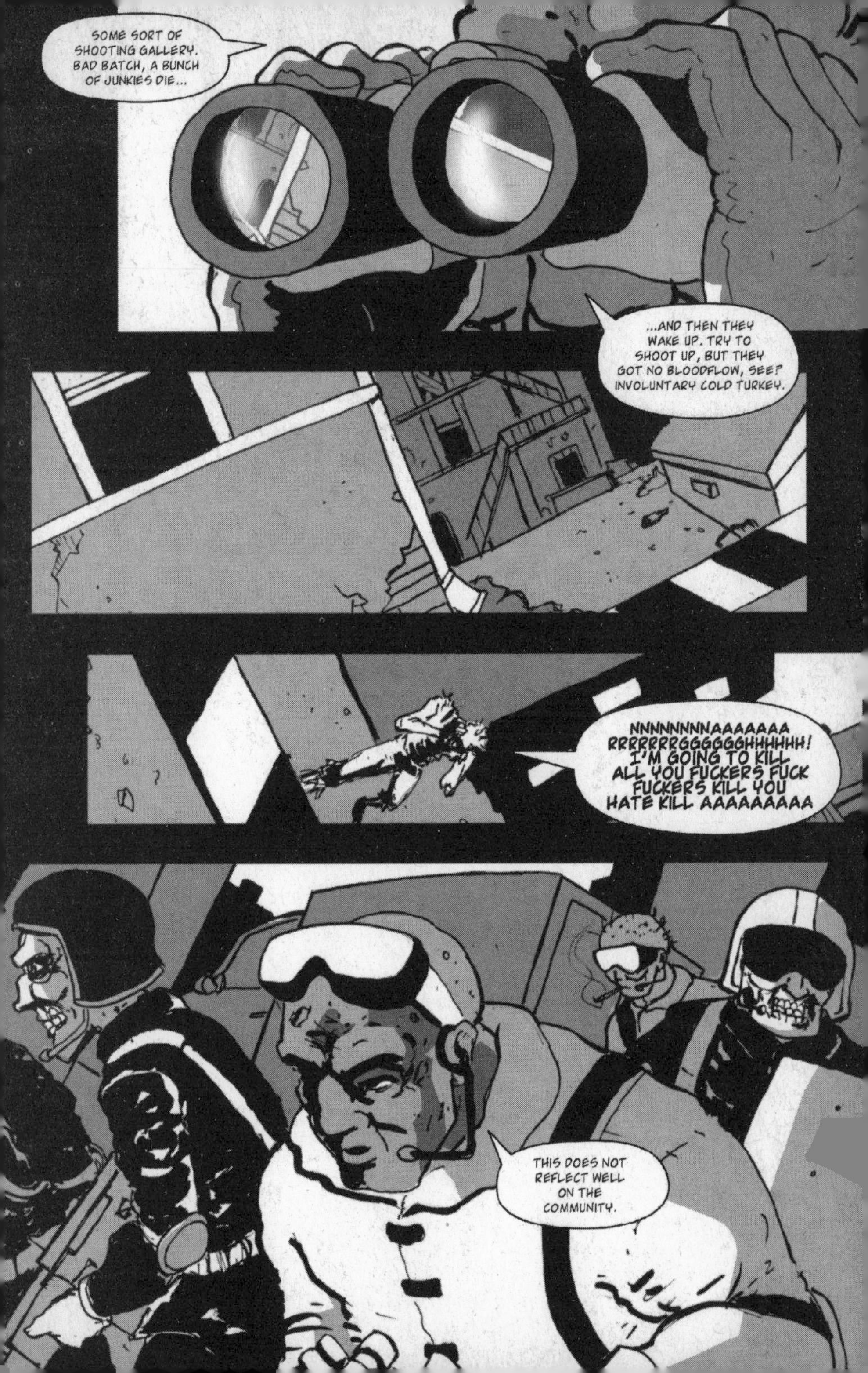
SOME SORT OF SHOOTING GALLERY. BAD BATCH, A BUNCH OF JUNKIES DIE...
...AND THEN THEY WAKE UP. TRY TO SHOOT UP, BUT THEY GOT NO BLOODFLOW, SEE? INVOLUNTARY COLD TURKEY.
NNNNNNNAAAAAAA RRRRRRRGGGGGGHHHHHH! I'M GOING TO KILL ALL YOU FUCKERS FUCK FUCKERS KILL YOU HATE KILL AAAAAAAAA
THIS DOES NOT REFLECT WELL ON THE COMMUNITY.

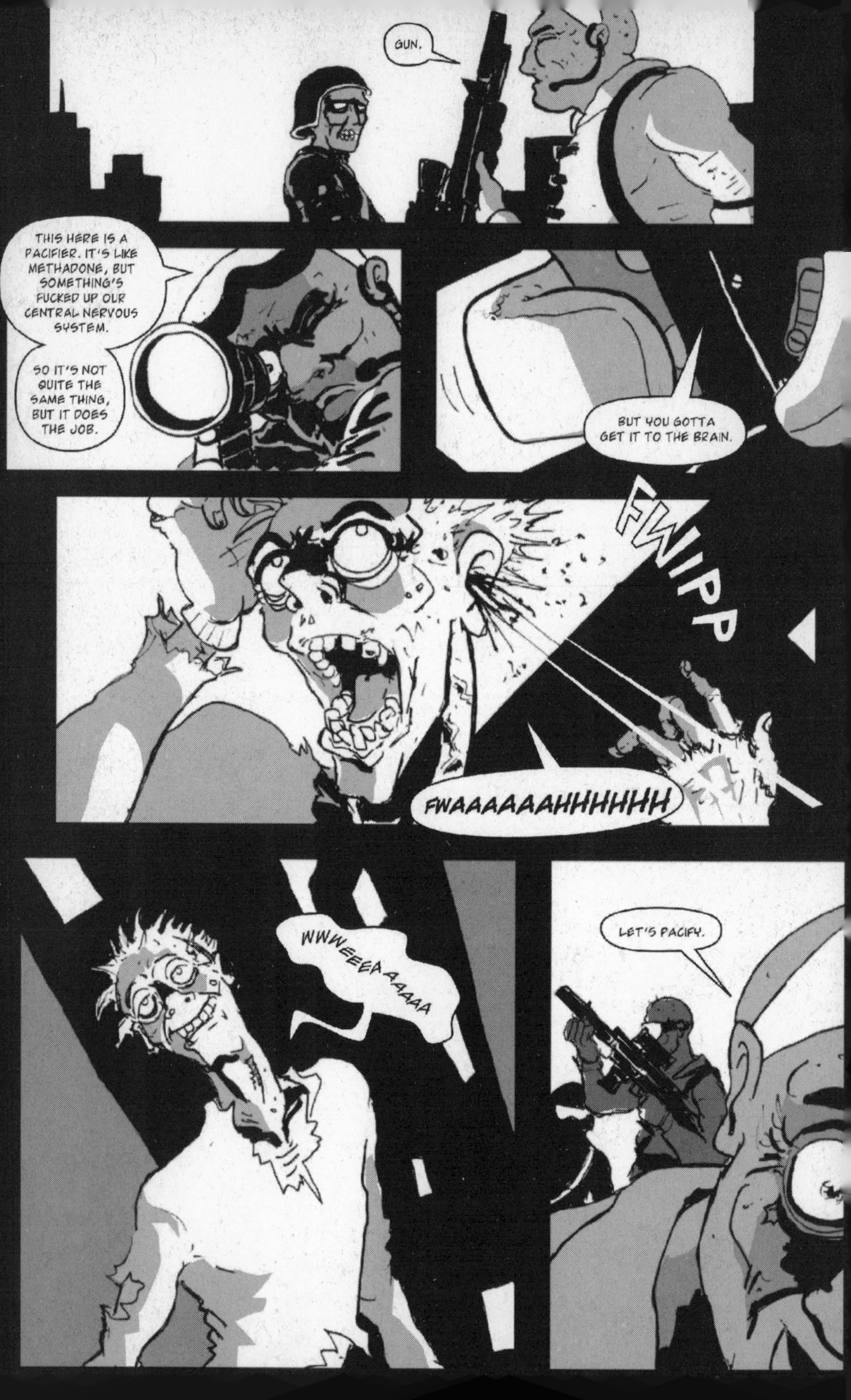
GUN.
THIS HERE IS A PACIFIER. IT'S LIKE METHADONE, BUT SOMETHING'S FUCKED UP OUR CENTRAL NERVOUS SYSTEM.
SO IT'S NOT QUITE THE SAME THING, BUT IT DOES THE JOB.
BUT YOU GOTTA GET IT TO THE BRAIN.
FWIPP
FWAAAAAAHHHHHH
WWWEEEAAAAAA
LET'S PACIFY.

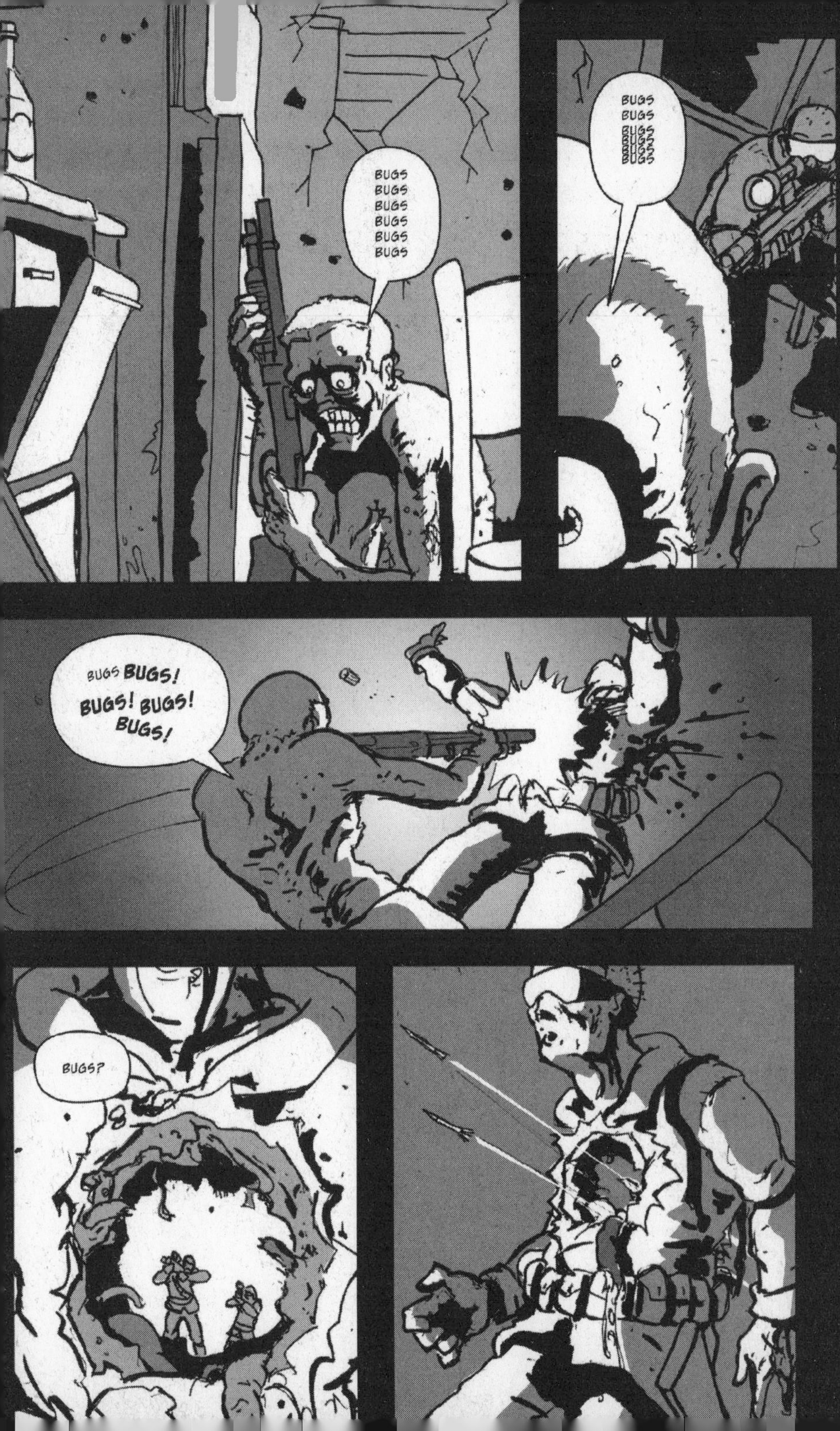
BUGS
BUGS
BUGS
BUGS
BUGS
BUGS
BUGS
BUGS
BUGS
BUGS
BUGS
BUGS
BUGS BUGS!
BUGS! BUGS!
BUGS!
BUGS?

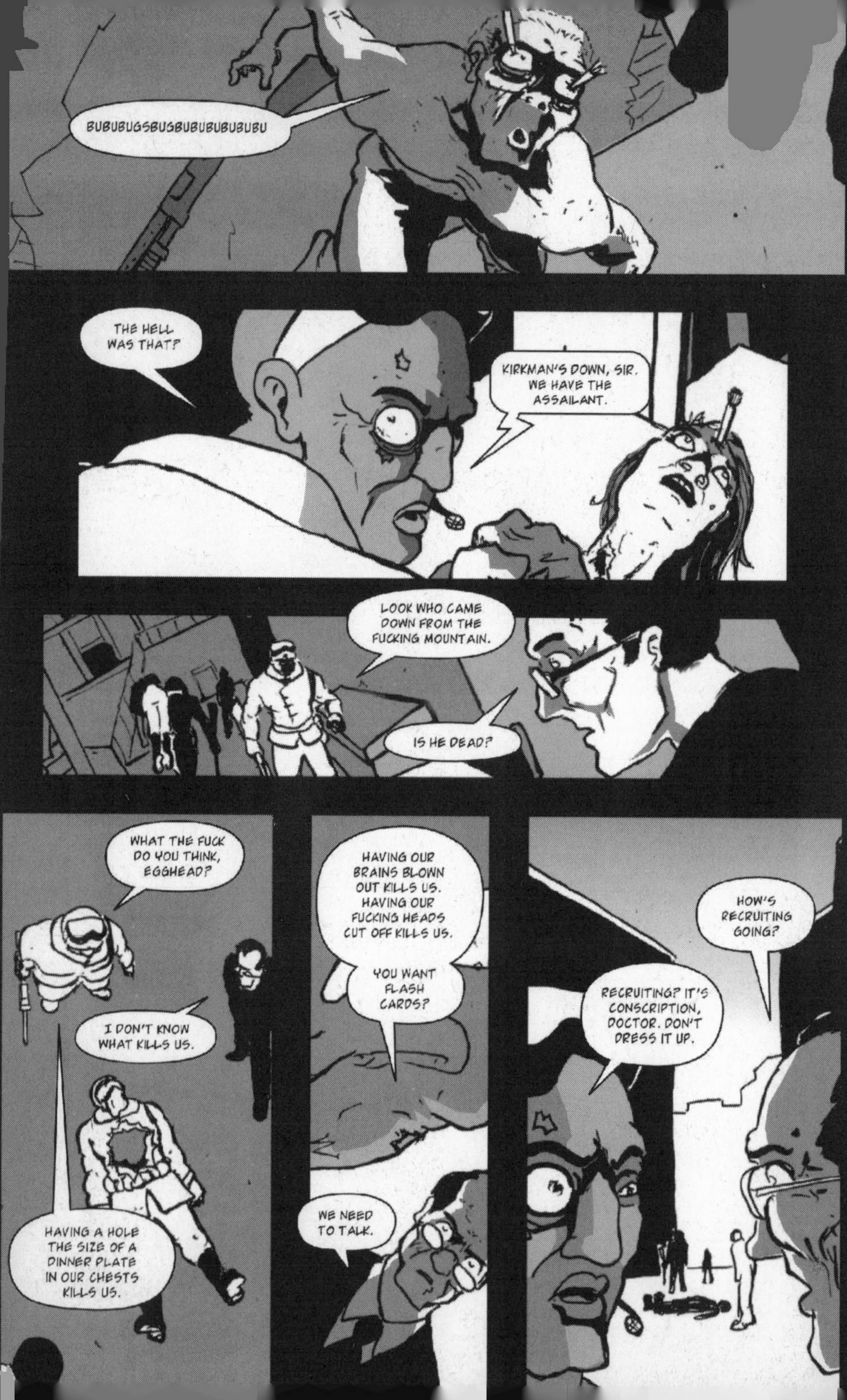
BUBUBUGSBUGBUBUBUBUBU
THE HELL WAS THAT?
KIRKMAN'S DOWN, SIR. WE HAVE THE ASSAILANT.
LOOK WHO CAME DOWN FROM THE FUCKING MOUNTAIN.
IS HE DEAD?
WHAT THE FUCK DO YOU THINK, EGGHEAD?
I DON'T KNOW WHAT KILLS US.
HAVING A HOLE THE SIZE OF A DINNER PLATE IN OUR CHESTS KILLS US.
HAVING OUR BRAINS BLOWN OUT KILLS US. HAVING OUR FUCKING HEADS CUT OFF KILLS US.
YOU WANT FLASH CARDS?
WE NEED TO TALK.
HOW'S RECRUITING GOING?
RECRUITING? IT'S CONSCRIPTION, DOCTOR. DON'T DRESS IT UP.

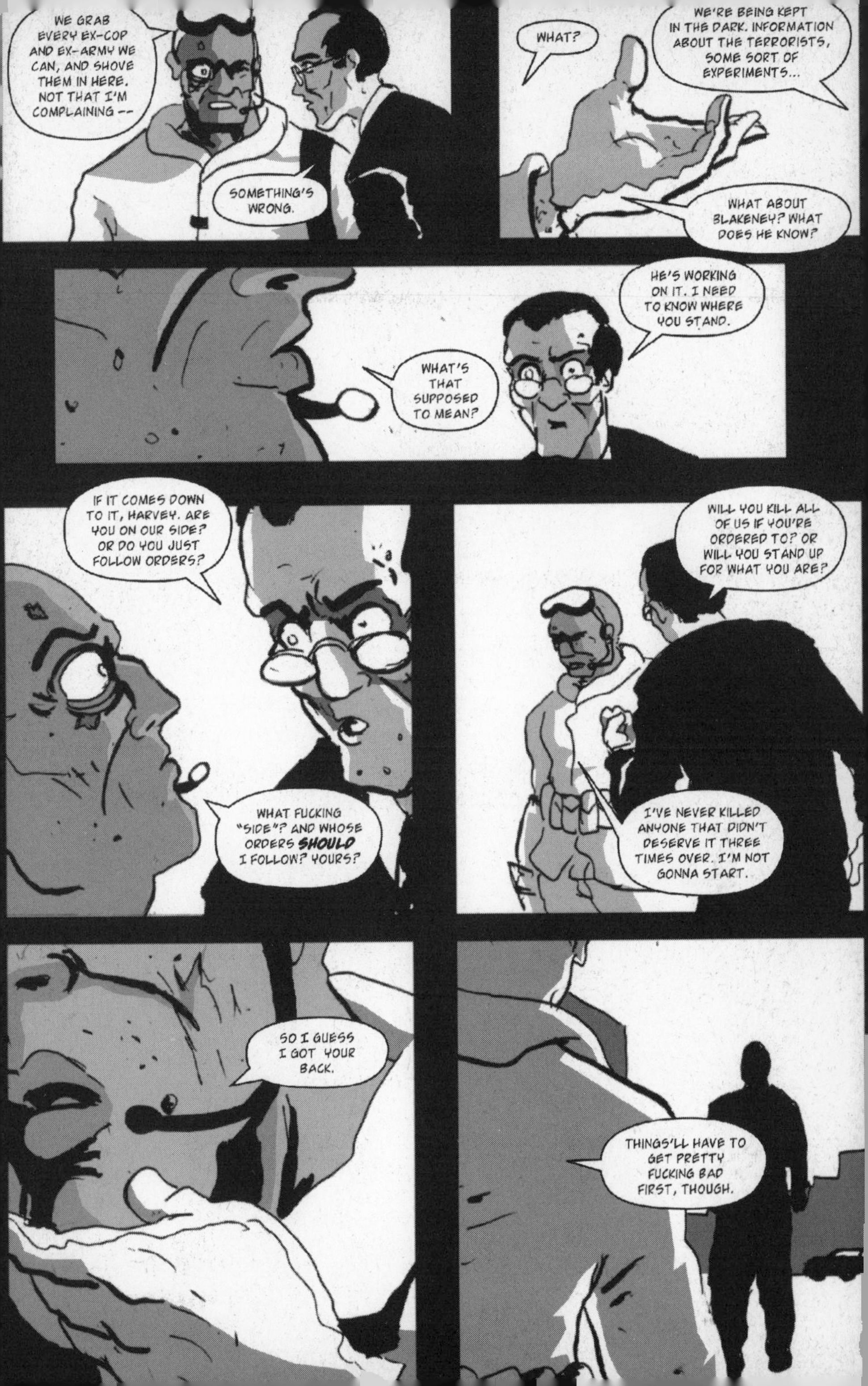
WE GRAB EVERY EX-COP AND EX-ARMY WE CAN, AND SHOVE THEM IN HERE. NOT THAT I'M COMPLAINING --
SOMETHING'S WRONG.
WHAT?
WE'RE BEING KEPT IN THE DARK. INFORMATION ABOUT THE TERRORISTS, SOME SORT OF EXPERIMENTS...
WHAT ABOUT BLAKENEY? WHAT DOES HE KNOW?
HE'S WORKING ON IT. I NEED TO KNOW WHERE YOU STAND.
WHAT'S THAT SUPPOSED TO MEAN?
IF IT COMES DOWN TO IT, HARVEY. ARE YOU ON OUR SIDE? OR DO YOU JUST FOLLOW ORDERS?
WHAT FUCKING "SIDE"? AND WHOSE ORDERS SHOULD I FOLLOW? YOURS?
WILL YOU KILL ALL OF US IF YOU'RE ORDERED TO? OR WILL YOU STAND UP FOR WHAT YOU ARE?
I'VE NEVER KILLED ANYONE THAT DIDN'T DESERVE IT THREE TIMES OVER. I'M NOT GONNA START.
SO I GUESS I GOT YOUR BACK.
THINGS'LL HAVE TO GET PRETTY FUCKING BAD FIRST, THOUGH.

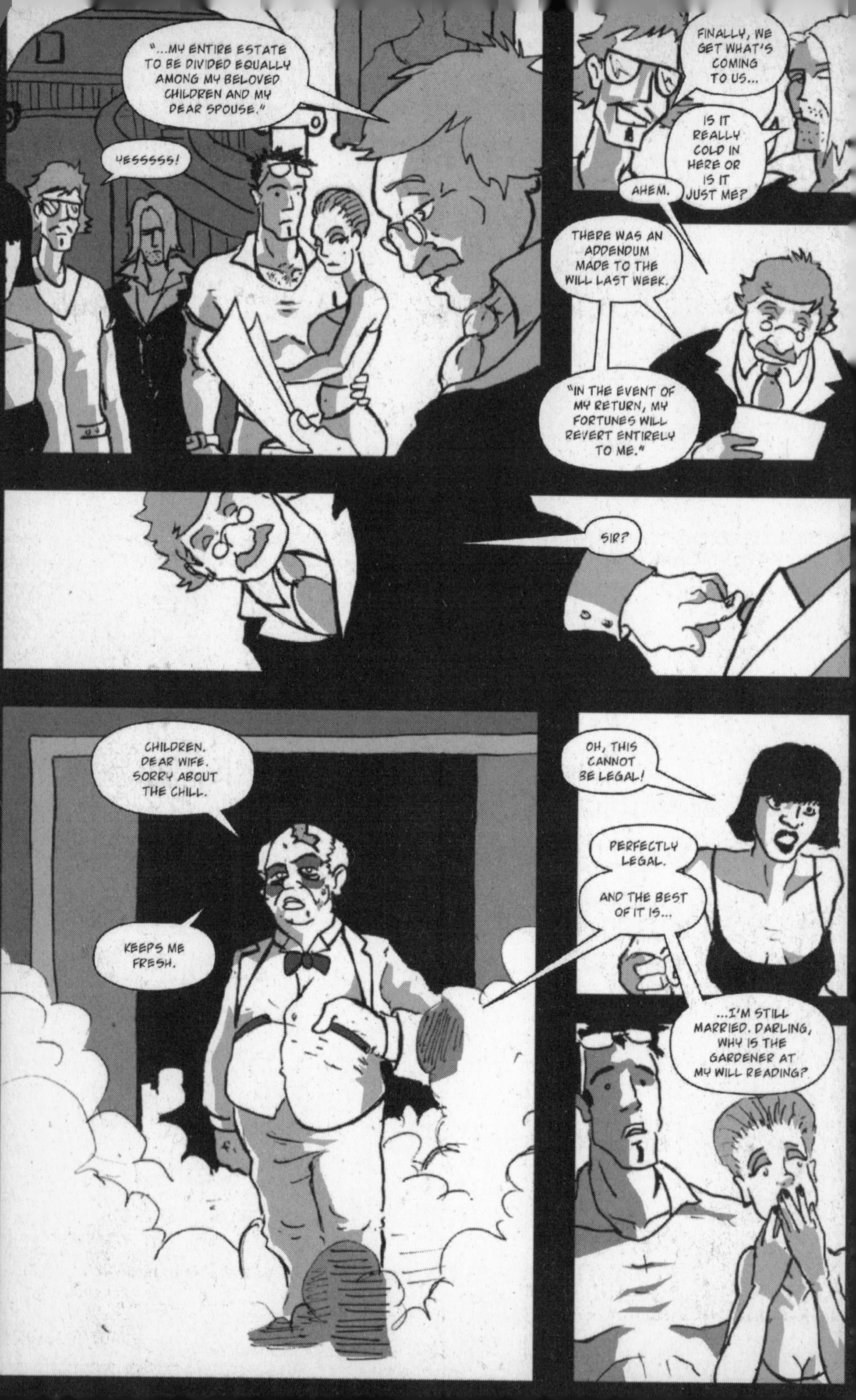
"...MY ENTIRE ESTATE TO BE DIVIDED EQUALLY AMONG MY BELOVED CHILDREN AND MY DEAR SPOUSE."
YESSSSS!
FINALLY, WE GET WHAT'S COMING TO US...
IS IT REALLY COLD IN HERE OR IS IT JUST ME?
AHEM.
THERE WAS AN ADDENDUM MADE TO THE WILL LAST WEEK.
"IN THE EVENT OF MY RETURN, MY FORTUNES WILL REVERT ENTIRELY TO ME."
SIR?
CHILDREN. DEAR WIFE. SORRY ABOUT THE CHILL.
KEEPS ME FRESH.
OH, THIS CANNOT BE LEGAL!
PERFECTLY LEGAL.
AND THE BEST OF IT IS...
...I'M STILL MARRIED. DARLING, WHY IS THE GARDENER AT MY WILL READING?

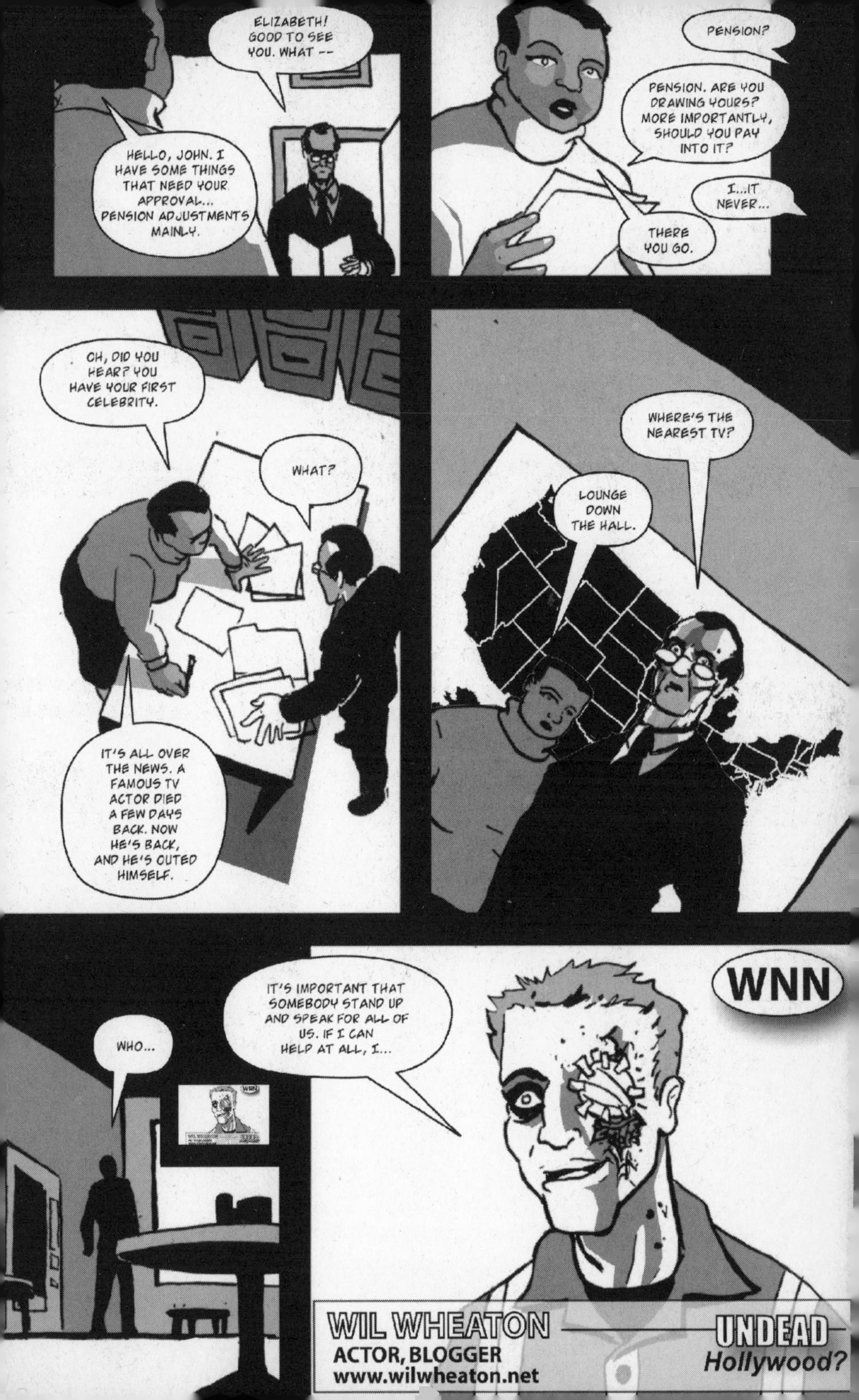
ELIZABETH! GOOD TO SEE YOU. WHAT --
HELLO, JOHN. I HAVE SOME THINGS THAT NEED YOUR APPROVAL... PENSION ADJUSTMENTS MAINLY.
PENSION?
PENSION. ARE YOU DRAWING YOURS? MORE IMPORTANTLY, SHOULD YOU PAY INTO IT?
I...IT NEVER...
THERE YOU GO.
OH, DID YOU HEAR? YOU HAVE YOUR FIRST CELEBRITY.
WHAT?
IT'S ALL OVER THE NEWS. A FAMOUS TV ACTOR DIED A FEW DAYS BACK. NOW HE'S BACK, AND HE'S OUTED HIMSELF.
WHERE'S THE NEAREST TV?
LOUNGE DOWN THE HALL.
WHO...
IT'S IMPORTANT THAT SOMEBODY STAND UP AND SPEAK FOR ALL OF US. IF I CAN HELP AT ALL, I...
WNN
WIL WHEATON
ACTOR, BLOGGER
www.wilwheaton.net
UNDEAD
Hollywood?

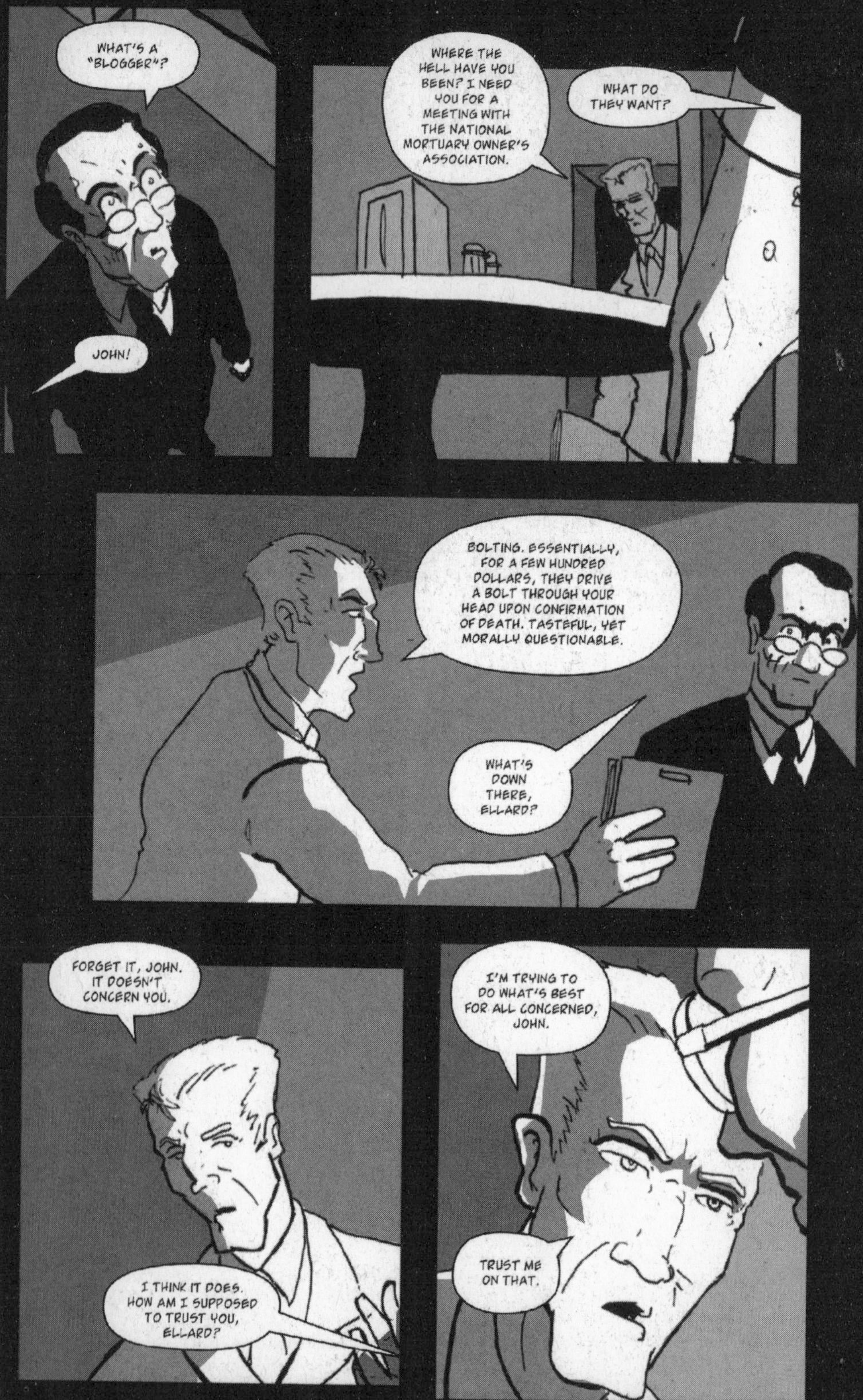

WHAT'S A "BLOGGER"?
JOHN!
WHERE THE HELL HAVE YOU BEEN? I NEED YOU FOR A MEETING WITH THE NATIONAL MORTUARY OWNER'S ASSOCIATION.
WHAT DO THEY WANT?
BOLTING. ESSENTIALLY, FOR A FEW HUNDRED DOLLARS, THEY DRIVE A BOLT THROUGH YOUR HEAD UPON CONFIRMATION OF DEATH. TASTEFUL, YET MORALLY QUESTIONABLE.
WHAT'S DOWN THERE, ELLARD?
FORGET IT, JOHN. IT DOESN'T CONCERN YOU.
I THINK IT DOES. HOW AM I SUPPOSED TO TRUST YOU, ELLARD?
I'M TRYING TO DO WHAT'S BEST FOR ALL CONCERNED, JOHN.
TRUST ME ON THAT.

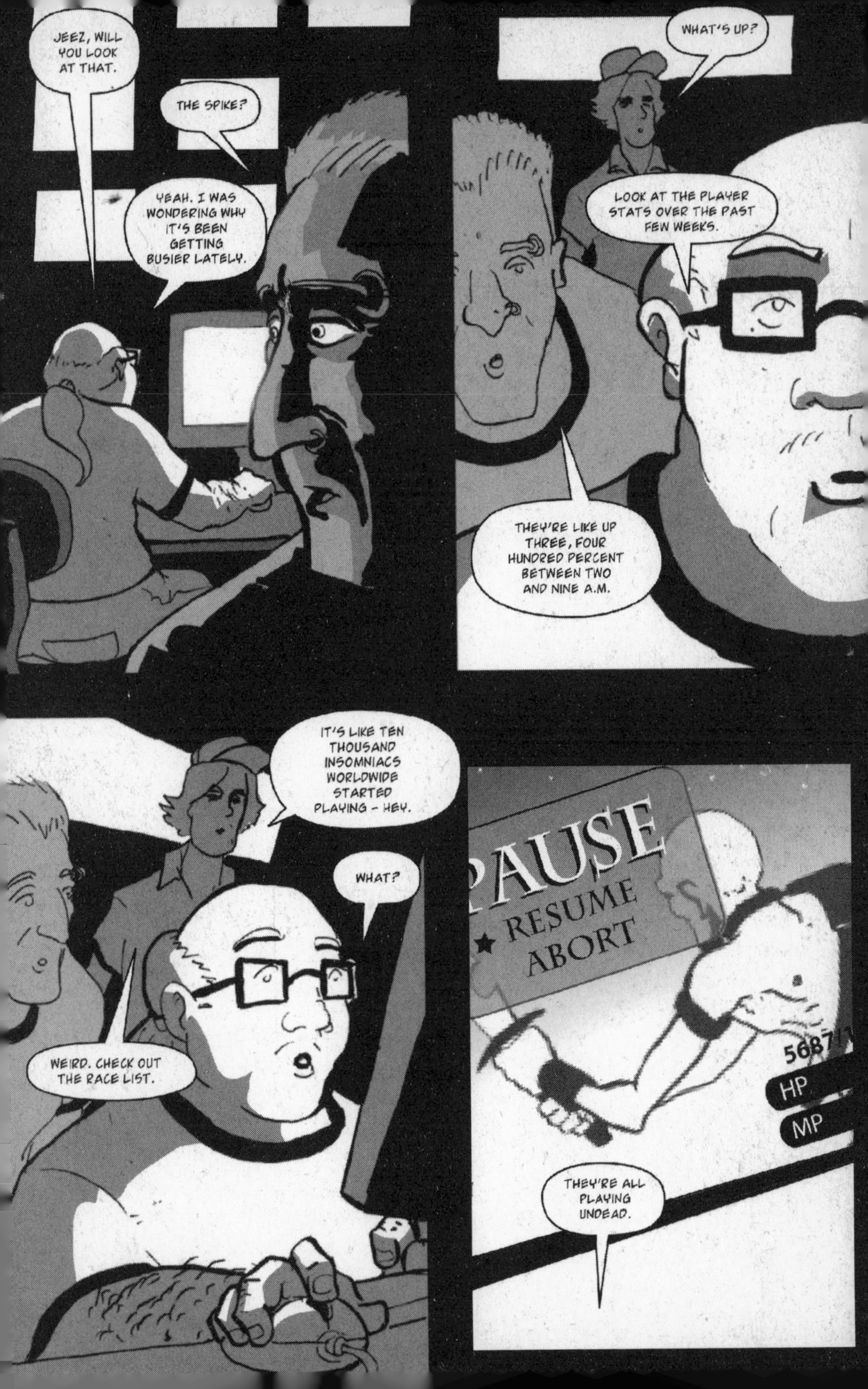

JEEZ, WILL YOU LOOK AT THAT.
THE SPIKE?
YEAH. I WAS WONDERING WHY IT'S BEEN GETTING BUSIER LATELY.
WHAT'S UP?
LOOK AT THE PLAYER STATS OVER THE PAST FEW WEEKS.
THEY'RE LIKE UP THREE, FOUR HUNDRED PERCENT BETWEEN TWO AND NINE A.M.
IT'S LIKE TEN THOUSAND INSOMNIACS WORLDWIDE STARTED PLAYING – HEY.
WHAT?
WEIRD. CHECK OUT THE RACE LIST.
PAUSE
RESUME
ABORT
HP
MP
THEY'RE ALL PLAYING UNDEAD.

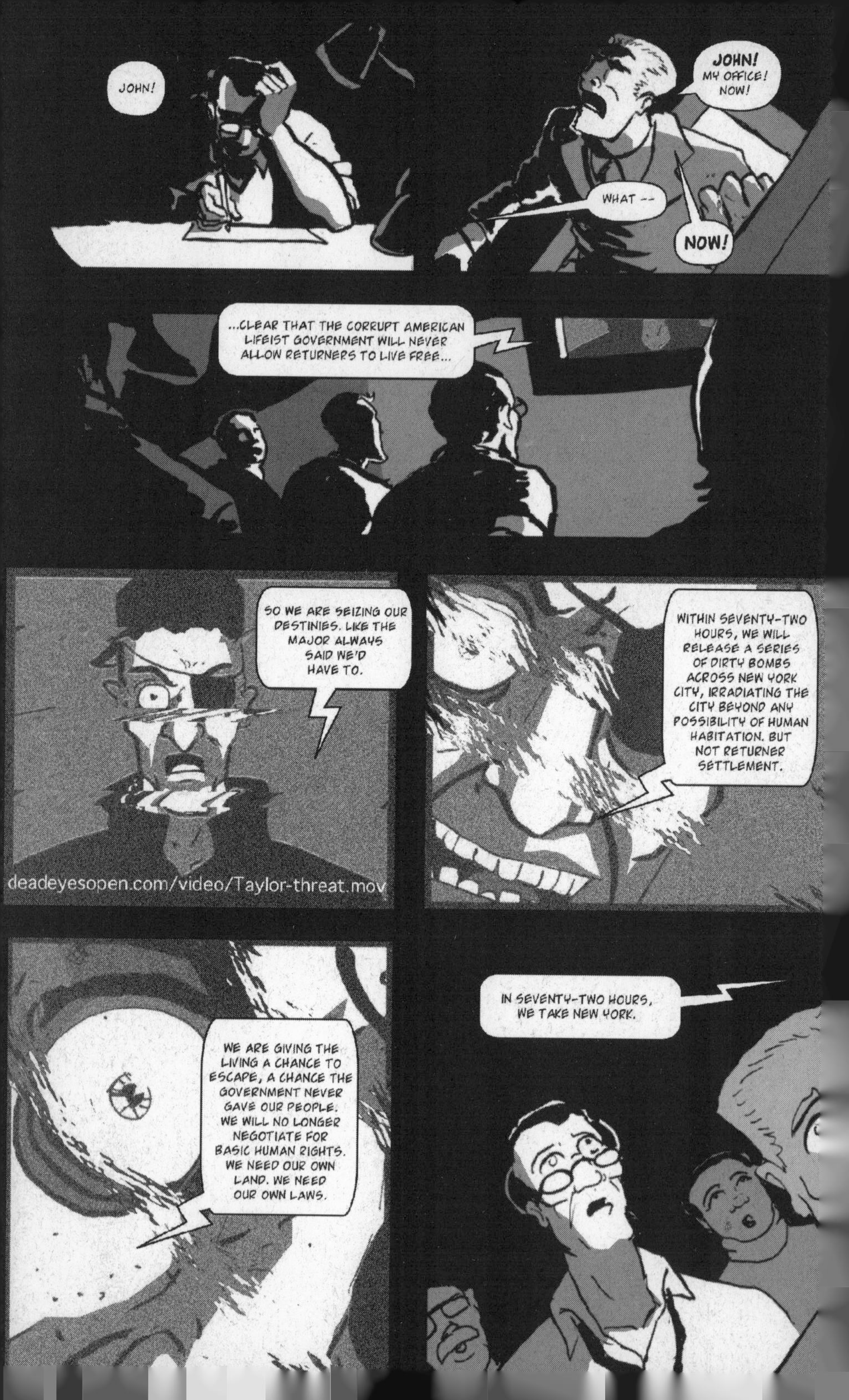
JOHN!
JOHN! MY OFFICE! NOW!
WHAT --
NOW!
...CLEAR THAT THE CORRUPT AMERICAN LIFEIST GOVERNMENT WILL NEVER ALLOW RETURNERS TO LIVE FREE...
SO WE ARE SEIZING OUR DESTINIES. LIKE THE MAJOR ALWAYS SAID WE'D HAVE TO.
deadeyesopen.com/video/Taylor-threat.mov
WITHIN SEVENTY-TWO HOURS, WE WILL RELEASE A SERIES OF DIRTY BOMBS ACROSS NEW YORK CITY, IRRADIATING THE CITY BEYOND ANY POSSIBILITY OF HUMAN HABITATION. BUT NOT RETURNER SETTLEMENT.
WE ARE GIVING THE LIVING A CHANCE TO ESCAPE, A CHANCE THE GOVERNMENT NEVER GAVE OUR PEOPLE. WE WILL NO LONGER NEGOTIATE FOR BASIC HUMAN RIGHTS. WE NEED OUR OWN LAND. WE NEED OUR OWN LAWS.
IN SEVENTY-TWO HOURS, WE TAKE NEW YORK.

CHAPTER
FIVE

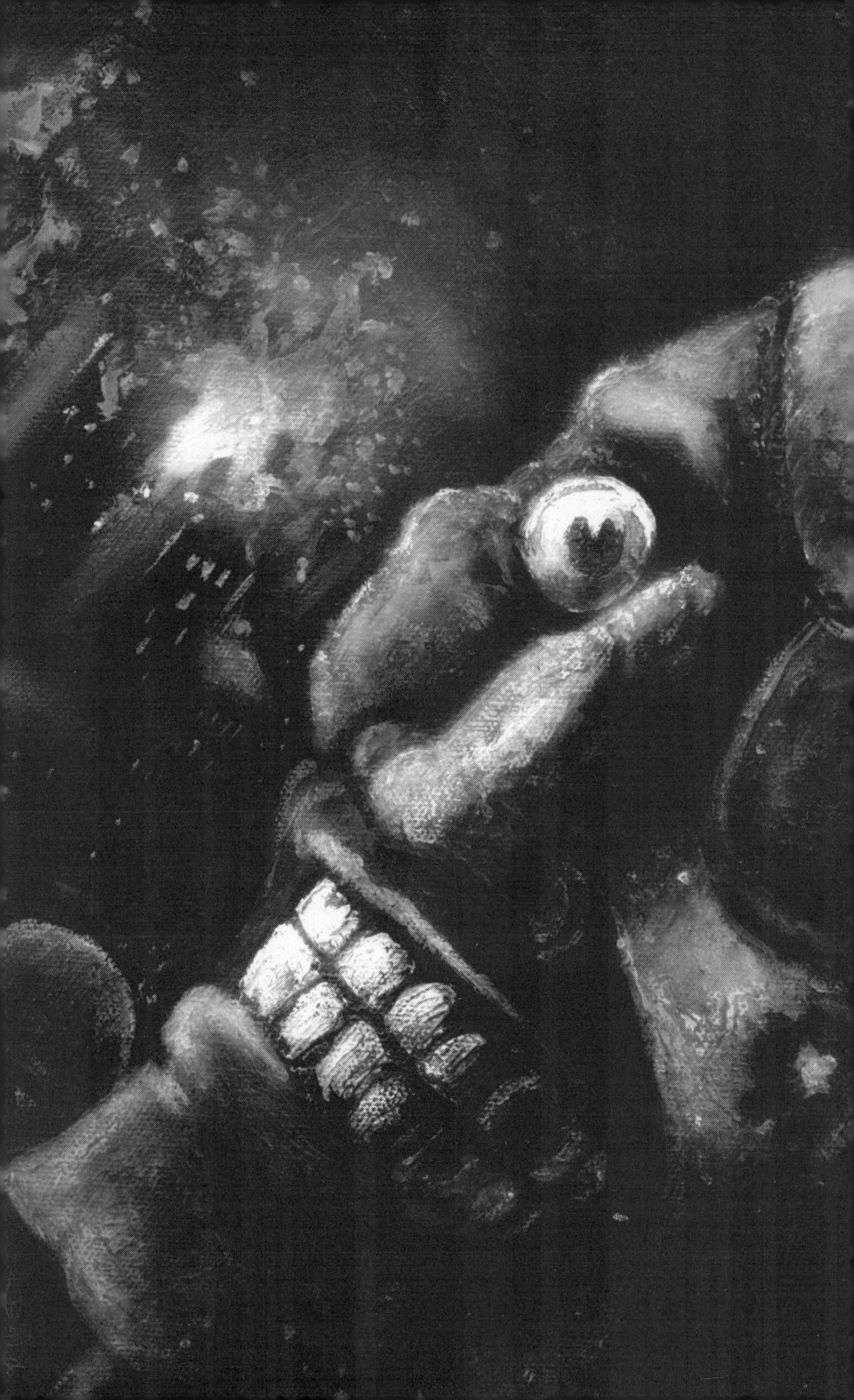

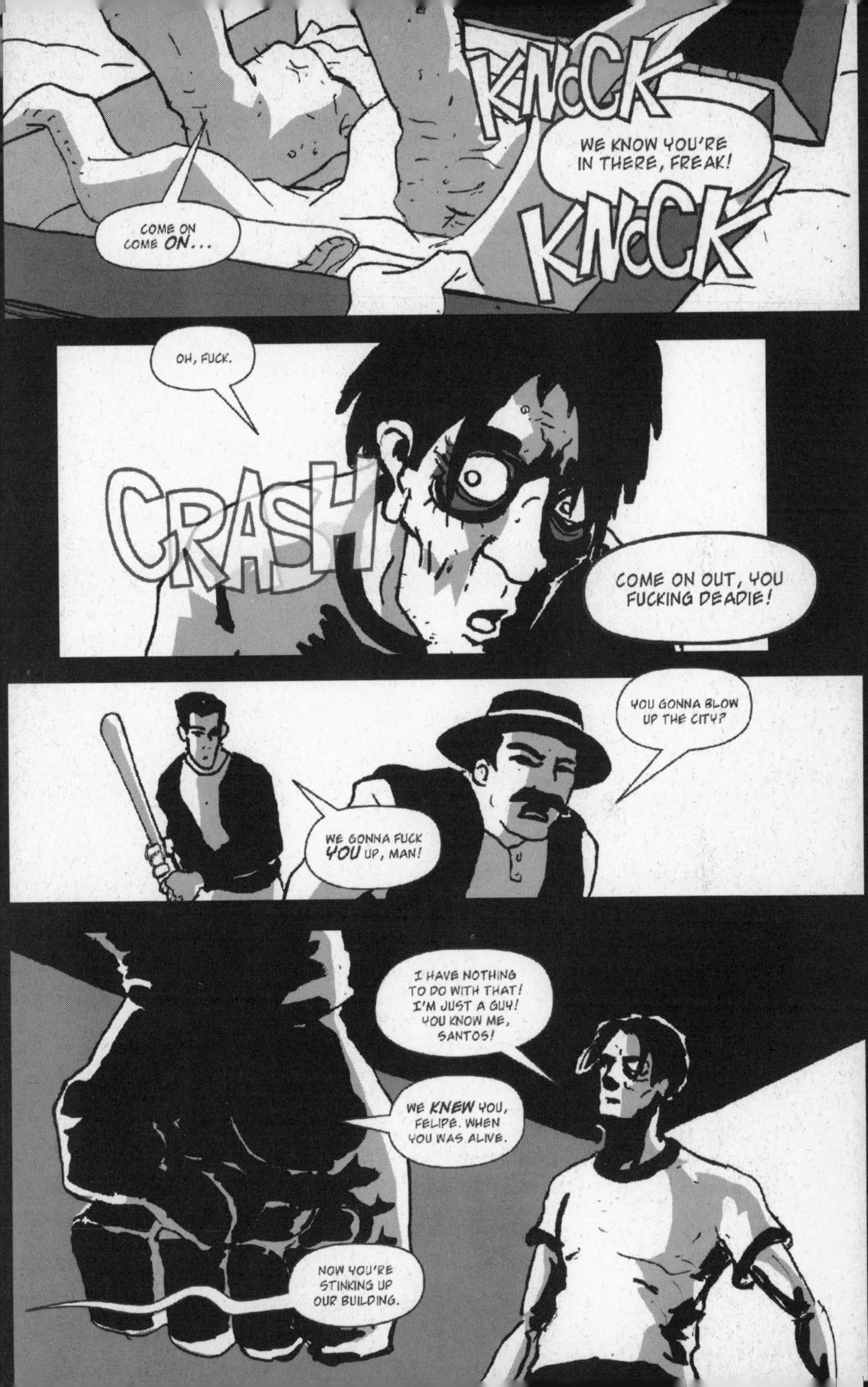

KNOCK
WE KNOW YOU'RE IN THERE, FREAK!
KNOCK
COME ON COME ON...
OH, FUCK.
CRASH
COME ON OUT, YOU FUCKING DEADIE!
YOU GONNA BLOW UP THE CITY?
WE GONNA FUCK YOU UP, MAN!
I HAVE NOTHING TO DO WITH THAT! I'M JUST A GUY! YOU KNOW ME, SANTOS!
WE KNEW YOU, FELIPE. WHEN YOU WAS ALIVE.
NOW YOU'RE STINKING UP OUR BUILDING.

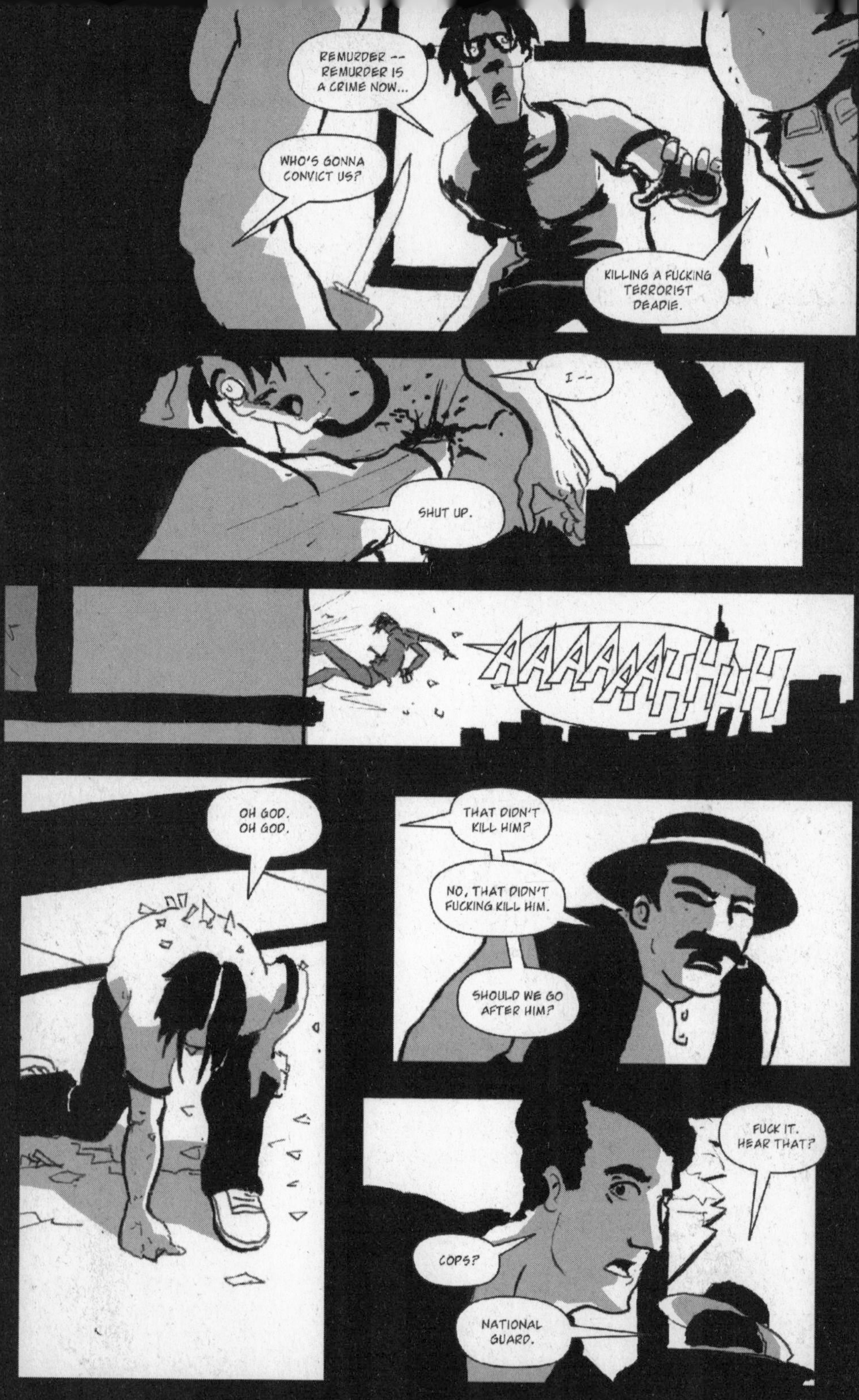
REMURDER -- REMURDER IS A CRIME NOW...
WHO'S GONNA CONVICT US?
KILLING A FUCKING TERRORIST DEADIE.
I --
SHUT UP.
AAAAAAHHHH
OH GOD. OH GOD.
THAT DIDN'T KILL HIM?
NO, THAT DIDN'T FUCKING KILL HIM.
SHOULD WE GO AFTER HIM?
FUCK IT. HEAR THAT?
COPS?
NATIONAL GUARD.

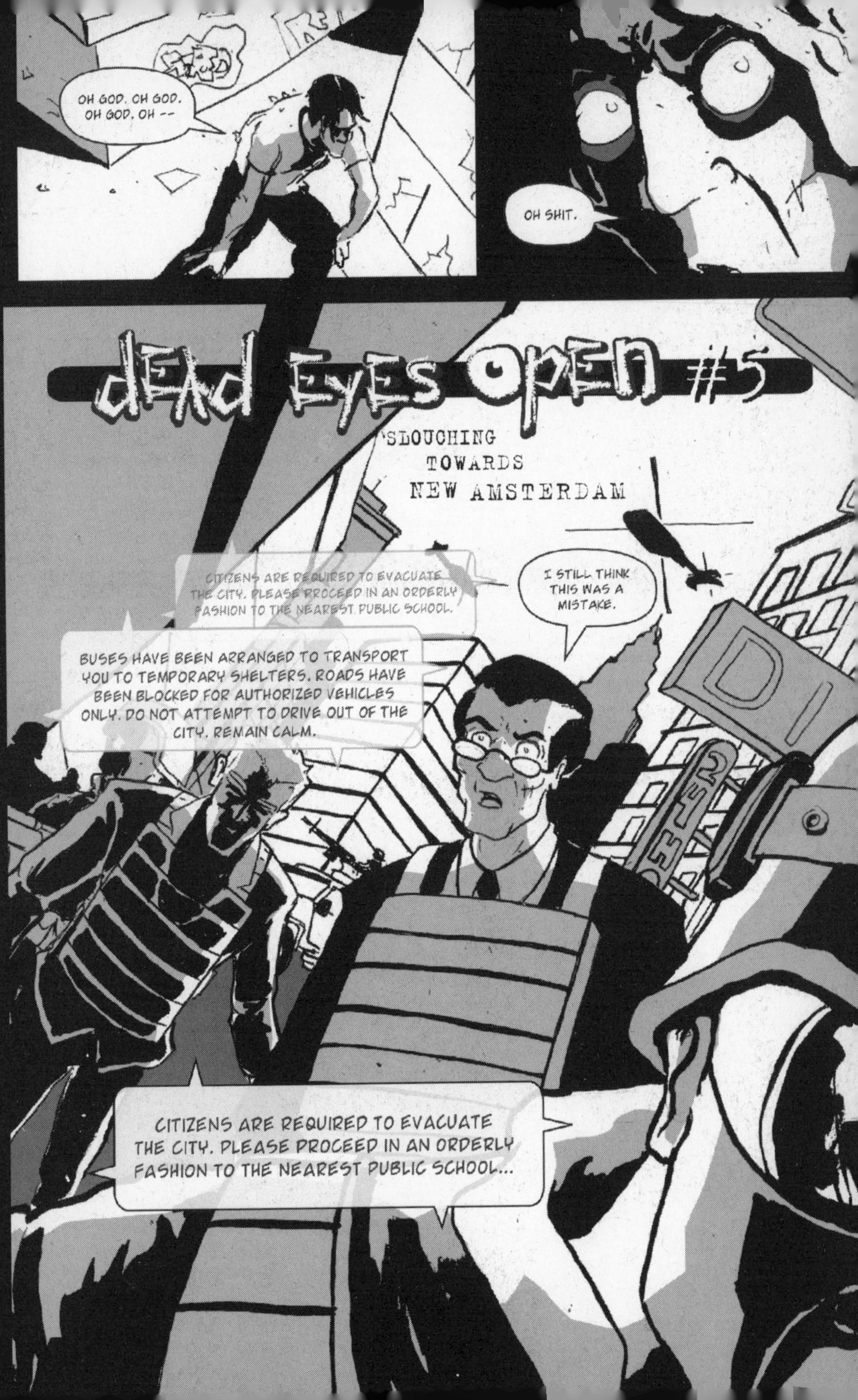
OH GOD. OH GOD. OH GOD. OH --
OH SHIT.
dEAd EyES OpEN #5
SLOUCHING TOWARDS NEW AMSTERDAM
CITIZENS ARE REQUIRED TO EVACUATE THE CITY. PLEASE PROCEED IN AN ORDERLY FASHION TO THE NEAREST PUBLIC SCHOOL.
I STILL THINK THIS WAS A MISTAKE.
BUSES HAVE BEEN ARRANGED TO TRANSPORT YOU TO TEMPORARY SHELTERS. ROADS HAVE BEEN BLOCKED FOR AUTHORIZED VEHICLES ONLY. DO NOT ATTEMPT TO DRIVE OUT OF THE CITY. REMAIN CALM.
CITIZENS ARE REQUIRED TO EVACUATE THE CITY. PLEASE PROCEED IN AN ORDERLY FASHION TO THE NEAREST PUBLIC SCHOOL...

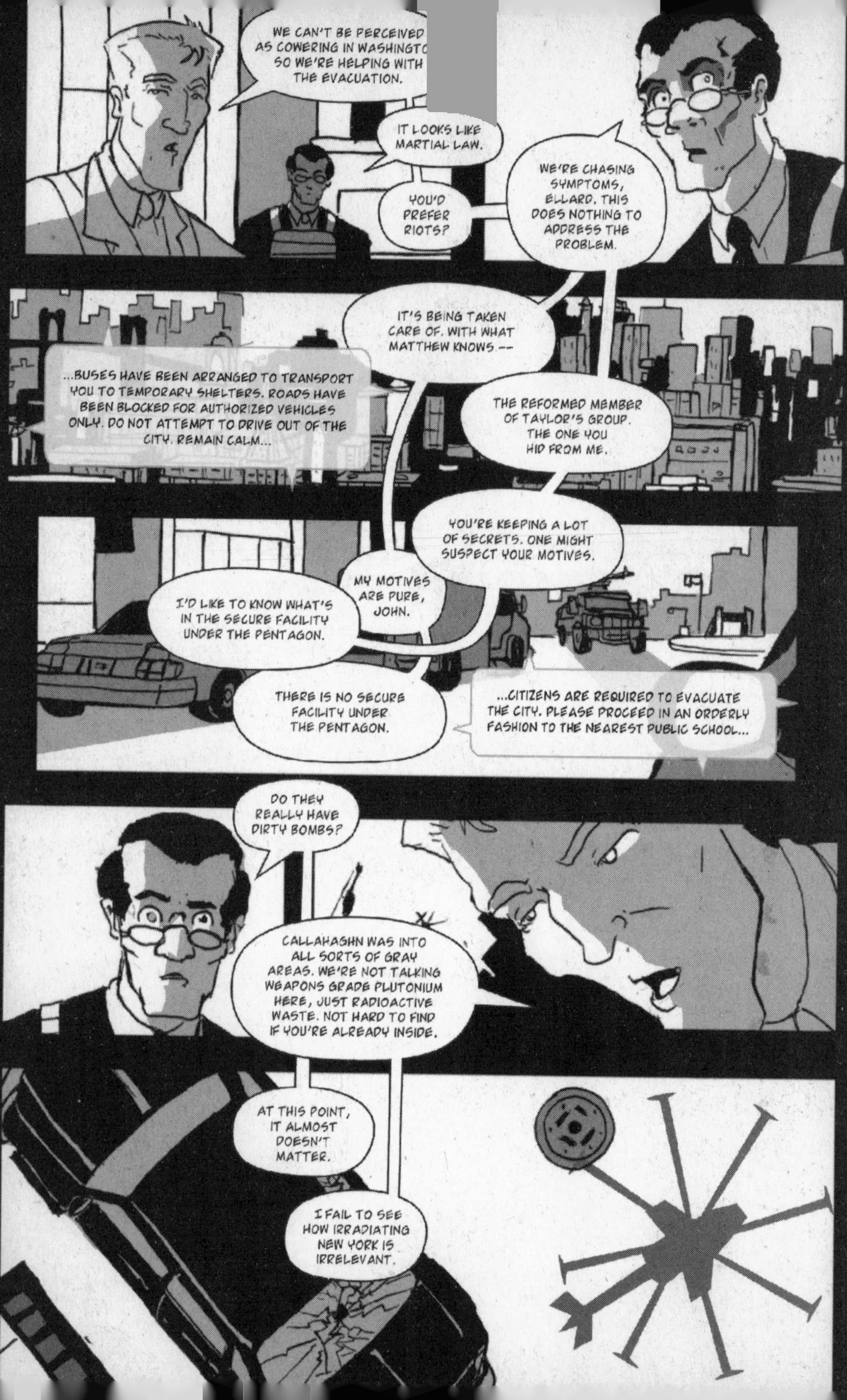
WE CAN'T BE PERCEIVED AS COWERING IN WASHINGTON, SO WE'RE HELPING WITH THE EVACUATION.
IT LOOKS LIKE MARTIAL LAW.
YOU'D PREFER RIOTS?
WE'RE CHASING SYMPTOMS, ELLARD. THIS DOES NOTHING TO ADDRESS THE PROBLEM.
IT'S BEING TAKEN CARE OF. WITH WHAT MATTHEW KNOWS.--
...BUSES HAVE BEEN ARRANGED TO TRANSPORT YOU TO TEMPORARY SHELTERS. ROADS HAVE BEEN BLOCKED FOR AUTHORIZED VEHICLES ONLY. DO NOT ATTEMPT TO DRIVE OUT OF THE CITY. REMAIN CALM...
THE REFORMED MEMBER OF TAYLOR'S GROUP. THE ONE YOU HID FROM ME.
YOU'RE KEEPING A LOT OF SECRETS. ONE MIGHT SUSPECT YOUR MOTIVES.
MY MOTIVES ARE PURE, JOHN.
I'D LIKE TO KNOW WHAT'S IN THE SECURE FACILITY UNDER THE PENTAGON.
THERE IS NO SECURE FACILITY UNDER THE PENTAGON.
...CITIZENS ARE REQUIRED TO EVACUATE THE CITY. PLEASE PROCEED IN AN ORDERLY FASHION TO THE NEAREST PUBLIC SCHOOL...
DO THEY REALLY HAVE DIRTY BOMBS?
CALLAHASHN WAS INTO ALL SORTS OF GRAY AREAS. WE'RE NOT TALKING WEAPONS GRADE PLUTONIUM HERE, JUST RADIOACTIVE WASTE. NOT HARD TO FIND IF YOU'RE ALREADY INSIDE.
AT THIS POINT, IT ALMOST DOESN'T MATTER.
I FAIL TO SEE HOW IRRADIATING NEW YORK IS IRRELEVANT.

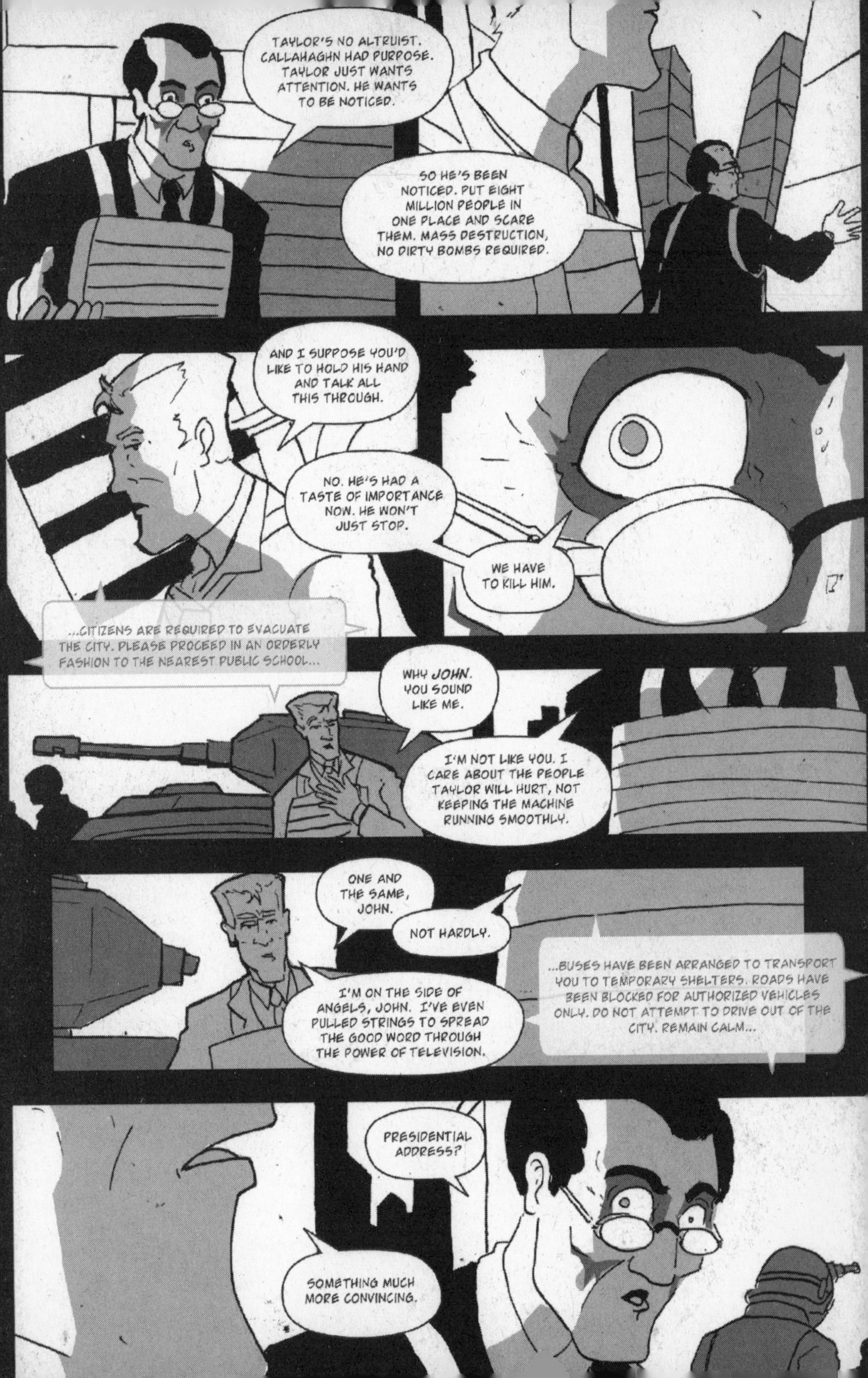
TAYLOR'S NO ALTRUIST. CALLAHAGHN HAD PURPOSE. TAYLOR JUST WANTS ATTENTION. HE WANTS TO BE NOTICED.
SO HE'S BEEN NOTICED. PUT EIGHT MILLION PEOPLE IN ONE PLACE AND SCARE THEM. MASS DESTRUCTION, NO DIRTY BOMBS REQUIRED.
AND I SUPPOSE YOU'D LIKE TO HOLD HIS HAND AND TALK ALL THIS THROUGH.
NO. HE'S HAD A TASTE OF IMPORTANCE NOW. HE WON'T JUST STOP.
WE HAVE TO KILL HIM.
...CITIZENS ARE REQUIRED TO EVACUATE THE CITY. PLEASE PROCEED IN AN ORDERLY FASHION TO THE NEAREST PUBLIC SCHOOL...
WHY *JOHN*. YOU SOUND LIKE ME.
I'M NOT LIKE YOU. I CARE ABOUT THE PEOPLE TAYLOR WILL HURT, NOT KEEPING THE MACHINE RUNNING SMOOTHLY.
ONE AND THE SAME, JOHN.
NOT HARDLY.
I'M ON THE SIDE OF ANGELS, JOHN. I'VE EVEN PULLED STRINGS TO SPREAD THE GOOD WORD THROUGH THE POWER OF TELEVISION.
...BUSES HAVE BEEN ARRANGED TO TRANSPORT YOU TO TEMPORARY SHELTERS. ROADS HAVE BEEN BLOCKED FOR AUTHORIZED VEHICLES ONLY. DO NOT ATTEMPT TO DRIVE OUT OF THE CITY. REMAIN CALM...
PRESIDENTIAL ADDRESS?
SOMETHING MUCH MORE CONVINCING.

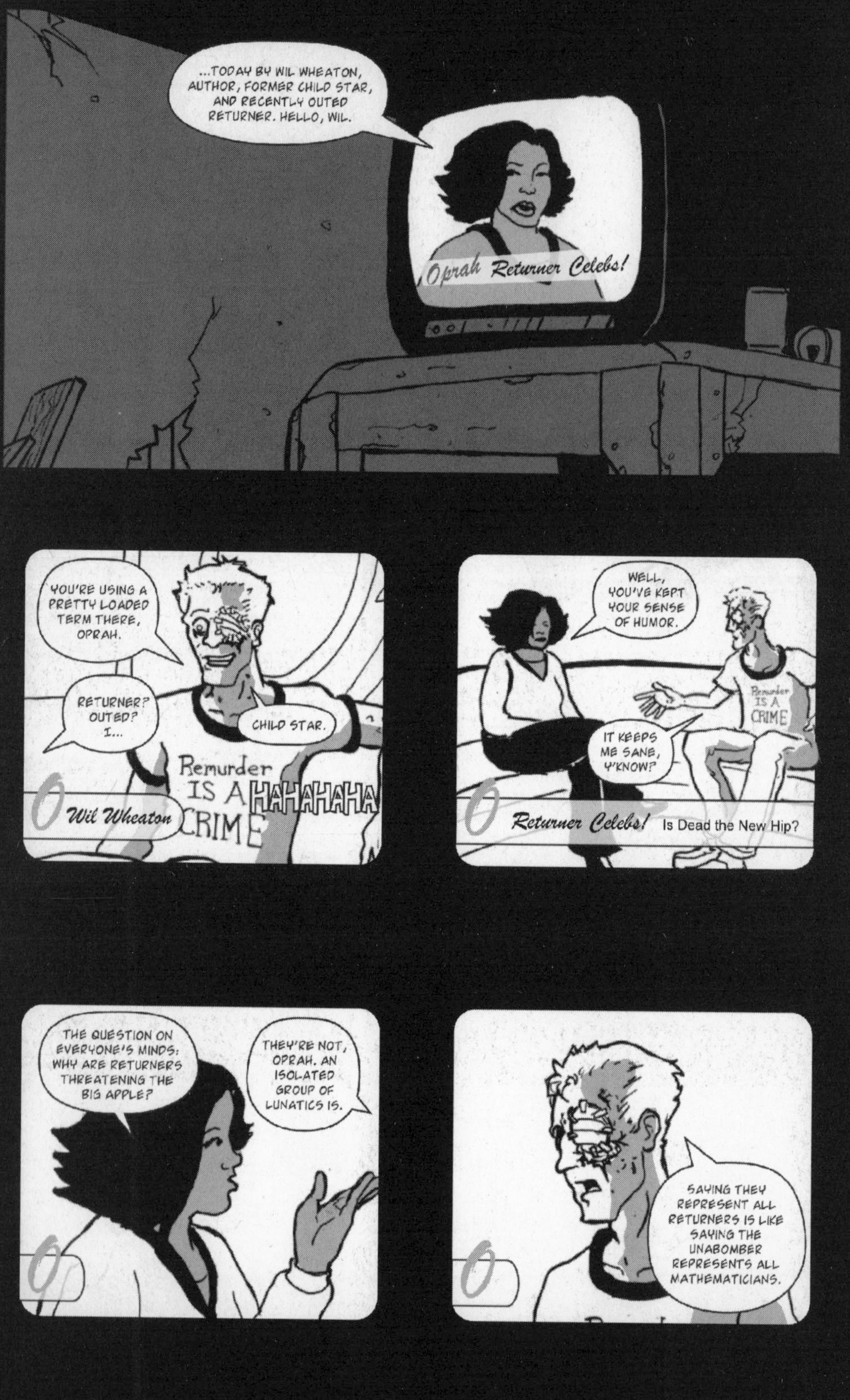
...TODAY BY WIL WHEATON, AUTHOR, FORMER CHILD STAR, AND RECENTLY OUTED RETURNER. HELLO, WIL.
Oprah Returner Celebs!
YOU'RE USING A PRETTY LOADED TERM THERE, OPRAH.
RETURNER? OUTED? I...
CHILD STAR.
Remurder IS A CRIME
HAHAHAHA
Wil Wheaton
WELL, YOU'VE KEPT YOUR SENSE OF HUMOR.
IT KEEPS ME SANE, Y'KNOW?
Remurder IS A CRIME
Returner Celebs! Is Dead the New Hip?
THE QUESTION ON EVERYONE'S MINDS: WHY ARE RETURNERS THREATENING THE BIG APPLE?
THEY'RE NOT, OPRAH. AN ISOLATED GROUP OF LUNATICS IS.
SAYING THEY REPRESENT ALL RETURNERS IS LIKE SAYING THE UNABOMBER REPRESENTS ALL MATHEMATICIANS.

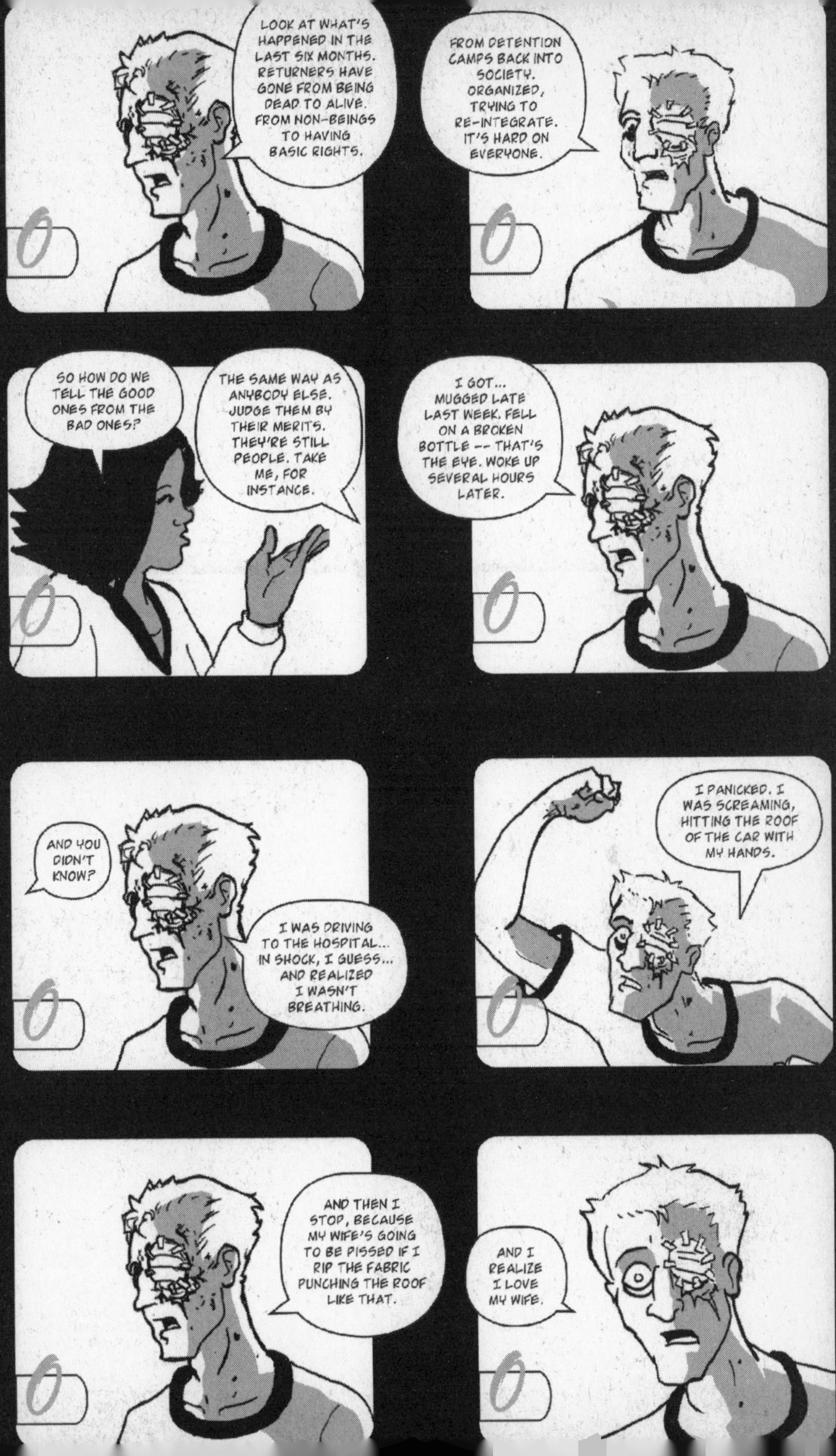
LOOK AT WHAT'S HAPPENED IN THE LAST SIX MONTHS. RETURNERS HAVE GONE FROM BEING DEAD TO ALIVE. FROM NON-BEINGS TO HAVING BASIC RIGHTS.
FROM DETENTION CAMPS BACK INTO SOCIETY. ORGANIZED, TRYING TO RE-INTEGRATE. IT'S HARD ON EVERYONE.
SO HOW DO WE TELL THE GOOD ONES FROM THE BAD ONES?
THE SAME WAY AS ANYBODY ELSE. JUDGE THEM BY THEIR MERITS. THEY'RE STILL PEOPLE. TAKE ME, FOR INSTANCE.
I GOT... MUGGED LATE LAST WEEK. FELL ON A BROKEN BOTTLE -- THAT'S THE EYE. WOKE UP SEVERAL HOURS LATER.
AND YOU DIDN'T KNOW?
I WAS DRIVING TO THE HOSPITAL... IN SHOCK, I GUESS... AND REALIZED I WASN'T BREATHING.
I PANICKED. I WAS SCREAMING, HITTING THE ROOF OF THE CAR WITH MY HANDS.
AND THEN I STOP, BECAUSE MY WIFE'S GOING TO BE PISSED IF I RIP THE FABRIC PUNCHING THE ROOF LIKE THAT.
AND I REALIZE I LOVE MY WIFE.

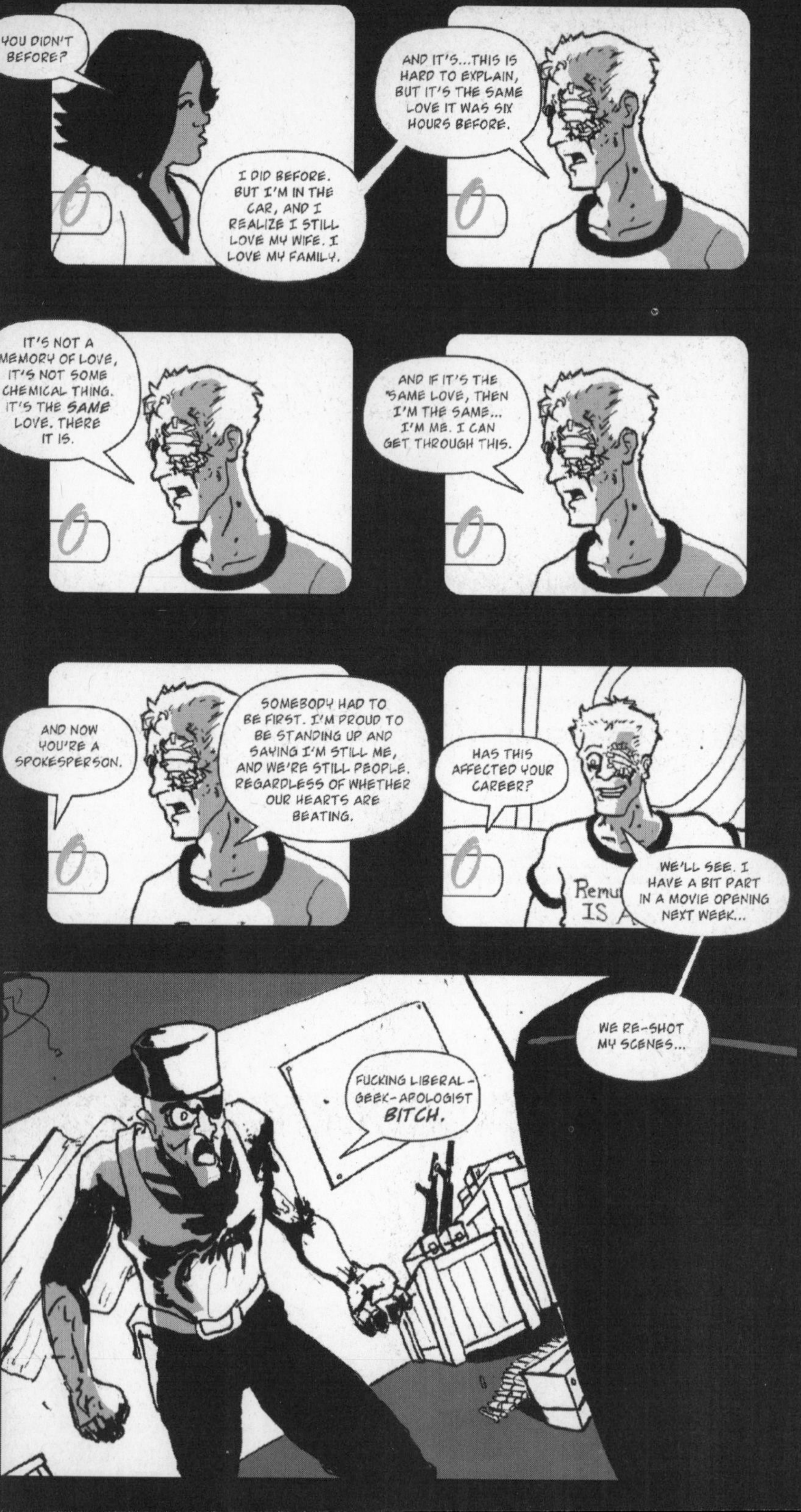
YOU DIDN'T BEFORE?
I DID BEFORE. BUT I'M IN THE CAR, AND I REALIZE I STILL LOVE MY WIFE. I LOVE MY FAMILY.
AND IT'S...THIS IS HARD TO EXPLAIN, BUT IT'S THE SAME LOVE IT WAS SIX HOURS BEFORE.
IT'S NOT A MEMORY OF LOVE, IT'S NOT SOME CHEMICAL THING. IT'S THE *SAME* LOVE. THERE IT IS.
AND IF IT'S THE SAME LOVE, THEN I'M THE SAME... I'M ME. I CAN GET THROUGH THIS.
AND NOW YOU'RE A SPOKESPERSON.
SOMEBODY HAD TO BE FIRST. I'M PROUD TO BE STANDING UP AND SAYING I'M STILL ME, AND WE'RE STILL PEOPLE. REGARDLESS OF WHETHER OUR HEARTS ARE BEATING.
HAS THIS AFFECTED YOUR CAREER?
WE'LL SEE. I HAVE A BIT PART IN A MOVIE OPENING NEXT WEEK...
WE RE-SHOT MY SCENES...
FUCKING LIBERAL-GEEK-APOLOGIST **BITCH.**

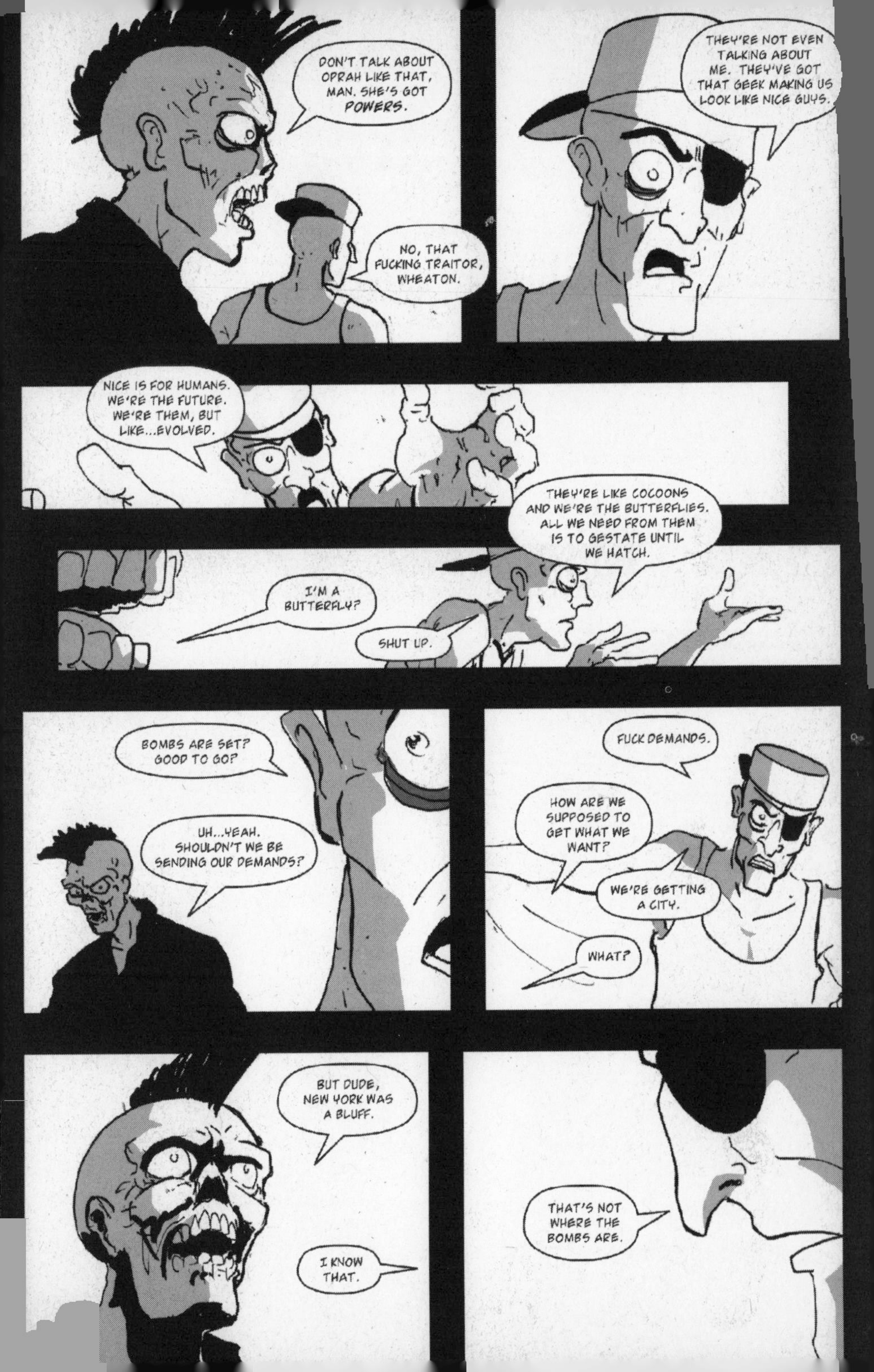
DON'T TALK ABOUT OPRAH LIKE THAT, MAN. SHE'S GOT POWERS.
NO, THAT FUCKING TRAITOR, WHEATON.
THEY'RE NOT EVEN TALKING ABOUT ME. THEY'VE GOT THAT GEEK MAKING US LOOK LIKE NICE GUYS.
NICE IS FOR HUMANS. WE'RE THE FUTURE. WE'RE THEM, BUT LIKE...EVOLVED.
THEY'RE LIKE COCOONS AND WE'RE THE BUTTERFLIES. ALL WE NEED FROM THEM IS TO GESTATE UNTIL WE HATCH.
I'M A BUTTERFLY?
SHUT UP.
BOMBS ARE SET? GOOD TO GO?
UH...YEAH. SHOULDN'T WE BE SENDING OUR DEMANDS?
FUCK DEMANDS.
HOW ARE WE SUPPOSED TO GET WHAT WE WANT?
WE'RE GETTING A CITY.
WHAT?
BUT DUDE, NEW YORK WAS A BLUFF.
I KNOW THAT.
THAT'S NOT WHERE THE BOMBS ARE.

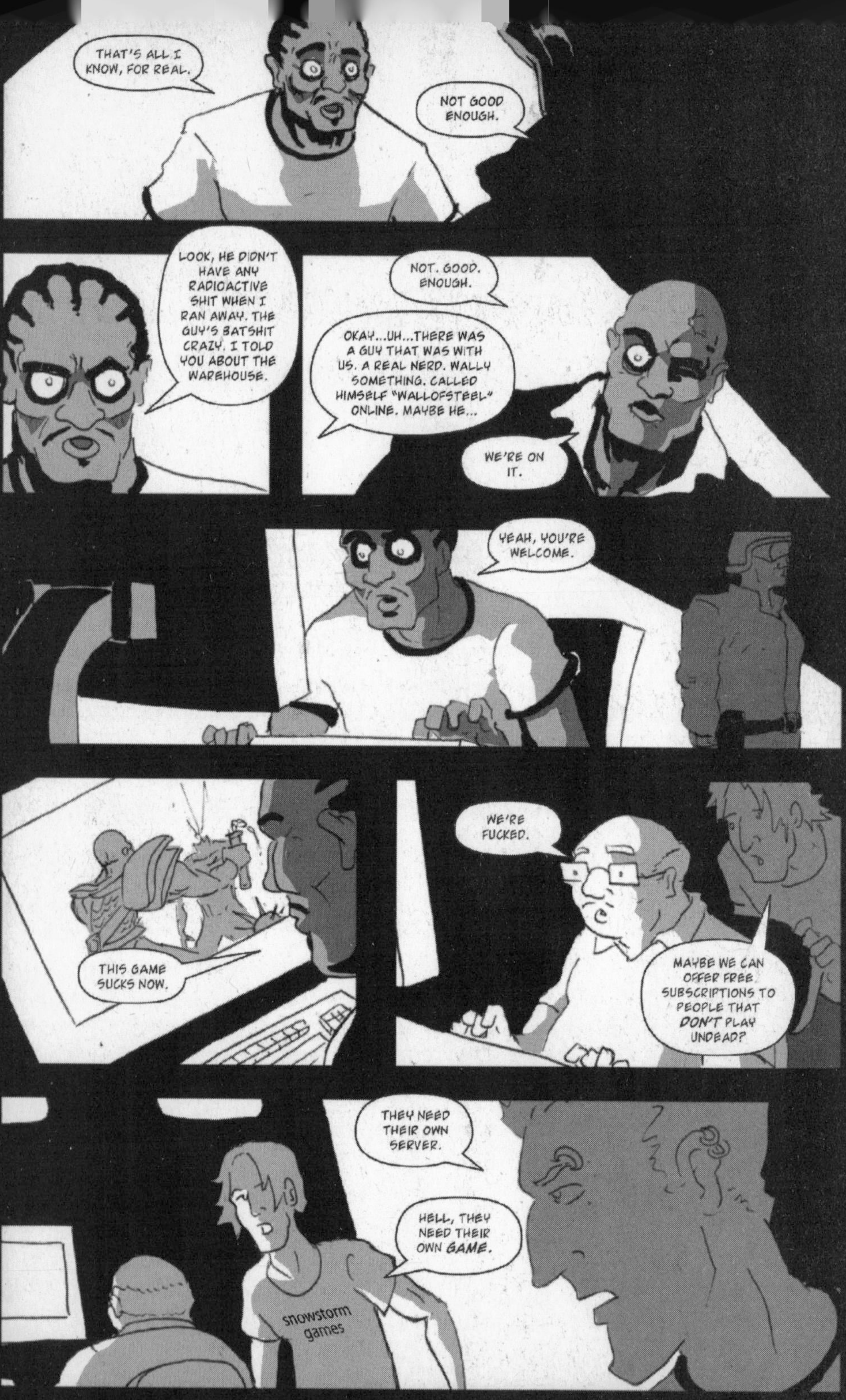
THAT'S ALL I KNOW, FOR REAL.
NOT GOOD ENOUGH.
LOOK, HE DIDN'T HAVE ANY RADIOACTIVE SHIT WHEN I RAN AWAY. THE GUY'S BATSHIT CRAZY. I TOLD YOU ABOUT THE WAREHOUSE.
NOT. GOOD. ENOUGH.
OKAY...UH...THERE WAS A GUY THAT WAS WITH US. A REAL NERD. WALLY SOMETHING. CALLED HIMSELF "WALLOFSTEEL" ONLINE. MAYBE HE...
WE'RE ON IT.
YEAH, YOU'RE WELCOME.
THIS GAME SUCKS NOW.
WE'RE FUCKED.
MAYBE WE CAN OFFER FREE SUBSCRIPTIONS TO PEOPLE THAT **DON'T** PLAY UNDEAD?
THEY NEED THEIR OWN SERVER.
HELL, THEY NEED THEIR OWN **GAME**.
snowstorm games

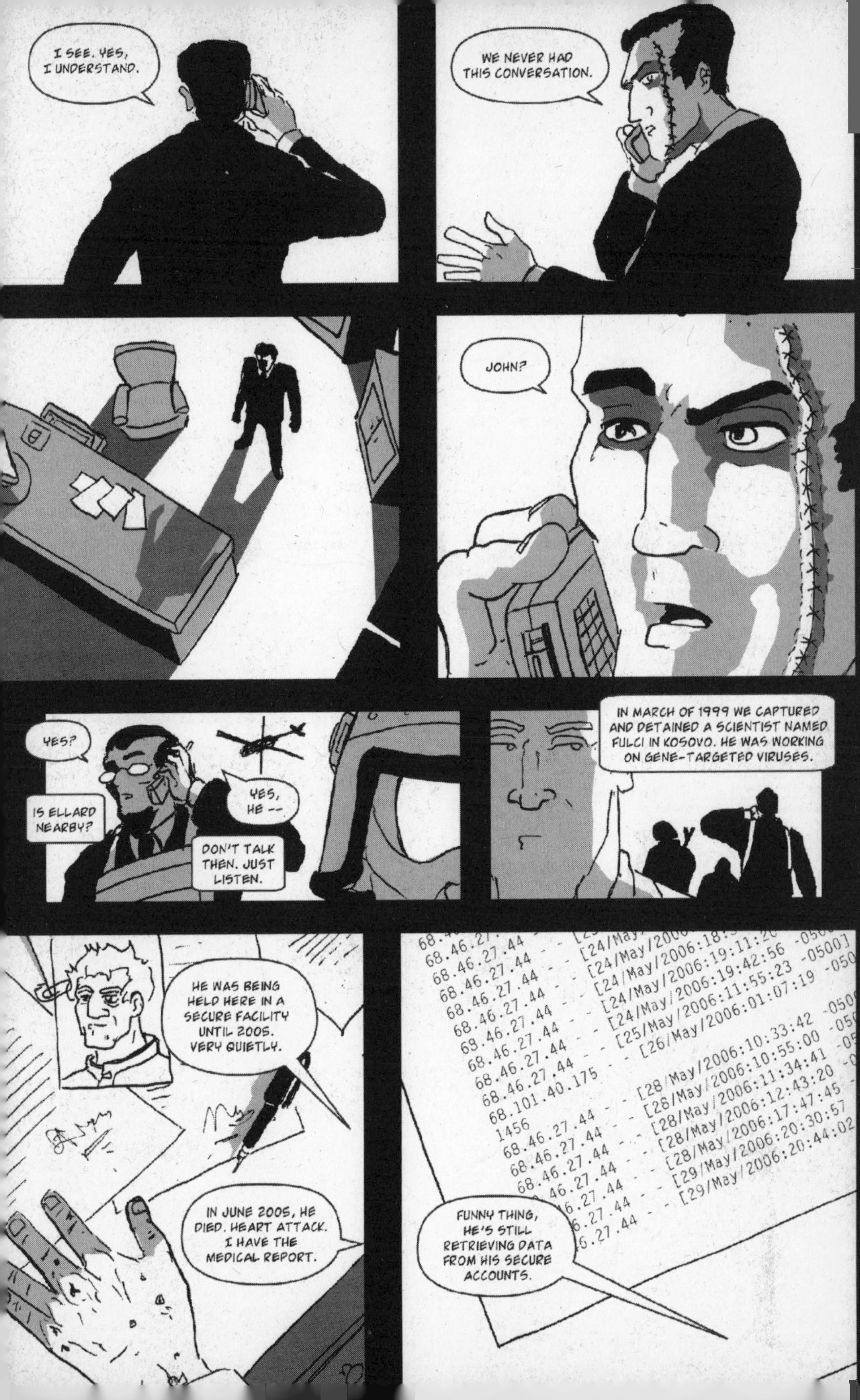
I SEE. YES, I UNDERSTAND.
WE NEVER HAD THIS CONVERSATION.
JOHN?
YES?
IS ELLARD NEARBY?
YES, HE --
DON'T TALK THEN. JUST LISTEN.
IN MARCH OF 1999 WE CAPTURED AND DETAINED A SCIENTIST NAMED FULCI IN KOSOVO. HE WAS WORKING ON GENE-TARGETED VIRUSES.
HE WAS BEING HELD HERE IN A SECURE FACILITY UNTIL 2005. VERY QUIETLY.
IN JUNE 2005, HE DIED. HEART ATTACK. I HAVE THE MEDICAL REPORT.
FUNNY THING, HE'S STILL RETRIEVING DATA FROM HIS SECURE ACCOUNTS.

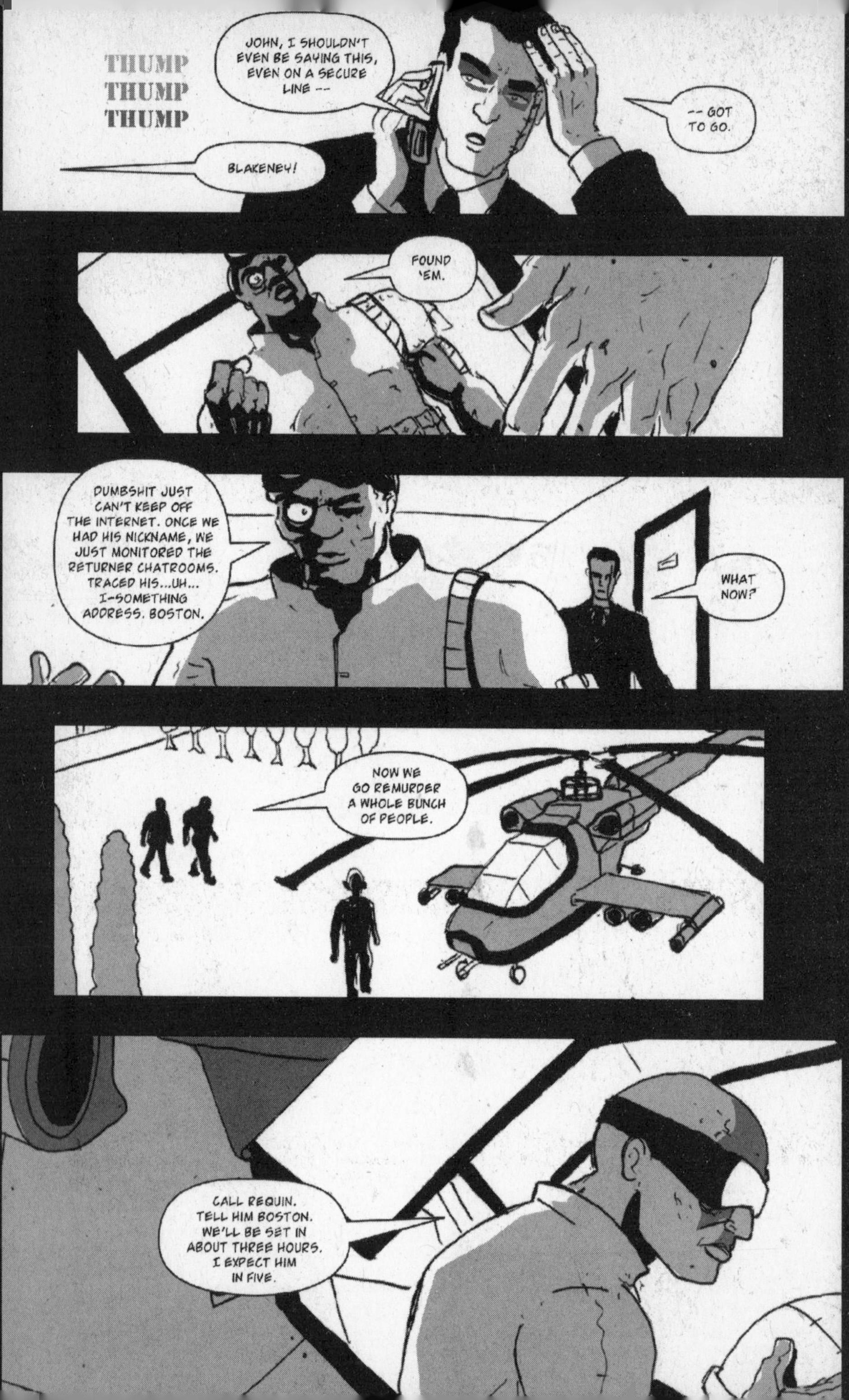
THUMP
THUMP
THUMP
JOHN, I SHOULDN'T EVEN BE SAYING THIS, EVEN ON A SECURE LINE --
-- GOT TO GO.
BLAKENEY!
FOUND 'EM.
DUMBSHIT JUST CAN'T KEEP OFF THE INTERNET. ONCE WE HAD HIS NICKNAME, WE JUST MONITORED THE RETURNER CHATROOMS. TRACED HIS...UH... I-SOMETHING ADDRESS. BOSTON.
WHAT NOW?
NOW WE GO REMURDER A WHOLE BUNCH OF PEOPLE.
CALL REQUIN. TELL HIM BOSTON. WE'LL BE SET IN ABOUT THREE HOURS. I EXPECT HIM IN FIVE.

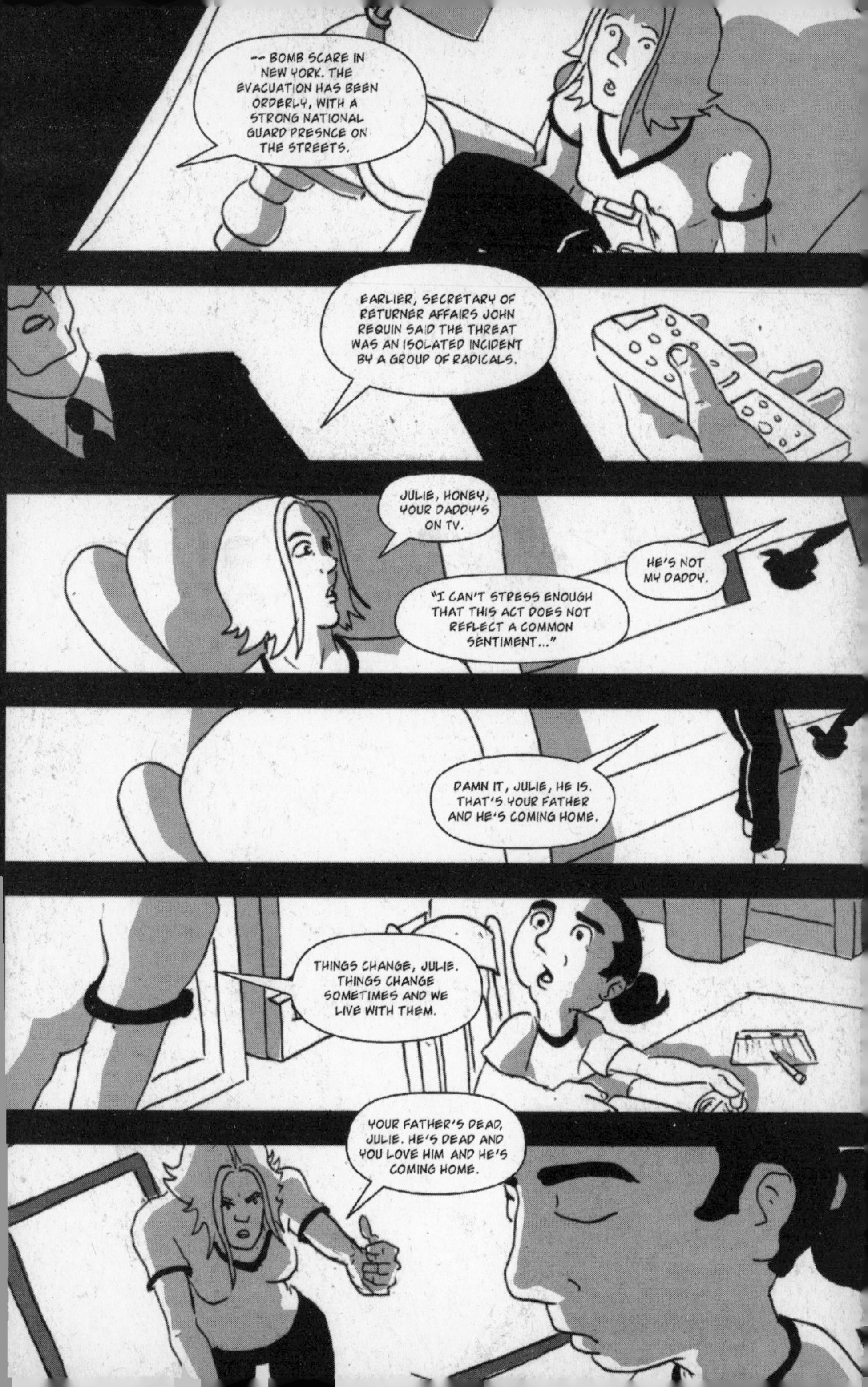
-- BOMB SCARE IN NEW YORK. THE EVACUATION HAS BEEN ORDERLY, WITH A STRONG NATIONAL GUARD PRESNCE ON THE STREETS.
EARLIER, SECRETARY OF RETURNER AFFAIRS JOHN REQUIN SAID THE THREAT WAS AN ISOLATED INCIDENT BY A GROUP OF RADICALS.
JULIE, HONEY, YOUR DADDY'S ON TV.
HE'S NOT MY DADDY.
"I CAN'T STRESS ENOUGH THAT THIS ACT DOES NOT REFLECT A COMMON SENTIMENT..."
DAMN IT, JULIE, HE IS. THAT'S YOUR FATHER AND HE'S COMING HOME.
THINGS CHANGE, JULIE. THINGS CHANGE SOMETIMES AND WE LIVE WITH THEM.
YOUR FATHER'S DEAD, JULIE. HE'S DEAD AND YOU LOVE HIM AND HE'S COMING HOME.

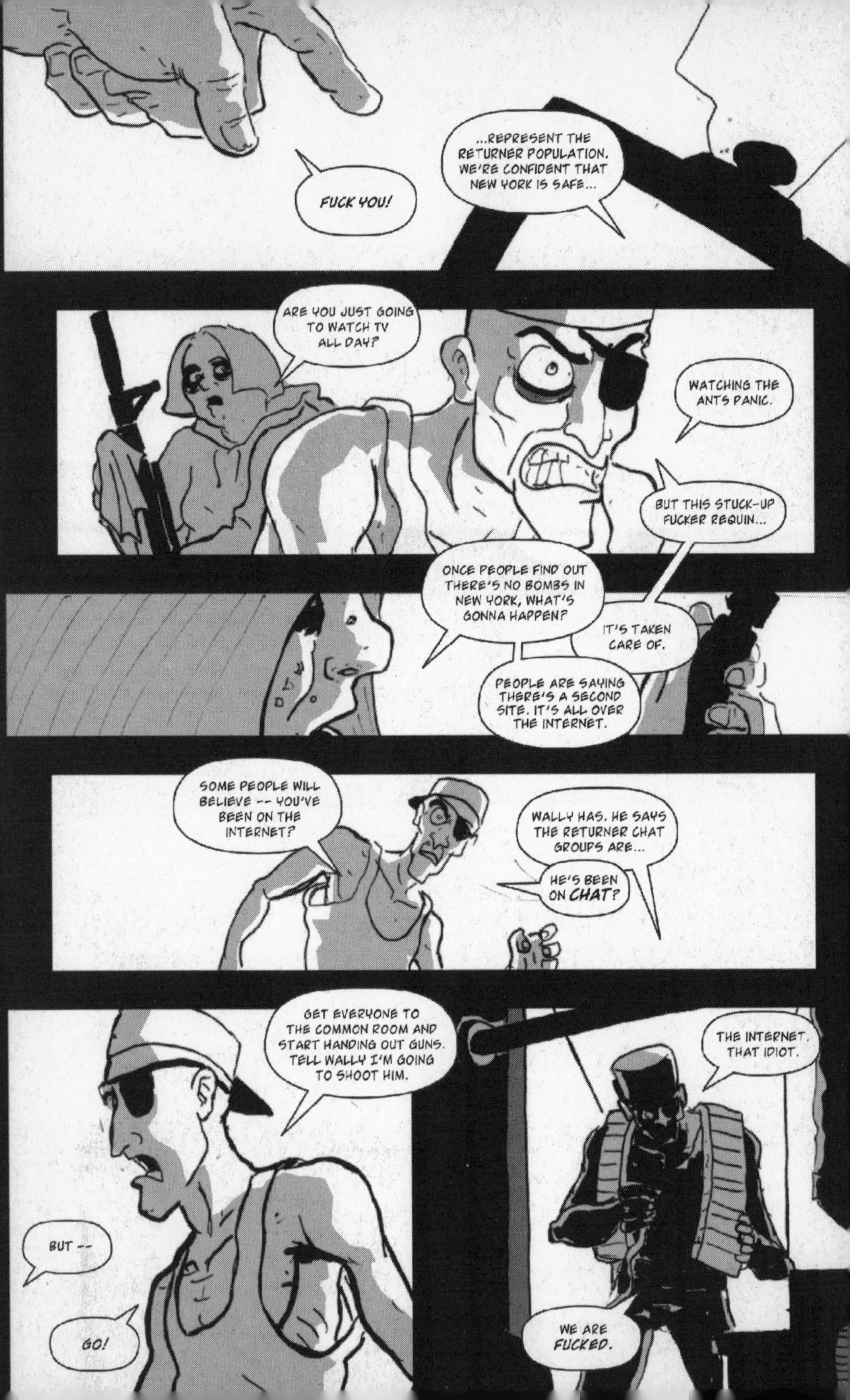
...REPRESENT THE RETURNER POPULATION. WE'RE CONFIDENT THAT NEW YORK IS SAFE...
FUCK YOU!
ARE YOU JUST GOING TO WATCH TV ALL DAY?
WATCHING THE ANTS PANIC.
BUT THIS STUCK-UP FUCKER REQUIN...
ONCE PEOPLE FIND OUT THERE'S NO BOMBS IN NEW YORK, WHAT'S GONNA HAPPEN?
IT'S TAKEN CARE OF.
PEOPLE ARE SAYING THERE'S A SECOND SITE. IT'S ALL OVER THE INTERNET.
SOME PEOPLE WILL BELIEVE -- YOU'VE BEEN ON THE INTERNET?
WALLY HAS. HE SAYS THE RETURNER CHAT GROUPS ARE...
HE'S BEEN ON CHAT?
GET EVERYONE TO THE COMMON ROOM AND START HANDING OUT GUNS. TELL WALLY I'M GOING TO SHOOT HIM.
BUT --
GO!
THE INTERNET. THAT IDIOT.
WE ARE FUCKED.

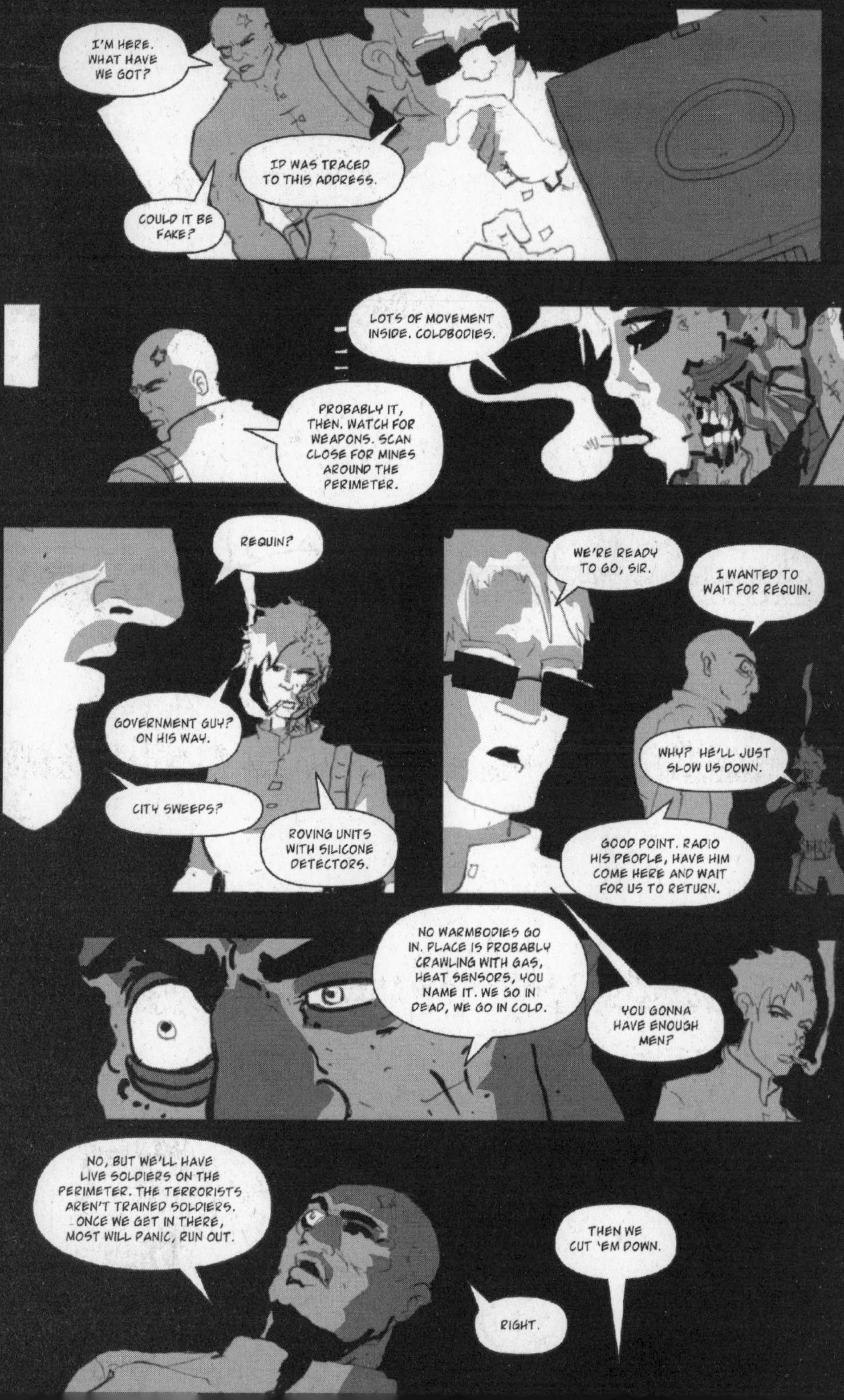
I'M HERE. WHAT HAVE WE GOT?
ID WAS TRACED TO THIS ADDRESS.
COULD IT BE FAKE?
LOTS OF MOVEMENT INSIDE. COLDBODIES.
PROBABLY IT, THEN. WATCH FOR WEAPONS. SCAN CLOSE FOR MINES AROUND THE PERIMETER.
REQUIN?
GOVERNMENT GUY? ON HIS WAY.
CITY SWEEPS?
ROVING UNITS WITH SILICONE DETECTORS.
WE'RE READY TO GO, SIR.
I WANTED TO WAIT FOR REQUIN.
WHY? HE'LL JUST SLOW US DOWN.
GOOD POINT. RADIO HIS PEOPLE, HAVE HIM COME HERE AND WAIT FOR US TO RETURN.
NO WARMBODIES GO IN. PLACE IS PROBABLY CRAWLING WITH GAS, HEAT SENSORS, YOU NAME IT. WE GO IN DEAD, WE GO IN COLD.
YOU GONNA HAVE ENOUGH MEN?
NO, BUT WE'LL HAVE LIVE SOLDIERS ON THE PERIMETER. THE TERRORISTS AREN'T TRAINED SOLDIERS. ONCE WE GET IN THERE, MOST WILL PANIC, RUN OUT.
THEN WE CUT 'EM DOWN.
RIGHT.

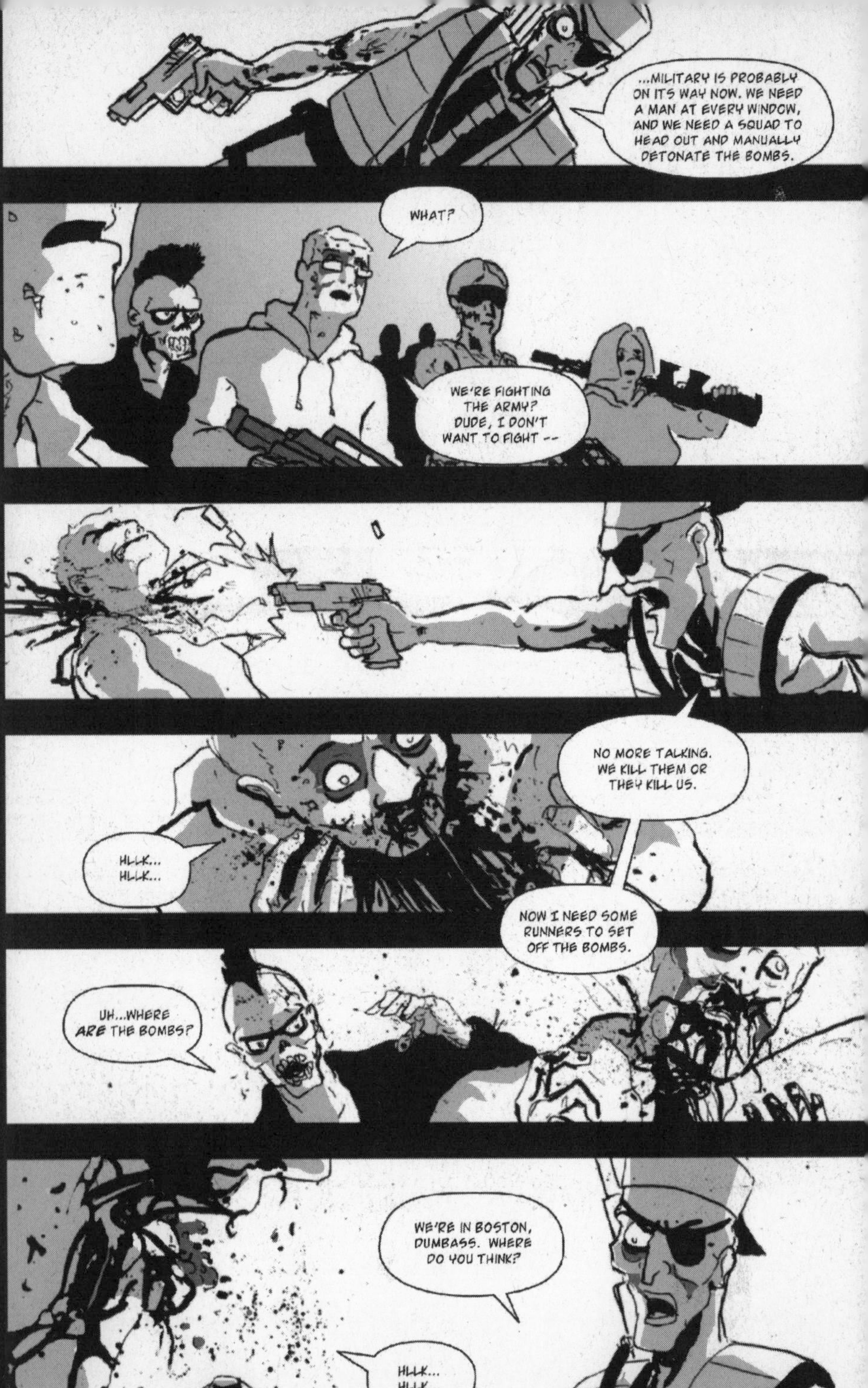
...MILITARY IS PROBABLY ON ITS WAY NOW. WE NEED A MAN AT EVERY WINDOW, AND WE NEED A SQUAD TO HEAD OUT AND MANUALLY DETONATE THE BOMBS.
WHAT?
WE'RE FIGHTING THE ARMY? DUDE, I DON'T WANT TO FIGHT --
NO MORE TALKING. WE KILL THEM OR THEY KILL US.
HLLK... HLLK...
NOW I NEED SOME RUNNERS TO SET OFF THE BOMBS.
UH...WHERE *ARE* THE BOMBS?
WE'RE IN BOSTON, DUMBASS. WHERE DO YOU THINK?
HLLK... HLLK...

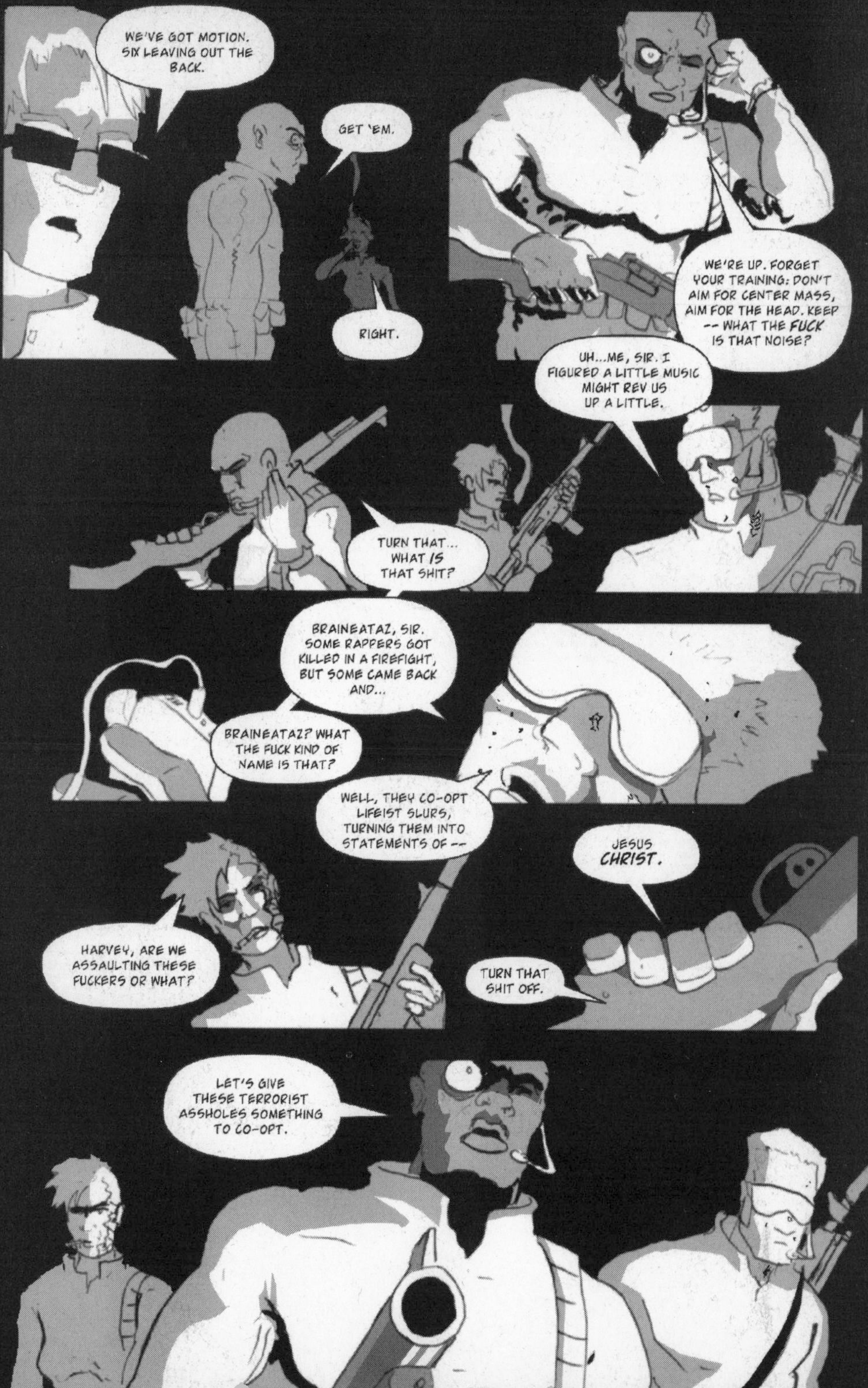
WE'VE GOT MOTION. SIX LEAVING OUT THE BACK.
GET 'EM.
RIGHT.
WE'RE UP. FORGET YOUR TRAINING: DON'T AIM FOR CENTER MASS, AIM FOR THE HEAD. KEEP -- WHAT THE FUCK IS THAT NOISE?
UH...ME, SIR. I FIGURED A LITTLE MUSIC MIGHT REV US UP A LITTLE.
TURN THAT... WHAT IS THAT SHIT?
BRAINEATAZ, SIR. SOME RAPPERS GOT KILLED IN A FIREFIGHT, BUT SOME CAME BACK AND...
BRAINEATAZ? WHAT THE FUCK KIND OF NAME IS THAT?
WELL, THEY CO-OPT LIFEIST SLURS, TURNING THEM INTO STATEMENTS OF --
JESUS CHRIST.
HARVEY, ARE WE ASSAULTING THESE FUCKERS OR WHAT?
TURN THAT SHIT OFF.
LET'S GIVE THESE TERRORIST ASSHOLES SOMETHING TO CO-OPT.

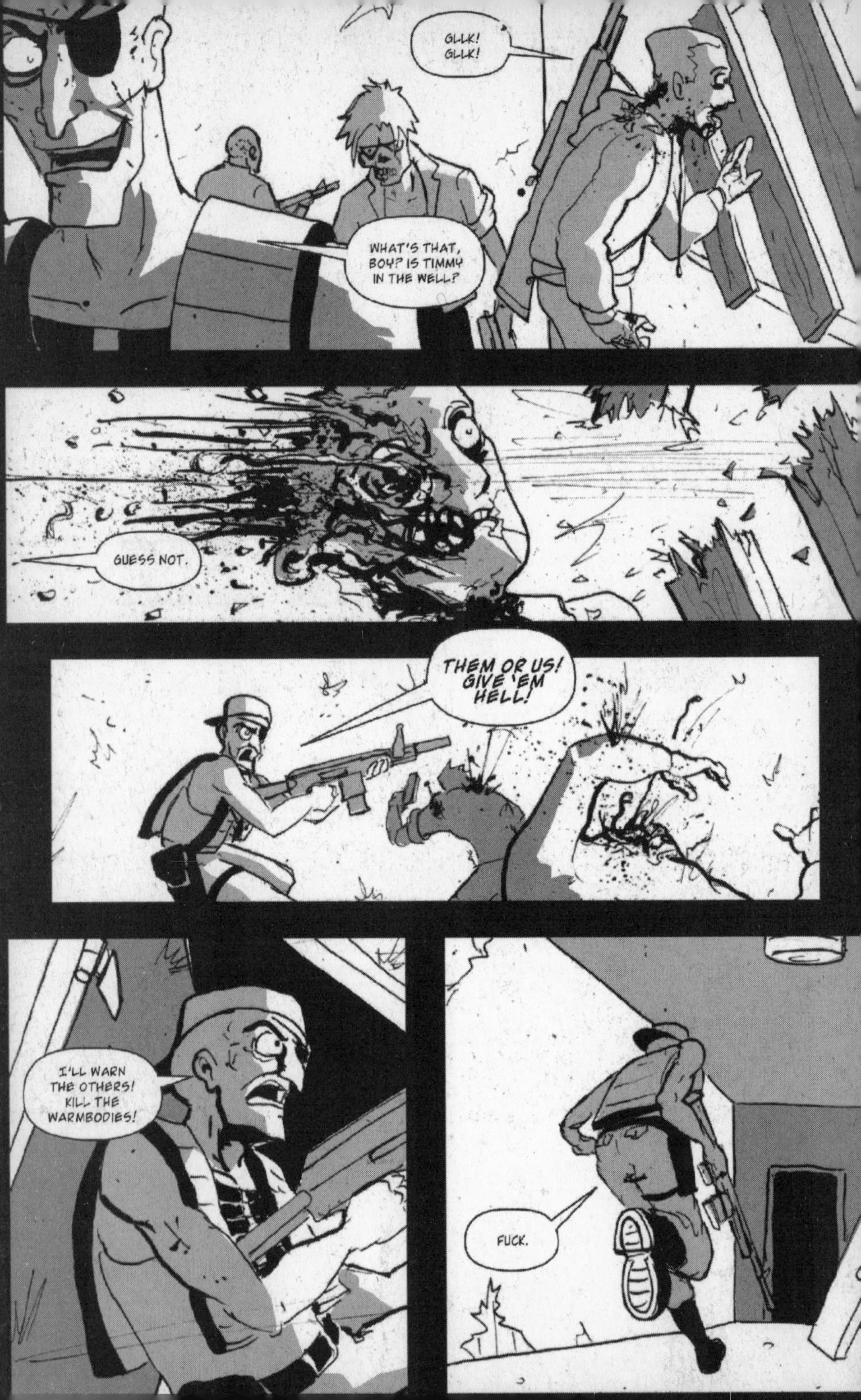
GLLK! GLLK!
WHAT'S THAT, BOY? IS TIMMY IN THE WELL?
GUESS NOT.
THEM OR US! GIVE 'EM HELL!
I'LL WARN THE OTHERS! KILL THE WARMBODIES!
FUCK.

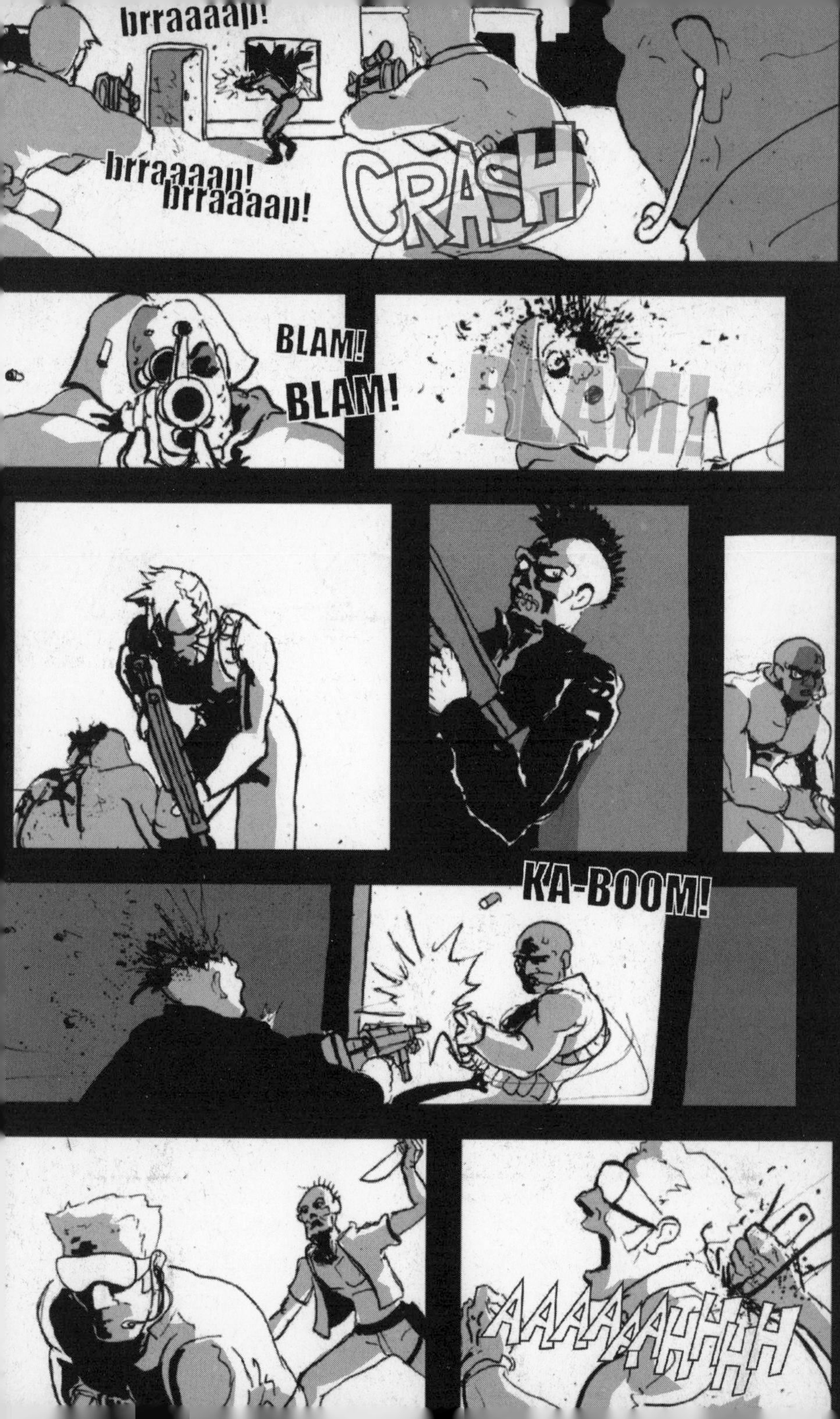
brraaaap!
brraaaap!
brraaaap!
CRASH
BLAM!
BLAM!
BLAM!
KA-BOOM!
AAAAAAHHH

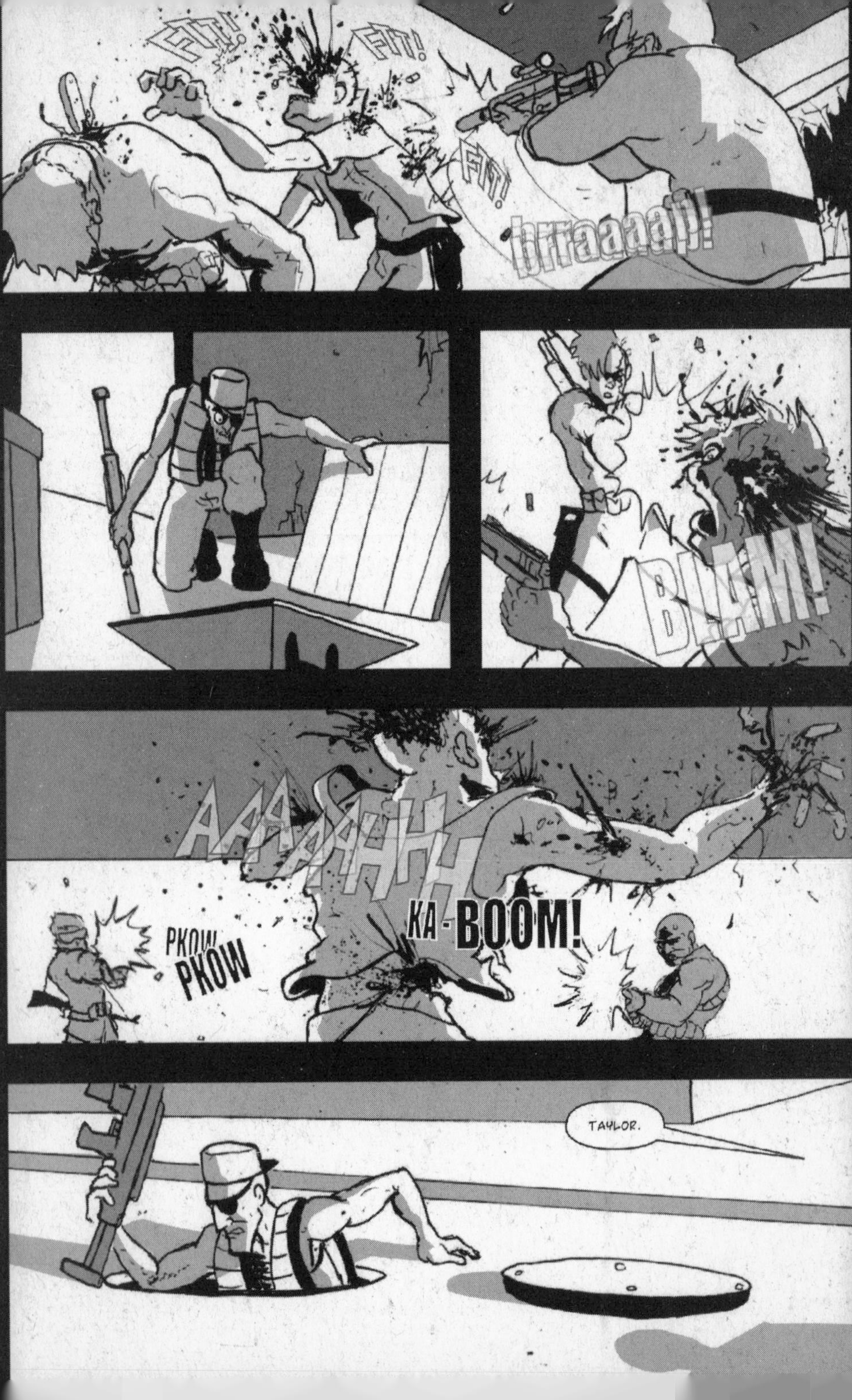
FTT!
FTT!
FTT!
brraaaap!
BLAM!
AAAAAHHH
PKOW PKOW
KA-BOOM!
TAYLOR.

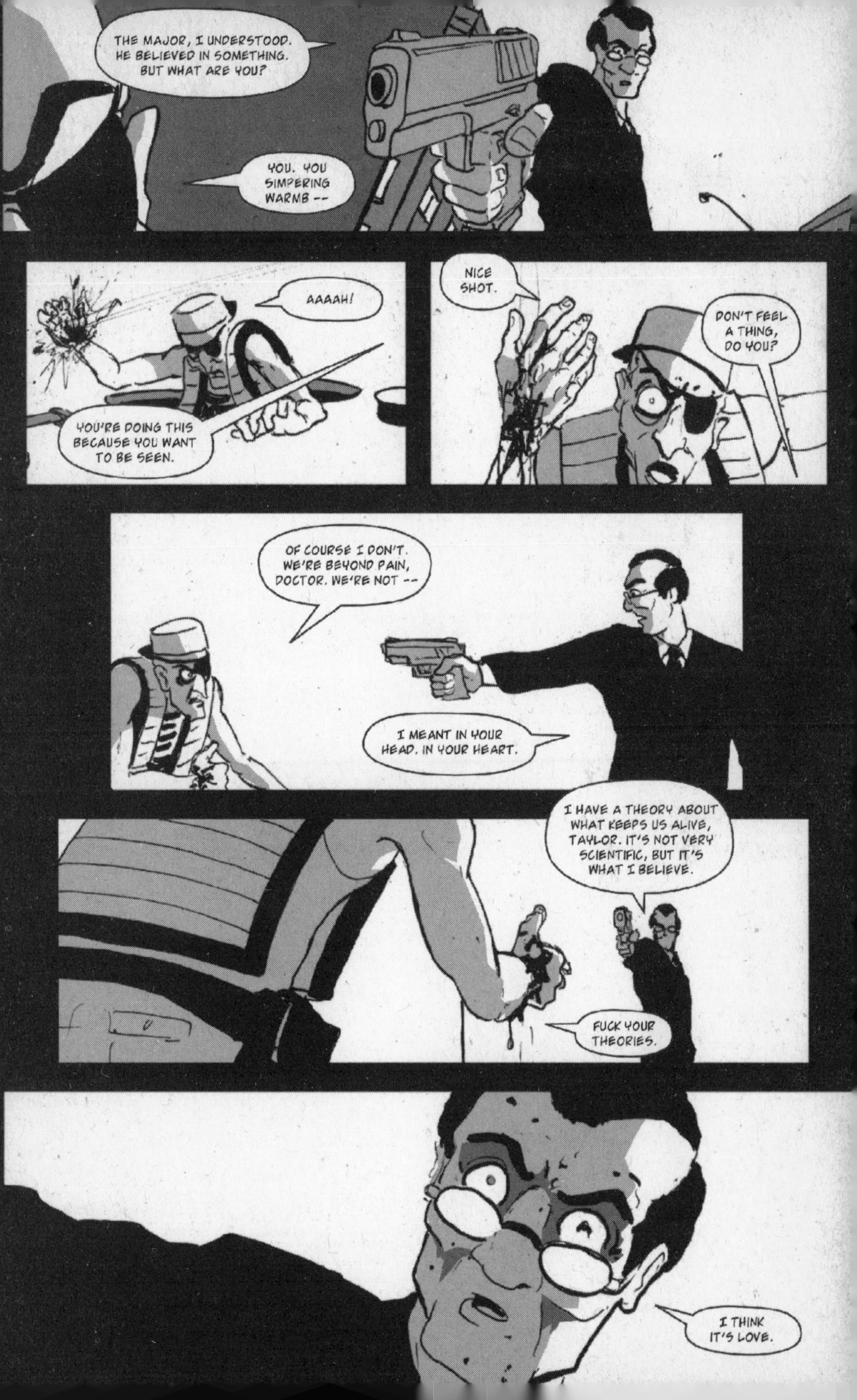
THE MAJOR, I UNDERSTOOD. HE BELIEVED IN SOMETHING. BUT WHAT ARE YOU?
YOU. YOU SIMPERING WARMB --
AAAAH!
YOU'RE DOING THIS BECAUSE YOU WANT TO BE SEEN.
NICE SHOT.
DON'T FEEL A THING, DO YOU?
OF COURSE I DON'T. WE'RE BEYOND PAIN, DOCTOR. WE'RE NOT --
I MEANT IN YOUR HEAD. IN YOUR HEART.
I HAVE A THEORY ABOUT WHAT KEEPS US ALIVE, TAYLOR. IT'S NOT VERY SCIENTIFIC, BUT IT'S WHAT I BELIEVE.
FUCK YOUR THEORIES.
I THINK IT'S LOVE.

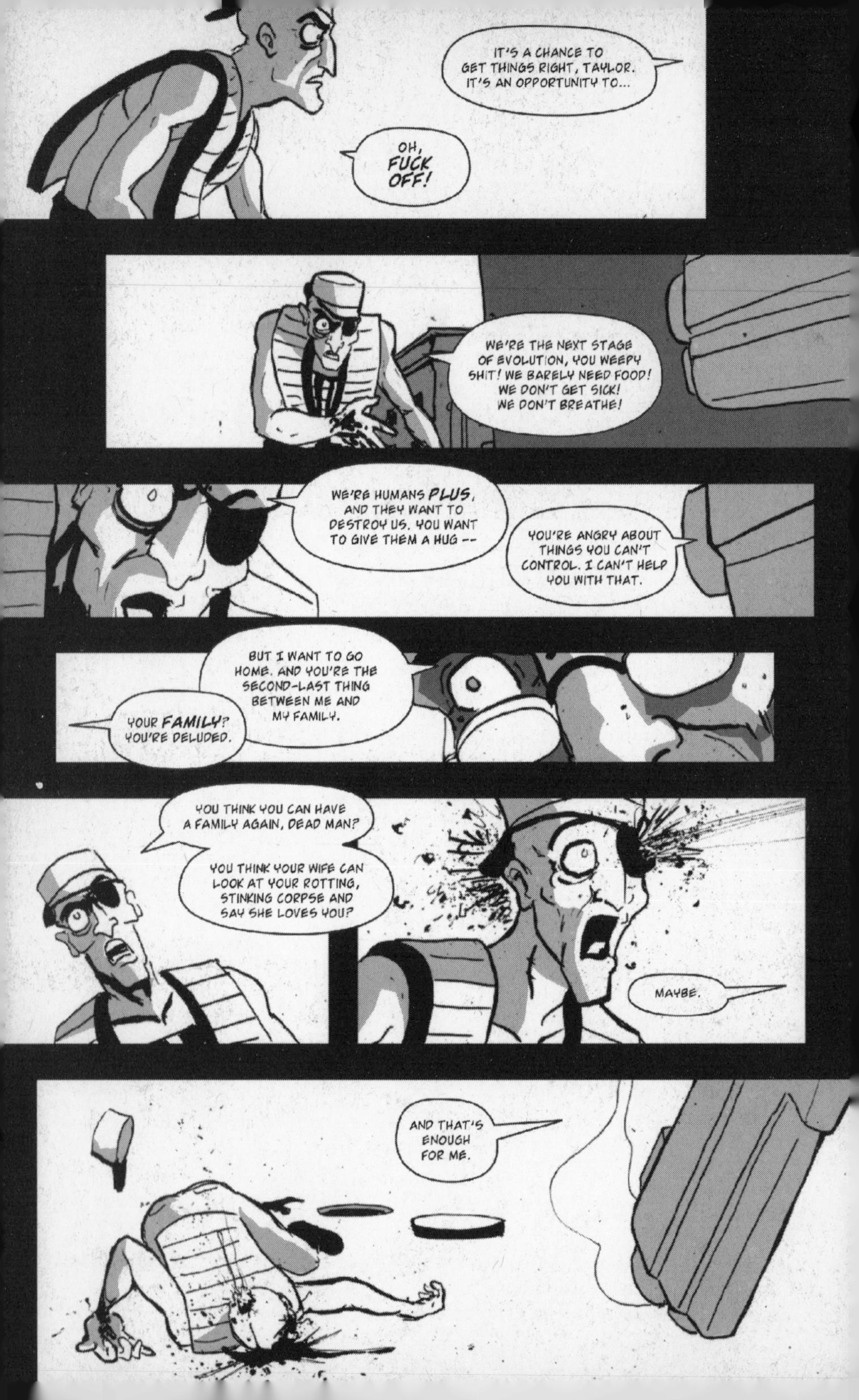
IT'S A CHANCE TO GET THINGS RIGHT, TAYLOR. IT'S AN OPPORTUNITY TO...
OH, FUCK OFF!
WE'RE THE NEXT STAGE OF EVOLUTION, YOU WEEPY SHIT! WE BARELY NEED FOOD! WE DON'T GET SICK! WE DON'T BREATHE!
WE'RE HUMANS PLUS, AND THEY WANT TO DESTROY US. YOU WANT TO GIVE THEM A HUG --
YOU'RE ANGRY ABOUT THINGS YOU CAN'T CONTROL. I CAN'T HELP YOU WITH THAT.
BUT I WANT TO GO HOME. AND YOU'RE THE SECOND-LAST THING BETWEEN ME AND MY FAMILY.
YOUR FAMILY? YOU'RE DELUDED.
YOU THINK YOU CAN HAVE A FAMILY AGAIN, DEAD MAN?
YOU THINK YOUR WIFE CAN LOOK AT YOUR ROTTING, STINKING CORPSE AND SAY SHE LOVES YOU?
MAYBE.
AND THAT'S ENOUGH FOR ME.

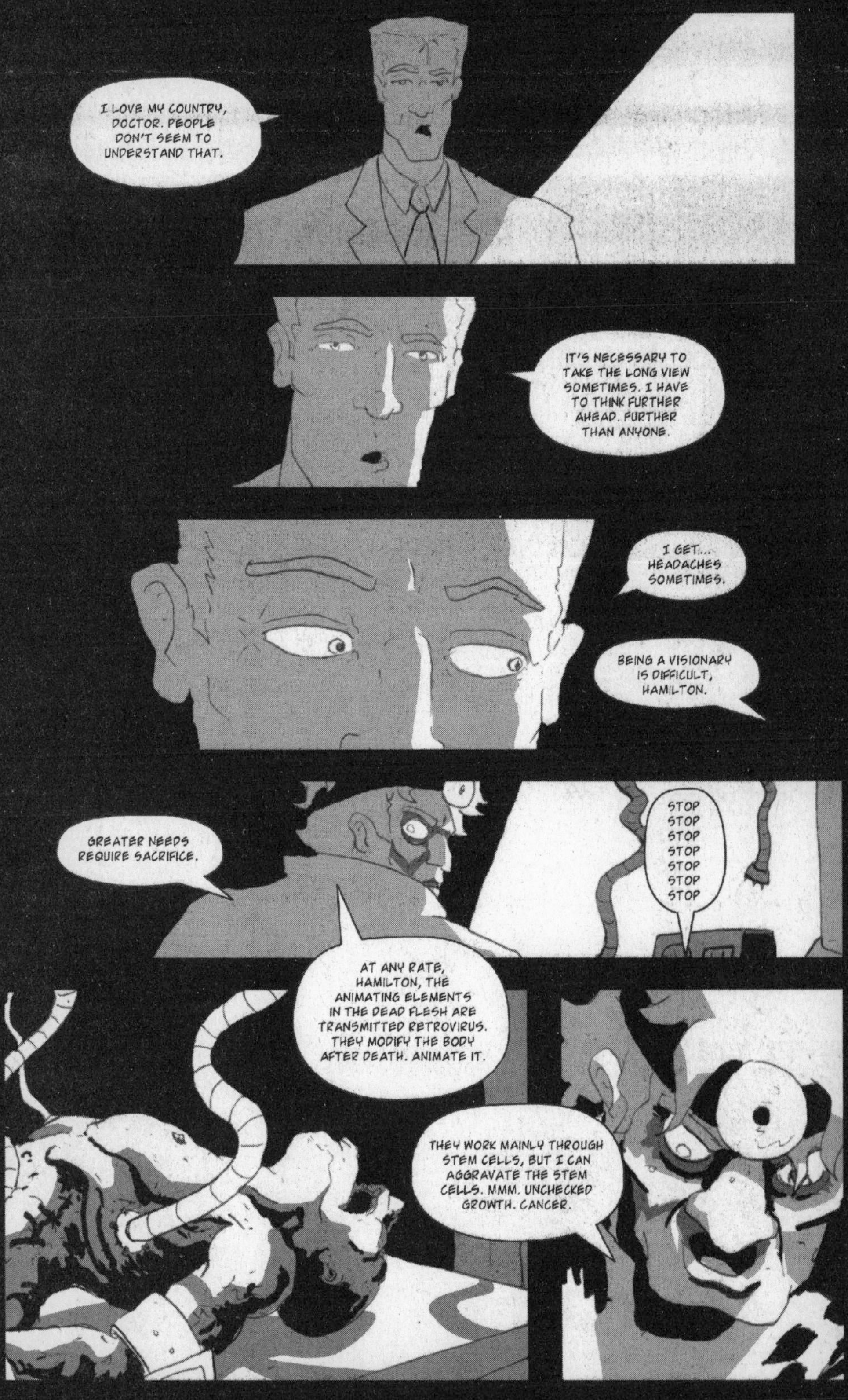
I LOVE MY COUNTRY, DOCTOR. PEOPLE DON'T SEEM TO UNDERSTAND THAT.
IT'S NECESSARY TO TAKE THE LONG VIEW SOMETIMES. I HAVE TO THINK FURTHER AHEAD. FURTHER THAN ANYONE.
I GET... HEADACHES SOMETIMES.
BEING A VISIONARY IS DIFFICULT, HAMILTON.
GREATER NEEDS REQUIRE SACRIFICE.
STOP STOP STOP STOP STOP STOP STOP
AT ANY RATE, HAMILTON, THE ANIMATING ELEMENTS IN THE DEAD FLESH ARE TRANSMITTED RETROVIRUS. THEY MODIFY THE BODY AFTER DEATH. ANIMATE IT.
THEY WORK MAINLY THROUGH STEM CELLS, BUT I CAN AGGRAVATE THE STEM CELLS. MMM. UNCHECKED GROWTH. CANCER.

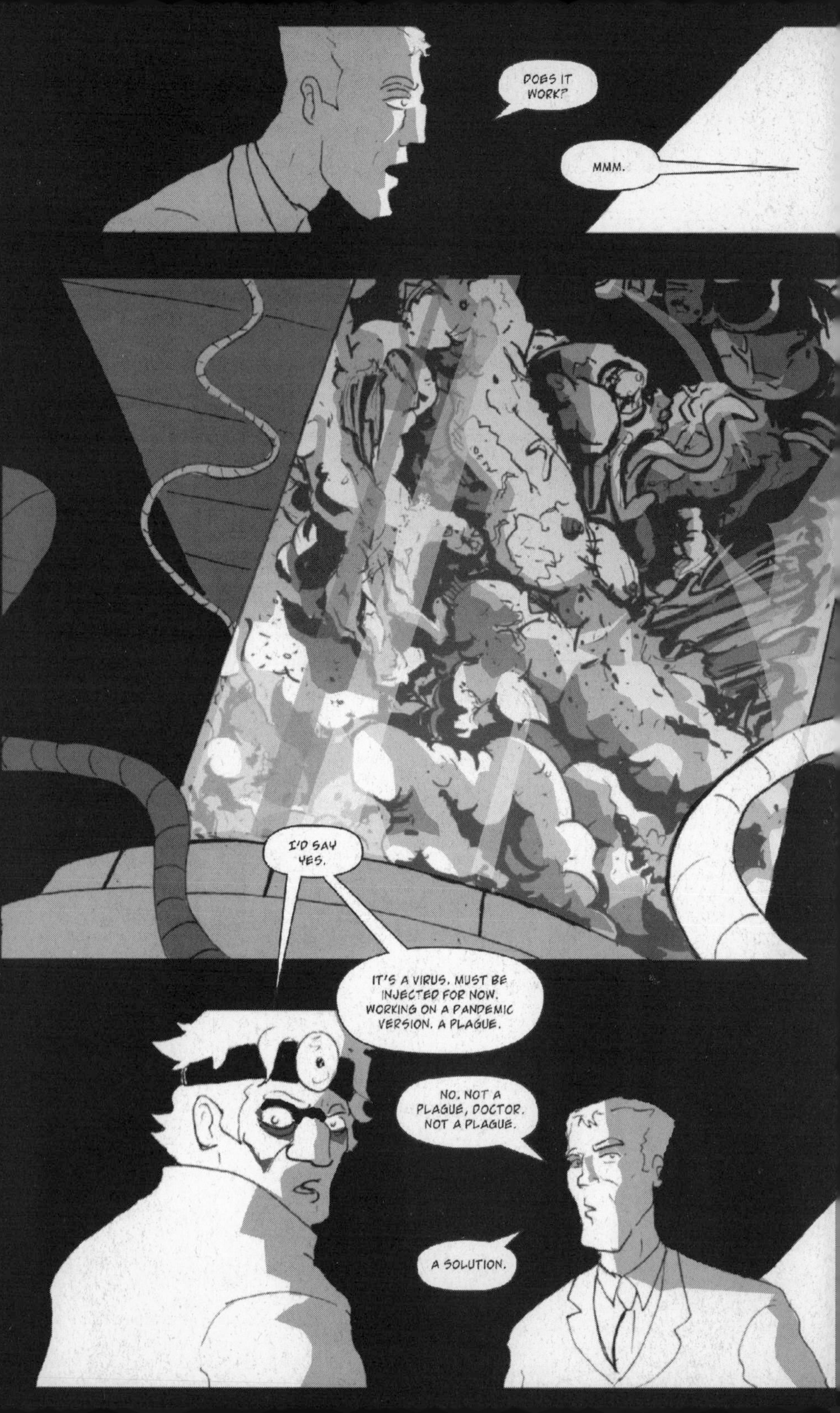
DOES IT WORK?
MMM.
I'D SAY YES.
IT'S A VIRUS. MUST BE INJECTED FOR NOW. WORKING ON A PANDEMIC VERSION. A PLAGUE.
NO. NOT A PLAGUE, DOCTOR. NOT A PLAGUE.
A SOLUTION.

CHAPTER
SIX

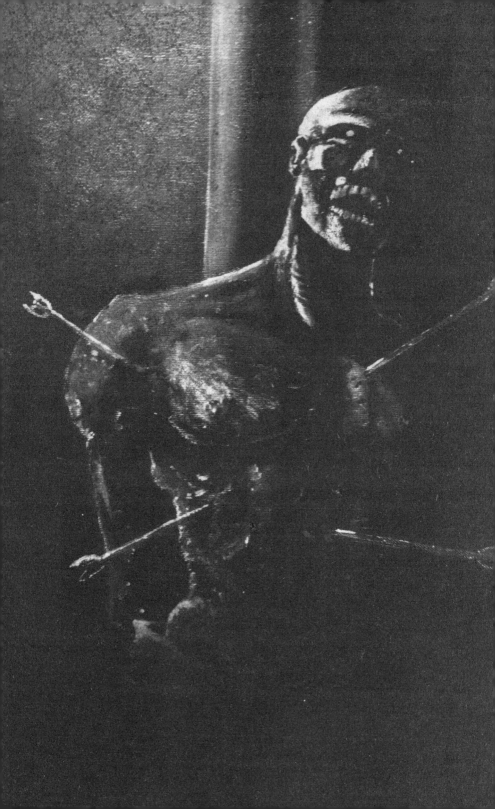

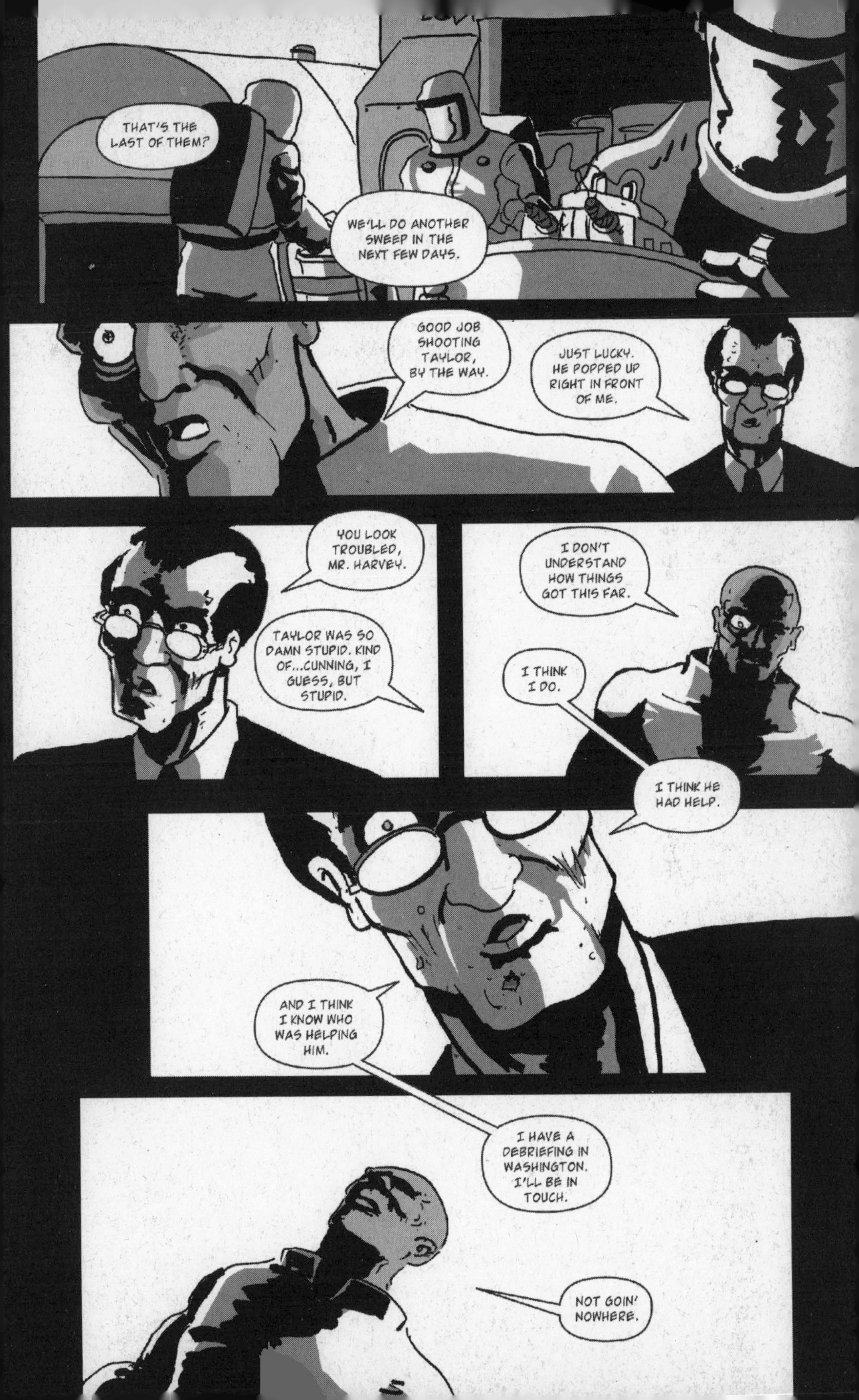
THAT'S THE LAST OF THEM?
WE'LL DO ANOTHER SWEEP IN THE NEXT FEW DAYS.
GOOD JOB SHOOTING TAYLOR, BY THE WAY.
JUST LUCKY. HE POPPED UP RIGHT IN FRONT OF ME.
YOU LOOK TROUBLED, MR. HARVEY.
TAYLOR WAS SO DAMN STUPID. KIND OF...CUNNING, I GUESS, BUT STUPID.
I DON'T UNDERSTAND HOW THINGS GOT THIS FAR.
I THINK I DO.
I THINK HE HAD HELP.
AND I THINK I KNOW WHO WAS HELPING HIM.
I HAVE A DEBRIEFING IN WASHINGTON. I'LL BE IN TOUCH.
NOT GOIN' NOWHERE.

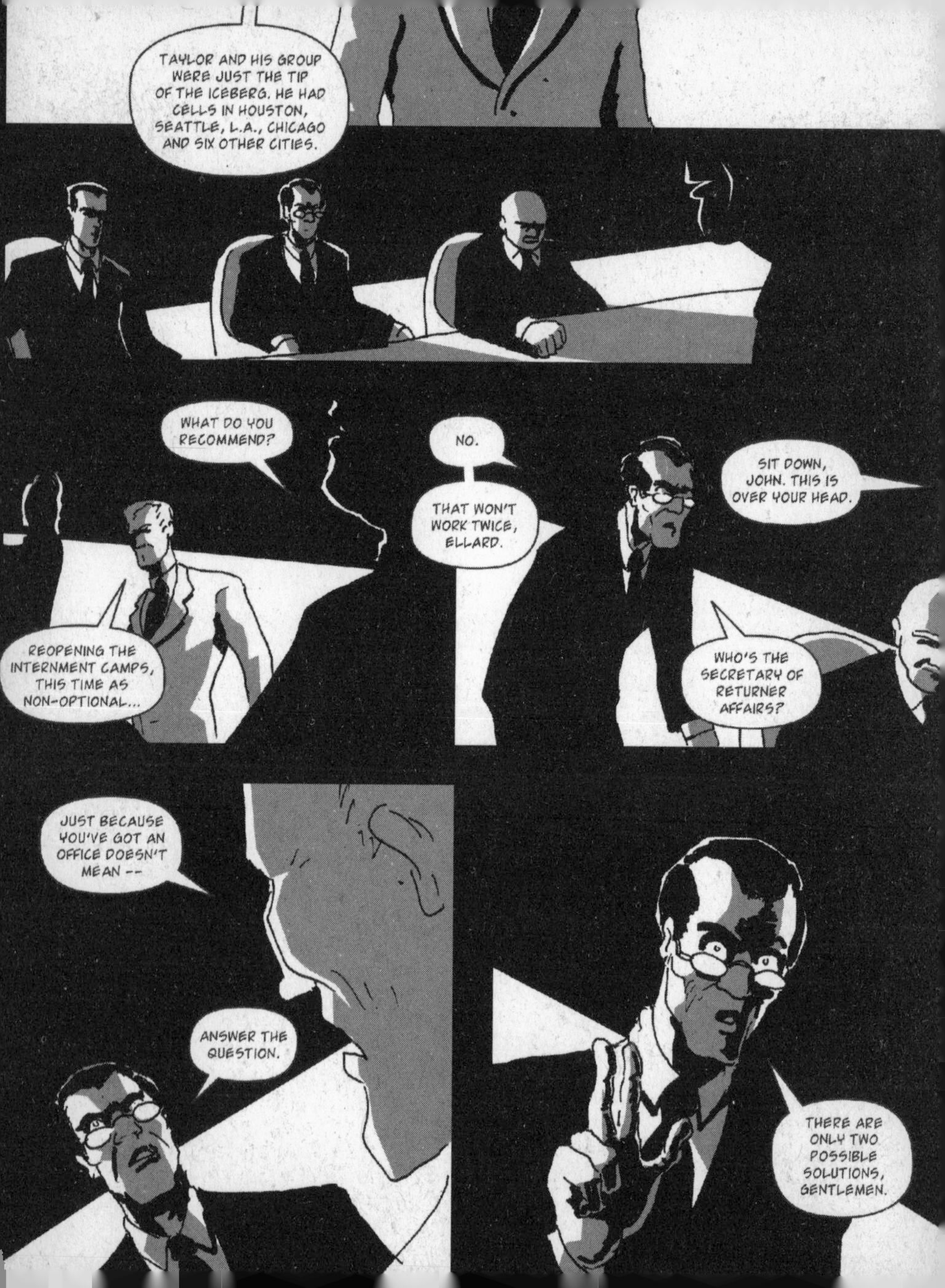
TAYLOR AND HIS GROUP WERE JUST THE TIP OF THE ICEBERG. HE HAD CELLS IN HOUSTON, SEATTLE, L.A., CHICAGO AND SIX OTHER CITIES.
WHAT DO YOU RECOMMEND?
REOPENING THE INTERNMENT CAMPS, THIS TIME AS NON-OPTIONAL...
NO.
THAT WON'T WORK TWICE, ELLARD.
SIT DOWN, JOHN. THIS IS OVER YOUR HEAD.
WHO'S THE SECRETARY OF RETURNER AFFAIRS?
JUST BECAUSE YOU'VE GOT AN OFFICE DOESN'T MEAN --
ANSWER THE QUESTION.
THERE ARE ONLY TWO POSSIBLE SOLUTIONS, GENTLEMEN.

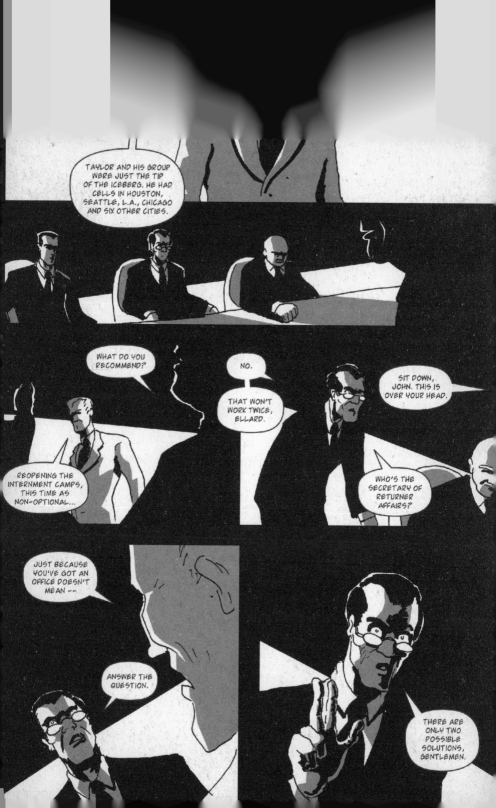

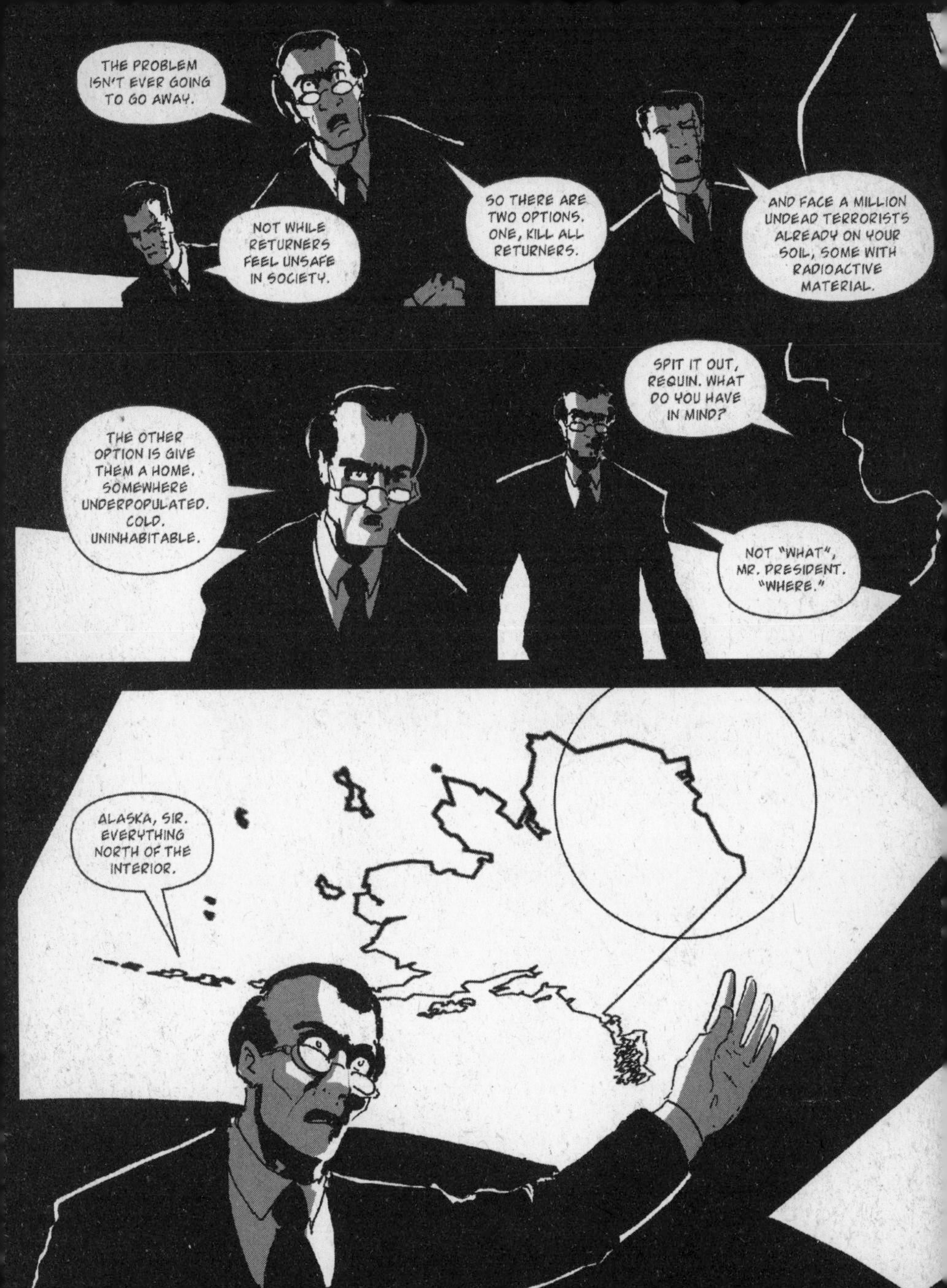
THE PROBLEM ISN'T EVER GOING TO GO AWAY.
NOT WHILE RETURNERS FEEL UNSAFE IN SOCIETY.
SO THERE ARE TWO OPTIONS. ONE, KILL ALL RETURNERS.
AND FACE A MILLION UNDEAD TERRORISTS ALREADY ON YOUR SOIL, SOME WITH RADIOACTIVE MATERIAL.
THE OTHER OPTION IS GIVE THEM A HOME. SOMEWHERE UNDERPOPULATED. COLD. UNINHABITABLE.
SPIT IT OUT, REQUIN. WHAT DO YOU HAVE IN MIND?
NOT "WHAT", MR. PRESIDENT. "WHERE."
ALASKA, SIR. EVERYTHING NORTH OF THE INTERIOR.

dead EYES open

by
matthew shepherd
& roy boney, jr.

chapter six:
PROMISED LANDS

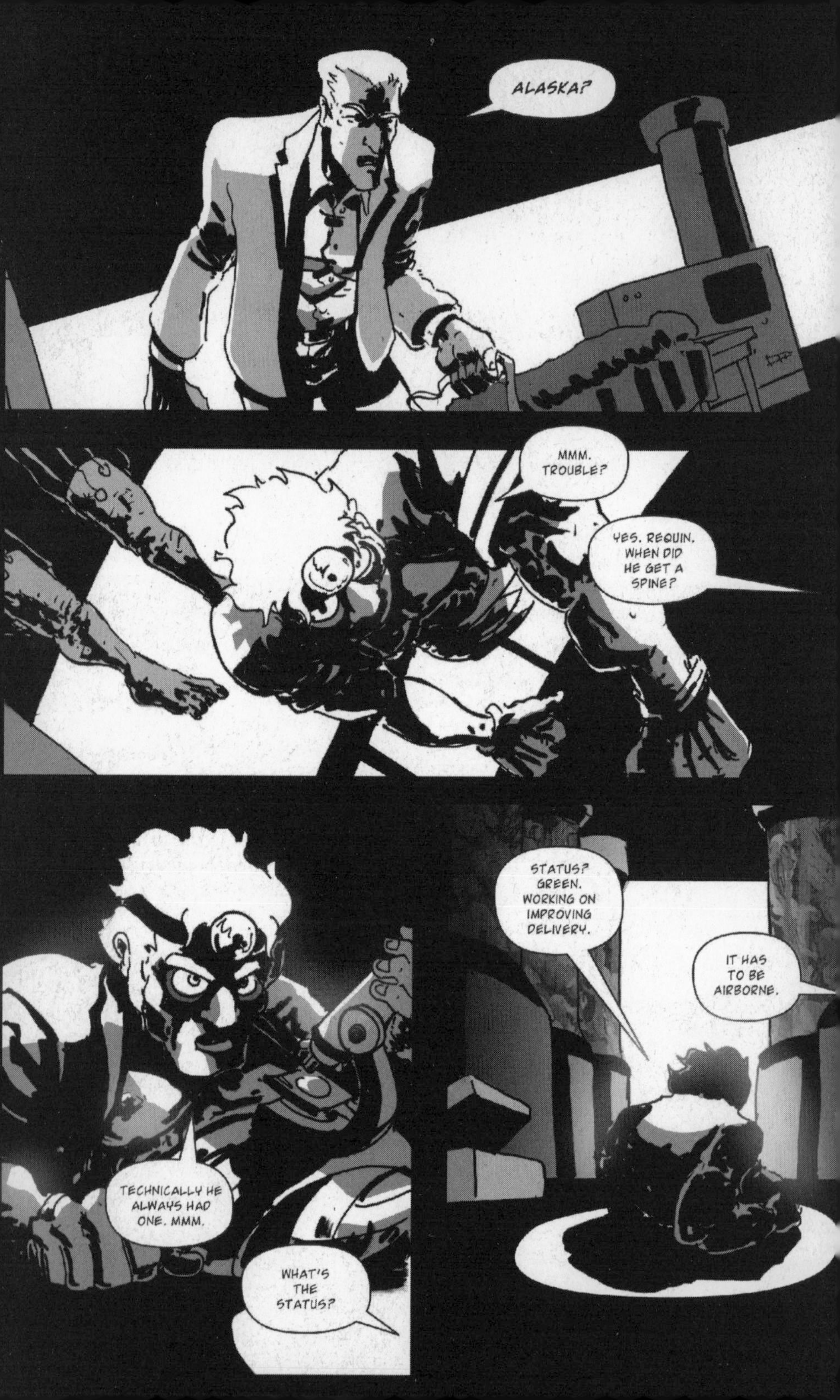
ALASKA?
MMM. TROUBLE?
YES. REQUIN. WHEN DID HE GET A SPINE?
TECHNICALLY HE ALWAYS HAD ONE. MMM.
WHAT'S THE STATUS?
STATUS? GREEN. WORKING ON IMPROVING DELIVERY.
IT HAS TO BE AIRBORNE.

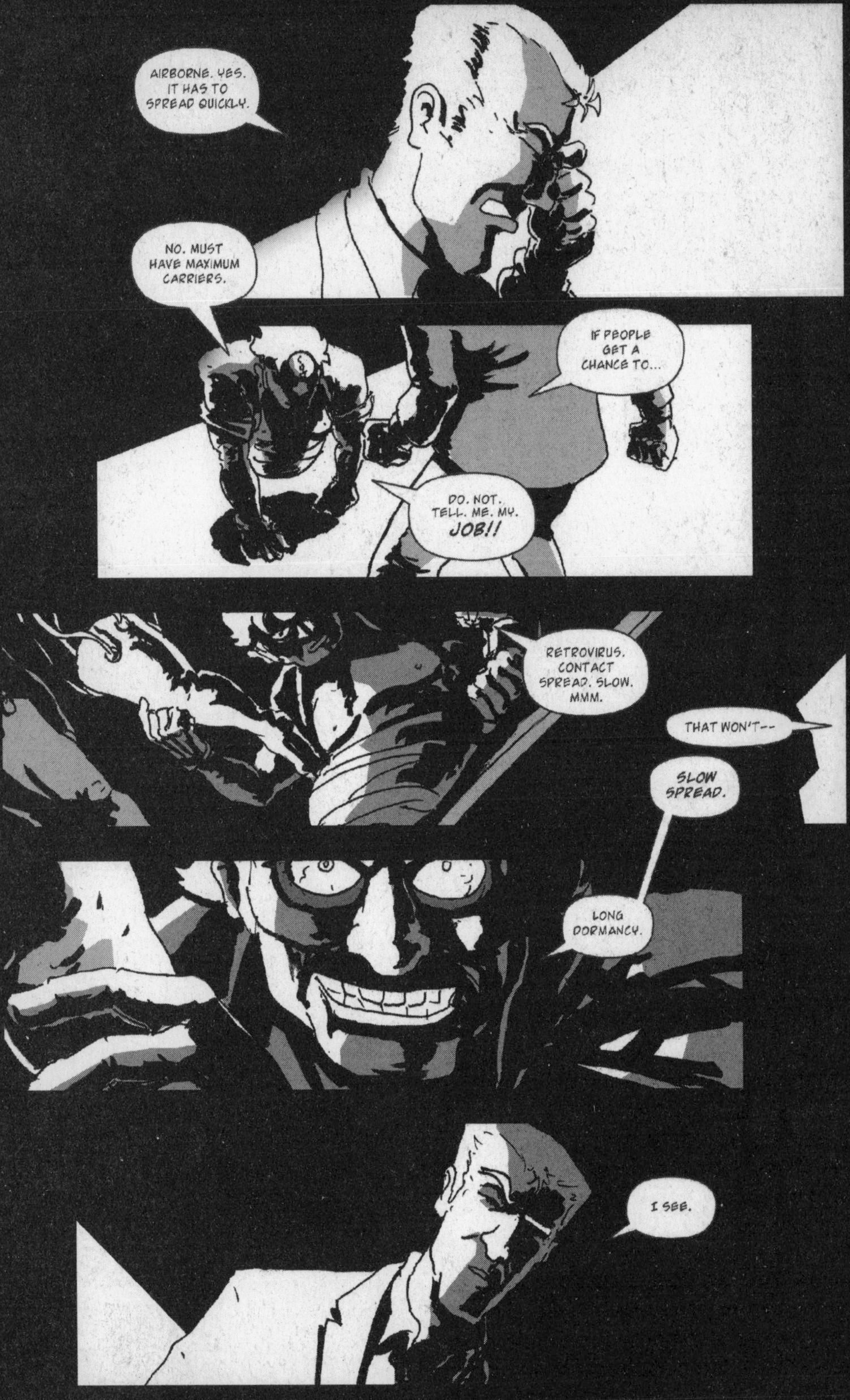
AIRBORNE. YES. IT HAS TO SPREAD QUICKLY.
NO. MUST HAVE MAXIMUM CARRIERS.
IF PEOPLE GET A CHANCE TO...
DO. NOT. TELL. ME. MY. JOB!!
RETROVIRUS. CONTACT SPREAD. SLOW. MMM.
THAT WON'T--
SLOW SPREAD.
LONG DORMANCY.
I SEE.

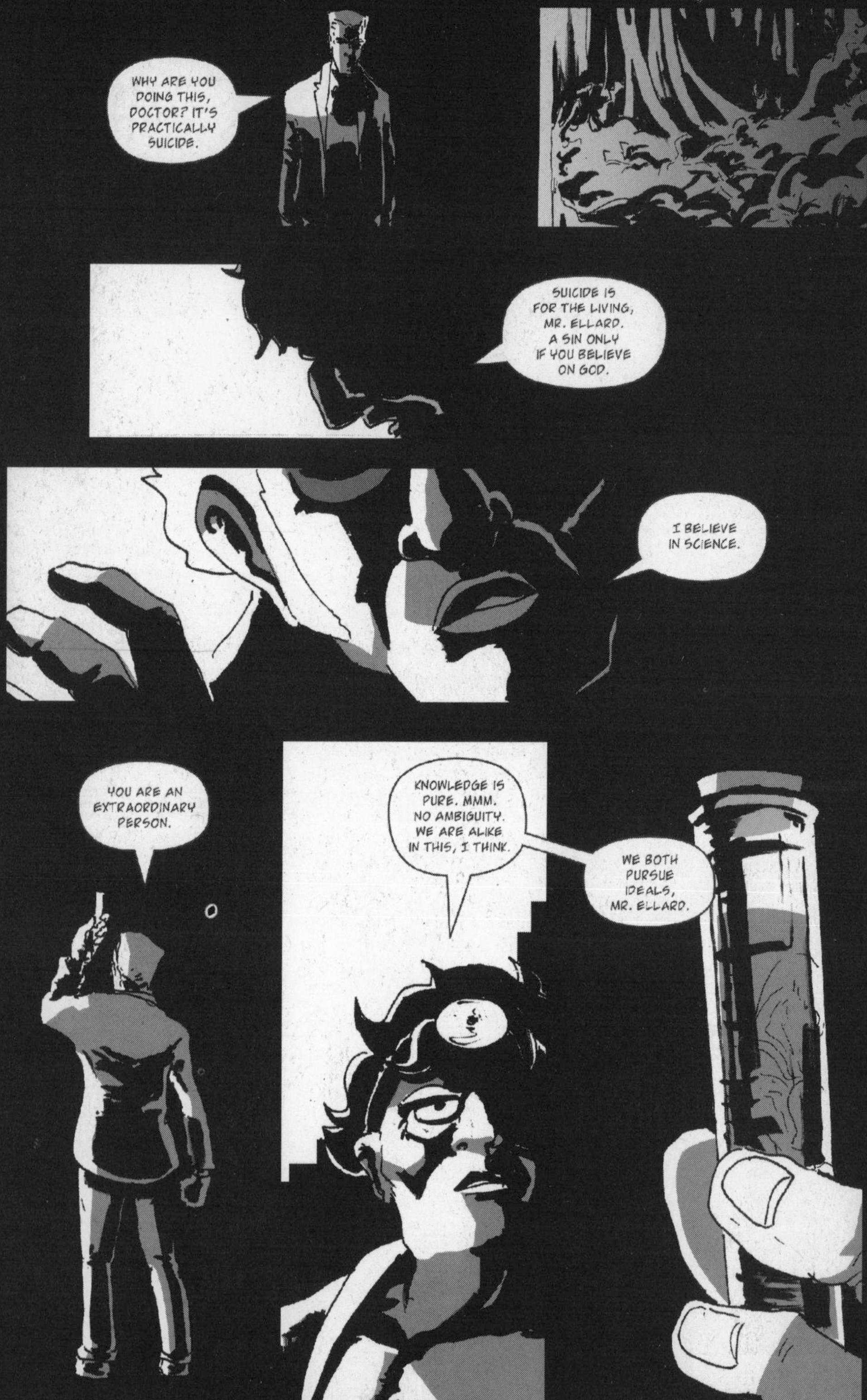
WHY ARE YOU DOING THIS, DOCTOR? IT'S PRACTICALLY SUICIDE.
SUICIDE IS FOR THE LIVING, MR. ELLARD. A SIN ONLY IF YOU BELIEVE ON GOD.
I BELIEVE IN SCIENCE.
YOU ARE AN EXTRAORDINARY PERSON.
KNOWLEDGE IS PURE. MMM. NO AMBIGUITY. WE ARE ALIKE IN THIS, I THINK.
WE BOTH PURSUE IDEALS, MR. ELLARD.

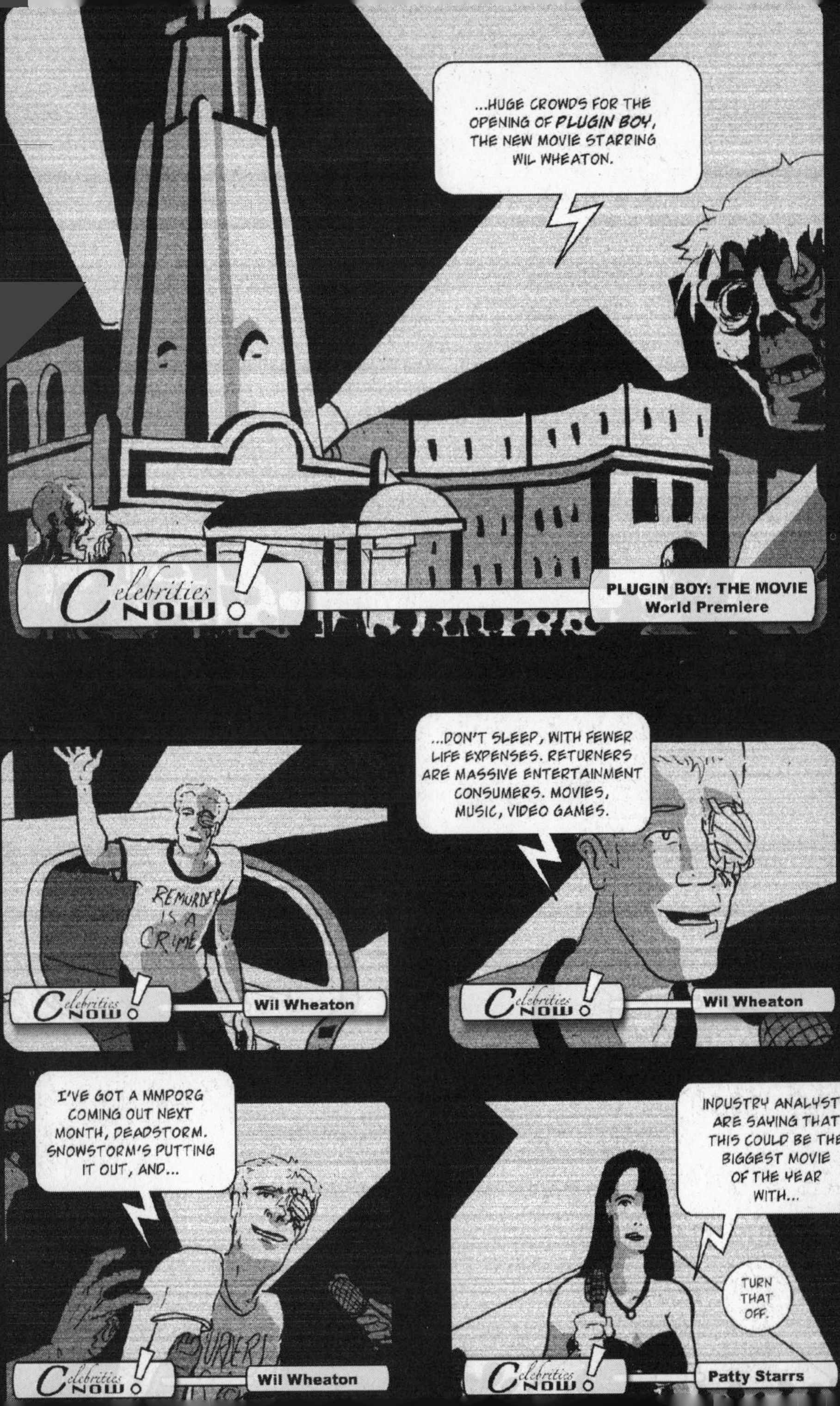
...HUGE CROWDS FOR THE OPENING OF PLUGIN BOY, THE NEW MOVIE STARRING WIL WHEATON.
Celebrities NOW!
PLUGIN BOY: THE MOVIE
World Premiere
REMURDER IS A CRIME
Celebrities NOW!
Wil Wheaton
...DON'T SLEEP, WITH FEWER LIFE EXPENSES. RETURNERS ARE MASSIVE ENTERTAINMENT CONSUMERS. MOVIES, MUSIC, VIDEO GAMES.
Celebrities NOW!
Wil Wheaton
I'VE GOT A MMPORG COMING OUT NEXT MONTH, DEADSTORM. SNOWSTORM'S PUTTING IT OUT, AND...
Celebrities NOW!
Wil Wheaton
INDUSTRY ANALYSTS ARE SAYING THAT THIS COULD BE THE BIGGEST MOVIE OF THE YEAR WITH...
TURN THAT OFF.
Celebrities NOW!
Patty Starrs

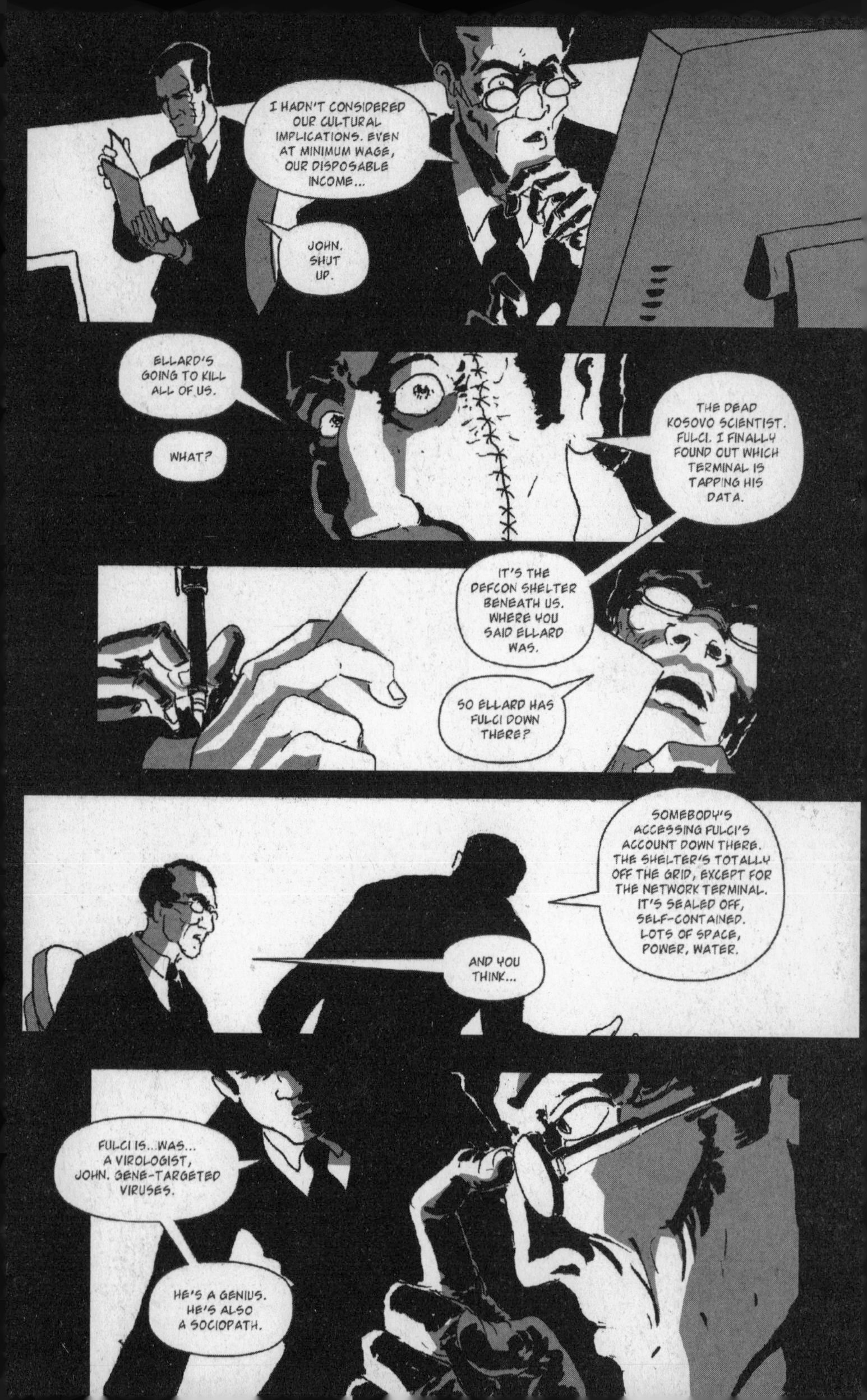
I HADN'T CONSIDERED OUR CULTURAL IMPLICATIONS. EVEN AT MINIMUM WAGE, OUR DISPOSABLE INCOME...
JOHN. SHUT UP.
ELLARD'S GOING TO KILL ALL OF US.
WHAT?
THE DEAD KOSOVO SCIENTIST. FULCI. I FINALLY FOUND OUT WHICH TERMINAL IS TAPPING HIS DATA.
IT'S THE DEFCON SHELTER BENEATH US. WHERE YOU SAID ELLARD WAS.
SO ELLARD HAS FULCI DOWN THERE?
SOMEBODY'S ACCESSING FULCI'S ACCOUNT DOWN THERE. THE SHELTER'S TOTALLY OFF THE GRID, EXCEPT FOR THE NETWORK TERMINAL. IT'S SEALED OFF, SELF-CONTAINED. LOTS OF SPACE, POWER, WATER.
AND YOU THINK...
FULCI IS...WAS... A VIROLOGIST, JOHN. GENE-TARGETED VIRUSES.
HE'S A GENIUS. HE'S ALSO A SOCIOPATH.

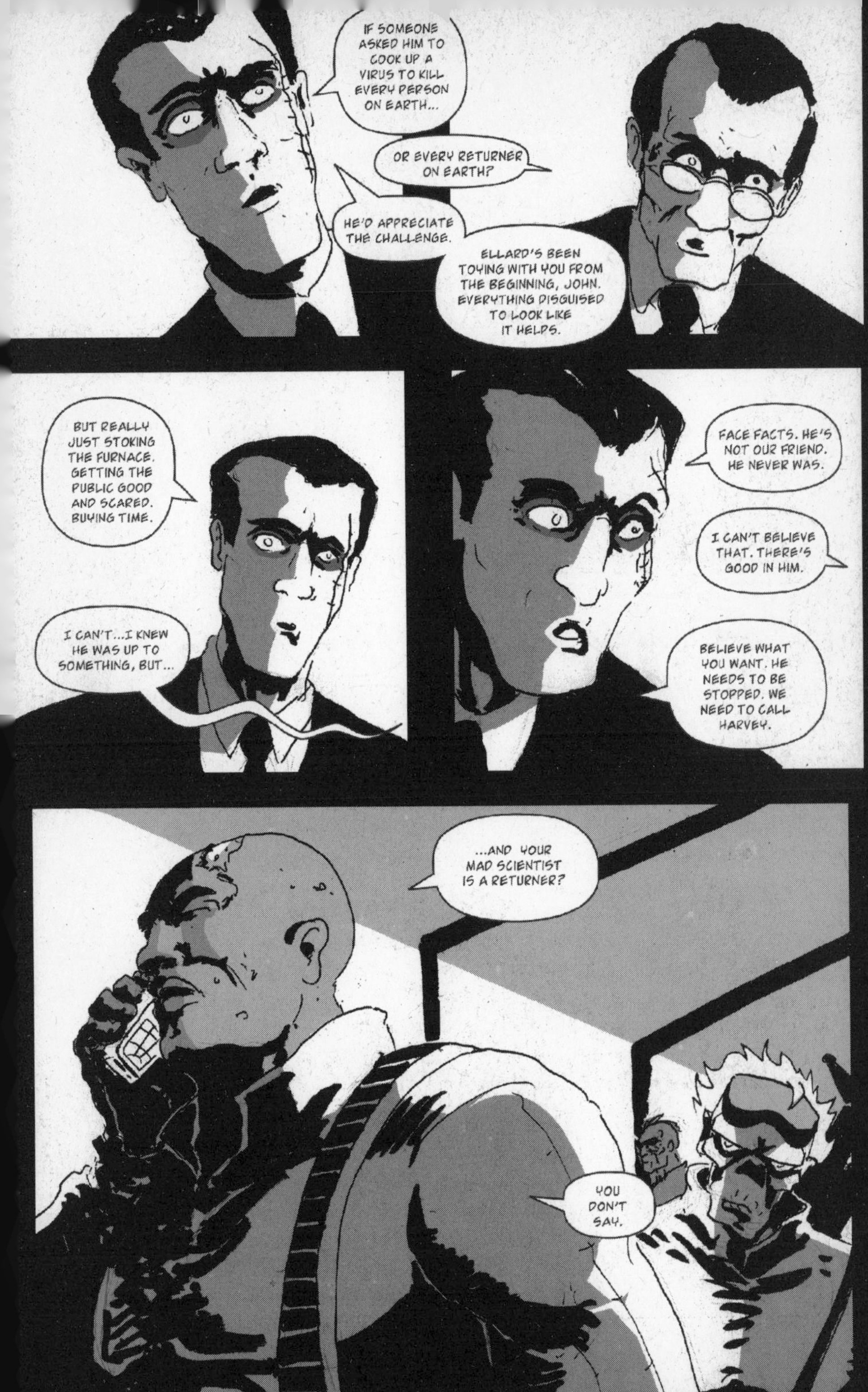
IF SOMEONE ASKED HIM TO COOK UP A VIRUS TO KILL EVERY PERSON ON EARTH...
OR EVERY RETURNER ON EARTH?
HE'D APPRECIATE THE CHALLENGE.
ELLARD'S BEEN TOYING WITH YOU FROM THE BEGINNING, JOHN. EVERYTHING DISGUISED TO LOOK LIKE IT HELPS.
BUT REALLY JUST STOKING THE FURNACE. GETTING THE PUBLIC GOOD AND SCARED. BUYING TIME.
I CAN'T...I KNEW HE WAS UP TO SOMETHING, BUT...
FACE FACTS. HE'S NOT OUR FRIEND. HE NEVER WAS.
I CAN'T BELIEVE THAT. THERE'S GOOD IN HIM.
BELIEVE WHAT YOU WANT. HE NEEDS TO BE STOPPED. WE NEED TO CALL HARVEY.
...AND YOUR MAD SCIENTIST IS A RETURNER?
YOU DON'T SAY.

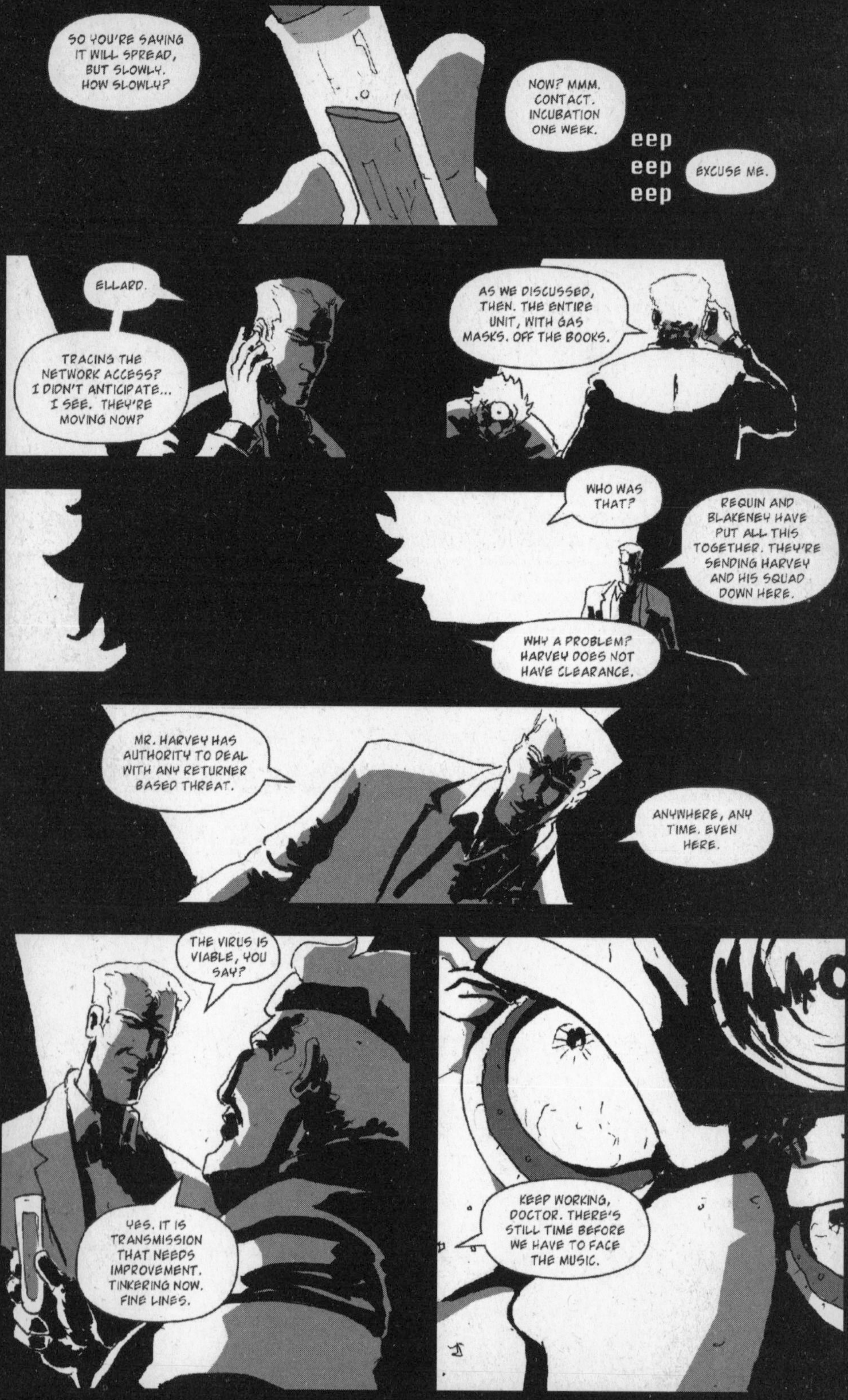
SO YOU'RE SAYING IT WILL SPREAD, BUT SLOWLY. HOW SLOWLY?
NOW? MMM. CONTACT. INCUBATION ONE WEEK.
eep
eep
eep
EXCUSE ME.
ELLARD.
TRACING THE NETWORK ACCESS? I DIDN'T ANTICIPATE... I SEE. THEY'RE MOVING NOW?
AS WE DISCUSSED, THEN. THE ENTIRE UNIT, WITH GAS MASKS. OFF THE BOOKS.
WHO WAS THAT?
REQUIN AND BLAKENEY HAVE PUT ALL THIS TOGETHER. THEY'RE SENDING HARVEY AND HIS SQUAD DOWN HERE.
WHY A PROBLEM? HARVEY DOES NOT HAVE CLEARANCE.
MR. HARVEY HAS AUTHORITY TO DEAL WITH ANY RETURNER BASED THREAT.
ANYWHERE, ANY TIME. EVEN HERE.
THE VIRUS IS VIABLE, YOU SAY?
YES. IT IS TRANSMISSION THAT NEEDS IMPROVEMENT. TINKERING NOW. FINE LINES.
KEEP WORKING, DOCTOR. THERE'S STILL TIME BEFORE WE HAVE TO FACE THE MUSIC.

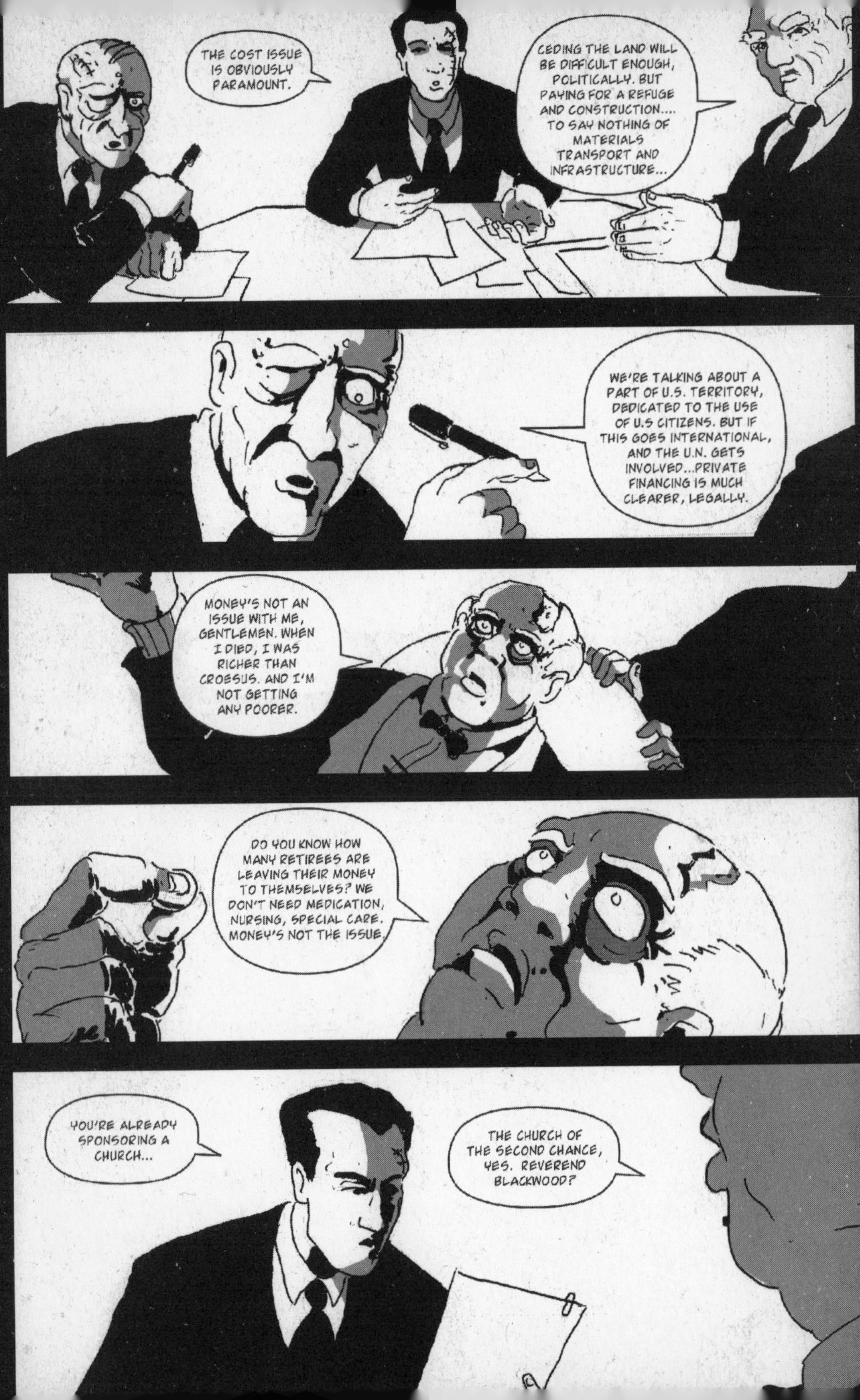
THE COST ISSUE IS OBVIOUSLY PARAMOUNT.
CEDING THE LAND WILL BE DIFFICULT ENOUGH, POLITICALLY. BUT PAYING FOR A REFUGE AND CONSTRUCTION.... TO SAY NOTHING OF MATERIALS TRANSPORT AND INFRASTRUCTURE...
WE'RE TALKING ABOUT A PART OF U.S. TERRITORY, DEDICATED TO THE USE OF U.S CITIZENS. BUT IF THIS GOES INTERNATIONAL, AND THE U.N. GETS INVOLVED...PRIVATE FINANCING IS MUCH CLEARER, LEGALLY.
MONEY'S NOT AN ISSUE WITH ME, GENTLEMEN. WHEN I DIED, I WAS RICHER THAN CROESUS. AND I'M NOT GETTING ANY POORER.
DO YOU KNOW HOW MANY RETIREES ARE LEAVING THEIR MONEY TO THEMSELVES? WE DON'T NEED MEDICATION, NURSING, SPECIAL CARE. MONEY'S NOT THE ISSUE.
YOU'RE ALREADY SPONSORING A CHURCH...
THE CHURCH OF THE SECOND CHANCE, YES. REVEREND BLACKWOOD?

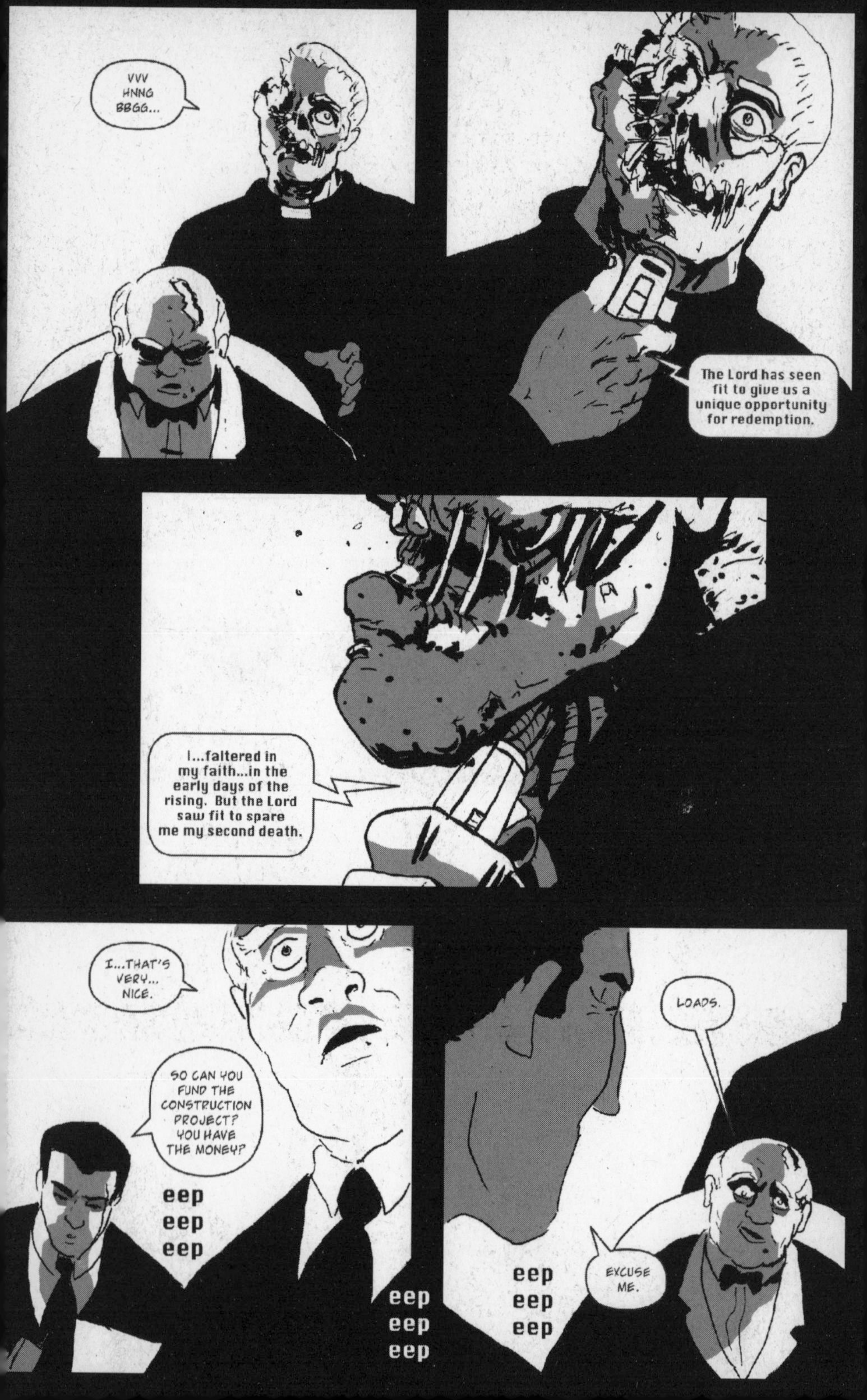
VVV
HNNG
BBGG...
The Lord has seen fit to give us a unique opportunity for redemption.
I...faltered in my faith...in the early days of the rising. But the Lord saw fit to spare me my second death.
I...THAT'S VERY... NICE.
SO CAN YOU FUND THE CONSTRUCTION PROJECT? YOU HAVE THE MONEY?
eep
eep
eep
eep
eep
eep
LOADS.
eep
eep
eep
EXCUSE ME.

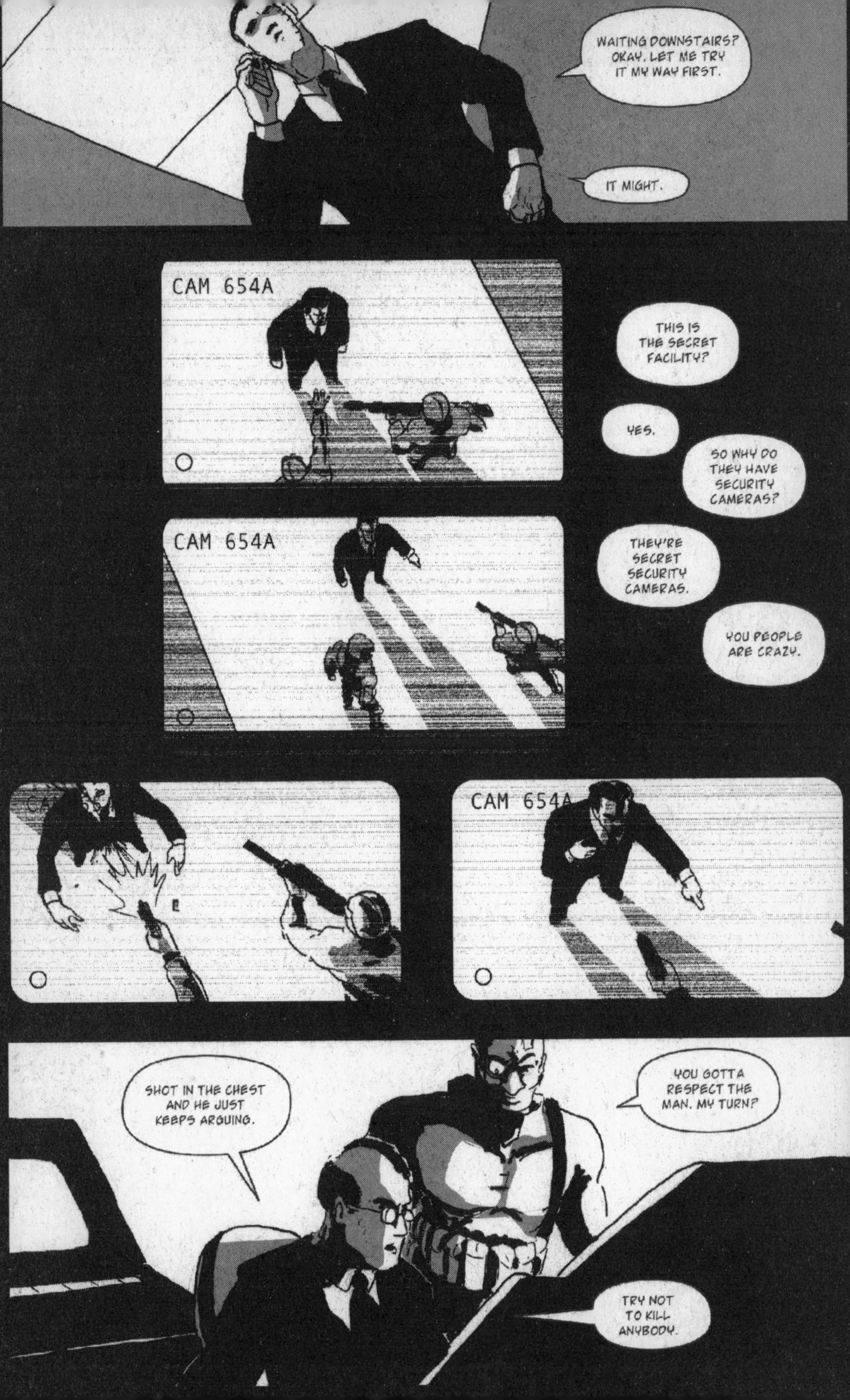
WAITING DOWNSTAIRS? OKAY. LET ME TRY IT MY WAY FIRST.
IT MIGHT.
CAM 654A
THIS IS THE SECRET FACILITY?
YES.
SO WHY DO THEY HAVE SECURITY CAMERAS?
CAM 654A
THEY'RE SECRET SECURITY CAMERAS.
YOU PEOPLE ARE CRAZY.
CAM 654A
SHOT IN THE CHEST AND HE JUST KEEPS ARGUING.
YOU GOTTA RESPECT THE MAN. MY TURN?
TRY NOT TO KILL ANYBODY.

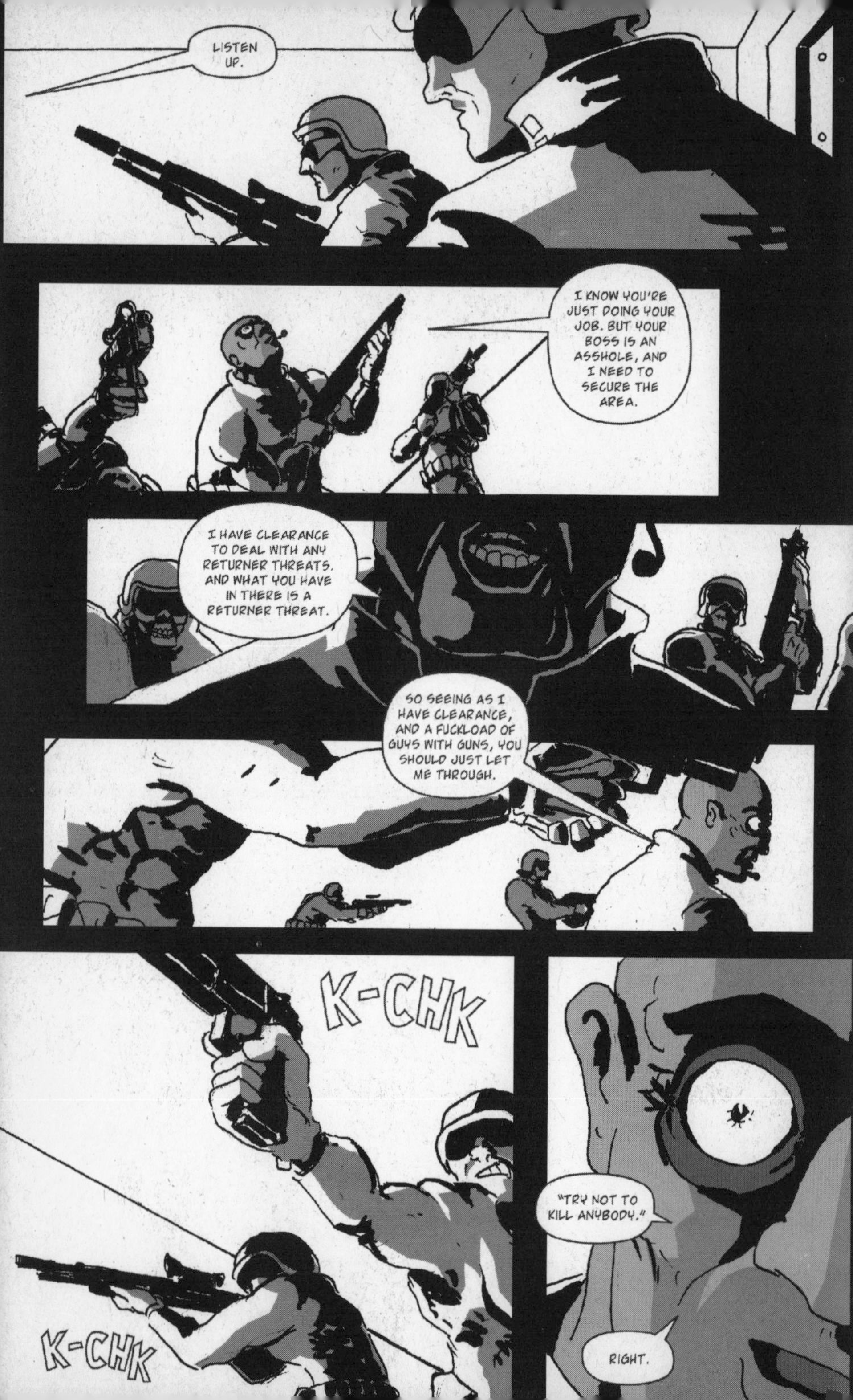
LISTEN UP.
I KNOW YOU'RE JUST DOING YOUR JOB. BUT YOUR BOSS IS AN ASSHOLE, AND I NEED TO SECURE THE AREA.
I HAVE CLEARANCE TO DEAL WITH ANY RETURNER THREATS. AND WHAT YOU HAVE IN THERE IS A RETURNER THREAT.
SO SEEING AS I HAVE CLEARANCE, AND A FUCKLOAD OF GUYS WITH GUNS, YOU SHOULD JUST LET ME THROUGH.
K-CHK
K-CHK
"TRY NOT TO KILL ANYBODY."
RIGHT.

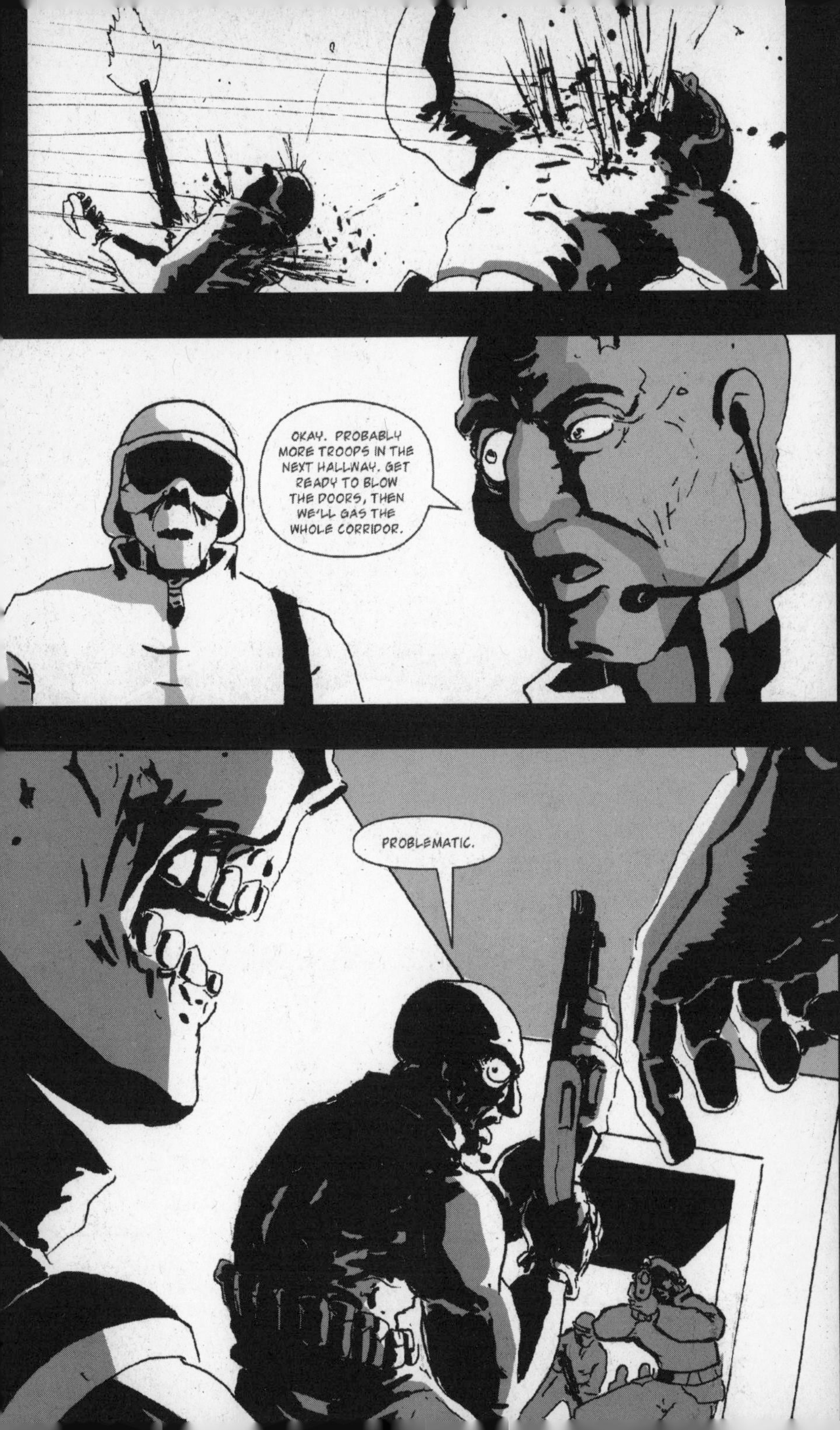
OKAY. PROBABLY MORE TROOPS IN THE NEXT HALLWAY. GET READY TO BLOW THE DOORS, THEN WE'LL GAS THE WHOLE CORRIDOR.
PROBLEMATIC.

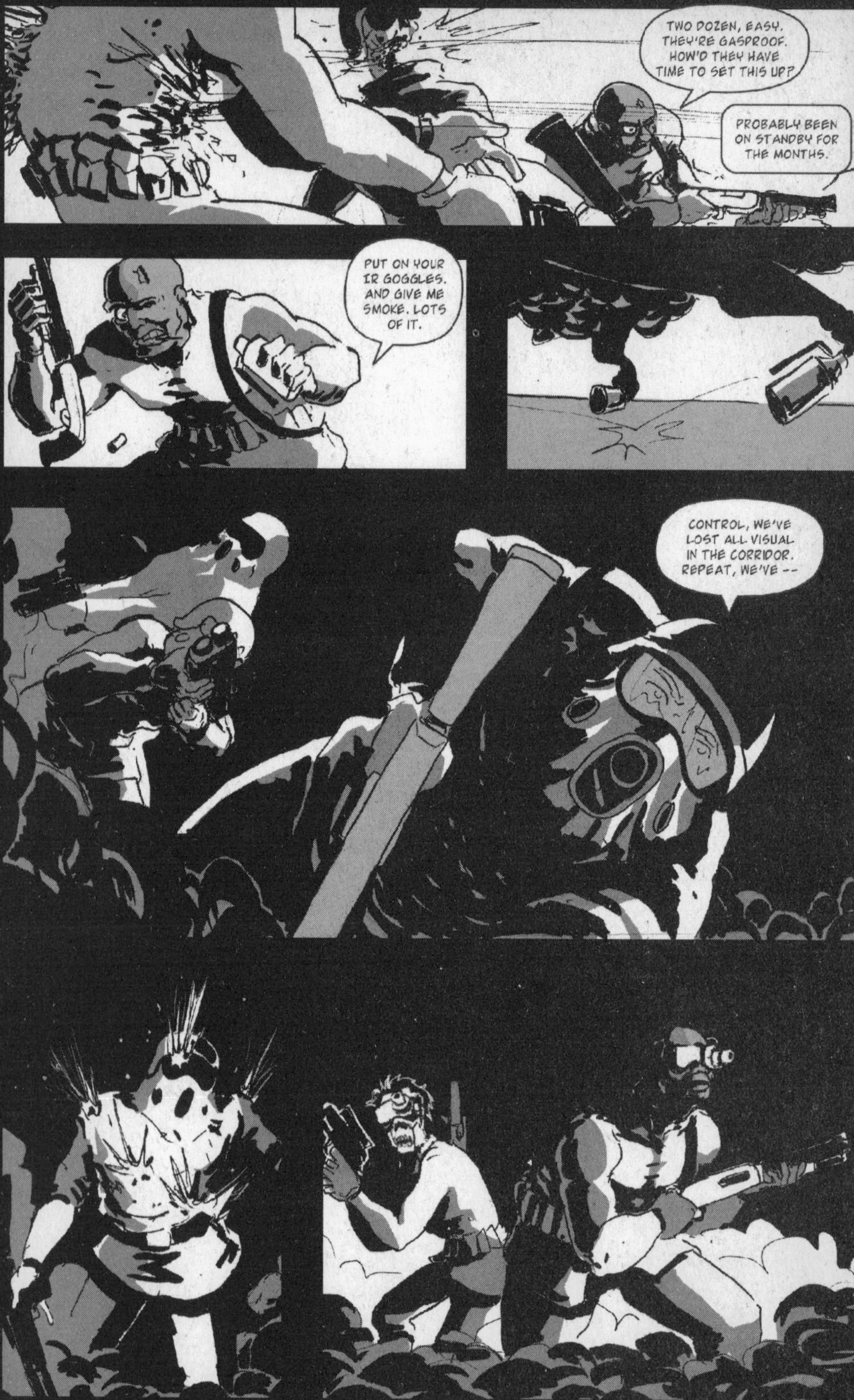
TWO DOZEN, EASY. THEY'RE GASPROOF. HOW'D THEY HAVE TIME TO SET THIS UP?
PROBABLY BEEN ON STANDBY FOR THE MONTHS.
PUT ON YOUR IR GOGGLES. AND GIVE ME SMOKE. LOTS OF IT.
CONTROL, WE'VE LOST ALL VISUAL IN THE CORRIDOR. REPEAT, WE'VE --

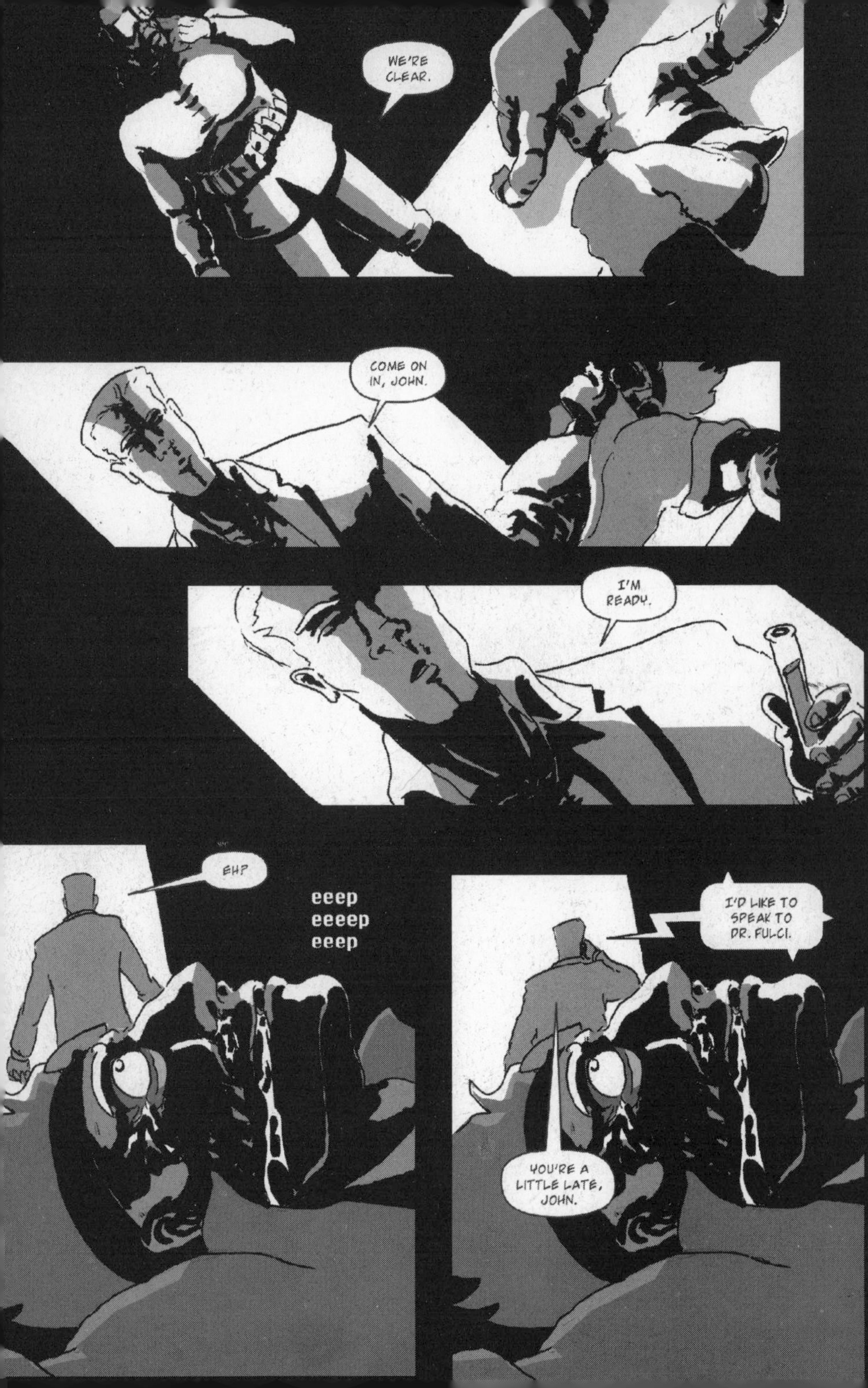
WE'RE CLEAR.
COME ON IN, JOHN.
I'M READY.
EH?
eeep
eeeep
eeep
I'D LIKE TO SPEAK TO DR. FULCI.
YOU'RE A LITTLE LATE, JOHN.

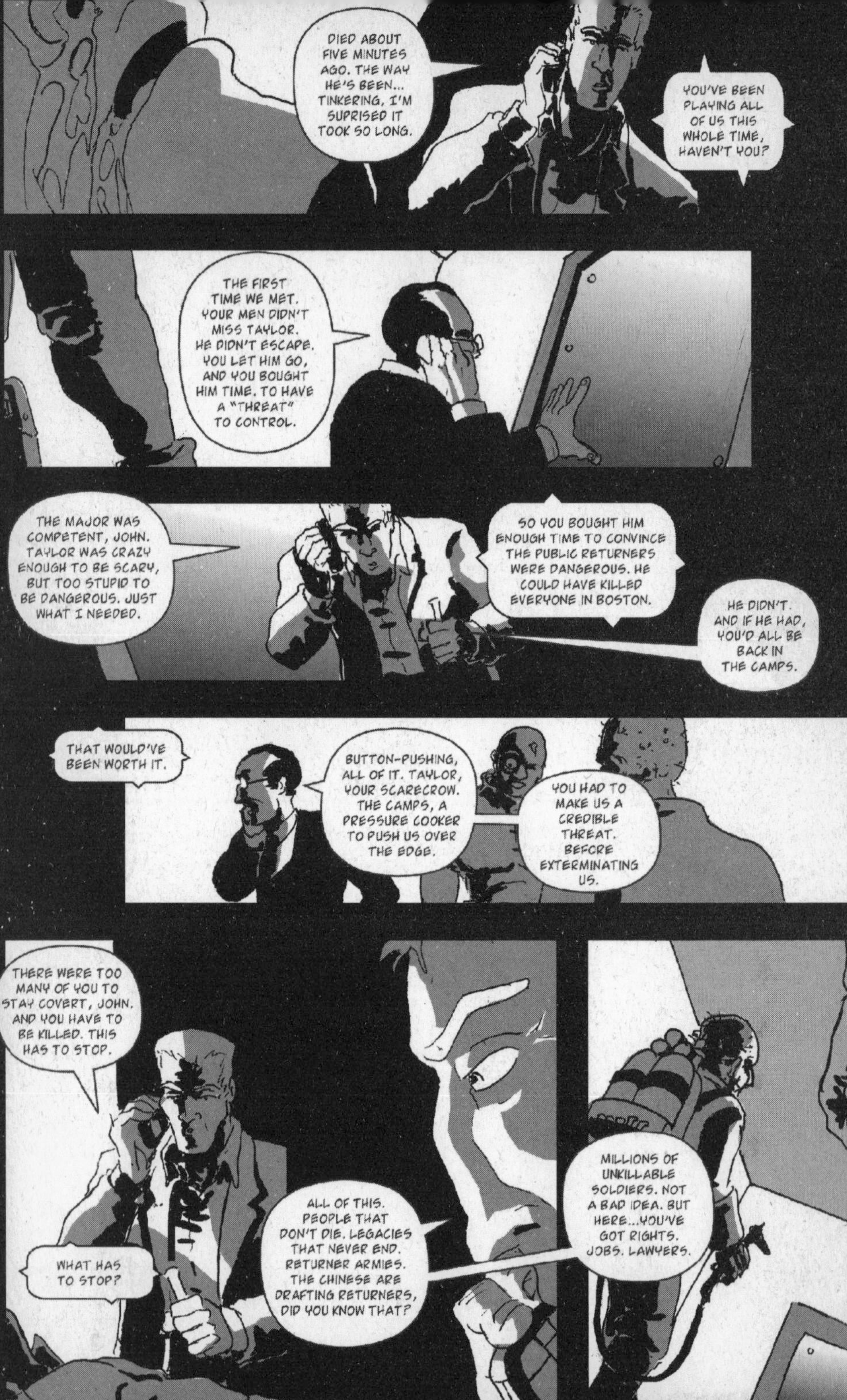
DIED ABOUT FIVE MINUTES AGO. THE WAY HE'S BEEN... TINKERING, I'M SUPRISED IT TOOK SO LONG.
YOU'VE BEEN PLAYING ALL OF US THIS WHOLE TIME, HAVEN'T YOU?
THE FIRST TIME WE MET. YOUR MEN DIDN'T MISS TAYLOR. HE DIDN'T ESCAPE. YOU LET HIM GO, AND YOU BOUGHT HIM TIME. TO HAVE A "THREAT" TO CONTROL.
THE MAJOR WAS COMPETENT, JOHN. TAYLOR WAS CRAZY ENOUGH TO BE SCARY, BUT TOO STUPID TO BE DANGEROUS. JUST WHAT I NEEDED.
SO YOU BOUGHT HIM ENOUGH TIME TO CONVINCE THE PUBLIC RETURNERS WERE DANGEROUS. HE COULD HAVE KILLED EVERYONE IN BOSTON.
HE DIDN'T. AND IF HE HAD, YOU'D ALL BE BACK IN THE CAMPS.
THAT WOULD'VE BEEN WORTH IT.
BUTTON-PUSHING, ALL OF IT. TAYLOR, YOUR SCARECROW. THE CAMPS, A PRESSURE COOKER TO PUSH US OVER THE EDGE.
YOU HAD TO MAKE US A CREDIBLE THREAT. BEFORE EXTERMINATING US.
THERE WERE TOO MANY OF YOU TO STAY COVERT, JOHN. AND YOU HAVE TO BE KILLED. THIS HAS TO STOP.
WHAT HAS TO STOP?
ALL OF THIS. PEOPLE THAT DON'T DIE. LEGACIES THAT NEVER END. RETURNER ARMIES. THE CHINESE ARE DRAFTING RETURNERS, DID YOU KNOW THAT?
MILLIONS OF UNKILLABLE SOLDIERS. NOT A BAD IDEA. BUT HERE...YOU'VE GOT RIGHTS. JOBS. LAWYERS.

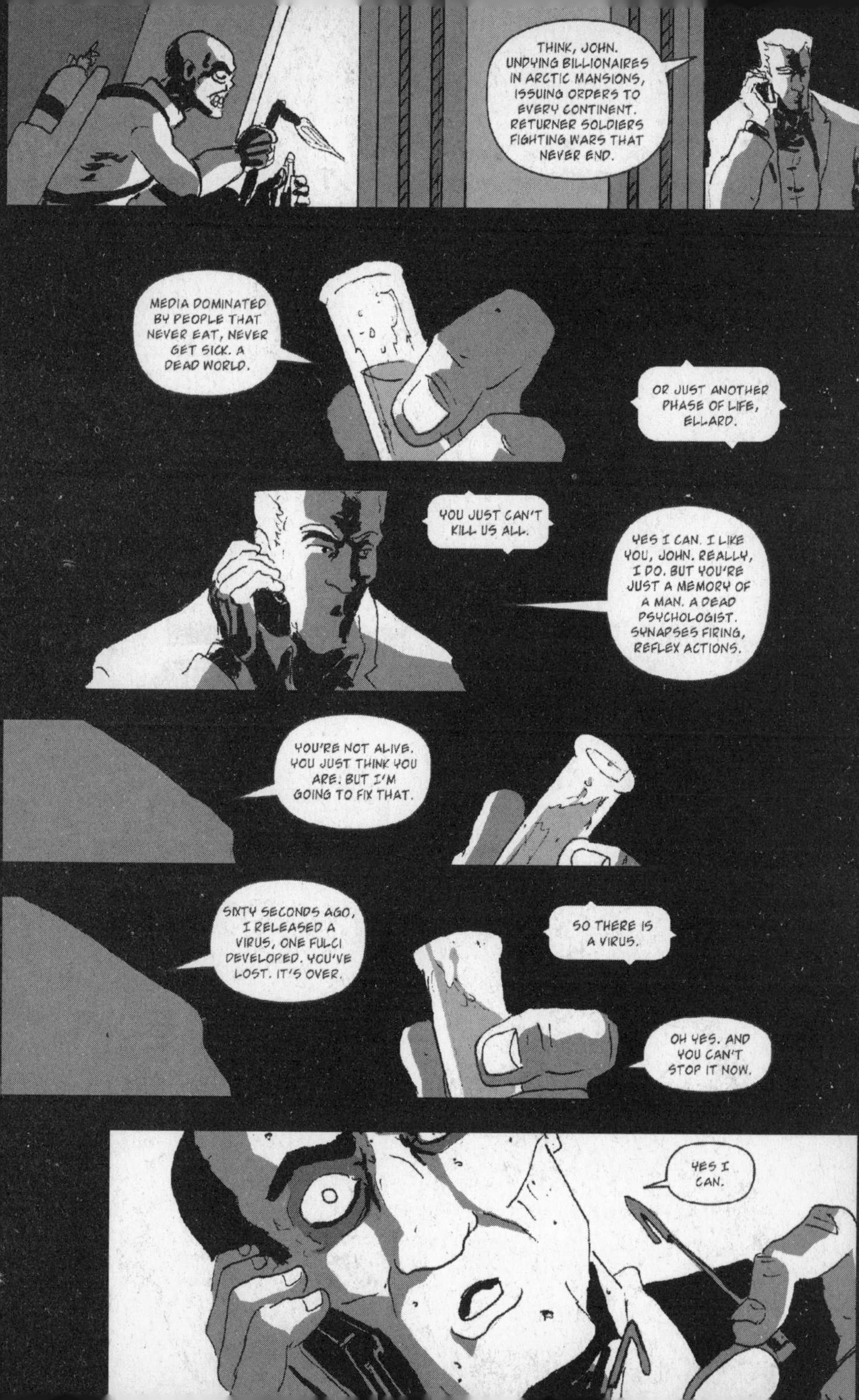
THINK, JOHN. UNDYING BILLIONAIRES IN ARCTIC MANSIONS, ISSUING ORDERS TO EVERY CONTINENT. RETURNER SOLDIERS FIGHTING WARS THAT NEVER END.
MEDIA DOMINATED BY PEOPLE THAT NEVER EAT, NEVER GET SICK. A DEAD WORLD.
OR JUST ANOTHER PHASE OF LIFE, ELLARD.
YOU JUST CAN'T KILL US ALL.
YES I CAN. I LIKE YOU, JOHN. REALLY, I DO. BUT YOU'RE JUST A MEMORY OF A MAN. A DEAD PSYCHOLOGIST. SYNAPSES FIRING, REFLEX ACTIONS.
YOU'RE NOT ALIVE. YOU JUST THINK YOU ARE. BUT I'M GOING TO FIX THAT.
SIXTY SECONDS AGO, I RELEASED A VIRUS, ONE FULCI DEVELOPED. YOU'VE LOST. IT'S OVER.
SO THERE IS A VIRUS.
OH YES. AND YOU CAN'T STOP IT NOW.
YES I CAN.

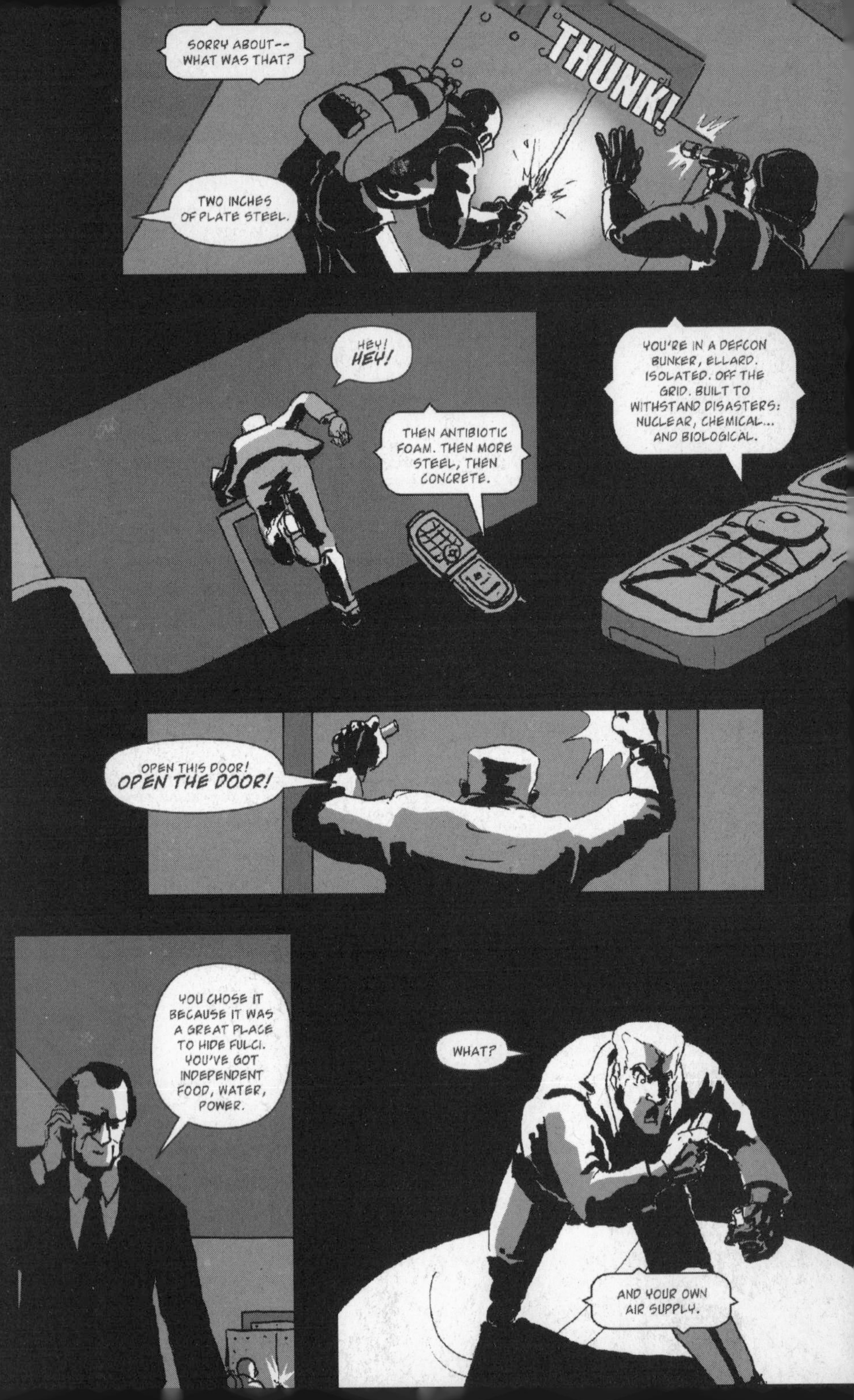
SORRY ABOUT-- WHAT WAS THAT?
THUNK!
TWO INCHES OF PLATE STEEL.
HEY! HEY!
THEN ANTIBIOTIC FOAM. THEN MORE STEEL, THEN CONCRETE.
YOU'RE IN A DEFCON BUNKER, ELLARD. ISOLATED. OFF THE GRID. BUILT TO WITHSTAND DISASTERS: NUCLEAR, CHEMICAL... AND BIOLOGICAL.
OPEN THIS DOOR! OPEN THE DOOR!
YOU CHOSE IT BECAUSE IT WAS A GREAT PLACE TO HIDE FULCI. YOU'VE GOT INDEPENDENT FOOD, WATER, POWER.
WHAT?
AND YOUR OWN AIR SUPPLY.

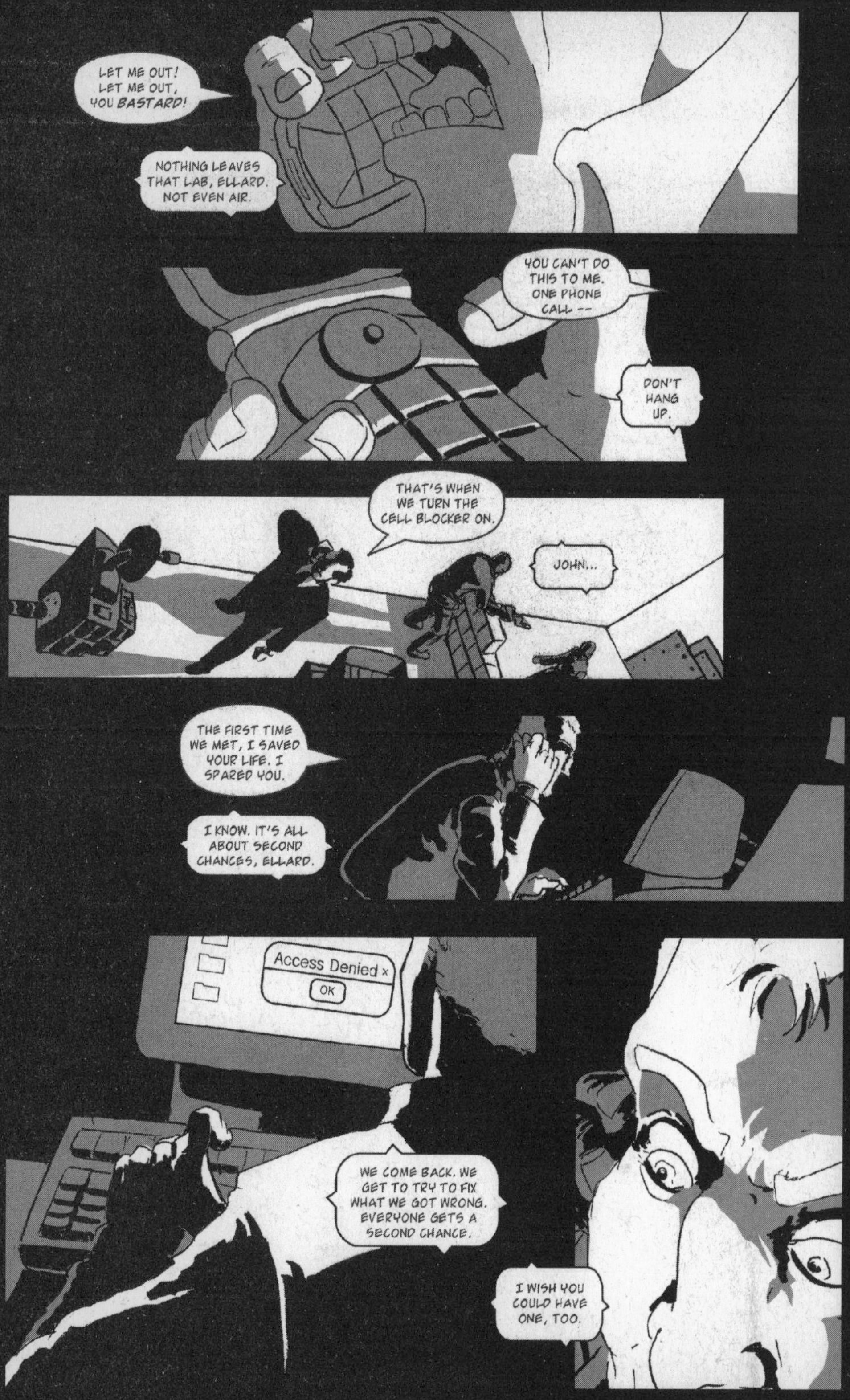
LET ME OUT! LET ME OUT, YOU BASTARD!
NOTHING LEAVES THAT LAB, ELLARD. NOT EVEN AIR.
YOU CAN'T DO THIS TO ME. ONE PHONE CALL --
DON'T HANG UP.
THAT'S WHEN WE TURN THE CELL BLOCKER ON.
JOHN...
THE FIRST TIME WE MET, I SAVED YOUR LIFE. I SPARED YOU.
I KNOW. IT'S ALL ABOUT SECOND CHANCES, ELLARD.
Access Denied x
OK
WE COME BACK. WE GET TO TRY TO FIX WHAT WE GOT WRONG. EVERYONE GETS A SECOND CHANCE.
I WISH YOU COULD HAVE ONE, TOO.

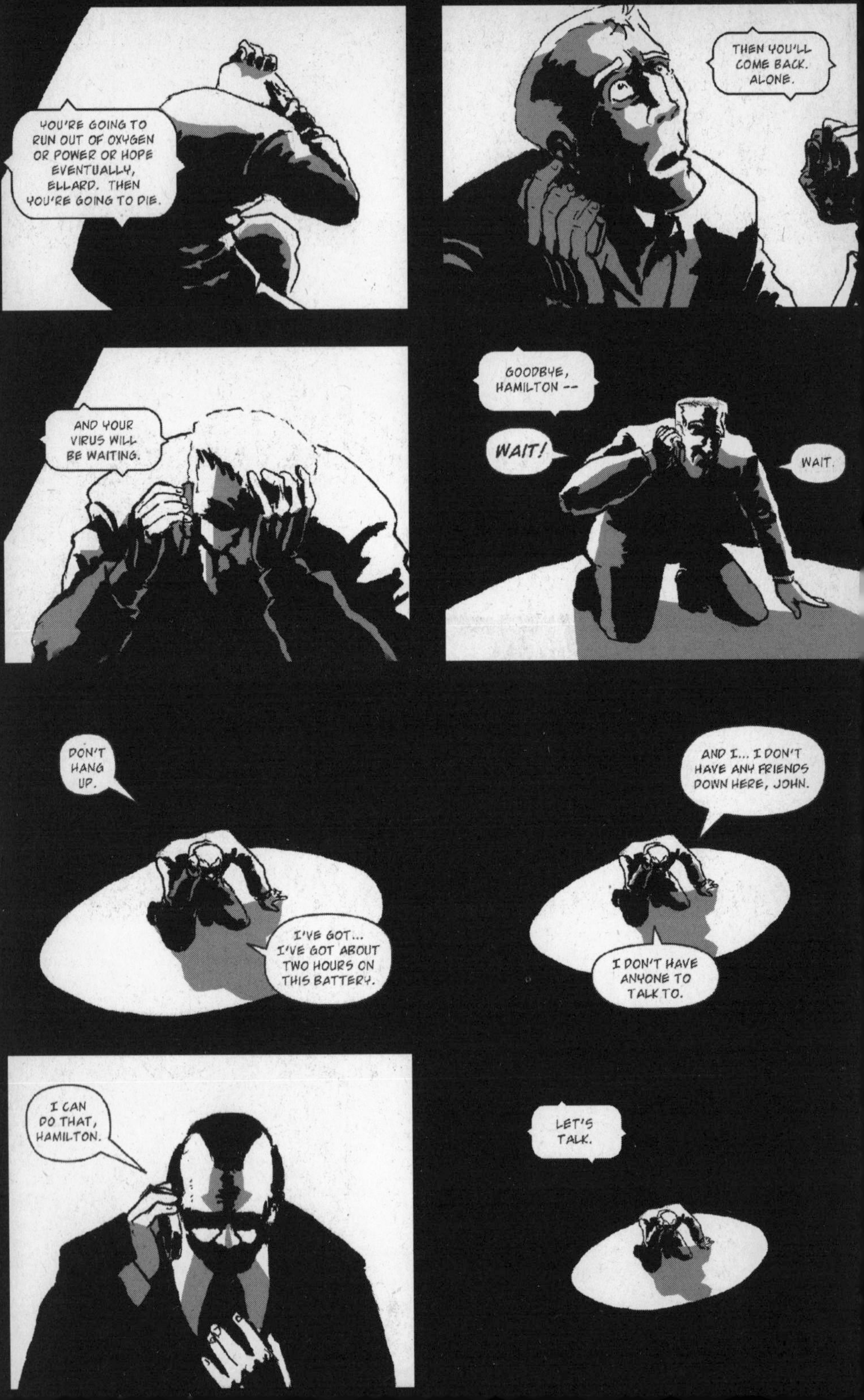
YOU'RE GOING TO RUN OUT OF OXYGEN OR POWER OR HOPE EVENTUALLY, ELLARD. THEN YOU'RE GOING TO DIE.
THEN YOU'LL COME BACK. ALONE.
AND YOUR VIRUS WILL BE WAITING.
GOODBYE, HAMILTON --
WAIT!
WAIT.
DON'T HANG UP.
I'VE GOT... I'VE GOT ABOUT TWO HOURS ON THIS BATTERY.
AND I... I DON'T HAVE ANY FRIENDS DOWN HERE, JOHN.
I DON'T HAVE ANYONE TO TALK TO.
I CAN DO THAT, HAMILTON.
LET'S TALK.

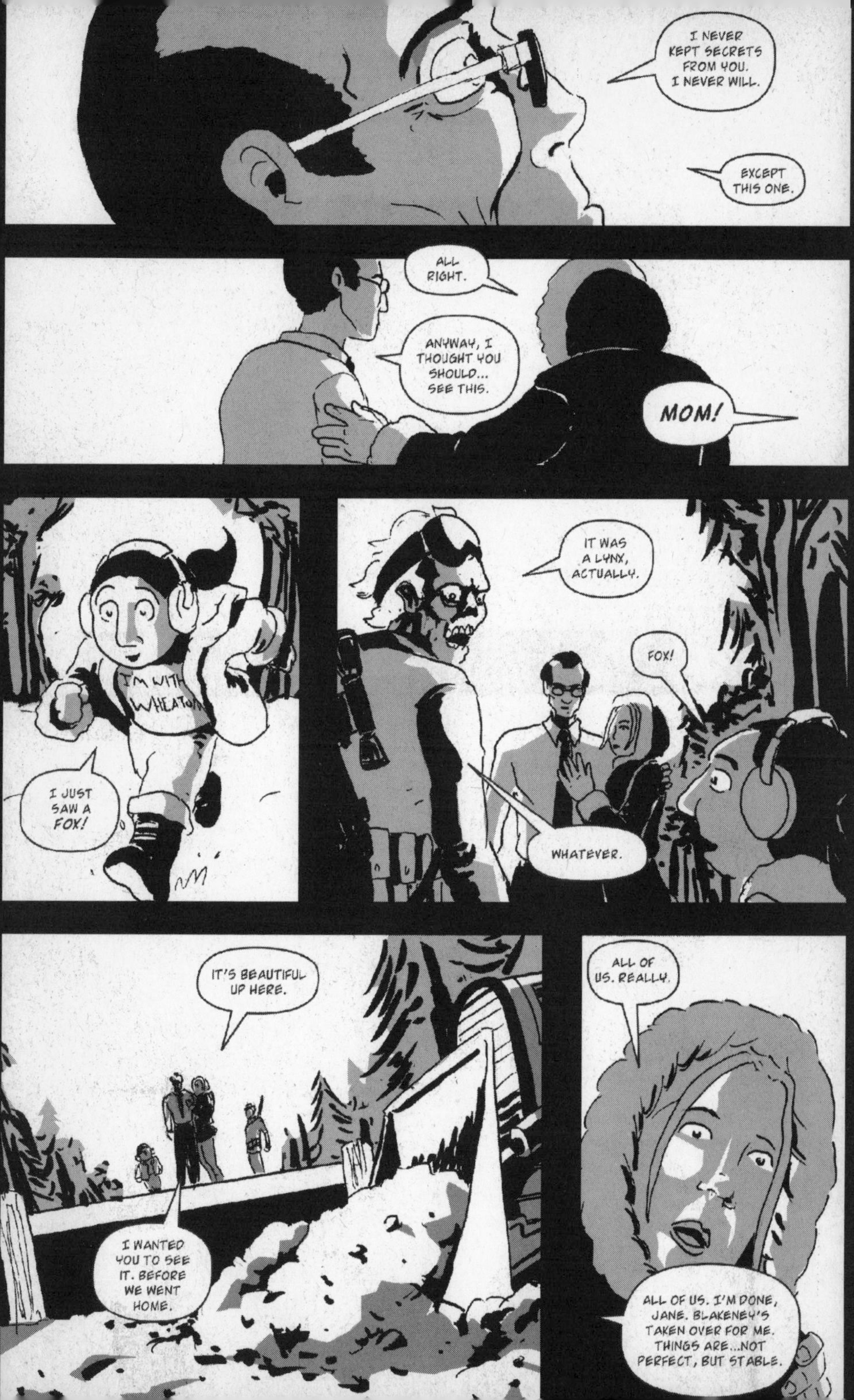
I NEVER KEPT SECRETS FROM YOU. I NEVER WILL.
EXCEPT THIS ONE.
ALL RIGHT.
ANYWAY, I THOUGHT YOU SHOULD... SEE THIS.
MOM!
I'M WITH WHEATON
I JUST SAW A FOX!
IT WAS A LYNX, ACTUALLY.
FOX!
WHATEVER.
IT'S BEAUTIFUL UP HERE.
I WANTED YOU TO SEE IT. BEFORE WE WENT HOME.
ALL OF US. REALLY.
ALL OF US. I'M DONE, JANE. BLAKENEY'S TAKEN OVER FOR ME. THINGS ARE...NOT PERFECT, BUT STABLE.

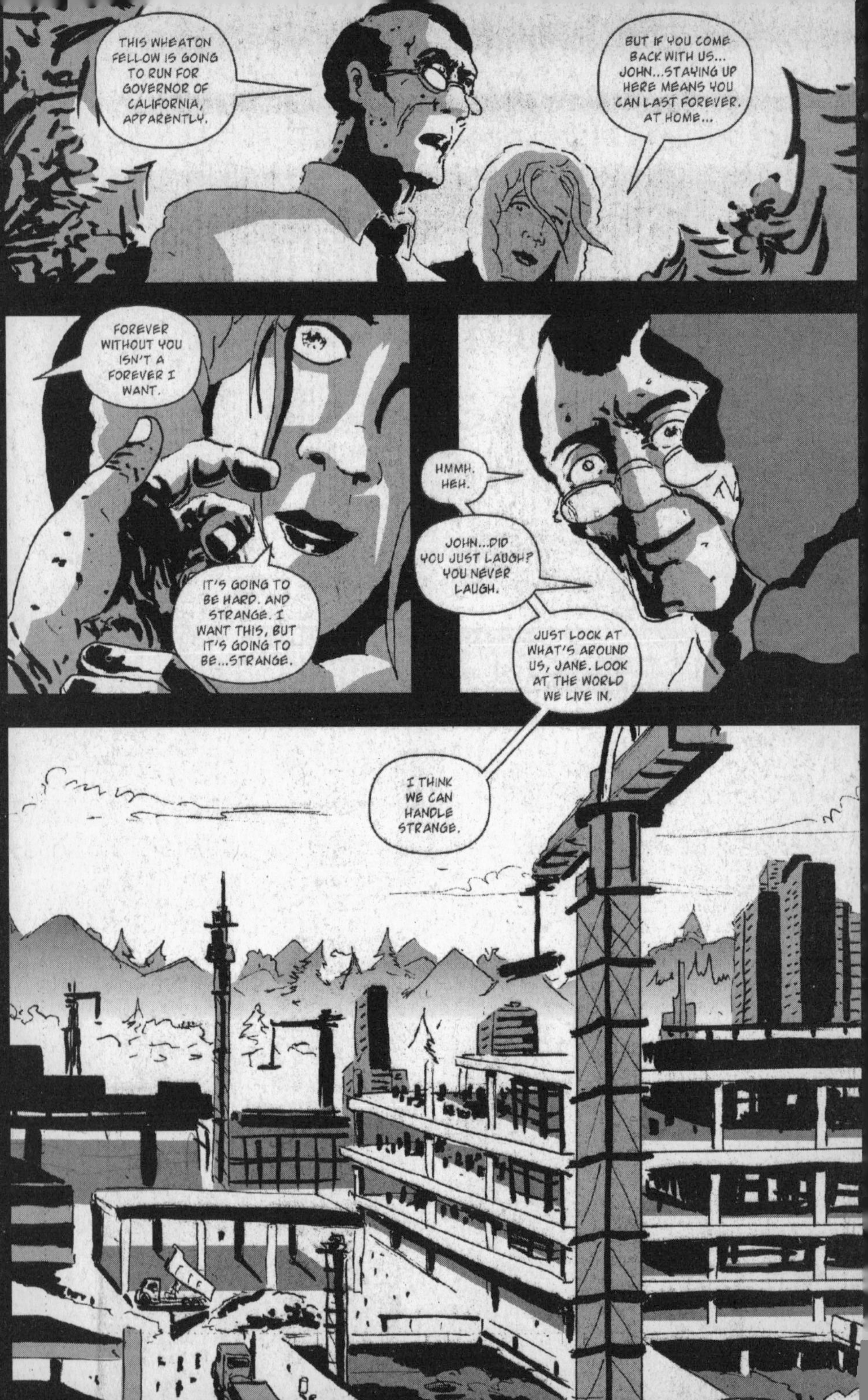
THIS WHEATON FELLOW IS GOING TO RUN FOR GOVERNOR OF CALIFORNIA, APPARENTLY.
BUT IF YOU COME BACK WITH US... JOHN...STAYING UP HERE MEANS YOU CAN LAST FOREVER. AT HOME...
FOREVER WITHOUT YOU ISN'T A FOREVER I WANT.
IT'S GOING TO BE HARD. AND STRANGE. I WANT THIS, BUT IT'S GOING TO BE...STRANGE.
HMMH. HEH.
JOHN...DID YOU JUST LAUGH? YOU NEVER LAUGH.
JUST LOOK AT WHAT'S AROUND US, JANE. LOOK AT THE WORLD WE LIVE IN.
I THINK WE CAN HANDLE STRANGE.